Springer Proceedings in Mathematics & Statistics

Volume 506

This book series features volumes composed of selected contributions from workshops and conferences in all areas of current research in mathematics and statistics, including data science, operations research and optimization. In addition to an overall evaluation of the interest, scientific quality, and timeliness of each proposal at the hands of the publisher, individual contributions are all refereed to the high quality standards of leading journals in the field. Thus, this series provides the research community with well-edited, authoritative reports on developments in the most exciting areas of mathematical and statistical research today.

Paolo Landa · André Côté · Jean-Baptiste Gartner ·
Géraldine Layani · Julien Husson ·
Jean-Baptiste Capgras · Célia Lemaire
Editors

Operations Research and Artificial Intelligence in Healthcare Management

SSHSM, Québec, Canada, June 2022, and Lyon, France, June 2023

Springer

Editors
See next page

ISSN 2194-1009 ISSN 2194-1017 (electronic)
Springer Proceedings in Mathematics & Statistics
ISBN 978-3-031-95658-4 ISBN 978-3-031-95659-1 (eBook)
https://doi.org/10.1007/978-3-031-95659-1

Mathematics Subject Classification: 62P10, 90C90, 90-10, 90C35, 68T01

Faculté des Sciences de l'Administration, Soutien à la recherche (SAR) FSA—Volet 3: Aide à la publication

This Springer imprint is published by the registered company Springer Nature Switzerland AG
The registered company address is: Gewerbestrasse 11, 6330 Cham, Switzerland

Editors
Paolo Landa
Department of Operations and Decision Systems
Laval University
Québec City, QC, Canada

Jean-Baptiste Gartner
Department of Management
Laval University
Québec City, QC, Canada

Julien Husson
School of Management
Université Lorraine
Metz, Moselle, France

Célia Lemaire
IAE Lyon School of Management
Université Jean Moulin Lyon 3
Lyon, Rhône, France

André Côté
Department of Management
Laval University
Québec City, QC, Canada

Géraldine Layani
Département de médecine de famille et de médecine d'urgence
University of Montreal
Montreal, QC, Canada

Jean-Baptiste Capgras
IFROSS
Université Jean Moulin Lyon 3
Lyon, Rhône, France

Preface

This work is a collection of papers presented at the two editions of the Francophone summer school on health service management. The second edition held in 2022 at Laval University in Quebec City (Canada) focused on innovation in healthcare organizations in a post-pandemic context. The third edition, for its part, was held in 2023 at Jean-Moulin University in Lyon 3 (France). The two editions had the same main theme, the redefinition of healthcare organizations through today's complexity.

The COVID-19 pandemic has highlighted many issues in adapting healthcare and social services establishments (health and medico-social establishments). More than ever, European and Canadian facilities have to undergo major transformations and face major challenges if they are to respond to these concerns. Innovative solutions can only be found through a detailed understanding of the many particularities of the environment and context. Sharing knowledge and experience to question the many facets of these challenges better is therefore all the more relevant and important.

To address this issue, the second edition of the summer school, focused on the theme: "Innovation in a post-pandemic health and social services system", analyzing the following subjects: (1) The patient at the heart of the reorganization of healthcare and services, (2) Healthcare organization, (3) Innovation in care trajectories, (4) Digital transformation and artificial intelligence serving health and social care institutions, (5) Learning health systems—operationalization and evaluation.

The third edition focused on the rethinking of healthcare organizations. Indeed, in the last decades, healthcare organizations have been going through a period of turmoil. Staff shortages, overcrowding in hospitals and primary care, supply disruptions, computer hacking, funding problems, and abuse scandals are all having a profound effect on health establishments and services, giving rise not only to unease among staff but also in society as a whole, and to questions about the missions of institutions and the resources needed to carry them out effectively and efficiently. While most of these crises are not new, their combination and the scale of their repercussions highlight the need to think differently about organizations to heal the damage and make them more resilient in the face of future challenges. To answer these challenges, several perspectives were approached by the participants of the Summer schools.

Beyond the themes explored during both editions of the summer school, the chapters gathered in this book illustrate several complementary avenues through which healthcare organizations can be reimagined and strengthened. A central dimension concerns the contribution of innovation approaches grounded in operations research and artificial intelligence. These methodologies offer powerful analytical and decision-support tools capable of guiding managers through complex environments, optimizing resource allocation, and improving the performance of healthcare services.

Another key perspective highlighted in this volume relates to recent advances in the modelling of healthcare trajectories and clinical pathways. Understanding how patients navigate the system, how services are coordinated, and where inefficiencies or vulnerabilities emerge provides a crucial foundation for redesigning processes and enhancing continuity of care. Equally essential is the attention paid to patient-centered approaches in the management and transformation of healthcare organizations.

By integrating patient experience, expectations, and participation, institutions can develop more responsive, equitable, and effective models of care, an imperative that became even more evident in the post-pandemic era.

Together, these contributions illustrate the richness and potential of combining operations research, artificial intelligence, and patient-centered management to rethink healthcare delivery. They demonstrate how such approaches can drive innovation in a context where organizations must adapt rapidly to heightened constraints, fluctuating demand, and new societal expectations.

When supported by rigorous analytical tools and informed by qualitative insights from the field, the reconfiguration of healthcare systems becomes not only possible but also more sustainable and resilient, ultimately benefiting managers, professionals, patients, and all stakeholders involved.

Québec City, Canada Paolo Landa
Québec City, Canada Jean-Baptiste Gartner
Québec City, Canada André Côté
Lyon, France Célia Lemaire
Lyon, France Jean-Baptiste Capgras
Metz, France Julien Husson
Montreal, Canada Géraldine Layani

Contents

Staffing Healthcare Personnel Combining Petri Nets and Optimisation

Bernardetta Addis, Roberto Aringhieri, Marco Gribaudo, and Andrea Grosso

Abstract Healthcare services are usually delivered by teams, each one composed of individuals working together sharing knowledge, experiences and skills. The staffing problem consists in finding an optimal set of teams with respect to a given performance metrics in such a way to meet a forecasted service demand, which determines the workload level. Various metrics can be used to measure the efficiency of one individual, and to evaluate the overall team performance. The random nature of the problem requires the introduction of random variables, and the characterisation of the overall team behaviour with a stochastic process. We propose hybrid algorithms based on generalised stochastic petri nets (GSPN) and optimisation. The basic idea is to exploit the GSPN model as a black box to evaluate a solution computed by an optimisation algorithm, that is the team performance under several demand scenarios. We test the proposed algorithms on a case study arising from an Italian Emergency Medical Services. The insights from the computational analysis confirm the validity of the proposed algorithms.

Keywords Workforce management · Staffing · Patient flow · Petri nets · Metaheuristics · Set partitioning

1 Introduction

Healthcare services are usually delivered by teams, each one composed of individuals working together sharing knowledge, experiences and skills. Approaches to the medical workforce management capable to guarantee the efficiency and fairness of

B. Addis
University of Lorraine-CNRS-LORIA, Nancy Cedex, France

R. Aringhieri (✉) · A. Grosso
Department of Computer Science, University of Turin, Turin, Italy
e-mail: roberto.aringhieri@unito.it

M. Gribaudo
Department of Electronics, Information and Bioengineering, Polytechnic University of Milan, Milan, Italy

P. Landa et al. (eds.), *Operations Research and Artificial Intelligence in Healthcare Management*, Springer Proceedings in Mathematics & Statistics 506,
https://doi.org/10.1007/978-3-031-95659-1_2

the delivered service becomes crucial [3]. In [13] the authors argued that skill maximisation (e.g., increasing the responsibilities of healthcare practitioners) is the key to increase productivity and care quality. They also argued that to increase output (represented by volumes of cases treated) and quality of care is not just necessary, but essential. For these main reasons, the authors concluded that the key to address the future of healthcare is the maximisation of the use of human resource.

In this work we focus on staffing stage in accordance with the classification proposed in [17]: the staffing problem consists in finding an optimal set of teams with respect to a given performance metrics in such a way to meet the forecasted service demand. Since the service demand determines the workload level, a good demand prevision plays a fundamental role when healthcare managers are interested in guaranteeing the efficiency and fairness of the provided service: for instance, the solutions computed by the algorithm proposed in [12] caused under-staffing because of inadequate forecasts.

Various metrics can be used to measure the efficiency of one individual and exploit such measures to evaluate the overall team performance with respect to the forecasted service demand. The random nature of the problem requires the introduction of random variables, and the characterisation of the overall team behaviour with a stochastic process in order to have a more accurate team performance evaluation. Generalized Stochastic Petri Nets (GSPN) allow to deal with such a requirement guaranteeing an accurate team performance evaluation: a GSPN allows a direct mapping from a high level representation to a Continuous Time Markov Chain (CTMC) that can be solved to evaluate the team performance under several demand scenarios. The review [9] considers the literature on staffing and scheduling approaches that account for non-stationary demand, that is when the number of "*customers*" fluctuates over time according to a stochastic pattern. In their conclusions, the authors indicated two important aspects, that is (i) the opportunity to model human behaviour, as handling speed may be influenced by workload and other factors, and (ii) the need of addressing the computational requirements of the performance evaluation methods. We consider both aspects in our work.

In this paper we propose hybrid algorithms based on the GSPN and optimisation whose underlying idea is to exploit the GSPN model as a black box to evaluate a solution computed by an optimisation algorithm. We present two hybrid algorithms, that is an exact one based on a partitioning model, and a metaheuristic based on a Local Search. We test the proposed algorithms on a case study arising from an Italian Emergency Medical Services whose features make it the ideal case study, as we will show in Sect. 2. The proposed Generalized Stochastic Petri Nets (GSPN) model evaluates the composition of a team analysing the EMS request flow at the Operation Centre (OC). It takes into account both the characterisation of the team members (by exploiting parameters obtained from the statistics on their previous activities), and of the specific situation (workload, team cardinality, members busy or free) in which the team is going to operate.

The paper is organised as follows. In Sect. 2, we describe the case study considered and report the problem statement. In Sect. 3 we describe our GSPN model through its evolution towards a more computationally efficient model. The hybrid GSPN and optimisation algorithms are proposed in Sect. 4. Insights from the computational analysis of the proposed solution algorithms are discussed in Sect. 5. Finally, Sect. 6 closes the paper.

2 Problem Statement

The main performance measure for the EMS providers is the *response time*, which is defined as the time elapsed between the call arrival and the arrival of the ambulance at the patient, as depicted in Fig. 1.

The service quality of an EMS is therefore directly connected to the promptness of the assistance. Of course, the ambulance availability plays a fundamental role in the service provided by an EMS, but the first answer to patients (triage and dispatch in Fig. 1) is given by the OC operators. Therefore, the promptness of the assistance can highly depend on how fast is the answer provided by the OC operators.

The OC of the Milano EMS is in charge of receiving the phone calls from citizens who need immediate medical assistance. The staff employed at the OC is organised in teams composed of operators; such teams are then scheduled following a cyclic pattern over a given time horizon. Due to legal obligation, the EMS keeps daily logs of the emergency calls, with time and duration of each call, and the operator "id" who handled the call. From this set of information, it is possible to derive both a measure of the efficiency of each operator and an evaluation of the variable demand characterising EMS workload. The answer to a call consists in three phases: (i) to determine where to send the ambulance, (ii) to perform the triage, and (iii) to dispatch an ambulance. The triage is a procedure which allow the operator to determine the seriousness of the emergency request, and to assign a colour-code to the request: white and green for non-urgent requests, yellow and red for the urgent ones.

The efficiency of an operator is set to the average duration of a call handled by the operator disregarding the urgency of the emergency request. This assumption is due to the fact that the urgency is defined at the end of the triage procedure, and not

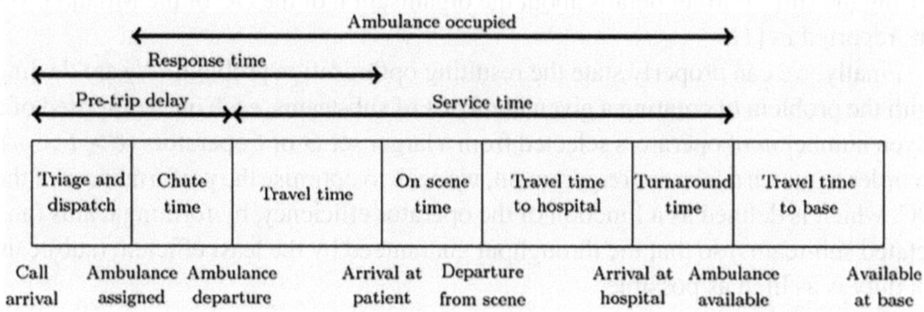

Fig. 1 The emergency response process (from [15])

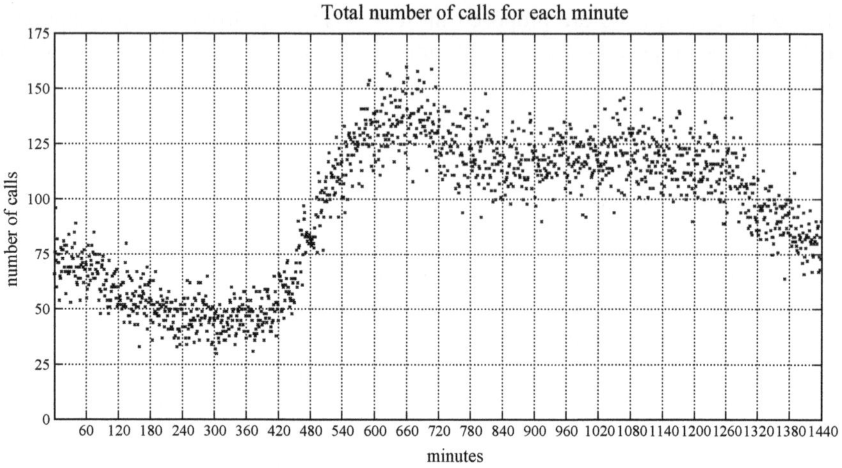

Fig. 2 Emergency demand (number of calls per day)

before the call. Therefore, the operator behaves as if they was managing an urgent request.

The demand is forecasted as follows: the 24 hours time horizon is divided in a set of time intervals for each of which the maximum number of simultaneous calls is computed. Then, the forecasted demand is computed as the maximum number of calls within a given time span. Figure 2 reports the emergency demand in terms of number of calls received during each time interval over a period of three months. We would like to point out the generality of the profile shown in Fig. 2, as shown for instance in [2, 10, 11].

Beside processing the emergency calls, the OC is in charge of other tasks, such as managing the transport of organs from organ donations, or keeping contact with the volunteering associations operating on the ambulances. Thus, the set of operators on work is constantly split into two "sub-teams", whose members alternate day by day in managing the phone calls. Each of the two sub-teams will be engaged at the phone during the shift. Further details about the organisation of the OC of the Milano EMS are reported in [1].

Finally, we can properly state the resulting optimisation problem. We are dealing with the problem of creating a given number t of sub-teams, each one composed of a given number m of operators selected from a larger set O of ℓ operators ($\ell \geq t \times m$). In order to match a fairness requirement, we seek to optimise the performances of the OC, which is defined as a function of the operator efficiency, by forming teams (and related sub-teams) so that the throughput guaranteed by the least efficient (sub)team on duty is as high as possible.

3 Modelling the EMS Patient Flow Using GSPN

We present two GSPN models to evaluate the performance of a group of operators. To help the reader, an introduction to the Petri Net methodology is reported in Appendix.

An initial GSPN model. As already discussed in Sect. 2, the service quality of an EMS is directly connected to the promptness of the assistance. In the following, we will consider the worst scenario, that is we are interested in observing the system during a peak of emergency requests and to evaluate its efficiency under the peak. This is required to address the need of fairness of the service. During a demand peak, a common procedure, called *cutoff priority queue*, is to postpone non-urgent requests in order to have enough free ambulances for the upcoming urgent requests [6, 18]. From a practical point of view, postponing means that those requests are managed by other operators (usually the other sub team) whose main task is to call back in order to verify if the emergency request is getting worse (in this case, the request become urgent and an ambulance will be sent as soon as one is available) or, on the contrary, if it is solved (the patient has been transported autonomously to a hospital).

We used the GSPN reported in Fig. 3 to model the behaviour of a team working at the OC. Transition `Arrival` represents the arrival of an emergency request call. The OC is able to handle only a maximum number of calls n: this is modelled by the marking of place n. Remember that all teams have the same number of operators as m, each team member is represented by a set of places and transitions: to simplify the model description, only the primitives corresponding to a single operator have been shown, which are then replied m times in Fig. 3. Therefore, the following describes the process of managing a call by the same operator operator by doing the three phases described in Sect. 2.

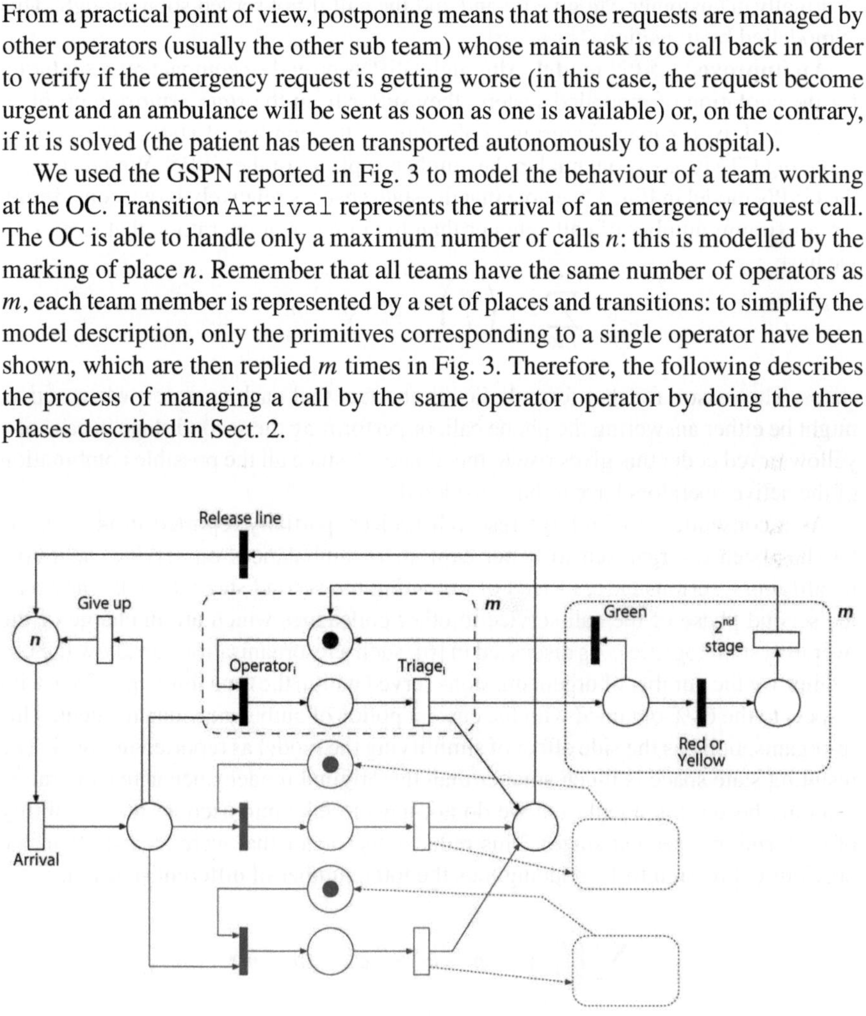

Fig. 3 An initial GSPN model of the OC

If a member is available, its corresponding place is marked. This allows new incoming call to be assigned randomly to any of the available operators. If all the operators are busy, the caller is forced to wait. The number of waiting calls is represented by the marking of the place immediately connected to the `Arrival` transition. The triage stage is represented by the transition `Triage`$_i$, that fires with an exponentially distributed firing time which defines the efficiency of an operator. At the end of the triage, the outcome of the process is modelled by two immediate transitions. If it is a green or white code, transition `Green` fires, freeing the operator for the next call. Otherwise, transition `Yellow or Red` fires, transferring the call to the second stage to dispatch an ambulance. In both cases the call is ended immediately and the line returns available to other callers.

Finally, a customer can give up and end the call if not served soon enough. This is modelled by transition `Give up`.

An improved GSPN model. Although GSPNs provide a compact representation for the evolution of modelled system, they suffer from the *state explosion* problem (see, e.g., [16] for manufacturing applications): the number of states of the corresponding CTMC is exponential in the number of places of the GSPN. With respect to the GSPN model in Fig. 3, we note that the state space is relatively large: considering the maximum number of calls greater than the number of operators, that is $n > m$, we have

$$\sum_{i=0}^{m} 2^i \cdot \binom{m}{i} + 2^m \cdot (n - m)$$

states. The reason for that formula lies in the fact that each operator, when active, might be either answering the phone call, or performing the second stage in case of a yellow or red code: this gives rise to the 2^i and 2^m since all the possible combination of the active operators have to be considered.

As a consequence of a large research project (partially reported in [4, 5]), the OC has been re-organised to better exploit the ambulances on service: operators identifying a serious case, instead of executing the second stage directly, they pass the second phase of the call service to other colleagues which are in charge of the overall system logistics. As discussed in [6], such a re-organisation can allow the OC to improve the number of urgent missions served within the time limit up to 75% with respect to the 61% obtained with the current policy of ambulance management. This re-organisation has the side effect of simplifying the model as reported in Fig. 4. The resulting state space is much smaller than the original model since active operators can only be serving a call (and we do not have to take into account the possibility of performing a second stage). This reduces the factor that were 2^i and 2^m in the previous expression to 1, reducing thus the total number of different states to:

$$\sum_{i=0}^{m} \binom{m}{i} + (n - m) = 2^m + (n - m).$$

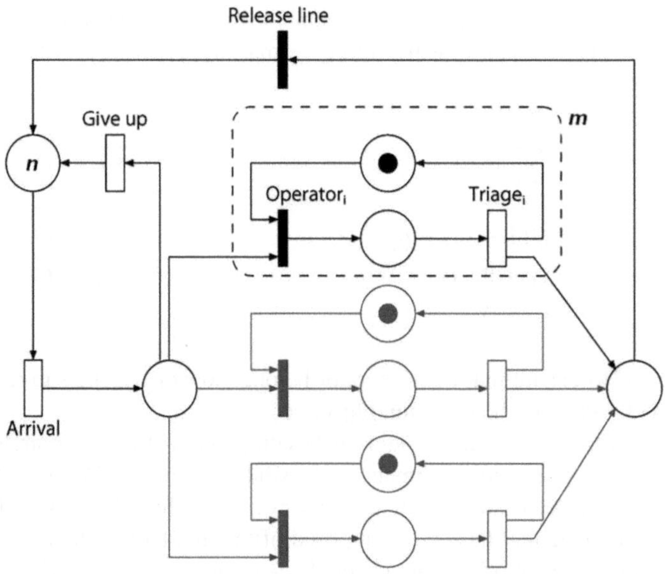

Fig. 4 An improved GSPN model of the OC

4 Hybrid GSPN and Optimisation Algorithms

The main concern of this section is to evaluate how to combine GSPN solutions and optimisation algorithms in an efficient and a proper way. To this purpose, we propose an exact method based on partitioning models, and a simple local search based metaheuristic. Apart of their effectiveness in computing good quality solutions, we are also interested in the feasibility of exploiting Petri Nets within an optimisation algorithm framework, and to address some computational issues.

The improved GSPN model discussed in Sect. 3 estimates the efficiency of a team by computing its throughput X. We seek to optimise the OC performances by forming teams (and related sub-teams) so that the throughput guaranteed by the least efficient (sub)team on duty is as high as possible. This matches a fairness requirement in order to avoid strong losses of performances through the shifts. We recall that the sub-team approach allows also to avoid that only the best operators answer to emergency calls: if we ask for optimal peak performances, without any additional constraints on shift, we would find solutions with always the same operators assigned to emergency calls; on the contrary, considering two (sub)teams for each team, we find solutions that still exhibit good performances, but take into account the necessary rotation in the service, allowing an alternation in phone call service, that is the most heavy job in the OC.

A set partitioning approach. The problem boils down to partitioning the set of operators into equally-sized sub-teams of fixed cardinality. We formulate the problem with a set O of operators, a set J of $\binom{\ell}{m}$ sub-teams and a coverage matrix $A = [a_{ij}]$ where $a_{ij} = 1$ if operator i belongs to sub-team $j \in J$. A number q_j measures the expected throughput guaranteed by sub-team j – this is computed by means of the GSPN model. The constant Q is fixed to $Q = \max_{j \in J}\{q_j\}$.

$$
\begin{aligned}
\max \quad & z^e && && \text{(1a)}\\
\text{s.t.} \quad & \sum_{j \in J} a_{ij} x_j = 1 && \forall\, i \in O && \text{(1b)}\\
& Q(1 - x_j) + q_j x_j \geq z^e && \forall\, j \in J && \text{(1c)}\\
& x_j \in \{0, 1\} && \forall\, j \in J && \text{(1d)}\\
& z^e \geq 0. && && \text{(1e)}
\end{aligned}
$$

Constraints (1b) ensure that each operator belongs to exactly one sub-team, while constraints (1c) capture the max-min objective.

The optimal solution of the problem can be computed with a simple strategy based on solving a sequence of lower dimension feasibility problems. We order the teams according to their decreasing efficiency, then we apply the following dichotomous search: it starts selecting the set J' composed of the first half of the possible teams (i.e., those having better efficiency); check if a feasible solution exists in J'; it exists, then half again the considered subset of teams, otherwise add half of the unused set. The procedure stops when the smallest set J' for which exists a feasible solution is found. The worst team in this set is the bottleneck one and gives the value of the optimal solution. In the worst case we solve $\log_2(|J|)$ feasibility problems of dimension at most $|J|$. At each iteration, in order to check feasibility, we solve the following reduced problem:

$$
\begin{aligned}
\min \quad & \sum_{j \in J'} x_j && \\
\text{s.t.} \quad & \sum_{j \in J'} a_{ij} x_j = 1 && \forall i \in O\\
& x_j \in \{0, 1\} && \forall j \in J'
\end{aligned}
$$

The illustrated approach is exact in nature.

A metaheuristic approach. We propose a simple but effective metaheuristic based on a straightforward neighbourhood exploration. Let us consider the following formulation of the original staffing problem. Let x_{ij} be a decision variable assuming value 1 if the operator $i = 1, \ldots, \ell$ is assigned to sub-team $j = 1, \ldots, t$, and 0 otherwise. The model follows:

$$
\begin{aligned}
\max \quad & z^m = \min_{j=1,\ldots,t} \{q_j(x)\} && && \text{(2a)}\\
\text{s.t.} \quad & \sum_{j=1}^{t} x_{ij} \leq 1 && i = 1, \ldots, \ell && \text{(2b)}
\end{aligned}
$$

$$\sum_{i=1}^{\ell} x_{ij} = m \qquad j = 1, \ldots, t \tag{2c}$$

$$x_{ij} \in \{0, 1\} \qquad i = 1, \ldots, \ell,\ j = 1, \ldots, t \tag{2d}$$

The function (2a) captures the max-min objective while constraints (2b) and (2c) model the team composition. Note that $q_j(x)$ is a function of the individual efficiency, denoted by e_i, and its value is determined by solving the corresponding GSPN.

We denote a solution as a set of teams C^j having efficiency $E^j \equiv q_j(x)$ for any $j = 1, \ldots, t$. Let z be equal to min $\{E^1, \ldots, E^t\}$. After computing the initial solution randomly assigning individuals to teams, such a solution is improved by a straightforward local search: at each iteration, the team C^w having the worst efficiency E^w is considered; then, we find a pair (i, h) of individuals giving the best solution improvement in such a way that i belongs to C^w and h to any other teams; after reaching a local optima, a random restart is performed to diversify the search following the insights reported in [7, 8] for combinatorial problems with a simple mathematical structure. The total number of restarts is determined by the parameter R.

5 Insights from the Computational Analysis

The main concern of this section is to validate the hybrid algorithms discussed in Sect. 4, and to provide some insights from the analysis of their results in order to better understand their computational behaviour.

The GSPN and the optimisation algorithms have been coded in C standard and compiled by `gcc 4.1.2`. They run on a 2.1 GHz AMD Opteron 8425HE with 16 GB of memory. Cplex with default configuration has been embedded in the exact algorithm.

We generated the benchmark instances as follows. The raw data is composed of a set of 45 operators and a list composed of calls collected during three months of OC activity. Each call is associated to an operator through an operator "id". The number of calls for each operator are about 1000. Further information available are instant time and duration of the call. Then, we compute an estimation of the operator efficiency as the average value of call duration measured in minutes. Finally, we generate 10 different instances (denoted by 0 to 9) selecting randomly $\ell = 30$ operators and their associated efficiency and setting $t = 10$ and $m = 3$. Different scenarios are also considered by varying the arrival rate, that is 1.5, 1.7 and 2.0, measured as call per minute.

GSPN solver performance. As discussed in Sect. 3, the computational efficiency of a GSPN model depends on the number of states in the corresponding CTMC. Here we would evaluate the running time behaviour of such a GSPN solver. Table 1 reports the average running time estimated by running the metaheuristic setting $R = 1000$: as a matter of fact, the number of restart R determines the total number of moves performed by the local search and, by consequence, the number of calls to the GSPN

Table 1 GSPN solver: average running time

	Rate 1.5			Rate 1.7			Rate 2.0		
	# moves	# GSPN	avg. ms.	# moves	# GSPN	avg. ms.	# moves	# GSPN	avg. ms.
0	20659	3346758	0.3399	21262	3444444	0.3821	21493	3481866	0.4599
1	2039	330318	0.5849	2189	354618	0.6462	2417	391554	0.7479
2	19099	3094038	0.3338	19336	3132432	0.3783	19054	3086748	0.4541
3	2464	399168	0.5518	2797	453114	0.6029	3249	526338	0.7013
4	22019	3567078	0.3401	22059	3573558	0.3877	21877	3544074	0.4672
5	2442	395604	0.5453	2866	464292	0.5906	3365	545130	0.6741
6	18083	2929446	0.3361	18093	2931066	0.3786	17771	2878902	0.4603
7	1907	308934	0.6004	2080	336960	0.6592	2319	375678	0.7552
8	3178	514836	0.5071	3800	615600	0.5486	4808	778896	0.6189
9	19060	3087720	0.3363	19089	3092418	0.3776	18962	3071844	0.4543
	Average time		0.4476	Average time		0.4952	Average time		0.5793

solver. For each scenario, three columns of data are reported: the number of local search moves, the number of calls to the GSPN solver, and the GSPN solver average running time in milliseconds. Last row reports the average running time among the different instances.

Results in Table 1 shows that, on average, a GSPN solution requires from 0.4476 to 0.5793 milliseconds. We remark that the average computing time increases as the arrival rate increases, that is when the system more easily saturates and, by consequence, it is harder to find a stationary solution of the corresponding CTMC.

Exact solutions. Table 2 reports the solutions computed by the exact algorithm reported in Sect. 4. For each scenario, three columns of data are reported: the sub-team "Id", the value z^e of the optimal solution and the running time in seconds. The last row reports the average running time. Ranking the sub-teams by decreasing value of their efficiency, the "Id" represents the position of that sub-team in the ranking. Note that the overall number of possible sub-teams are 4060.

The results in Table 2 highlight an average running time that decreases as soon as the arrival rate increases, which is in contrast to those in Table 1. When the arrival rate increases, the number of different teams having the same maximal throughput increases as soon as the probability to saturate the system increased. This implies that it is easier and faster to identify an optimal solution for our exact algorithm based on a dichotomous search. On the contrary, when the arrival rate decreases it could be possible to have a large bunch of similar teams having similar solution values, close to the optimal one. This is due to a sort of replacement effect for which changing an operator with another one having better (worse) efficiency could slightly increase (decrease) the team throughput. In such a situation is clearly harder for our exact algorithm to identify the optimal solution.

Metaheuristic solutions. Tables 3 and 4 report the solutions computed by the metaheuristic algorithm depicted in Sect. 4. The results reported in the two tables

Table 2 Results for the exact algorithm under the 3 scenarios

	Rate 1.5			Rate 1.7			Rate 2.0		
	Id	z^e	s	Id	z^e	s	Id	z^e	s
0	2118	1.45914	829.18	2126	1.67751	1074.02	2126	1.88112	1039.06
1	1997	1.46528	1180.68	1984	1.68847	1125.93	1986	1.89863	941.11
2	2091	1.46366	91.22	2071	1.68570	94.93	2073	1.89430	79.93
3	2045	1.46161	90.66	2045	1.68211	73.84	2035	1.88882	85.34
4	2099	1.45835	88.81	2099	1.67623	70.67	2097	1.87908	85.54
5	2040	1.46299	92.95	2037	1.68445	83.14	2029	1.89206	79.43
6	2013	1.46218	104.20	2011	1.68289	1003.58	2003	1.88982	7.44
7	2046	1.46498	1225.14	2020	1.68790	862.88	2022	1.89765	90.62
8	2008	1.45968	893.35	2008	1.67861	69.68	2006	1.88272	965.51
9	2058	1.46246	829.81	2055	1.68352	77.43	2053	1.89086	76.45
	Average time		542.60	Average time		453.61	Average time		345.04

differ from the number of restart R performed by the metaheuristic, that is $R = 10$ and $R = 100$, respectively. For each scenario, four columns of data are reported: the value z^m of the best solution computed, the number of moves performed by the local search, the running time in seconds and the relative gap with respect to the corresponding optimal solution. The last two rows report the average running time, the average relative gap and the number of optimal solution computed.

The reported results prove the good quality of the solution computed by the metaheuristic also considering the average running time which is respectively two (Table 3) and one (Table 4) order of magnitude below of the average running time of the exact method reported in Table 2. It is worth noting that the number of restart does not really influence the quality of the solution: as a matter of fact, the solution values z^m slightly improves when R increases and, by consequence, the average gap slightly decreases. This seems to indicate the need of more some intensification and diversification strategies to further improve the solution quality.

From a computational point of view, we observe that the number of moves (see also the corresponding column in Table 1) and the corresponding running time grow up proportionally to the number of restart R, as one can expect.

Looking at different scenarios, we can observe that the scenario with arrival rate 1.7 seems the hardest for the proposed metaheuristic. We observed that the number of similar teams having similar solution values, close to the optimal, can increase when the arrival rate decrease. A similar effect can be observed when the arrival rate increases determining (because of the system saturation) many teams having the same maximal throughput. In such situations is easier for a local search to determine a local optimum whose value is close to the optimal one.

Table 3 Results for the metaheuristic algorithm under the 3 scenarios and $R = 10$

	Rate 1.5				Rate 1.7				Rate 2.0			
	z^m	moves	s	gap %	z^m	moves	s	gap %	z^m	moves	s	gap %
0	1.45914	231	12.70	0.0000	1.63492	235	14.60	2.5389	1.88112	243	18.08	0.0000
1	1.43558	20	1.93	2.0269	1.60379	21	2.27	5.0152	1.83660	25	3.04	3.2671
2	1.46366	209	11.22	0.0000	1.64215	201	12.26	2.5835	1.89390	192	14.10	0.0211
3	1.42968	24	2.18	2.1846	1.59502	26	2.59	5.1774	1.82193	29	3.38	3.5414
4	1.45824	199	11.04	0.0075	1.63360	223	13.96	2.5432	1.87877	217	16.57	0.0165
5	1.43558	20	1.92	1.8736	1.60379	23	2.38	4.7885	1.83660	31	3.46	2.9312
6	1.46205	211	11.42	0.0089	1.63965	210	12.94	2.5694	1.88939	194	14.34	0.0228
7	1.43558	21	1.99	2.0069	1.60379	22	2.32	4.9831	1.83660	23	2.88	3.2171
8	1.43558	37	2.96	1.6510	1.60379	37	3.33	4.4573	1.83660	48	4.86	2.4496
9	1.46230	183	10.01	0.0109	1.64016	190	11.80	2.5756	1.89056	198	14.59	0.0159
	Average values		6.74	0.9770	Average values		7.85	3.7232	Average values		9.53	1.5483
	No. of best solutions			2	No. of best solutions			0	No. of best solutions			1

Table 4 Results for the metaheuristic algorithm under the 3 scenarios and $R = 100$

	Rate 1.5				Rate 1.7				Rate 2.0			
	z^m	moves	s	gap %	z^m	moves	s	gap %	z^m	moves	s	gap %
0	1.45914	2008	109.94	0.0000	1.63492	2128	131.76	2.5389	1.88112	2188	163.42	0.0000
1	1.43558	201	19.02	2.0269	1.60379	215	22.73	5.0152	1.83660	236	28.82	3.2671
2	1.46366	1879	101.34	0.0000	1.64229	1904	116.65	2.5752	1.89408	1830	134.09	0.0116
3	1.42968	241	21.65	2.1846	1.59502	278	27.08	5.1774	1.82193	322	36.38	3.5414
4	1.45833	2233	123.61	0.0014	1.63369	2262	141.66	4.7885	1.87895	2223	166.85	0.0069
5	1.43558	246	21.89	1.8736	1.60379	288	27.66	4.7885	1.83660	342	37.32	2.9312
6	1.46209	1849	100.75	0.0062	1.63974	1830	112.5	2.5640	1.88950	1792	133.35	0.0169
7	1.43558	200	18.96	2.0069	1.60379	221	23.09	4.9831	1.83660	240	29.38	3.2171
8	1.43558	326	26.68	1.6510	1.60379	375	33.29	4.4573	1.83660	481	48.46	2.4496
9	1.46239	2055	110.94	0.0048	1.64016	2029	124.72	2.5756	1.89086	2069	151.74	0.0000
	Average values		65.48	0.9755	Average values		76.11	3.7213	Average values		92.98	1.5442
	No. of best solutions			2	No. of best solutions			0	No. of best solutions			2

6 Conclusions

Workforce planning and scheduling based on forecasted demand is a topic that is receiving a growing attention by the research community. In this paper, we deal with a staffing problem based on forecasted demand arising in the personnel management of the Emergency Medical Service in Milano, Italy. This problem is the opportunity to propose and to test new hybrid algorithms that combines Petri Nets and optimisation. The basic idea is to exploit Petri Nets capability—if compared with other *classic* metrics—to evaluate the team performance with respect to a forecasted demand while an optimisation engine tries to compose the optimal set of teams. We proposed two algorithms to prove the feasibility of such an idea. The insights from the computational analysis confirm the validity of the proposed hybrid algorithms highlighting also the different computational behaviour of the two proposed hybrid algorithms.

Appendix: Short Introduction to Petri Net Modelling

The Petri Net (PN) approach is a graphical formalism used to represent models characterised by parallelism and synchronisation. A PN can be represented by a bipartite graph, whose nodes are divided in two classes called respectively *Places* (graphically represented by circles) and *Transitions* (drawn as boxes). Places and transitions are connected with two different types of arcs: *Standard Arcs* (drawn as arrows) and *Inhibitor Arcs* (represented by lines with a circular end). Each arc has associated an integer weight with default value equal to 1. Places may contain an integer number of objects called *Tokens* (drawn as black discs). Figure 5 presents a simple PN that shows all the primitives just described.

A PN represents a set of possible evolutions of a system through *enabling* and *firing* rules. A transition is said to be *enabled* if all the places, to which it is connected via an incoming standard arc (i.e., an arc directed from a place to a transition), contain a number of token *greater than or equal to* the weight of the connecting arc, and if all the places, to which it is connected with an inhibitor arc, contain a number of tokens which is *strictly less* than the weight of the arc. Standard arcs are thus guards that enables the transitions to which they point, provided that the starting places have

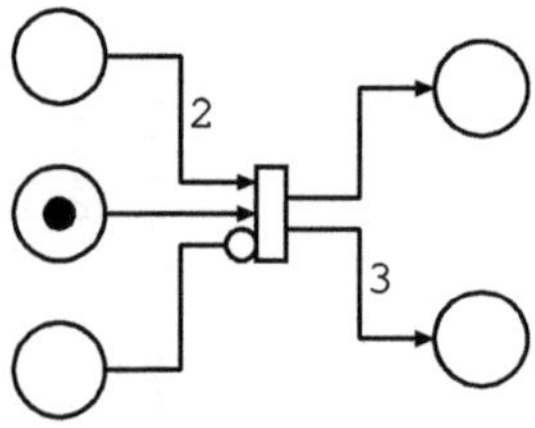

Fig. 5 A simple Petri Net model

enough tokens. On the other hand, an inhibitor arc prevents a transition from being enabled if the place from which it starts has more tokens than required. Inhibitor arcs are necessary to give to a PN the computational power of a Turing machine [14, Sect. 7.3]. If a transition is enabled, it may fire. When it fires, it removes from the input places as many tokens as the weight of the incoming arcs. Then the transition puts as many tokens as the weight of the outgoing arcs in all the places to which it is connected. Places connected with inhibitor arcs are unaffected by the firing of a transition.

In SPN (Stochastic Petri Nets), all the transition have associated a *firing rate*. When a transition becomes enabled, it fires after an exponentially distributed random amount of time, whose mean is inversely proportional to the firing rate. In a time instant more than one transition may be enabled: this is called a *conflict* and it allows to model several different evolutions of the system. Only a transition will fire, and it will be selected using *race policy*: all the transitions draw a sample from an exponential distribution according to their rate. The one with the shortest firing time is selected: since the probability of extracting exactly the same value from two independent exponential distributions is zero, race policy can always resolve the conflict.

Generalized Stochastic Petri Nets (GSPN), beside exponential transitions, allows a second type of transitions: *immediate transitions*. These transitions fire as soon as they become enabled and do not have any waiting time associated with them. While exponential transitions are used to model timed events, immediate transitions are used to model choices. Immediate transitions have associated a *weight* expressed by a continuous number. If more than one immediate transitions are enabled at the same time, weights are used to solve the conflict. The transition that fires is chosen probabilistically, according to the respective weights.

References

1. Addis, B., Aringhieri, R., Carello, G., Grosso, A., Maffioli, F.: Workforce management based on forecasted demand. In: Tanfani, E., Testi, A. (eds.) Advanced Decision Making Methods Applied to Health Care.International Series in Operations Research & Management Science, vol. 173, pp. 1–11. Springer (2012)
2. Argiento, R., Guglielmi, A., Lanzarone, E., Nawajah, I.: A Bayesian framework for describing and predicting the stochastic demand of home care patients. Flex. Serv. Manuf. J. **28**(1–2), 254–279 (2016)
3. Aringhieri, R.: Composing medical crews with equity and efficiency. CEJOR **17**(3), 343–357 (2009)
4. Aringhieri, R.: An integrated DE and AB simulation model for EMS management. In: IEEE Workshop on Health Care Management (2010). https://doi.org/10.1109/WHCM.2010.5441260
5. Aringhieri, R., Berchi, R., Carello, G., Fragnelli, F., Morale, D., Pagliosa, A., Righini, G., Sesana, G.: Il ruolo della ricerca operativa nell'organizzazione di un sistema di pronto intervento di soccorso sanitario. In: Sciomachen, A., Felici, G. (eds.) Scienza delle decisioni in Italia: applicazioni della ricerca operativa a problemi aziendali. ECIG, Genova (2008)

6. Aringhieri, R., Carello, G., Morale, D.: Supporting decision making to improve the performance of an Italian emergency medical service. Ann. Oper. Res. **236**(1), 131–148 (2016)
7. Aringhieri, R., Cordone, R.: Comparing local search metaheuristics for the maximum diversity problem. J. Oper. Res. Soc. **62**(2), 266–280 (2011)
8. Aringhieri, R., Cordone, R., Grosso, A.: Construction and improvement algorithms for dispersion problems. Eur. J. Oper. Res. **242**, 21–33 (2015)
9. Defraeye, M., Nieuwenhuyse, I.V.: Staffing and scheduling under nonstationary demand for service: a literature review. Omega **58**, 4–25 (2016)
10. Duma, D., Aringhieri, R.: An ad hoc process mining approach to discover patient paths of an emergency department. Flex. Serv. Manuf. J. **32**(1), 6–34 (2020)
11. Duma, D., Aringhieri, R.: Real-time resource allocation in the emergency department: a case study. Omega (United Kingdom) **117** (2023)
12. Mason, A.J., Ryan, D.M., Panton, D.M.: Integrated simulation, heuristic and optimisation approaches to staff scheduling. Oper. Res. **46**(2), 161–175 (1998)
13. McIntosh, B., Sheppy, B.: Skill maximisation: the future of healthcare. Br. J. Health Care Manag. **19**(3), 118–122 (2013)
14. Peterson, J.: Petri Net Theory and the Modeling of Systems. Prentice Hall (1981)
15. Reuter-Oppermann, M., Berg, P.L., Vile, J.L.: Logistics for emergency medical service systems. Health Syst. **6**(3), 187–208 (2017)
16. Tuncel, G., Bayhan, G.: Applications of petri nets in production scheduling: a review. Int. J. Adv. Manuf. Technol. **34**, 762–773 (2007)
17. Turner, J., Mehrotra, S., Daskin, M.S.: Perspectives on health-care resource management problems. In: Sodhi, M.S., Tang, C.S. (eds.) A Long View of Research and Practice in Operations Research and Management Science. International Series in Operations Research & Management Science, vol. 148, pp. 231–247. Springer (2010)
18. Yoon, S., Albert, L.A.: An expected coverage model with a cutoff priority queue. Health Care Manag. Sci. **21**(4), 517–533 (2018)

Exploring the Recent Applications of Artificial Intelligence Techniques for Type-1 Diabetes Management

Anas Nuemann, Marzia Angela Cremona, Adnène Haji, Michael Morin, and Monia Rekik

Abstract Type-1 Diabetes (T1D) is a chronic autoimmune disease affecting millions of patients worldwide. The pancreas of T1D patients no longer produces the insulin responsible for regulating blood glucose levels. Therefore, T1D patients must inject insulin themselves either through multiple daily injections or continuous subcutaneous insulin infusion (insulin pumps). They must daily manage their diabetes to

A. Nuemann (✉) · M. A. Cremona · A. Haji · M. Morin · M. Rekik
Department of Operations and Decision Systems, Laval University, Quebec City, Canada
e-mail: anas.neumann@polymtl.ca

M. A. Cremona
e-mail: marzia.cremona@fsa.ulaval.ca

A. Haji
e-mail: adnene.hajji@fsa.ulaval.ca

M. Morin
e-mail: michael.morin@fsa.ulaval.ca

M. Rekik
e-mail: monia.rekik@fsa.ulaval.ca

A. Nuemann
Department of Mathematical and Industrial Engineering, Polytechnic School of Montreal, Montreal, Canada

M. A. Cremona · M. Morin · M. Rekik
Diabetes, and Obesity (CMDO), The Research Network On Cardiometabolic Health, Quebec City, Canada

M. A. Cremona · M. Morin
Institute Intelligence and Data (IID), Quebec City, Canada

A. Nuemann · M. A. Cremona · A. Haji · M. Rekik
Interuniversity Research Center On Enterprise Networks, Logistics, and Transportation (CIRRELT), Quebec City, Canada

M. A. Cremona · M. Morin · M. Rekik
University Hospital Center of Quebec City, Laval University Research Center (CHUL), Quebec City, Canada

P. Landa et al. (eds.), *Operations Research and Artificial Intelligence in Healthcare Management*, Springer Proceedings in Mathematics & Statistics 506,
https://doi.org/10.1007/978-3-031-95659-1_3

reach the advised blood glucose targets and avoid short-term and long-term complications. With the technological advances achieved in the last decades in diabetes- and non-diabetes-oriented technologies, a large amount of data has become available. This has encouraged researchers to apply artificial intelligence techniques to improve diabetes management by predicting blood glucose levels or recommending actions for better control of T1D. Our paper reviews recent contributions in this area focusing on data-driven approaches for blood glucose prediction. It highlights future research avenues to better exploit the new advances in machine learning and deep learning models.

Keywords Type-1 diabetes · Literature review · Prediction · Machine learning · Deep learning

1 Introduction

Type-1 Diabetes (T1D) is a chronic condition affecting millions of patients worldwide. It is an autoimmune disease that destroys the pancreatic beta cells responsible for producing insulin. People living with T1D continuously need insulin injections to regulate their blood glucose level and achieve advised glucose targets. High blood glucose levels, also known as hyperglycemia, can lead to serious health complications over time, such as heart diseases, stroke, blindness, and kidney diseases. Low blood glucose levels, also known as hypoglycemia, affect physical and mental health and decrease the quality of life of T1D patients. Predicting and preventing hyperglycemia and hypoglycemia events is still challenging despite ongoing research efforts. T1D management, and more precisely the prediction of future blood glucose levels to ultimately prevent hypoglycemia and hyperglycemia, relies on the precise understanding of each T1D patient's glycemic behavior. The latter can be influenced by various factors such as physical activity, diet, stress, or lifestyle habits. With the growing popularity of Artificial Intelligence (AI) applications in all fields, including T1D management, it becomes very challenging for both researchers and practitioners to be constantly up to date with the latest advances in AI applied to the T1D field.

1.1 Methodology and Objectives

Our paper presents and discusses the recent scientific literature related to the management of T1D based on data-driven approaches, especially machine and deep learning models. Our objectives are threefold: (i) reporting globally accepted concepts, practices, and techniques; (ii) synthesizing the recent advances in the literature; and (iii) identifying gaps and opportunities for future research. Our paper presents a general overview of the recent literature addressing T1D management with data-driven approaches but emphasizes recently reported data-driven models for Blood

Glucose Level (BGL) prediction. This is motivated by two main reasons. First, we observed that most of the recent papers in T1D management based on data-driven approaches address BGL prediction. Second, BGL prediction is a main step for T1D management: predicting blood glucose levels with a reasonable precision not only enables straightforwardly predicting hypoglycemia and hyperglycemia events and other metrics commonly used for T1D management but is also a mandatory step to recommend actions (recommender systems) for better T1D control.

To carry on this review, we selected three main types of papers. First, we analyzed very recent contributions that used data-driven methods to predict BGL. To do so, we employed all 74 databases connected to the Sofia tool[1] and retrieved 17 papers. The keywords used were (blood glucose OR sugar) AND (Type 1 diabetes) AND (Prediction OR Forecasting) AND (Artificial intelligence OR learning OR data-driven OR AI). We only selected peer-reviewed papers published in English and in or after 2022. We also excluded papers that focused exclusively on (i) type-2 diabetes; (ii) detection of pre-diabetes; and (iii) prediction related to covid-19. Second, the analysis of four recent systematic literature reviews and tutorial papers on type-1 diabetes management yielded the selection of additional well-cited papers published before 2022. Finally, to deepen the analysis on recent contributions evoked in reviewed papers, we conducted a series of research on more precise topics such as "meta-learning", "biology-informed neural network", or "explainability" using Google Scholar.[2] This literature review ultimately covers a corpus of 76 articles.

1.2 Main Results

Our literature review reveals that recent contributions are mainly related to the explainability of the prediction or recommendation, the ability of the model to provide a level of confidence associated with its outputs, and its capacity to adapt (using meta-learning) to new patients with specific Blood Glucose (BG) dynamics. The other contributions are rather related to the integration of one or several absorption models for insulin, carbohydrates (CHO) intake, and activity-related effects yet or still active in the plasma. These absorption curves are respectively called Insulin-On-Board (IOB), Carbohydrates-On-Board (COB), and Exercise-On-Board (EOB).

Our literature review enables us to point out four main research avenues. First, the effects of Multiple Daily Injections of insulin (MDI), Continuous Subcutaneous Insulin Infusion (CSII), and Physical Activities (PA) on hypoglycemia and, especially, Nocturnal Hypoglycemia (NH). Second, the conception of a universal method to integrate IOB, COB, and EOB into data-driven models. Third, further experimentation on real patients in Real World free-living Condition (RWC)—since many contributions have been tested exclusively on virtual patients through simulators.

[1] https://ulaval.on.worldcat.org/discovery/.

[2] https://scholar.google.com/.

Finally, and most importantly, the ability of the proposed models to adapt to the characteristics of each patient. Indeed, the BG dynamic varies between patients, as well as for the same patient in different conditions or over time. A practical solution, intended to help T1D patients, or to be integrated into insulin pumps, should be able to make accurate predictions and recommendations for all users.

1.3 Remainder

The remainder of the paper is as follows. Section 2 presents a general overview of the data-driven algorithms recently proposed for T1D management, their objectives, their architectures, and the most used data for algorithms training. Section 3 details recent contributions, particularly for BGL prediction. Section 4 summarizes research gaps and opportunities that still need further investigation.

2 Overview and Modern Practices

2.1 Data-Driven Models and Their Objectives

The most prevalent predictive models related to T1D management are regression models that capture BG dynamics to predict future BGLs. The Prediction Horizon (PH) usually varies from 15 to 60 min [33, 57, 59], and sometimes reaches 2 h [25, 54, 66]. While most models are designed to predict a specific PH, some can predict multiple PHs at the same time [7, 23, 27, 34]. Several models also use Kalman Filter algorithms to predict and adjust each time new data is provided [23, 69]. The second most frequent predictive models are classification models used as alarm systems for hypoglycemia (BGL < 70 mg/dL or 3.9 mmol/L) and hyperglycemia (BGL > 180–200 mg/dL or 10 mmol/L at any time) events [11, 23, 33, 59, 61]. In general, these models especially focus on hypoglycemia and Time Below Range (TBR) since these episodes are more dangerous for T1D patients than hyperglycemia ones [69, 73]. Other data-driven models are used as personalized recommender systems [21, 33]. However, they are less common and more challenging to design because the expected results involve: (i) predicting a BGL or an event, (ii) understanding and ranking the multiple causes, and (iii) selecting an action or policy adapted to the patient and his/her current state. To build more robust models, a few papers like [36, 42, 61] predict a risk score instead of actual blood concentration. Several types of scores have been proposed in the literature. For instance, the Coefficient of Variation (CV), which is a ratio between the standard deviation and the mean value of BGLs, measures the degree of glucose mismanagement resulting in hypoglycemia and hyperglycemia [61].

2.2 *Types of Algorithms and Models*

2.2.1 Pure Data-Driven Models

A wide range of data-driven and learning algorithms have been used in the context of T1D management: Decision Tree (DT), Native Bayes (NB), K-Nearest Neighbors (KNN), Support Vector Machine (SVM), XGBoost, or AutoRegressive Integrated Moving Average (with eXogenous input) (ARIMA/ARIMAX) [4, 5, 21, 23, 50, 57, 59, 70]. However, Artificial Neural Networks (ANN), and deep learning models in general, represent the most frequent algorithms reported in the literature. They were used by 45% of papers in the field, according to a recent systematic literature review [66]. These algorithms also represent (one of) the best-performing approaches according to several comparative studies [1, 27, 59]. Finally, Genetic Algorithms (GA) [47] and Fuzzy-logic approaches [54] were scarcely used.

Some ANN models are simple fully connected Feed-Forward Multi-Layered Perceptron (FF-MLP) and use the SoftMax function in the classification context [5, 59]. Given that the information exploited as input features is time series (heartbeat, BGL over time, etc.), several deep learning models are Recurrent Neural Networks (RNN), use Long-Short Time Memory (LSTM) cells [1, 33, 47, 61, 71] and Gated Recurrent Units (GRUs) [33, 61, 73, 74]. Those units are adapted for sequential data requiring memory since they partially solve the problems of vanishing and exploding gradients. An Enhanced Personalized LSTM (EP-LSTM) adapted to the studied context has also been proposed [33]. Besides, some papers demonstrate that feature-extraction models like Temporal Convolutional Networks (TCN) outperform RNN and LSTM models [8, 68]. Finally, some models use attention layers or encoder-decoder architectures [6, 44, 73, 74].

2.2.2 Hybrid Models

Many data-driven approaches proposed in the literature are hybrid. Besides common pre-processing steps used to standardize or to resample input data [35, 57], hybrid models use physiological models to extract high-level features (such as absorption curves, IOB, COB, or EOB) to be used in one of the deep learning models reported above. In general, physiological models consist of differential equations and are divided into two parts: an absorption model and a kinetic model. Hybrid data-driven models consider only the absorption model [25, 47]. While many physiological models dedicated to insulin [31, 36, 52, 65] and CHO intake [31, 41, 60] have been proposed in the literature, fewer are dedicated to PA or blood glucose dynamics [22]. Prior to the recent advances in the field of machine learning, physiological models were directly used as predictors. However, the parameters of those models (peak time, peak decay rate, etc.) were generally difficult to estimate because of the intra- and inter-patient variability [47]. As detailed in Sect. 4.2, a few recent contributions propose innovative ways to integrate known dynamics and physiological systems into fully deep learning models, trained end-to-end, instead of building hybrid approaches.

2.2.3 Population-Based Versus Personalized Models

Population-based models are trained on the data of several T1D patients. They are intended to be robust and perform well for different patients [25]. Yet, they sometimes fail to adapt to individuals with specific blood glucose patterns. Some papers propose to use patient clustering techniques to improve population-based models [25, 43]. However, the intra- and inter-patient variability make personalized models mandatory to build an artificial pancreas [23, 44]. Obtaining enough RWC data to train a personalized model is difficult, in practice. Thus, as detailed in [38], there is a small number of fully personalized models, like [23, 47], reported in the literature. This type of models performs well for the patient under study, but risk overfitting [1, 25]. To reduce the quantity of needed data, pre-trained population-based models are often used to perform transfer learning and fine-tuning [62]. As detailed in Sect. 3.2, some recent papers exploit modern techniques like meta-learning to reuse personalized models for different patients. For instance, [6] uses the embedding vector built by an encoder sub-network to identify the current patient and adapt the prediction.

2.3 Input Data and Features

This section presents the data that are the most considered in data-driven models and the challenges related to their use in machine learning and deep learning models.

2.3.1 Most Used Input Data

The principal data used is the previous BGL, usually collected by Continuous Glucose Monitoring (CGM) sensors [66]. The number of BGL points used for prediction, or the length of the BGL sequence, depends on the capability of the proposed model. The second most exploited feature is the quantity of insulin injected. Some models integrate the type of administered insulin (basal and bolus) or distinguish between fast-acting and slow-acting insulin [34, 40]. The third most frequently used feature is physical activity [55, 56, 61, 62]. Several analyses demonstrate the impact of PA on blood glucose concentration and variability and the importance of considering PA to predict future BGL [14, 19, 37]. PA and energy expenditure are measured using several metrics like heartbeat frequency (bpm), skin temperature, number of steps, or speed. These metrics are generally collected as structured data (CSV files) by smartwatches, like the one proposed by Fitbit or SenseWear [11, 66], and Achtigraphs [46]. Some papers also differentiate between (i) aerobic exercises and High-Intensity Interval Training (HIIT) and between (ii) trained and untrained patients

[62]. The fourth most exploited type of data is CHO intake, usually measured in grams. Some papers also distinguish between dietary nutrients and energy sources, e.g. monosaccharides, starch, lipids, protein, and fiber [34]. The model proposed in the DIabetes Advisory System (DIAS) [6] is often used to predict the quantity of each nutrient [34]. Also, the physiological Lehman's compartmental model [39] has been widely used to build hybrid data-driven models [3, 15, 28, 29, 63]. Some papers also consider personal information like the enrollment and diagnosis ages, the gender, or the patient's weight [21]. Finally, fewer models consider stress-related data, like Acute Psychological Stress (APS), measured with signals like skin temperature and conductivity, eye movement, or heartbeat variability [54].

2.3.2 Multivariate Inputs and Related Challenges

The data collected have different units of measure and magnitude. Hence, they usually need a standardization step either by using the z-score or the min–max method. The latter outputs a percentage between 0 (lowest possible value) and 1 (highest possible value). Not all types of information are collected periodically. For instance, while CGM and heartbeats are usually collected continuously (every 5 min for CGM and every minute for heartbeats), PAs and meals are collected as discrete events. Periodic data are also collected at different frequencies. Another challenge is that the different sensors are often not synchronized. Hence, a resampling step is often mandatory [11, 68, 73]. Sometimes pre-processing steps are also mandatory to reduce collinearity in inputs. This is especially important between insulin and carbohydrate intake signals [57]. Moreover, insulin doses, PAs, and CHOs do not directly enter the plasma and do not instantly affect the BGL. This explains why physiological models are used to model the three respective absorption curves and the previous IOB, COB, and EOB still active in the plasma [11, 47].

2.4 Training and Validation

Most regression models used to predict future BGL are evaluated using common statistical metrics like Mean Square Error (MSE), Root Mean Square Error (RMSE), Mean Absolute Error (MAE), or Mean Absolute Relative Difference (MARD) [7, 33, 38, 66, 68]. Recent papers, such as [56], also use the Coefficient of determination (R^2). Event classification and alarm systems are rather evaluated using true-positive rate or Sensitivity (SN), true-negative rate or Specificity (SP), F1-Score, and Gmean (that considers both SN and SP with the same weight) [11, 23, 59]. In both contexts, the p-value, or the probability of observing the actual data assuming that a null hypothesis is true, has also been widely used [10, 54].

Besides statistical measures and loss functions, several papers also use clinical tools and metrics like the IndexJ [58, 66], temporal gain (the time between the prediction of a hypo/hyperglycemia event and its occurrence) [68], or the Clarke

Error Grid Analysis (CEGA) [23, 58, 61, 64, 71]. The Clarke Grid, defined in [16, 17], is divided into five error zones ranked by the level of risk. The worst zones, called E, correspond to the prediction of (i) an event of hypoglycemia when the patient was, in fact, in hyperglycemia or (ii) hyperglycemia when the patient was, in fact, in hypoglycemia.

To assess the impact of each input data and the effect of a specific architectural part of the model or hyperparameter (number of layers, activation function, etc.) on the prediction, some authors enable/disable inputs or components and compare several versions of the model [7, 47, 71]. This practice is called ablation experiments [71]. While considering PA, measures are usually taken before and after the exercise to analyze variations between patients and intra-patients over time [34].

The type and quantity (number of patients and sampling duration) of training data also vary between papers. Some use simulators of virtual patients or open-source in-silico datasets like UVA/Padova [33, 38], DirectNet [7], OhioT1DM [71, 73], ARISE [73], or ABC4D [73]. Others choose to assess the performance of their models on real patients in free-living conditions [10, 66]. Unlike past experiments, some of the most recent papers collected up to 4–5 months of data, including PA and meal information.

3 Recent Contributions

Despite the vast number of contributions made in the field, many gaps still needed to be filled whereas new advanced diabetes- and non-diabetes-oriented technologies appeared in the last five years. This section details some recent contributions.

3.1 Physical Activity, Nocturnal Hypoglycemia, and Absorption Models

Annuzzi et al. [7] proposed a detailed analysis of the postprandial glucose response and the effect of different nutritional factors. According to their results: (i) proteins and fibers have a short-term effect (15 min), (ii) fibers and lipids affect the BGL in the middle term (30–45 min), and (iii) all nutrients and sources of energy (including CHO) impact BGL in the long term (60 min). The FF-MLP proposed by Karim et al. [34] predicts BGL up to 4 h in advance. The complete approach is hybridized with a physiological model that differentiates between various types of nutrients and simulates their absorption over time.

Several recent works focused on PAs and their effect on BGL and NH. Indeed, more than 50% of severe hypoglycemia occur during the night [11]. Besides, the absence of visible symptoms is a common effect of NH, especially for patients under MDI [11]. This phenomenon is called the Impaired Awareness Hypoglycemic

(IAH) syndrome. A comparative and statistical study by Montt-Blanchard et al. [46] highlights the need for long-term predictions and a personalized post-PA strategy. Exploiting the data of real patients over 14 days, they demonstrated that exercise did not impact the Time In Range (TIR) and the Time Above Range (TAR) metrics but caused high TBRs at night.

The results were even more evident for groups doing high-intensity workouts. Parcerisas et al. [49] experimented on virtual patients under MDI to analyze the importance of considering CHOs and PA to predict NH, using several population-based and personalized models built with an optimization stage. Bertachi et al. [10] designed a Repeated Measures Random Forest to predict hypoglycemia risk during exercise.

They trained their model on 459 patients in free-living conditions for a total of 8,827 exercise sessions. Repeated measures enable classical machine learning models like RF and DT to integrate within-subject (like sequential data) and non-linear correlations. In this context, this technique was used as a component for explainability, helping identify the predictor that impacted the outcomes the most. Their results emphasize the importance of maintaining high BGL before exercise to avoid hypoglycemia episodes.

They also demonstrated the influence of the evolution trend of the BGL (direction and growth/decay rate) on future levels. In addition, their results highlight a higher risk for free-living exercises (hiking, walking, physical labor, etc.) than structured activities (workout, aerobic, etc.), regardless of the intensity. Finally, they noted a slightly higher risk when exercises are performed during the night.

Instead of forecasting a future BGL, the model proposed in [2] uses previous BGL, stress-related information, and PA to predict the insulin still active in the plasma (IOB). The proposed model reuses two previous pharmacokinetic models found in [50, 67]. The relations between the different input variables being non-linear, they also designed their approach as an Extended Kalman Filter. The deep neural network proposed by Muñoz-Organero et al. [47] consists of a combination of LSTM and dense (fully connected) layers. They also use several parametric physiological models to integrate input information related to CHO, fast, and slow insulin and operate a GA to optimize their parameters (peak time and decay rate). The model proposed in [11] predicts and avoids, in 70% of cases, NH caused by MDI and PA in RWC. In their experiments, SVM provided better population outcomes than the FF-MLP model. Both approaches used three physiological absorption models to integrate the IOB [65], EOB [48], and COB [9].

3.2 *Advanced Deep Learning Methods: Explainability and Meta-Learning*

The lack of data, especially RWC data, is a common problem in the field of T1D. For instance, CGM sensors typically collect 288 entries per day (one every 5 min).

While many previous studies, e.g. [45, 53], used transfer learning to adapt population-based and personalized models to new patients, the model proposed in [38] uses meta-learning. Meta-learning consists of learning to learn and proposing models able to adapt to new tasks [76]. More specifically, Langarica et al. [38] use the well-known optimization-based algorithm named Model-Agnostic Meta-Learning (MAML) proposed in [26]. MAML exploits two training stages. The first stage uses two optimization loops to find an initialization (weight and bias) of the network that is adapted to learn new tasks without requiring a large dataset. An inner loop optimizes a copy of the model on a small batch of tasks and an outer loop updates the actual model using a cumulative loss computed across the multiple tasks. The second training stage (executed at each new task) performs fine-tuning to adapt the model [38, 76]. In the T1D context, tasks usually correspond to predicting BGL of one patient or group of patients sharing a similar profile. In comparison with traditional transfer learning techniques, the use of MAML avoids the biases yielded by combining the data of many patients into a unique dataset. In [38], authors also propose a new network architecture composed of sub-networks. While the first one uses LSTM cells and is optimized only by the outer loop of MAML, the second one is an FF-MLP and is updated for each new patient. The models proposed in [73, 74] also use MAML to adapt a pre-trained population-based model to each new patient with minimal data requirements. They also use evidential deep learning techniques to associate the outcome (prediction or recommendation) with a level of confidence. This could indeed help the acceptability of the model in such a sensitive context. Technically, the level of confidence is based on an aggregated hidden state computed by a many-to-one attention layer at the end of a network composed of several layers of bidirectional GRUs. Duckworth et al. [21] proposed an explainable classical machine learning model (XGBoost) using the SHapley Additive exPlanation (SHAP) algorithm to retrieve the most responsible features in case of predicting an event of hypoglycemia or hyperglycemia. The use of SHAP allowed Shilo et al. [56] to rank input features by contribution while predicting BGLs. Especially, PA-related features were less influential than glucose and nutritional information such as glucose trend prior to meals and carbohydrate-to-fat ratio. Being able to explain a prediction could enable feature-oriented recommendations.

3.3 Algorithmic Mechanisms to Better Adapt the Models to T1D

Del Favero et al. [24] proposed a new loss function called glucose-specific MSE (gMSE). gMSE is based on the Clark Error Grid and applies penalties for overestimating the BGL during hypoglycemia (with a factor up to 2.5) and underestimating the BGL during hyperglycemia (with a factor up to 2). gMSE also respects the recommendations for effective loss functions: no local minima and smooth transitions using sigmoid-like functions. gMSE has also been used in recent papers, e.g. [23, 74], in its glucose-specific RMSE (gRMSE) form. Faccioli et al. [23] propose an alarm system with multiple PH and an aggregation funnel to build the final prediction.

While most reviewed models use the same time window for all input information, Yang et al. [71] use an autonomous channel network to consider the time-dependent scale discrepancy, incompletion, and redundancy of the different time series variables.

While the slow insulin impacts BGL for 1–24 h, the effect of meals on BGL lasts for only 3 h. Each channel has a multi-lag structure to extract features, has an adapted length, and is used for a different type of input. In the end, all channels connect to form a unique LSTM-based network. They also use IOB and COB physiological models from [12, 18] as preprocessing steps.

4 Scientific Gaps and Future Research Opportunities

Based on their experiments, some authors made observations regarding what aspects they consider to be the next research agenda requiring further investigation. In the following sections, we summarize key research avenues highlighted by recent papers.

4.1 Physical Activity and Nocturnal Hypoglycemia

To date, there is no universal method to measure the impact of PA on future blood glucose levels and variability [66, 68]. Results from recent studies, e.g. [10, 46, 54], contradict previous experiments that highlighted only the effects of energy expenditure and intensity. Several authors argue that current methods are not sufficient to handle the high inter- and intra-patient variability in RWC [30, 62]. Furthermore, existing predictive models only forecast blood glucose up to 2 h ahead, which is not enough to anticipate NHs [10, 46]. Finally, some potentially important data are missing from the current experiments [10]. For example, a PA session could have been prematurely stopped due to BGL concerns or the onset of symptoms [10].

4.2 Recommender Systems: Explainability, Evidential Learning, and Use of Absorption Models to Inform Neural Networks

Besides PA, there is also no universal method to accurately measure the quantity of CHO and nutrients eaten [66]. Some authors consider the modeling of personalized CHO and insulin absorption curves as an aspect needing improvement [2, 34]. Some of the proposed BGL or IOB prediction models and alarm systems could be integrated with a recommender system to propose a complete proactive-reactive strategy [2, 13]. However, very few recommender systems have been proposed in the literature. Fewer consider absorption models and CHO, insulin, or exercise still active in the plasma (on-board) [2]. Also, while most machine learning-based models proposed in the literature perform well for predicting BGLs, they are less reliable for providing therapy treatments recommendations. This is because fully data-driven models cannot learn biologically possible patterns absent from past data (due for example to patient habits). As a result, they also lack the ability to precisely model the impact of individual phenomena (eating, increasing the delivery rate of insulin, etc.) on glycemic variations. This is one of the reasons why recommender systems are rare in the scientific literature (another being the inherent risks of testing such systems on real patients). To solve this problem, two recent papers [20, 75] propose a new generation of hybrid models that inform deep learning models with biological laws. To do so, they bias the learning process toward known dynamics using System-Biology Informed Neural Network (SBINN) loss functions [72] and ODE-based physiological models (such as Roy and Parker's model proposed in [51]). The approach proposed in [20] not only predicts BGL but offers recommendations on insulin dosage.

Explainability in deep learning, or eXplainable Artificial Intelligence (XAI), remains a challenging and dynamic field of research [1]. Some modern techniques, like Layer-wise Relevance Propagation (LRP), enable measuring the relationships between the result and each feature and combination of features. Other approaches make it possible to describe the model and extract the decision rules that it would have learned. For T1D management, explainability is crucial to understanding the reasons behind the recommendations made, profiling each patient, and gaining the trust of patients and doctors [7, 73]. However, even if some attempts have been made on classical machine learning models [21], no concrete proposition has been made for complex deep learning and RNN-based models [7, 73]. The integration of PA and absorption models with XAI and evidential learning is also an interesting avenue of research [21].

4.3 Better Models and Practical Usability: Free-Living Conditions and Meta-Learning

In addition to explainability and evidential learning, other factors could enhance the practical usability of the proposed models in RWC. First, many models have only been tested with simulated in-silico data. However, existing simulators do not consider all sources of uncertainty and variability [32]. T1D patients can deal with harmful situations caused, or not, by their condition [32]. Hence, they could benefit from further experimentation and training on real patients [32]. Second, very few models focus on the portability of personalized models [32, 66]. Transfer learning and meta-learning are promising approaches but still need further research in the context of T1D [66]. This is also true for cluster analysis and patient profiling [32].

Glycemic homeostasis consists of two complementary processes: (i) alpha cells secreting glucagon, a peptide hormone that increases BGL, and (ii) beta cells producing amylin and insulin, a hormone that reduces BGL. T1D is an immune disease that destroys beta cells, resulting in deficient glycemic homeostasis. To the best of our knowledge, while recent advances have been made in dual-hormone artificial pancreas injecting insulin and glucagon, no data-driven model considers glucagon as input information or possible decision.

5 Conclusion

In this paper, we reviewed recent papers from the scientific literature related to the management of T1D based on data-driven approaches, especially machine and deep learning models. We classified our findings into three main categories.

First, we mapped out the globally accepted concepts and practices: (i) the types and purposes of reviewed studies (alarm systems and prediction models), (ii) the most used information to build input features (insulin, CHO intakes, past CGM, physical activities, etc.), and (iii) the statistical and clinical metrics used to evaluate the quality of the predictions like gMSE or the Clarke Error Grid. This first analysis revealed three main challenges: the multivariate and time series nature of the inputs, the lack of available data, and the still not-well-understood impact of exercising. Additionally, we outlined common solutions such as the use of population data to pre-train models with more data.

Second, we synthesized several recent findings from the literature. Most recent papers aim to address the remaining challenges to increase the quality of the predictions. Some focus on refining input features and model architecture to integrate exercise-related information, insulin absorption, or meal digestion (e.g. autonomous channel networks, hybrid physiological and data-based approaches). Several recent papers also use meta-learning and the MAML algorithm to circumvent the lack of available data. Others also exploit modern deep learning approaches to propose a more practical model in real-life conditions but also in the context of a recommender system. In particular, explainability and evidential learning are crucial to understanding the reasons behind the recommendations made, profiling each patient, and gaining the trust of patients and doctors.

Third, we listed persisting gaps and opportunities for research reported in recent papers. We noticed that there is still no universal method to measure the impact of physical activity and related information (duration, intensity, type of activity, etc.) on future blood glucose levels and variability. Also, some XAI approaches have only been tested on traditional machine learning models (with flattened time-lag features). They could be adapted for more modern deep learning recurrent models. Finally, several recent contributions, especially regarding recommender systems, have only been tested on simulated virtual patients and should be experimented with real patients.

Disclosure of Interest The authors declare no conflict of interest.

References

1. Afsaneh, E., Sharifdini, A., Ghazzaghi, H., Ghobadi, M.Z.: Recent applications of machine learning and deep learning models in the prediction, diagnosis, and management of diabetes: a comprehensive review. Diabetol. Metab. Syndr. **14**(1), 196 (2022). https://doi.org/10.1186/s13098-022-00969-9
2. Aiello, E.M., Wolkowicz, K.L., Pinsker, J.E., Dassau, E., Doyle, F.J., III.: A novel model-based estimator for real-time prediction of insulin-on-board. Chem. Eng. Sci. **267**, 118321 (2023). https://doi.org/10.1016/j.ces.2022.118321
3. Alanis, A.Y., Sanchez, E.N., Ruiz-Velazquez, E., Leon, B.S.: Neural model of blood glucose level for Type 1 Diabetes Mellitus Patients. In: IEEE, The 2011 International Joint Conference on Neural Networks, 2018–2023 (2011). https://doi.org/10.1142/S0129065711003000
4. Alfian, G., Syafrudin, M., Anshari, M., Benes, F., Atmaji, F.T.D., Fahrurrozi, I., Fathan, A., Rhee, J.: Blood glucose prediction model for type 1 diabetes based on artificial neural network with time-domain features. Biocybern. Biomed. Eng. **40**(4), 1586–1599 (2020). https://doi.org/10.1016/j.bbe.2020.10.004
5. Aljihmani, L., Kerdjidj, O., Petrovski, G., Erraguntla, M., Sasangohar, F., Mehta, R.K., Qaraqe, K.: Hand tremor-based hypoglycemia detection and prediction in adolescents with type 1 diabetes. Biomed. Signal Process. Control **78**, 103869 (2022). https://doi.org/10.1016/j.bspc.2022.103869
6. Andreassen, S., Hejlesen, O.K., Hovorka, R., Cavan, D.A.: The diabetes advisory system-an IT approach to the management of insulin dependent diabetes. In: IOS Press, Medical Informatics Europe'96, pp. 1079–1083 (1996). https://doi.org/10.3233/978-1-60750-878-6-1079
7. Annuzzi, G., Apicella, A., Arpaia, P., Bozzetto, L., Criscuolo, S., De Benedetto, E., Pesola, M., Prevete, R., Vallefuoco, E.: Impact of nutritional factors in blood glucose prediction in type 1 diabetes through machine learning. IEEE Access **11**, 17104–17115 (2023). https://doi.org/10.1109/ACCESS.2023.3244712
8. Bai, S., Kolter, J.Z., Koltun, V.: An empirical evaluation of generic convolutional and recurrent networks for sequence modeling (2018). arXiv:1803.01271. https://doi.org/10.48550/arXiv.1803.01271
9. Beneyto, A., Bertachi, A., Bondia, J., Vehi, J.: A new blood glucose control scheme for unannounced exercise in type 1 diabetic subjects. IEEE Trans. Control Syst. Technol. **28**(2), 593–600 (2018). https://doi.org/10.1109/TCST.2018.2878205
10. Bergford, S., Riddell, M.C., Jacobs, P.G., Li, Z., Gal, R., Clements, M.A., Martin, C.K., Patton, S.R., Castle, J.R., Gillingham, M.B., Beck, R.W., Calhoun, P.: The type 1 diabetes and exercise initiative (T1DEXI): predicting hypoglycemia risk during exercise for participants with type 1 diabetes using repeated measures random forest. Diabetes Technol. Ther. (2023). https://doi.org/10.1089/dia.2023.0140
11. Bertachi, A., Viñals, C., Biagi, L., Contreras, I., Vehí, J., Conget, I., Giménez, M.: Prediction of nocturnal hypoglycemia in adults with type 1 diabetes under multiple daily injections using continuous glucose monitoring and physical activity monitor. Sensors **20**(6), 1705 (2020). https://doi.org/10.3390/s20061705
12. Bertachi, A., Biagi, L., Contreras, I., Luo, N., & Vehí, J.: Prediction of blood glucose levels and nocturnal hypoglycemia using physiological models and artificial neural networks. In: KHD@IJCAI, pp. 85–90 (2018)

13. Bertachi, A., Ramkissoon, C.M., Bondia, J., Vehí, J.: Automated blood glucose control in type 1 diabetes: a review of progress and challenges. Endocrinología, Diabetes y Nutrición (English ed.) **65**(3), 172–181 (2018). https://doi.org/10.1109/TCST.2018.2878205
14. Breton, M.D., Brown, S.A., Karvetski, C.H., Kollar, L., Topchyan, K.A., Anderson, S.M., Kovatchev, B.P.: Adding heart rate signal to a control-to-range artificial pancreas system improves the protection against hypoglycemia during exercise in type 1 diabetes. Diabetes Technol. Ther. **16**(8), 506–511 (2014). https://doi.org/10.1089/dia.2013.0333
15. de Canete, J.F., Gonzalez-Perez, S., Ramos-Diaz, J.C.: Artificial neural networks for closed loop control of in silico and ad hoc type 1 diabetes. Comput. Methods Progr. Biomed. **106**(1), 55–66 (2012). https://doi.org/10.1016/j.cmpb.2011.11.006
16. Clarke, W.L.: The original Clarke error grid analysis (EGA). Diabetes Technol. Ther. **7**(5), 776–779 (2005). https://doi.org/10.1089/dia.2005.7.776
17. Clarke, W.L., Cox, D., Gonder-Frederick, L.A., Carter, W., Pohl, S.L.: Evaluating clinical accuracy of systems for self-monitoring of blood glucose. Diabetes Care **10**(5), 622–628 (1987). https://doi.org/10.2337/diacare.10.5.622
18. Contreras, I., Bertachi, A., Biagi, L., Vehí, J., Oviedo, S.: Using grammatical evolution to generate short-term blood glucose prediction models. In KHD@ IJCAI, pp. 91–96 (2018)
19. Dadlani, V., Levine, J.A., McCrady-Spitzer, S.K., Dassau, E., Kudva, Y.C.: Physical activity capture technology with potential for incorporation into closed-loop control for type 1 diabetes. J. Diabetes Sci. Technol. **9**(6), 1208–1216 (2015). https://doi.org/10.1177/1932296815609949
20. Deng, Y., Arao, K., Mantzoros, C.S., Karniadakis, G.E.: Patient-specific deep offline artificial pancreas for blood glucose regulation in type 1 diabetes. bioRxiv (2022). https://doi.org/10.1101/2022.10.21.513303
21. Duckworth, C., Guy, M.J., Kumaran, A., O'Kane, A.A., Ayobi, A., Chapman, A., Marshall P., Boniface, M.: Explainable machine learning for real-time hypoglycemia and hyperglycemia prediction and personalized control recommendations. J. Diabetes Sci. Technol. (2022). https://doi.org/10.1177/19322968221103561
22. Duke, D.L.: Intelligent Diabetes Assistant: a Telemedicine System for Modeling and Managing Blood Glucose. Carnegie Mellon University (2010)
23. Faccioli, S., Prendin, F., Facchinetti, A., Sparacino, G., Del Favero, S.: Combined use of glucose-specific model identification and alarm strategy based on prediction-funnel to improve online forecasting of hypoglycemic events. J. Diabetes Sci. Technol. (2022). https://doi.org/10.1177/19322968221093665
24. Del Favero, S., Facchinetti, A., Cobelli, C.: A glucose-specific metric to assess predictors and identify models. IEEE Trans. Biomed. Eng. **59**(5), 1281–1290 (2012). https://doi.org/10.1109/TBME.2012.2185234
25. Felizardo, V., Garcia, N.M., Pombo, N., Megdiche, I.: Data-based algorithms and models using diabetics real data for blood glucose and hypoglycaemia prediction-a systematic literature review. Artif. Intell. Med. **118**, 102120 (2021). https://doi.org/10.1016/j.artmed.2021.102120
26. Finn, C., Abbeel, P., Levine, S.: Model-agnostic meta-learning for fast adaptation of deep networks. In: International Conference on Machine Learning (PMLR), pp. 1126–1135 (2017)
27. Fox, I., Ang, L., Jaiswal, M., Pop-Busui, R., Wiens, J.: Deep multi-output forecasting: learning to accurately predict blood glucose trajectories. In: Proceedings of the 24th ACM SIGKDD International Conference on Knowledge Discovery & Data Mining, pp. 1387–1395 (2018). https://doi.org/10.1145/3219819.3220102
28. Georga, E.I., Protopappas, V.C., Fotiadis, D.I.: Predictive metabolic modeling for type 1 diabetes using free-living data on mobile devices. In: Wireless Mobile Communication and Healthcare: Second International ICST Conference, MobiHealth 2010, Ayia Napa, Cyprus, pp. 187–193. Springer (2011). https://doi.org/10.1007/978-3-642-20865-2_24
29. Georga, E.I., Protopappas, V.C., Polyzos, D., Fotiadis, D.I.: A predictive model of subcutaneous glucose concentration in type 1 diabetes based on random forests. In: IEEE, 2012 Annual International Conference of the IEEE Engineering in Medicine and Biology Society, pp. 2889–2892 (2012). https://doi.org/10.1109/EMBC.2012.6346567

30. Hobbs, N., Hajizadeh, I., Rashid, M., Turksoy, K., Breton, M., Cinar, A.: Improving glucose prediction accuracy in physically active adolescents with type 1 diabetes. J. Diabetes Sci. Technol. **13**(4), 718–727 (2019). https://doi.org/10.1177/1932296818820550
31. Hovorka, R., Canonico, V., Chassin, L.J., Haueter, U., Massi-Benedetti, M., Federici, M.O., Pieber, T.R., Schaller, H.C., Schaupp, L., Vering, T., Wilinska, M.E.: Nonlinear model predictive control of glucose concentration in subjects with type 1 diabetes. Physiol. Meas. **25**(4), 905 (2004). https://doi.org/10.1088/0967-3334/25/4/010
32. Iacono, F., Magni, L., Toffanin, C.: Personalized LSTM-based alarm systems for hypoglycemia and hyperglycemia prevention. biomedical signal processes and control (2023). SSRN 4402867. https://doi.org/10.1016/j.bspc.2023.105167
33. Kalita, D., Mirza, K.B.: LS-GRUNet: glucose forecasting using deep learning for closed-loop diabetes management. In: IEEE, 7th International Conference for Convergence in Technology (I2CT), pp. 1–6 (2022). https://doi.org/10.1109/I2CT54291.2022.9824867
34. Karim, R.A., Vassányi, I., Kósa, I.: After-meal blood glucose level prediction using an absorption model for neural network training. Comput. Biol. Med. **125**, 103956 (2020). https://doi.org/10.1016/j.compbiomed.2020.103956
35. Kovatchev, B.P., Breton, M., Dalla Man, C., Cobelli, C.: In silico preclinical trials: a proof of concept in closed-loop control of type 1 diabetes. J. Diabetes Sci. Technol. (2009). https://doi.org/10.1177/193229680900300106
36. Kovatchev, B.P., Cox, D.J., Gonder-Frederick, L.A., Clarke, W.: Symmetrization of the blood glucose measurement scale and its applications. Diabetes Care **20**(11), 1655–1658 (1997). https://doi.org/10.2337/diacare.20.11.1655
37. Kudva, Y.C., Carter, R.E., Cobelli, C., Basu, R., Basu, A.: Closed-loop artificial pancreas systems: physiological input to enhance next-generation devices. Diabetes Care **37**(5), 1184–1190 (2014). https://doi.org/10.2337/dc13-2066
38. Langarica, S., Rodriguez-Fernandez, M., Núñez, F., Doyle, F.J., III.: A meta-learning approach to personalized blood glucose prediction in type 1 diabetes. Control. Eng. Pract. **135**, 105498 (2023). https://doi.org/10.1016/j.conengprac.2023.105498
39. Lehmann, E.D., Deutsch, T.: A physiological model of glucose-insulin interaction in type 1 diabetes mellitus. J. Biomed. Eng. **14**(3), 235–242 (1992). https://doi.org/10.1016/0141-5425(92)90058-S
40. Liu, C., Vehí, J., Avari, P., Reddy, M., Oliver, N., Georgiou, P., Herrero, P.: Long-term glucose forecasting using a physiological model and deconvolution of the continuous glucose monitoring signal. Sensors **19**(19), 4338 (2019). https://doi.org/10.3390/s19194338
41. Man, C.D., Rizza, R.A., Cobelli, C.: Meal simulation model of the glucose-insulin system. IEEE Trans. Biomed. Eng. **54**(10), 1740–1749 (2007). https://doi.org/10.1109/TBME.2007.893506
42. Mayo, M., Koutny, T.: Neural multi-class classification approach to blood glucose level forecasting with prediction uncertainty visualisation. In: CEUR Workshop Proceedings, KDH 2020, vol. 2675, pp. 80–84 (2020)
43. Mhaskar, H.N., Pereverzyev, S.V., Van der Walt, M.D.: A deep learning approach to diabetic blood glucose prediction. Front. Appl. Math. Stat. **3**, 14 (2017). https://doi.org/10.3389/fams.2017.00014
44. Mohammadreza, A., Kidd, B., Du, Y., Huang, J.Z.: Deep personalized glucose level forecasting using attention-based recurrent neural networks. In: IEEE, International Joint Conference on Neural Networks (2021). https://doi.org/10.1109/IJCNN52387.2021.9533897
45. Mohebbi, A., Johansen, A.R., Hansen, N., Christensen, P.E., Tarp, J.M., Jensen, M.L., Bengtsson H., Mørup, M.: Short term blood glucose prediction based on continuous glucose monitoring data. In: IEEE, 42nd Annual International Conference of the IEEE Engineering in Medicine & Biology Society (EMBC), pp. 5140–5145 (2020). https://doi.org/10.1109/EMBC44109.2020.9176695
46. Montt-Blanchard, D., Sánchez, R., Dubois-Camacho, K., Leppe, J., Onetto, M.T.: Hypoglycemia and glycemic variability of people with type 1 diabetes with lower and higher physical activity loads in free-living conditions using continuous subcutaneous insulin infusion with

predictive low-glucose suspend system. BMJ Open Diabetes Res. Care **11**(2), e003082 (2023). https://doi.org/10.1136/bmjdrc-2022-003082
47. Muñoz-Organero, M., Queipo-Álvarez, P., García Gutiérrez, B.: Learning carbohydrate digestion and insulin absorption curves using blood glucose level prediction and deep learning models. Sensors **21**(14), 4926 (2021). https://doi.org/10.3390/s21144926
48. Ozaslan, B., Patek, S., Breton, M.: Quantifying the effect of antecedent physical activity on prandial glucose control in type 1 diabetes: defining exercise on board. In: Proceedings of the Abstracts from ATTD 2017 10th International Conference on Advanced Technologies & Treatments for Diabetes, pp. 5–18, Paris, France (2017)
49. Parcerisas, A., Contreras, I., Delecourt, A., Bertachi, A., Beneyto, A., Conget, I., Viñals, C., Giménez, M., Vehi, J.: A machine learning approach to minimize nocturnal hypoglycemic events in type 1 diabetic patients under multiple doses of insulin. Sensors **22**(4), 1665 (2022). https://doi.org/10.3390/s22041665
50. Prendin, F., Del Favero, S., Vettoretti, M., Sparacino, G., Facchinetti, A.: Forecasting of glucose levels and hypoglycemic events: head-to-head comparison of linear and nonlinear data-driven algorithms based on continuous glucose monitoring data only. Sensors **21**(5), 1647 (2021). https://doi.org/10.3390/s21051647
51. Roy, A., Parker, R.S.: Dynamic modeling of exercise effects on plasma glucose and insulin levels. J. Diabetes Sci. Technol. **1**(3), 338–347 (2007). https://doi.org/10.1177/193229680700100305
52. Schiavon, M., Dalla Man, C., Cobelli, C.: Modeling subcutaneous absorption of fast-acting insulin in type 1 diabetes. IEEE Trans. Biomed. Eng. **65**(9), 2079–2086 (2017). https://doi.org/10.1109/TBME.2017.2784101
53. Seo, W., Park, S.W., Kim, N., Jin, S.M., Park, S.M.: A personalized blood glucose level prediction model with a fine-tuning strategy: a proof-of-concept study. Comput. Methods Progr. Biomed. **211**, 106424 (2021). https://doi.org/10.1016/j.cmpb.2021.106424
54. Sevil, M., Rashid, M., Hajizadeh, I., Park, M., Quinn, L., Cinar, A.: Physical activity and psychological stress detection and assessment of their effects on glucose concentration predictions in diabetes management. IEEE Trans. Biomed. Eng. **68**(7), 2251–2260 (2021). https://doi.org/10.1109/TBME.2020.3049109
55. Shilo, S., Godneva, A., Rachmiel, M., Korem, T., Bussi, Y., Kolobkov, D., et al.: The gut microbiome of adults with type 1 diabetes and its association with the host glycemic control. Diabetes Care **45**(3), pp. 555–563 (2022). https://doi.org/10.2337/dc21-1656
56. Shilo, S., Godneva, A., Rachmiel, M., Korem, T., Kolobkov, D., Karady, T., et al.: Prediction of personal glycemic responses to food for individuals with type 1 diabetes through integration of clinical and microbial data. Diabetes Care **45**(3), 502–511 (2022). https://doi.org/10.2337/dc21-1048
57. Simone, F., Andrea, F., Giovanni, S., Gianluigi, P.: Linear model identification for personalized prediction and control in diabetes. IEEE Trans. Biomed. Eng. **69**(2), 558–568 (2021). https://doi.org/10.1109/TBME.2021.3101589
58. Sivananthan, S., Naumova, V., Man, C.D., Facchinetti, A., Renard, E., Cobelli, C., Pereverzyev, S.V.: Assessment of blood glucose predictors: the prediction-error grid analysis. Diabetes Technol. Ther. **13**(8), 787–796 (2011). https://doi.org/10.1089/dia.2011.0033
59. Syafrudin, M., Alfian, G., Fitriyani, N.L., Hadibarata, T., Rhee, J., Anshari, M.: Future glycemic events prediction model based on artificial neural network. In: IEEE, 2022 International Conference on Innovation and Intelligence for Informatics, Computing, and Technologies (3ICT), pp. 151–155 (2022). https://doi.org/10.1109/3ICT56508.2022.9990708
60. Tarin, C., Teufel, E., Picó, J., Bondia, J., Pfleiderer, H.J.: Comprehensive pharmacokinetic model of insulin glargine and other insulin formulations. IEEE Trans. Biomed. Eng. **52**(12), 1994–2005 (2005). https://doi.org/10.1109/TBME.2005.857681
61. Toledo-Marín, J.Q., Ali, T., van Rooij, T., Görges, M., Wasserman, W.W.: Prediction of blood risk score in diabetes using deep neural networks. J. Clin. Med. **12**(4), 1695 (2023). https://doi.org/10.3390/jcm12041695

62. Tyler, N.S., Mosquera-Lopez, C., Young, G.M., El Youssef, J., Castle, J.R., Jacobs, P.G.: Quantifying the impact of physical activity on future glucose trends using machine learning. Iscience **25**(3), 103888 (2022). https://doi.org/10.1016/j.isci.2022.103888
63. Valletta, J.J., Chipperfield, A.J., Byrne, C.D.: Gaussian process modelling of blood glucose response to free-living physical activity data in people with type 1 diabetes. In: IEEE, 2009 Annual International Conference of the IEEE Engineering in Medicine and Biology Society, pp. 4913–4916 (2009). https://doi.org/10.1109/IEMBS.2009.5332466
64. Wadghiri, M.Z., Idri, A., El Idrissi, T., Hakkoum, H.: Ensemble blood glucose prediction in diabetes mellitus: a review. Comput. Biol. Med. 105674 (2022). https://doi.org/10.1016/j.compbiomed.2022.105674
65. Wilinska, M.E., Chassin, L.J., Schaller, H.C., Schaupp, L., Pieber, T.R., Hovorka, R.: Insulin kinetics in type-1 diabetes: continuous and bolus delivery of rapid acting insulin. IEEE Trans. Biomed. Eng. **52**(1), 3–12 (2004). https://doi.org/10.1109/TBME.2004.839639
66. Woldaregay, A.Z., Årsand, E., Walderhaug, S., Albers, D., Mamykina, L., Botsis, T., Hartvigsen, G.: Data-driven modeling and prediction of blood glucose dynamics: machine learning applications in type 1 diabetes. Artif. Intell. Med. **98**, 109–134 (2019). https://doi.org/10.1016/j.artmed.2019.07.007
67. Wolkowicz, K.L., Deshpande, S., Iii, F.J.D., Dassau, E.: Towards insulin monitoring: infrequent kalman filter estimates for diabetes management. IFAC-PapersOnLine **53**(2), 15877–15883 (2020). https://doi.org/10.1016/j.ifacol.2020.12.279
68. Xie, J., Wang, Q.: Benchmarking machine learning algorithms on blood glucose prediction for type I diabetes in comparison with classical time-series models. IEEE Trans. Biomed. Eng. **67**(11), 3101–3124 (2020). https://doi.org/10.1109/TBME.2020.2975959
69. Yale, J.F., Paty, B., Senior, P.A.: Diabetes Canada clinical practice guidelines expert committee: hypoglycemia. Can. J. Diabetes **42**, S104–S108 (2018). https://doi.org/10.1016/j.jcjd.2017.10.010
70. Yang, J., Li, L., Shi, Y., Xie, X.: An ARIMA model with adaptive orders for predicting blood glucose concentrations and hypoglycemia. IEEE J. Biomed. Health Inform. **23**(3), 1251–1260 (2018). https://doi.org/10.1109/JBHI.2018.2840690
71. Yang, T., Yu, X., Ma, N., Wu, R., Li, H.: An autonomous channel deep learning framework for blood glucose prediction. Appl. Soft Comput. **120**, 108636 (2022). https://doi.org/10.1016/j.asoc.2022.108636
72. Yazdani, A., Lu, L., Raissi, M., Karniadakis, G.E.: Systems biology informed deep learning for inferring parameters and hidden dynamics. PLoS Comput. Biol. **16**(11), e1007575 (2020). https://doi.org/10.1371/journal.pcbi.1007575
73. Zhu, T., Li, K., Herrero, P., Georgiou, P.: Personalized blood glucose prediction for type 1 diabetes using evidential deep learning and meta-learning. IEEE Trans. Biomed. Eng. **70**(1), 193–204 (2022). https://doi.org/10.1109/TBME.2022.3187703
74. Zhu, T., Uduku, C., Li, K., Herrero, P., Oliver, N., Georgiou, P.: Enhancing self-management in type 1 diabetes with wearables and deep learning. NPJ Digit. Med. **5**(1), 78 (2022). https://doi.org/10.1038/s41746-022-00626-5
75. Zou, B.J., Levine, M.E., Zaharieva, D.P., Johari, R., Fox, E.: Hybrid2 neural ODE causal modeling and an application to glycemic response. In: The Forty-first International Conference on Machine Learning, p. 235. Vienna, Austria. PMLR (2024)
76. Zou, Y., Liu, F., Li, Q.: Unraveling model-agnostic meta-learning via the adaptation learning rate. In: International Conference on Learning Representations (2021)

An Overview of the Implementation of Artificial Intelligence in Clinical Pathways

Luca Murazzano and Paolo Landa

Abstract The increase in the use and development of artificial intelligence (AI) is a reality in the modern scientific community. In healthcare settings, the use of AI is spread in all areas and specialties, mostly given by the increase of big data and massive data sets available publicly and privately, together with the advance of computer technologies. Clinical pathways consist of a multidisciplinary, evidence-based approach to healthcare management that outlines the optimal sequence and timing of clinical interventions for the care of patients with a specific diagnosis or condition. The use of this evidence-based tool is related to data availability and impact on patient health outcomes. There are many contributions in the literature that analyze the impact and development of AI within clinical pathways. The objective of this study is to provide an overview of the literature on the application of AI to clinical pathways, analyzing the main characteristics, benefits, and limitations of part of the scientific contributions published in the last decade.

Keywords Artificial intelligence · Clinical pathways · Health trajectories

L. Murazzano · P. Landa (✉)
Department of Operations and Decision Systems, Laval University, 2325 Rue de la Terrasse, Quebec City, QC G1V 0A6, Canada
e-mail: paolo.landa@fsa.ulaval.ca

L. Murazzano
e-mail: luca.murazzano.1@ulaval.ca

Population Health and Optimal Health Practices Axis, Research Center of CHU de Québec, 1050 Chemin Sainte-Foy, Quebec City, QC G1S 4L8, Canada

Interuniversity Research Center on Enterprise Network, Logistics and Transportation (CIRRELT), Laval University, 2325 Rue de la Terrasse, Quebec City, QC G1V 0A6, Canada

Oral Ecology Research Group (GREB), Laval University, 2420 Rue de la Terrasse, Quebec City, QC G1V 0A6, Canada

P. Landa et al. (eds.), *Operations Research and Artificial Intelligence in Healthcare Management*, Springer Proceedings in Mathematics & Statistics 506,
https://doi.org/10.1007/978-3-031-95659-1_4

1 Introduction

Healthcare systems face complex challenges in managing patient care efficiently, handling large volumes of diverse data, and ensuring consistent treatment quality across different cases. Clinical pathways (CPs) have emerged as a solution to streamline healthcare by guiding clinicians through evidence-based, standardized processes that translate clinical guidelines into practical steps for patient care. CPs aim to optimize the sequence and quality of care, addressing specific conditions while adjusting to the local healthcare institution's structure [1].

In this demanding context, artificial intelligence (AI) has attracted significant attention for its potential to analyse large datasets and provide decision-support tools. AI, as a branch of computer science, has evolved significantly since its inception in the 1950s, with rapid advancements over the last two decades [2]. This growth has been driven by faster computing power, improved algorithms, and vast amounts of accessible data. In particular, the exponential increase in data sharing—from about 281 million gigabytes in 1986 to 65 billion gigabytes in 2014—has enabled the development of big data technologies that fuel AI's capabilities [3]. The combination of new hardware and software technologies, along with vast data availability, has empowered AI to analyse massive amounts of information, discover patterns, measure performance in complex systems, and predict future behaviours.

Since the beginning of AI's development, healthcare has stood out as one of its most promising application areas, owing to its complexity and the large variety of information it generates (e.g., hospital data, tests, imaging, clinical information). Governments and the private sector worldwide have recognized this potential, leading to increased investments in AI research and development within healthcare, including startup ventures focused on AI applications [4].

AI encompasses a range of techniques—including machine learning, deep learning, and natural language processing–that are robustly suited to tackle healthcare's unique challenges. Applications of AI in clinical pathways span diverse areas: from patient monitoring and disease diagnosis to treatment recommendations and risk prevention [4–7]. By leveraging healthcare data from Electronic Health Records (EHRs) and using process mining techniques, AI can identify inefficiencies, enhance patient flow, and ultimately support improved patient outcomes and resource allocation within healthcare systems.

Within healthcare, special attention has been given to applying AI to clinical pathways [8]. CPs are used to guide clinicians with evidence-based care and translate clinical practice guidelines into local structures. CPs define steps in a course of treatment or care, standardizing processes for specific clinical problems or procedures within defined patient populations [1]. In this complex environment, there is a pressing need for integrated decision-support systems to aid medical personnel in clinical work. Many AI implementations within CPs support various tasks, such as image recognition [5, 7, 9], disease diagnosis [5, 10], patient genome interpretation [5], treatment selection [5, 11], patient monitoring [4, 5], and patient risk prevention [5–7].

Beyond clinical support, AI can also assist in managing healthcare systems. For instance, by analysing EHR data and applying process mining techniques, AI can map the different clinical pathways patients undergo, identifying tasks that may hinder optimal care. This approach can improve patient care conditions, promote better staff workload distribution, and ensure more efficient resource use within hospital systems.

This study provides an overview of the literature on AI applications in clinical pathways, highlighting the benefits and limitations observed in recent years. Section 2 presents a literature review of recent studies on AI applications in CPs. Sections 3 and 4 analyse the benefits and limitations of these applications, and Sect. 5 concludes with future research directions.

2 Literature Review

Recent studies on AI in healthcare have explored various themes, including its potential benefits, implementation challenges, safety and ethical considerations, and regulatory frameworks. These themes highlight both the opportunities AI presents and the challenges that must be addressed to integrate AI effectively within healthcare systems.

Several studies emphasize the vast potential AI holds for improving healthcare delivery. For instance, Davenport and Kalakota [6] provide an extensive overview of AI applications in healthcare, focusing on how different AI technologies can support the diverse roles of medical staff. They emphasize the potential of AI to improve efficiency, support clinical decision-making, and enhance patient care outcomes. Similarly, Sunarti et al. [10] examine AI's opportunities to boost healthcare efficiency and outcomes, noting that AI-driven innovations could lead to better resource management and optimized care processes. Challen et al. [9] focus on machine learning systems specifically, underlining their benefits for clinical support across different medical contexts and emphasizing the gains in accuracy and reproducibility.

While AI presents promising applications, its integration into existing clinical workflows is fraught with challenges. He et al. [4] discuss practical barriers to AI implementation, including issues related to data privacy, algorithm transparency, data standardization, and interoperability across platforms. They also address patient safety and stress the need for frameworks to ensure AI systems integrate seamlessly within clinical workflows. Panch et al. [11] further explore the impact of machine learning on health systems, emphasizing the importance of fostering a receptive environment for AI adoption. They argue that creating supportive infrastructures and adapting organizational workflows are essential steps toward realizing AI's potential benefits in healthcare.

Ensuring the safety and ethical use of AI in healthcare is a prominent theme in the literature. Ellahham et al. [12] highlight concerns around security, proposing that strategies like safe design, fail-safe protocols, and procedural safeguards are vital to prevent potential risks associated with AI systems. They advocate for guidelines and regulatory frameworks to address security issues and ensure that AI is used responsibly. McCardden et al. [13] emphasize the need for robust validation processes for AI models used in clinical care, proposing a three-stage validation framework to ensure accuracy and reliability, with a focus on ethical review and oversight. Challen et al. [9] also address safety and ethical issues by discussing the need for frameworks to handle quality and safety concerns, especially for machine learning models, across different time horizons (short-, medium-, and long-term).

Studies also address the broader social and regulatory implications of AI in healthcare. Yu et al. [5] provide a comprehensive review that not only highlights AI's technological advancements but also discusses its economic, legal, and social impacts. They identify the necessity for regulatory standards that can adapt to the rapid development of AI-based systems. He et al. [4] similarly review the regulatory landscape, comparing the US with other regions and stressing the need for international standards to ensure safe and equitable AI implementation. Panch et al. [11] discuss the ethical implications of AI on the healthcare workforce, considering how AI might change the dynamics of healthcare provision and the importance of regulatory and ethical preparedness.

2.1 *Clinical Pathways and Health Trajectories*

Clinical pathways, also known as care pathways or critical pathways, are a multidisciplinary, evidence-based approach to healthcare management that outlines the optimal sequence and timing of clinical interventions for the care of patients with a specific diagnosis or condition. Clinical pathways aim to improve patient outcomes by promoting the delivery of consistent, high-quality care that is based on best practices and clinical guidelines [14]. Clinical pathways typically include a series of steps that healthcare providers follow in a standardized manner to diagnose, treat, and manage a patient's condition. These steps may include diagnostic tests, medication regimens, rehabilitation plans, and follow-up care.

The term healthcare trajectory focuses on the patient's care pathway across the continuum of care. Thus, it can be the clinical pathway when it focuses on the organizational scale, but also the care pathway when it focuses on the systemic scale. Furthermore, the concept of healthcare trajectory is not limited to the operational aspect of the care process and to the pathophysiological process of a patient's disease state but also refers to the total organization of work done throughout all medical workers and patient interactions, as well as the effectiveness of patient care processes on those interactions and the organization [15].

The benefits of clinical pathways include improved patient outcomes, increased patient satisfaction, reduced healthcare costs, and enhanced communication and collaboration among healthcare providers. Clinical pathways can also help to standardize care delivery across different healthcare settings and providers, reducing variations in care and improving the efficiency of healthcare delivery.

3 Benefits of AI in Clinical Pathways

AI-based systems have a transformative impact on healthcare, enhancing the efficiency, accuracy, and responsiveness of patient care across various clinical pathways [16]. Crucially, AI acts as an augmentation tool rather than a replacement, working alongside healthcare professionals to optimize care delivery. By supporting medical and administrative teams, AI helps healthcare systems meet patient needs more effectively, creating a collaborative approach to care [7].

One of the most impactful applications of AI in healthcare is in clinical diagnosis [17–19], particularly in specialities reliant on imaging, such as radiology, dermatology, ophthalmology, and pathology. AI-powered image recognition tools are trained on millions of images to accurately detect signs of diseases in medical scans, such as tumours in radiology or diabetic retinopathy in ophthalmology. For instance, a study found that AI can help detect skin cancers as effectively as experienced dermatologists [17], significantly reducing diagnostic errors and accelerating the time from screening to diagnosis. This capability enables healthcare providers to prioritize complex cases and spend more time on patient interactions, with AI handling initial screenings and flagging high-risk images [5].

Natural language processing (NLP) is another powerful AI tool with wide-reaching applications in clinical documentation. NLP systems can analyse and organize unstructured text from patient records, which helps in preparing reports, extracting relevant information, and even generating structured clinical summaries automatically. For example, an NLP-based tool can scan physician notes to identify critical mentions of symptoms, medications, and diagnoses, structuring this information in ways that support efficient data retrieval and patient tracking [20]. This not only reduces the time clinicians spend on administrative tasks but also helps improve the consistency and accuracy of medical records, which are essential for continuity of care [6].

AI also plays a significant role in clinical decision support by leveraging electronic health records (EHRs) and advanced data extraction techniques. Clinical decision-support systems (CDSS) use machine learning and rule-based algorithms to assist healthcare providers in making informed treatment recommendations [21]. For instance, in oncology, AI-based CDSS can help recommend personalized treatment plans based on a patient's genetic makeup, predicting which therapies might be most effective for certain cancer types [22]. These systems also contribute to predictive analytics, identifying patients at risk for complications or readmissions, allowing for timely intervention and proactive management [6].

On the administrative side, robotic process automation (RPA) applications have introduced efficiencies by automating high-volume, repetitive tasks that consume significant resources. Tasks such as insurance claims processing, billing, patient scheduling, and updating EHRs can now be managed by RPA tools, which ensure consistency and speed in handling data. For example, an RPA system can automatically update patient records with recent lab results, minimizing clerical errors and freeing administrative staff to focus on more complex responsibilities. This approach not only improves operational efficiency but also reduces errors that could affect patient care outcomes [6].

Finally, AI-driven machine learning and process mining techniques provide powerful insights into patient care pathways by identifying patterns and bottlenecks in clinical workflows. Process mining, for instance, examines data from EHRs to map out how patients progress through treatments, uncovering delays in testing, consultations, or discharge processes [23]. In one healthcare system, process mining was used to analyse patient flow in emergency departments, revealing that lab processing delays were a key bottleneck. By addressing these specific points, hospitals can improve patient flow, reduce waiting times, and ensure that resources are used more effectively [24].

Through these applications, AI enables healthcare systems to offer faster, more accurate, and highly personalized patient care, supporting both clinicians and administrators in meeting the demands of an evolving healthcare landscape. These AI tools are integral to advancing healthcare efficiency, improving patient outcomes, and optimizing resource allocation, ultimately setting a new standard for quality in patient care.

4 Limitations of AI in Clinical Pathways

While AI has the potential to transform healthcare, numerous challenges impede its full integration into clinical pathways. These challenges are technical, legal, and societal and must be addressed to ensure the safe and effective use of AI in healthcare.

From a technical perspective, AI systems require enormous datasets to perform well, yet healthcare data is often fragmented and inconsistent. For instance, hospitals and clinics may use different electronic health record (EHR) systems, with variations in data formats, terminology, and structure. Consider a scenario where one hospital stores patient temperature data in Celsius and another in Fahrenheit; this inconsistency could lead to inaccuracies if not properly standardized. Furthermore, even within the same institution, data might be stored in text form, handwritten notes, or imaging files, complicating AI data processing. The process of data standardization, therefore, is critical, requiring that data be uniform and of high quality before it can be used in AI models [4].

Data quality and representativeness present additional challenges. If the data used to train an AI system doesn't reflect the diversity of real-world patients, the model may perform poorly or even produce biased results. For instance, in a study on AI for skin cancer detection, models trained on lighter skin tones had lower accuracy when used to diagnose conditions in people with darker skin tones. This lack of generalizability can lead to incorrect or delayed diagnoses for under-represented groups, underscoring the importance of training AI models on diverse datasets that reflect different demographics, lifestyles, and genetic backgrounds [5]. Ensuring that data includes representation from various populations is vital to avoid biases that may harm patient safety and trust.

System integration is another technical limitation. Many healthcare facilities lack the infrastructure to connect AI tools directly with clinical data systems. For example, a hospital may have a separate system for imaging, another for laboratory results, and a different one for EHRs, each operating independently. Integrating these systems with external AI-based applications would require substantial resources and expertise to ensure data can flow seamlessly, securely, and in real-time. Without effective integration, AI models may work with outdated or incomplete information, limiting their usefulness in critical clinical decisions. Moreover, AI's potential is often stunted by security and privacy concerns due to the sensitive nature of health data. The absence of a clear and effective regulatory framework complicates matters, as healthcare institutions are hesitant to share patient data without strict protocols that ensure patient confidentiality and data protection [12].

On the legal and regulatory side, AI in healthcare operates in a complex landscape where compliance with data privacy laws, like the General Data Protection Regulation (GDPR) in the EU or the Health Insurance Portability and Accountability Act (HIPAA) in the US, is critical. For example, AI algorithms may need access to sensitive patient information to function effectively, but if patient consent protocols are unclear, data access could violate privacy regulations. Additionally, AI systems must undergo rigorous validation and certification to meet medical device standards, a process that can be lengthy and expensive. For instance, AI diagnostic tools often require FDA or EMA approval, which involves extensive clinical testing to ensure safety and effectiveness. Without regulatory clarity and streamlined certification, hospitals and AI developers may hesitate to invest in AI, limiting its deployment [13].

From a societal perspective, both patients and medical staff harbour concerns about the transparency and accountability of AI systems. AI models, particularly those based on deep learning, often operate as "black boxes," providing outputs without clear explanations. This opacity can lead to mistrust among patients, as they may be uncomfortable with receiving a diagnosis or treatment recommendation that lacks a clear rationale. For example, an AI system might flag a patient as high-risk for a certain condition without explaining the specific factors that led to this classification, making it challenging for patients and providers to trust the result [25].

Privacy concerns also loom large for patients. As AI systems gather, analyse, and store vast amounts of personal health data, the risk of data breaches or misuse grows. A prominent example is the 2015 breach at Anthem, one of the largest health insurers in the US, where the personal information of nearly 80 million people was compromised. Such incidents heighten patients' fears about entrusting their health data to AI systems and may impact their willingness to engage with AI-driven healthcare solutions [26].

For medical professionals, there is apprehension regarding AI's potential impact on job security and workflow. Some clinicians worry that AI could replace certain roles, especially in specialities like radiology and pathology where AI is effective in analysing imaging data. For example, AI systems have shown strong performance in detecting lung nodules in CT scans, which traditionally would require a radiologist's expertise. Although these systems are intended to assist rather than replace medical staff, there remains a perception that certain roles could become redundant [6].

However, several factors should reassure healthcare workers. The deployment of AI in clinical practice is expected to be gradual, and most AI applications require extensive "labelled" data, meaning clinicians play a key role in preparing this data for AI training and validating the system's outputs. This collaboration underscores the importance of human oversight and expertise in AI-driven healthcare.

Additionally, there are ethical concerns tied to AI in healthcare, particularly around issues of accountability and decision-making. For example, if an AI system makes an incorrect diagnosis or treatment recommendation, it is often unclear who should bear responsibility—the developers of the AI, the healthcare institution, or the clinicians using it. This ambiguity creates challenges for healthcare providers, who may face legal risks if an AI-driven error leads to patient harm. The need for accountability frameworks that outline responsibilities in AI-supported decisions is therefore crucial [27].

In conclusion, while AI offers transformative potential in clinical pathways, these limitations underscore the importance of developing comprehensive strategies to address data quality, technical integration, regulatory compliance, and ethical considerations. By proactively managing these challenges, healthcare institutions can safely harness the power of AI to improve patient outcomes without compromising on quality, transparency, or human trust.

5 Conclusions

This paper has overviewed the use of artificial intelligence in healthcare trajectories. Implementations for clinical support systems and healthcare management have been presented. We can draw some conclusions from the work surveyed above. The rising of patients, service times and consequently the rising cost in healthcare services claim for solutions able to make the systems more efficient.

Many actions can be taken to reach a more efficient healthcare system, starting from using cutting edge facilities, but also digitalizing the system and so avoiding paper mistakes. This second choice makes it possible also to structure a data-based system on which is easier to act on, starting from the data monitoring. In this scenario the development of artificial intelligence finds rich terrains in which to act.

Artificial intelligence can help achieve a more efficient healthcare system by replacing all those repetitive tasks that make a patient's journey longer, and the work of doctors heavier. At the same time, it can be useful for all the repetitive administrative tasks which can be easily replaced. Although it is certain that AI can help to structure more efficient healthcare systems, it is equally true that many steps must be taken to arrive at reliable decision support tools. Starting with a clear regulatory framework that specifies the responsibilities and duties of all stakeholders. Continuing with the development of digitalized hospital systems capable of providing large amounts of good quality data. And finally, by making clear to patients the possibilities and risks in using these systems to reduce the fears that accompany the introduction of new technologies in such an important environment. As the world of AI is constantly and rapidly evolving, it will be the purpose of future research to investigate in more detail the application of such systems within healthcare systems.

References

1. Rotter, T., Jong, R.B., Lacko, S.E., et al.: Clinical pathways as a quality strategy. In: Busse, R., Klazinga, N., Panteli, D., et al. (eds.) Improving Healthcare Quality in Europe: Characteristics, Effectiveness and Implementation of Different Strategies. Health Policy Series, No. 53. European Observatory on Health Systems and Policies, Copenhagen, Denmark (2019). https://www.ncbi.nlm.nih.gov/books/NBK549262/
2. Russell, S.J., Norvig, P.: Artificial Intelligence: A Modern Approach, 3rd edn. Prentice Hall, New Jersey (2010)
3. Hilbert, M., López, P.: The world's technological capacity to store, communicate, and compute information. Science **332**(6025), 60–65 (2011)
4. He, J., Baxter, S.L., Xu, J., Xu, J., Zhou, X., Zhang, K.: The practical implementation of artificial intelligence technologies in medicine. Nat. Med. **25**(1), 30–36 (2019)
5. Yu, K.-H., Beam, A.L., Kohane, I.S.: Artificial intelligence in healthcare. Nat. Biomed. Eng. **2**(10), 719–731 (2018)
6. Davenport, T., Kalakota, R.: The potential for artificial intelligence in healthcare. Future Healthc. J. **6**(2), 94–98 (2019)
7. Panch, T., Pearson-Stuttard, J., Greaves, F., Atun, R.: Artificial intelligence: opportunities and risks for public health. Lancet Digit. Health **1**(1), 13–14 (2019)
8. Aspland, E., Gartner, D., Harper, P.: Clinical pathway modelling: a literature review. Health Syst. (Basingstoke) **10**(1), 1–23 (2019)
9. Challen, R., Denny, J., Pitt, M., Gompels, L., Edwards, T., Tsaneva-Atanasova, K.: Artificial intelligence, bias and clinical safety. BMJ Qual. Saf. **28**(3), 231–237 (2019)
10. Sunarti, S., Fadzlul Rahman, F., Naufal, M., Risky, M., Febriyanto, K., Masnina, R.: Artificial intelligence in healthcare: opportunities and risk for future. Gac. Sanit. **35**(Suppl 1), 67–70 (2021)
11. Panch, T., Szolovits, P., Atun, R.: Artificial intelligence, machine learning and health systems. J. Glob. Health **8**(2), 020303 (2018)
12. Ellahham, S., Ellahham, N., Simsekler, M.C.E.: Application of artificial intelligence in the health care safety context: opportunities and challenges. Am. J. Med. Qual. **35**(4), 341–348 (2020)
13. McCradden, M.D., Stephenson, E.A., Anderson, J.A.: Clinical research underlies ethical integration of healthcare artificial intelligence. Nat. Med. **26**(9), 1325–1326 (2020)
14. Kempa-Liehr, A.W., Lin, C.Y.-C., Britten, R., Armstrong, D., Wallace, J., Mordaunt, D., O'Sullivan, M.: Healthcare pathway discovery and probabilistic machine learning. Int. J. Med. Inf. **137**, 104087 (2020). https://doi.org/10.1016/j.ijmedinf.2020.104087
15. Gartner, J.-B., Abasse, K.S., Bergeron, F., Landa, P., Lemaire, C., Côté, A.: Definition and conceptualization of the patient-centered care pathway, a proposed integrative framework for consensus: a concept analysis and systematic review. BMC Health Serv. Res. **22**(1), 558 (2022)
16. Adwer, L., Whiting, E.: Exploring artificial intelligence solutions and challenges in healthcare administration. In: IEEE 12th International Conference on Healthcare Informatics (ICHI), pp. 528–530 (2024). https://doi.org/10.1109/ICHI61247.2024.00077
17. Liu, Y., Jain, A., Eng, C., Way, D.H., Lee, K., Bui, P., Kanada, K., Oliveira Marinho, G., Gallegos, J., Gabriele, S., et al.: A deep learning system for differential diagnosis of skin diseases. Nat. Med. **26**(6), 900–908 (2020)
18. Serte, S., Demirel, H.: Deep learning for diagnosis of COVID-19 using 3D CT scans. Comput. Biol. Med. **132**(104306), 104306 (2021)

19. De Fauw, J., Ledsam, J.R., Romera-Paredes, B., Nikolov, S., Tomasev, N., Blackwell, S., Askham, H., Glorot, X., O'Donoghue, B., Visentin, D., et al.: Clinically applicable deep learning for diagnosis and referral in retinal disease. Nat. Med. **24**(9), 1342–1350 (2018)
20. Zhou, B., Yang, G., Shi, Z., Ma, S.: Natural language processing for smart healthcare. IEEE Rev. Biomed. Eng. **17**, 4–18 (2024). https://doi.org/10.1109/RBME.2022.3210270
21. Prajapati, J.B., Prajapati, B.G.: Clinical decision support system braced with artificial intelligence: a review. In: Third International Conference on Image Processing and Capsule Networks. Lecture notes in networks and systems, pp. 531–540. Springer, Cham (2022)
22. Aznar-Gimeno, R., García-González, M.A., Muñoz-Sierra, R., Carrera-Lasfuentes, P., Rodrigálvarez-Chamarro, M.d.l.V., González-Muñoz, C., Meléndez-Estrada, E., Lanas, Á., Del Hoyo-Alonso, R.: Gastric AI tool: a clinical decision support tool for the diagnosis and prognosis of gastric cancer. Biomedicines **12**(9) (2024)
23. Guzzo, A., Rullo, A., Vocaturo, E.: Process mining applications in the healthcare domain: a comprehensive review. Wiley Interdiscip. Rev. Data Min. Knowl. Discov. **12**(2) (2022). https://doi.org/10.1002/widm.1442
24. Bose, R.P.J.C., Mans, R.S., Aalst, W.M.P.: Wanna improve process mining results? In: IEEE Symposium on Computational Intelligence and Data Mining (CIDM). IEEE (2013). https://doi.org/10.1109/CIDM.2013.6597227
25. Richardson, J.P., Smith, C., Curtis, S., Watson, S., Zhu, X., Barry, B., Sharp, R.R.: Patient apprehensions about the use of artificial intelligence in healthcare. NPJ Digit. Med. **4**(1), 140 (2021)
26. Ueda, D., Kakinuma, T., Fujita, S., Kamagata, K., Fushimi, Y., Ito, R., Matsui, Y., Nozaki, T., Nakaura, T., Fujima, N., Tatsugami, F., Yanagawa, M., Hirata, K., Yamada, A., Tsuboyama, T., Kawamura, M., Fujioka, T., Naganawa, S.: Fairness of artificial intelligence in healthcare: review and recommendations. Jpn. J. Radiol. **42**(1), 3–15 (2024)
27. Kumar, P., Chauhan, S., Awasthi, L.K.: Artificial intelligence in healthcare: review, ethics, trust challenges and future research directions. Eng. Appl. Artif. Intell. **120**(105894), 105894 (2023)

Economic Evaluation of Hospital Production: Analysis and Comparison of Different Models

Angela Testi, Paolo Landa, and Elena Tànfani

Abstract The growth of health care needs and the hospital establishment capacity has led to increased costs together with a deterioration in the finances of national health public systems. Hospitals need to understand how they can improve efficiency and service quality to survive and keep on operating with a sustainable activity for the future. Hospitals have to face hard budget constraints and on the other side maintain a high quality of care and improved health outcomes. The hospital production is a topic that the microeconomists analyzed in the last fifty years, looking at the hospital efficiency able to provide the best outputs and outcomes using limited number of inputs. The modelling of this function was mostly performed using parametric methods (such as Translog and Cobb-Douglas functional forms or Stochastic Frontiers), and later with non-parametric methods (such as Data Envelopment Analysis). The objective of this preliminary study consists in providing an overview of the economic evaluation of hospital production, comparing the two methods and showing the main benefits and limitations of each approach.

Keywords Hospital production function · Parametric models · Data envelopment analysis

A. Testi (✉)
Department of Internal Medicine (DIMI), University of Genoa, Genoa, Italy
e-mail: 5030@unige.it

P. Landa
Department of Operations and Decision Systems, Laval University, Quebec City, QC, Canada

Population Health and Optimal Health Practices Axis, Hospital Univeristy Research Center of Quebec City, Quebec City, QC, Canada

Oral Ecology Research Group, Laval Univeristy, Quebec City, QC, Canada

Interuniversity Research Centre for Enterprise Networks, Logistics and Transportation (CIRRELT), Quebec City, Canada

P. Landa
e-mail: paolo.landa@fsa.ulaval.ca

E. Tànfani
Department of Economics (DIEC), University of Genoa, Genoa, Italy

P. Landa et al. (eds.), *Operations Research and Artificial Intelligence in Healthcare Management*, Springer Proceedings in Mathematics & Statistics 506,
https://doi.org/10.1007/978-3-031-95659-1_5

1 Introduction

The growth of health care needs of the population in the last decades and the increase of hospital establishment capacity given by the increase of population and needs, has led to increased costs together with a deterioration in the finances of national health public systems. Cost containment is one of the main needs of health systems, a prerequisite for the survival of public health systems to provide health services to the population, maintaining high quality and equity in access. Measuring efficiency is therefore one of the essential steps to verify that all resources available are allocated in the best way.

In economics the problem of efficiency is given by the scarcity of resources (natural resources, labor, and capital) and by the unlimited needs of the economic agent. The challenge consists in allocating resources in the most efficient way to satisfy the needs of the largest number of individuals as possible. There is economic efficiency when resources are allocated in order to maximize the production of goods and services, meaning that resources are used in the most efficient manner possible without any waste. Economic efficiency enables the cost reduction and the increase of output of the production process, reducing market prices for goods and services and increasing economic growth [1–3].

There are three main efficiencies analyzed in health care literature: technical efficiency, productive efficiency and allocative efficiency [4]. Technical efficiency is the physical relation between resources and health outcome, it is achieved when he maximum possible improvement in outcome is obtained from a set of resource inputs [4]. Productive efficiency consists in the maximization of health outcome for a given cost, or the minimization of cost for a given outcome [4]. Finally, allocative efficiency considers productive efficiency together with the efficiency with which the outcomes are distributed among the community [5]. The first distinction is between allocative and productive efficiency. The allocative efficiency refers to the question *what to produce* (relates input and health outcomes such as QALY) and is studied with cost–benefit analysis (cost-effectiveness and cost-utility), and then the productive efficiency which refers to the question *how to produce* (the output that has proven to be cost-effective and sustainable/equitable from previous analysis). Productive efficiency, in turn, depends on three conditions: (1) technical efficiency (this means that production have to stay on an isoquant and does not take input prices into consideration); (2) managerial efficiency, it is needed to choose, among all possible production techniques in the isoquant, the one that costs the least, and (3) Scale efficiency, i.e., positioning myself on isoquant that allows me to decrease costs in the long run (when all inputs are variable) [4, 5]. In this study we will focus on technical efficiency and scale efficiency.

In traditional microeconomics, the study of productive efficiency originates in the production function, that correspond to how to utilize inputs to achieve the best result in terms of output. The functional form of the production function is the following

$$Q = f(X_1, X_2, \ldots X_n) \tag{1}$$

where Q represents the quantity of output and $X1, X2, \ldots, Xn$ is the vector the quantities of factor inputs, usually including capital, labour (hospital staff as physicians and nurses, hospital buildings and land, raw materials and other elements of that contribute to the production. Then starting from the production function and technically efficient combinations (those on the isoquant or frontier) and by applying input prices, it is possible to define the cost function. Since input prices are rather difficult to identify in hospitals (especially the capital), it is common use to turn the cost faction mainly as econometric estimation of the production function.

Measuring the efficiency of hospitals is, moreover, particularly difficult, although less difficult than for other health care facilities, such as general practitioners' offices or local health units working in the territory. There are multiple reasons for this difficult in measuring, some of which are the following:

- the output is multioutput (there are different types of outputs, for example, outpatient visits, day hospitalizations, surgeries, etc.), but even within the same type, we can have very different elements. For example, hospitalizations are very heterogeneous, and for these there are about 500 Diagnosis Related Groups (DRGs), but even within each DRG there can be several interventions.
- Part of the production is carried out by teamwork and the presence of teams;
- Hospital facilities require equipment and fixed capital to a sometimes-preponderant extent (such as wards and operating rooms);
- Rather fixed production coefficients are present (characterizing the low substitutability of inputs participating in production);
- As a measure for evaluation, not only the output is important (given, for example, by the number of interventions performed), but also the 'outcome (e.g., the final health impact of the interventions).
- There are different care strategies and different qualities;
- The production is multi-stage, several stages each involving a different production function, but they must be coordinated with each other, so each individual process rather than the global view of production takes on particular importance.
- Other presence of uncertainty about results (exogenous factors such as socioeconomic deprivation);

The objective of this preliminary study consists in presenting an overview of the hospital production function in economics, providing the analysis and the comparison of parametric and non-parametric models that were approached in the last fifty decades. The structure of this study is the following: in section two are reported the material and methods of the study based on the presentation of the parametric models, Data Envelopment Analysis and stochastic frontiers; in section three are reported the results of the comparison, showing the benefits and the limitations of each approach. Finally, in Section four are reported the conclusion and the future development of this study.

2 Material and Methods

2.1 *Parametric Models*

Economists have been grappling with this task since the 1970s when costs began to rise sharply, dragged down by several factors such as the technological innovation, the aging population, and a larger need of citizens in terms of health care and health services. In addition, both the quality and mode of treatment of hospital patients have changed, leading to increased costs [6]. Other factors that have led to the increase in spending over the past fifty years are the increase in GDP per capita and the reimbursement methodologies payment of health care service [7–9]. The issue is even more important today, as these factors have even accentuated their dynamics over time, posing serious challenges to public coverage of health care needs.

Early attempts to measure the efficiency of hospitals initiated in the 1970s both in the U.S. and in Europe [6, 10–15], used traditional production functions already found in the international literature, such as Cobb Douglas, Trans-Logarithmic and Leontief.

The estimation of production functions is based on a set of observations by taking explicit functional forms to describe the technology. The production function expresses output as a function of inputs and is defined by the following relationship where it is the dependent variable, while the vector of inputs is composed of the explanatory variables or regressors. As in all economic models, it is necessary to place assumptions and properties on the object of study. The production function, according to definitions posed in the literature [16] must be:

1. Monotonic, so if then;
2. Monotonic in the strict sense, so if then;
3. Let V be the set of input combinations that produce the output level y, the set must be convex and the production function must be nearly concave;
4. Concave, therefore for;
5. Weak essentiality, so where is the null vector;
6. Narrow essentiality, therefore;
7. The set $V(y)$ is closed and nonempty for every $y > 0$;
8. $f(x)$ is finite, nonnegative, real-valued and finite-valued for every finite and nonnegative value of x;
9. $f(x)$ is always continuous;
10. $f(x)$ is doubly differentiable at each of its points.

The output of functional forms is estimated through a relationship between the dependent variable and the regressors, where the parameters to be estimated can follow the following parametric forms: Linear, Cobb-Douglas, Quadratic, Normalized Quadratic, Trans-logarithmic, Leontief and Constant elasticity of substitution (CES) [16].

All these functional forms have the advantages of being flexible, linear in parameters, regular and parsimonious. The Cobb-Douglas functional form is very easy to estimate because its equation can be directly transformed into a linear equation in the logarithms of the variables.

$$Q(K, L) = AL^{\alpha} K^{\beta} \quad (2)$$

In this formulation Y represents the total production, while L and K are the labour and capital input, respectively. The parameter A is the total factor productivity, and α and β are the output elasticities of capital and labor, respectively (with $0 < \alpha < 1$ and $0 < \beta < 1$). The parameters obtained from the estimation are the elasticities of the product with respect to the individual factors. In the special case where the sum of the elasticities is equal to one, the elasticity of scale is equal to one and there are constant returns to scale, the elasticity of substitution between factors also becomes constant and is equal to unity. These elements lead to the limitation of this functional form in that prior to estimation one constrains the elasticity of substitution to unity and this results in good substitutability between inputs (which does not always correspond to reality).

Many studies of the production function seek to explain the relationships between production and which independent variables constrain production.

Goisis [15] defines hospital production through a Cobb-Douglas functional form, where production is measured by the number of admissions (dependent variable) and by a relationship between several independent variables such as beds, physicians and variables of convenience (dummy variables) that introduce the presence of teaching conventions with the university by the hospital. According to that study, the returns to scale are slightly increasing, furthermore, the size of the hospital affects the value of the elasticity of output with respect to inputs.

Feldstein [17] also defines output through a Cobb-Douglas where output is defined by the number of admissions per case mix (dependent variable) and a relationship between physicians, beds, nurses, and miscellaneous supplies. The study found that the largest elasticity is present in beds, while the only two significant inputs are beds and physicians. The returns to scale are moderately decrescent.

Lave and Lave [18] estimate the cost function capable of addressing the problems arising from the multi-output nature of production by analyzing the relationship between costs and output, looking in detail for explanatory variables to be used in the estimation. The authors address the problem of estimating the cost function under multioutput production through a Cobb-Douglas type function by developing two procedures and assuming that the output mix is constant within each hospital. The first procedure is based on a two-stage analysis and allows the cost function to differ across hospitals by estimating a relationship between average cost, factors utilization, size and time for each hospital. The second stage, on the other hand, searches for the causes of variations in parametric estimates among hospitals, assuming that all hospitals have the same cost function. The results obtained analyze the reasons why costs increase, showing that hospitals with teaching functions have faster cost increases. According to the study, marginal costs compose about half of the average costs (varying from 40 to 65%), furthermore in case economies of scale are present, they are not significant.

Finally, they point out that the rate of cost increases is greatly influenced by the cost per patient component.

Trans-logarithmic (or Translog) estimation is found in most of the work in the literature and is agreed to be the most valid functional form in the analysis of hospital output [19–22]. This function is much more flexible because it does not require the three elasticities to be constant. The more flexible a functional form is, the fewer restrictions one must assume a priori on the type of production process. From the estimated coefficients obtained from the Translog, it is possible to trace, through special formulations, the values of the relevant elasticities. However, the advantage of the greater flexibility of this form is counterbalanced by the disadvantage of a larger number of independent variables requiring much larger samples. A generalized example of a Translog production function, where y is the output produced, and x_n is the quantity of input n used in the production process, takes the form.

$$\text{In}\, y = \beta_0 + \sum_{n=1}^{N} \ln x_n + \frac{1}{2}\sum_{n=1}^{N}\sum_{m=1}^{M} \beta_{nm} \text{In}\, x_n\ \text{In}\, x_m \tag{3}$$

A form of estimation based on the Leontief functional form was proposed by Li and Rosenman [23], this choice lies in the fact that from an econometric point of view it is convenient when a set of conditions are met. The Leontief functional form has similarities to hospital production as production takes place through a high variety of intermediate products, from radiological diagnostics to physiotherapy, from outpatient medical visits to surgery.

The model proposed by Li and Rosenman makes it possible to analyze how, within the hospital, variations in the costs of different types of care affect the cost function for each individual patient. The econometric specification involves the use of a data panel framework to estimate the cost function through two models (one with fixed effects and one with random effects). The first estimation is done through the random-effects model and then it is validated through the use of the Breusch and Pagan test [24]. The formulation of the model considers many factors, such as patient days, discharge visits, factor prices of labor and capital, and error terms not attributable to production. This type of functional form provides flexibility in the economy of scale and does not impose a priori restrictions on the elasticity between factors of production. In addition, it is homogeneous in input prices (a necessary condition for the existence of duality between cost and transformation function), and in the cost function there are variables not related to inputs that can still have influence on costs, exactly the error on hospital specifications that does not vary over time and the error term that varies per hospital that varies over time. The authors, through the results obtained from this study, indicate that Leontief turns out to be a better functional form than Translog for estimating the hospital production function because it allows for the heterogeneity present among the hospitals surveyed in the study. Ultimately, it is inferred from the model that hospitals have significant economies of scale but limited economies of scope.

A different approach is that provided by Carey [25] where a multi-output cost function is estimated using a very large sample of hospitals, where they use a panel data methodology over five years. The choice of this technique allows them to understand the correlations between unobservable differences between hospitals and their observable determinants of hospital costs. The panel data technique is compared with a simple cross-sectional technique to illustrate the importance of separating individual ,effects from cost function parameters. This effect can be seen in the measurement of economies of scale in the two models: the cross-section estimation shows diseconomies of scale that remain stable throughout the five years, while the estimation using panel data shows economies of scale that decrease over time. The importance of the study performed lies in the fundamental choice of variables that will make up the econometric estimation of the hospital cost function.

Scuffham et al. [26] explore the structure of hospital costs, input substitutability, and economies of scale and scope by targeting what potential efficiencies are produced by these, through the use of a Translog cost function that provides model flexibility for handling multiple inputs and outputs. With regard to elasticities, it appears that Labor and material prices have cost effects are more than proportional, furthermore, substitutability of inputs is poor. Economies of scale are not present. The translog cost function reveals that hospitals have at least two options for improving hospital efficiency in the short run: either through variation in staff input mix or through variation in output levels relative to staffing levels present. Options for input substitution such as demand for medical staff increases when there are increases in supply prices (and not vice versa). Nurses, who account for 50% of hospital operating expenditures in the sample, are relatively less replaceable than other inputs. Nurses therefore have greater bargaining power, and a change in their salaries can have strong repercussions on hospital costs.

2.2 *Data Envelopment Analysis*

The peculiarity of hospital production and its difficulty encountered in the estimation considering the above described model and its limitations, prompted the search for other methods of evaluation. The research method was no more the identification of parametric methods, but the choice fell on a nonparametric method, such as the Data Envelopment Analysis (DEA), developed on the basis of Farrell's [27] ideas and the purely economic concept of Paretian optimum, by Charnes, Cooper and Rhodes [28], formulating a linear programming problem capable of calculating of a score (score) of efficiency for each observation in the sample (decision-making unit or DMU). This score represents the percentage reduction in the use of all inputs that can be achieved when compared with the best without reducing the amount of output. These scores can be calculated in the presence of both constant returns to scale (CRS) and variable returns to scale (VRS). Major developments in DEA in the 1970s and 1980s are documented by Seiford and Thrall [29] and several authors in the last two decades provided systematic literature reviews on the application of DEA to health care [30–33].

Given a sample containing K inputs, M outputs and N hospitals, where is the set of inputs for observation i for $k = 1, \ldots, K$ and is the set of outputs for observation i for $m = 1, \ldots, M$, the DEA problem definition with constant returns to scale for observation i is such that $r = 1, \ldots, M$; $s = 1, \ldots, K$; $j = 1, \ldots, N$. The efficiency score, where indicates a point on the frontier and is technically efficient if it takes the unit value.

The first application of DEA to health care is developed by Sherman [33], which employed DEA in hospital manufacturing to compare the efficiency of manufacturers with different control structures.

The use of DEA over other econometric methods is due to a number of advantages:

- the absence of restrictions on the functional form of the relationship linking inputs to outputs (production technology);
- being a deterministic method does not require the imposition of assumptions on the distribution function of efficiency scores [34, 35];
- ease in extending the method when there are technologies that use more than one input to obtain more than one output;
- the assumption of the lack of error terms in the data studied;
- DMUs are directly compared with other DMUs or combinations thereof;
- there are no constraints on the units of measurement of inputs and outputs (e.g., we can use the number of lives saved as output and for input we can use resource consumption in country currency);

However, the DEA approach has some disadvantages such as:

- the absence of an error term can create problems in error measurements;
- it is an excellent method for estimating the relative efficiency of a DMU but converges slowly to absolute efficiency because it lacks the theoretical best;
- being a nonparametric technique, it is difficult to perform statistical hypothesis testing;
- computationally, it can become a highly complex method if the problem is large, as there is a linear programming formulation for each DMU;
- in estimating "best practice" frontier produces indicators that are extremely sensitive to the choice of input and output variables and, consequently, easily affected by measurement error.

The main advantages are the ability of DEA to handle multiple input and multiple output models where input and outputs may have very different units. For DEA there is no need of any assumption of a functional form relating inputs to outputs, and in addition, the DMUS are compared against a peer or a combination of peers.

The applications of the DEA method to health care have multiplied especially over the years and worldwide [36–43] covering many aspects of the health care system, but especially the hospital sector was studied in two reviews [44, 46] that pointed out the main benefits and limitations. The problems addressed in the reviews were very different, and depending on the specific objectives, outputs and inputs were chosen appropriately. The second review [46] show the percentage of studies that use inpatients days as an output category, reporting a significant decline during the decades due to changes in reimbursement.

2.3 Stochastic Frontiers

Starting from dissatisfaction with some features of the DEA model, some authors have moved again in the direction of parametric models, proposing models that have been called "stochastic production frontiers" (SF). Such frontiers, however, again presuppose the choice of a functional form. They differ in several ways from DEA, with the potential advantage that random variations in catch can be accommodated, providing a more consistent measure with the potential harvest under normal working conditions. On the other hand, a disadvantage of SF is that, although it can model multiple output technologies, doing so is somewhat more complicated, requires stochastic multiple output distance functions, and raises problems for outputs that take zero values [45]. (to summarize something, e.g., to put first authors, to make the logic of double error understood, etc.) they are also real "frontiers" (and not averages… complete).

Stochastic frontiers is a method introduced in 1997 by Aigner, Lovell, and Schmidt [46] and Meuseen and Van Den Broeck [47], provide a measurement of technical efficiency by taking into account the possibility of unforeseen random shocks that cannot be controlled by producers and that can influence the level of output. Through such a tool, it is possible to separate the effects on output caused by changes in technical efficiency from those attributable to changes in input and environmental performance. The analysis of stochastic frontiers is done through the study of technical efficiency, given by the ratio of output produced to the maximum output obtainable.

The deterministic frontier consists of the production frontier where is the output produced by the *i*-th producer, is the vector of *N* inputs used by the producer, and β is an estimated vector of technological parameters, is the technical efficiency of the *i*-th producer. This assumption implies that any deviation from the observed output is to be attributed to the presence of technical inefficiency. In order to introduce the random shocks of each producer within the frontier we reformulate the frontier as follows:

$$\ln Q_{j,t} = \beta_0 + \sum_{n=1}^{N} \beta_n \ln x_{njt} + \frac{1}{2} \sum_{n=1}^{N} \sum_{m=1}^{M} \beta_{nm} \ln x_{njt} \ln x_{mjt} - u_{jt} + v_{jt} \quad (4)$$

In this formulation where $Q_{j,t}$ is the output of the hospital or unit j in period t and x_{njt} and x_{mjt} are the variable and fixed hospital or unit inputs (*n*, *m*) to the production process. The error term is separated into two components, where v_{jt} is the stochastic error term and u_{jt} is an estimate of technical inefficiency. The random component is specific to each producer, in addition, the evaluation of technical efficiency according to this model considers environmental variations, which, following the deterministic approach, would affect the estimate of efficiency itself.

For SF it is necessary to define the functional form described. In the case of assuming that the functional form is a Cobb-Douglas we will have where is the difference between the error term attributable to random disturbance and the error term due to technical inefficiency. These estimates of the production technology-related parameters (β) and the technical efficiency of each producer are calculated through the likelihood method because, given the skewness of and positivity of the functional form, the ordinary least squares (OLS) method provides only consistent estimates for the covariates and not for the intercept. For the evaluation of technical efficiency, estimates must be extracted, and this requires special assumptions about the distributions that characterize the two error components.

It quickly becomes apparent that one of the major problems with the stochastic frontier approach is the need to specify the distribution function of the compound error. Generally, it is assumed that the error term is distributed as a normal random variable, while for the term related to inefficiency one can have different specifications, although the most widely used in the empirical literature seems to be the half-normal distribution. One of the assumptions of the models is that the distributional hypotheses on inefficiency components adopted in the literature are the Exponential and Truncated Normal [48–50]. Some models using different distributional hypotheses on the inefficiency components and are the Normal-Half Normal, Normal-Exponential and the Normal Truncated Normal.

3 Results and Discussion

3.1 Comparison Between DEA and SF

Compared with the DEA method SF have the advantage of being stochastic, but also several disadvantages, such as the mandatory choice of the functional form, requiring a lot of data, and the assumptions concerning the distribution of the inefficiency term imposed in order to decompose the error [51, 52].

There has also been much debate in the literature whether DEA or SF is preferable. There is also a group of papers in which both methods have been applied [51, 53–56] although the results may vary between studies and its applications. All that can be said is that DEA methods are suitable as the number of assumptions is limited and it is easier in its development, while SF methods need several assumptions that are not easy to implement and that might not respect the real phenomena we are looking for modelling. DEA is a tool based on linear programming, and there is a possibility that the functions we are looking are not linear. In addition, made are not real since they are taken based on the elements in the given situation. Each method has particular strengths and weaknesses and potentially measure different aspects of efficiency.

3.2 Discussion on Economic Evaluation Methods

All these economic matrix methods, i.e., aimed at estimating efficiency basically as productivity and as the relationship between output and input, we could say that even in the diversity of the various specifications/methods have as their goal to compare production facilities with each other to give a score, to make a ranking. When hospitals or production units are not on the frontier and have a lower efficiency than the unit, the DEA method also succeeds in giving rather precise indications of the cause of the inefficiency, which can be ascribed, sometimes to an excess of some input, and sometimes, to too large or too small a scale of production.

Stochastic frontiers in this are coarser and fail to give these indications. The comparison in the DEA model is made with respect to one of the other units to be evaluated in the system, or to a linear combination of them. And there may also be different standards to copy. On the one hand this leaves some flexibility, but it is not always sufficient, or at least they are rather crude indications that often do not take other factors into account. That is why in the DEA model we usually proceed to a second stage, relating the obtained scores to other external and contextual variables that could be the causes of low scores; in that case the inefficiency of the operational units would not be attributable to mismanagement, but rather to other causes, for example using a regression approach in the second-phase [56–60].

In all cases, however, the DEA evaluation is a system-level, economic policy evaluation that fails to provide precise strategies to individual hospitals. You can inform with a detailed analysis that a hospital (or an operating unit) is not efficient, the DEA also provides some useful indication, but then from the operational point of view it doesn't provide a clear information on how the inefficiency should be improved or removed.

Further analysis needs to be done by delving into what is happening within individual hospitals, i.e., not just what goes in and what comes out, but considering a larger set of outcomes that might be difficult to collect and analyze.

Lack of effort in achieving efficiency was defined in a famous article by Leibenstein [61] and described as X-inefficiency, that occurs when a firm lacks the incentive to control costs. This causes the average production cost to be higher than necessary, this lack implies technically a non-efficient production. Much discussion has taken place as to what this should mean; a concept also heavily criticized by Stigler [62]. It has been said that there would be elements of x-inefficiency whenever there is no incentive for efficiency in the market (e.g., in monopoly), but this could also be the case with public enterprises, as theories of bureaucracy teach where every rational organization must have a set of rules and regulations. These rules and regulations must be followed without any fault, ensuring uniformity in the market and in the business, where the staff members know what is expected of them [63]. O'Neill et al. [46] says just that DEA was used to determine appropriate levels of care [46], while Chillingerian used DEA for many other scopes, such as to develop particular frontiers for primary care at physician level and practice patterns [64].

4 Conclusions and Future Works

The objective of this study was providing a preliminary analysis on the economic evaluation of hospital production and its efficiency analysis the international literature and showing the benefits and the limitations of the approaches described. Considering the large quantity of studies and the multiple approaches, two main approaches were identified: parametric and non-parametric approaches. Each one presented both benefits and limitations in both application and modelling assumptions. However, is not easy to prove the best methodology for estimate efficiency to provide an economic evaluation of hospital production.

Previously described techniques, in fact, referred to efficiency evaluation basically as productivity, that is, as the ratio of output to input. More complex methods such as for example the DEA share the main principles, indeed they have same approaches such as the use of multi-output and multi-input cases, weight assignment, as reported above.

In the case of hospitals, however, limiting to this is rather sterile. It is best to refer to the more general concept of "performance" [65, 66]. It is a multidimensional and interdisciplinary concept, not exclusive only to the economic sphere in the strict sense, but rather to the business or organizational spheres. It can be broadly defined as the measure of how well a facility satisfies its customers. In the case of healthcare, therefore, the concept of performance includes both efficiency and effectiveness. The most important thing in fact is effectiveness, that is the ability to meet needs and then efficiency, what justifies delegating to the public system, that is that needs are met efficiently. In universalistic public systems such, an additional factor is added, that of equity that is that the absence of unfair and avoidable differences among groups of people (socially, economically, demographically, or geographically or by other dimensions) of inequality health services.

The most appropriate and comprehensive approach, moreover, seems to be an approach based engineering and operational research methods. We refer, in particular, to those methodologies that belongs to operations management or industrial engineering [67, 68] and include many techniques. However, this preliminary study is not interested in showing these approaches, but future research will be dedicated to describe such models and understand whether they can help in assessing the efficiency or performance of hospitals.

References

1. Lang, M.G.: Economic efficiency and policy comparisons. Am. J. Agr. Econ. **62**(4), 772–777 (1980). https://doi.org/10.2307/1239779
2. Whittaker, W.: Resource allocation funding formulae, efficiency of. In: Culyer, A.J. (ed.) Encyclopedia of Health Economics, pp. 256–266. Elsevier (2014). ISBN 9780123756794
3. Jovanovic, B.: Economic growth: theory. In: Smelser, N.J., Baltes, P.B. (eds.) International Encyclopedia of the Social & Behavioral Sciences, Pergamon, pp. 40984101 (2001). ISBN 9780080430768, https://doi.org/10.1016/B0-08-043076-7/02309-3

4. Palmer, S., Torgerson, D.J.: Economic notes: definitions of efficiency. BMJ **318**(7191), 1136 (1999). https://doi.org/10.1136/bmj.318.7191.1136.PMID:10213735;PMCID:PMC1115526
5. Drummond, M.: Output measurement for resource-allocation decisions in health care. In: McGuire, A., Fenn, P., Mayhew, K. (eds.) Providing Health Care. The Economics of Alternative Systems of Finance and Delivery. Oxford University Press, Oxford (1991)
6. Feldstein, M.R., Lave, L.B.: Quality change and the demand for hospital care. Econometrica **45**(7), 1681–1702 (1970)
7. Newhouse, J.P.: Medical care expenditure: a cross-national survey. J. Hum. Resour. **12**(1), 115–125 (1977)
8. Swan, J.H., Harrington, C., Clemeña, W., Pickard, R.B., Studer, L., deWit, S.K.: Medicaid nursing facility reimbursement methods: 1979–1997. Med. Care Res. Rev. **57**(3), 361–378 (2000). https://doi.org/10.1177/107755870005700306
9. Casto, A.B., Forrestal, E.: Principles of Healthcare Reimbursement. American Health Information Management Association (2013)
10. Goisis, G., Molgora, M.M.: Oziosità degli impianti e distribuzione della domanda nel settore ospedaliero. Rivista Internazionale di Scienze Sociali **87**(4), 507–535 (1979)
11. Goisis, G., Parravicini, P.: Restraining public health expenditure. In: Operations Research Proceedings 1996. Operations Research Proceedings, vol. 1996. Springer, Berlin, Heidelberg (1997). https://doi.org/10.1007/978-3-642-60744-8_71
12. Sherman, H.D.: Hospital efficiency measurement and evaluation: empirical test of a new technique. Med. Care **22**(10), 922–938 (1984)
13. Wagstaff, A.: Estimating efficiency in the hospital sector: a comparison of three statistical cost frontier models. Appl. Econ. **21**(5), 659–672 (1989). https://doi.org/10.1080/758524897
14. Lave, J.R., Lave, L.B.: Economic analysis for health service efficiency: a review article. Appl. Econ. **1**(4), 293–305 (1970). https://doi.org/10.1080/00036847000000005
15. Goisis, G.: Rendimenti di scala ed efficienza economica nella produzione di servizi ospedalieri. Milano, Giuffré, vol. 8, p. 168 (1976)
16. Chambers, R.G.: Applied Production Analysis: a Dual Approach. Cambridge University Press (1988)
17. Feldstein, M.: Quality change and the demand for hospital care. Econometrica: JSTOR **45**(7), 1681–702 (1977). Accessed 8 Aug. 2023. https://doi.org/10.2307/1913959
18. Lave, J.R., Lave, L.B.: Hospital cost functions. Am. Econ. Rev. JSTOR **60**(3), 379–95 (1970). Accessed 8 Aug. 2023. http://www.jstor.org/stable/1817988
19. Sielska, A., Nojszewska, E.: Production function for modeling hospital activities. The case of Polish county hospitals. PLoS One **17**(5), e0268350 (2022). https://doi.org/10.1371/journal.pone.0268350. PMID: 35551295; PMCID: PMC9098024
20. Reyes Santías, F., Cadarso-Suárez, C., Rodríguez-Álvarez, M.X.: Estimating hospital production functions through flexible regression models. Math. Comput. Modell. **54**(7–8), 1760–1764 (2011). ISSN 0895-7177. https://doi.org/10.1016/j.mcm.2010.11.087
21. Reyes-Santías, F., Cordova-Arevalo, O., Rivo-Lopez, E.: Using flexible regression models for calculating hospital's production functions. BMC Health Serv. Res. **20**, 641 (2020). https://doi.org/10.1186/s12913-020-05465-2
22. Stadhouders, N., Koolman, X., van Dijk, C., Jeurissen, P., Adang, E.: The marginal benefitsof healthcare spending in the Netherlands: estimating cost-effectiveness thresholds using a translog production function. Health Econ. **28**, 1331–1344 (2019). https://doi.org/10.1002/hec.3946
23. Li, T., Rosenman, R.: Estimating hospital costs with a generalized Leontief function. Health Econ. **10**(6), 523–538 (2001). https://doi.org/10.1002/hec.605. PMID: 11550293
24. Breusch, T.S., Pagan, A.R.: A simple test for Heteroskedasticity and random coefficient variation. Econometrica **47**(5), 1287–1294 (1979). https://doi.org/10.2307/1911963.JSTOR1911963.MR0545960
25. Carey, K.: A panel data design for estimation of hospital cost functions. Rev. Econ. Stat. (MIT Press) **79**(3), 443–453

26. Scuffham, P.A., Devlin, N.J., Jaforullah, M.: The structure of costs and production in New Zealand public hospitals: and application of the transcendental logarithmic vaiable cost funcation. Appl. Econ. **28**(1), 75–85 (1996). https://doi.org/10.1080/00036849600000010
27. Farrell, M.J.: The measurement of productive efficiency. J. R. Stat. Soc.: Ser. A (General) **120**, 253–281 (1957). https://doi.org/10.2307/2343100
28. Charnes, A., Cooper, W.W., Rhodes, E.: Measuring the efficiency of decision making units. Eur. J. Oper. Res. **2**(6), 429–444 (1978). ISSN 0377-2217. https://doi.org/10.1016/0377-2217(78)90138-8
29. Seiford, L.M., Thrall, R.M.: Recent developments in DEA: the mathematical programming approach to frontier analysis. J. Econometr. **46**(1–2), 738 (1990). ISSN 0304-4076, https://doi.org/10.1016/0304-4076(90)90045-U
30. Zakowska, I., Godycki-Cwirko, M.: Data envelopment analysis applications in primary health care: a systematic review. Fam. Pract. **37**(2), 147–153 (2020). https://doi.org/10.1093/fampra/cmz057. PMID: 31605609
31. Jung, S., Son, J., Kim, C., Chung, K.: Efficiency measurement using data envelopment analysis (DEA) in public healthcare: research trends from 2017 to 2022. Processes **11**(3), 811 (2023). https://doi.org/10.3390/pr11030811
32. Mbau, R., Musiega, A., Nyawira, L., et al.: Analysing the efficiency of health systems: a systematic review of the literature. Appl. Health Econ. Health Policy **21**, 205–224 (2023). https://doi.org/10.1007/s40258-022-00785-2
33. Martins Drei, S., Angulo-Meza, L.: Data envelopment analysis (DEA) in health: a literary review of Latin America. Multidiscip. Rev. **6**(2), 2023011 (2023). https://doi.org/10.31893/multirev.2023011
34. Sherman, H.D.: Hospital efficiency measurement and evaluation. Empirical test of a new technique. Med. Care **22**(10), 922–38 (1984). https://doi.org/10.1097/00005650-198410000-00005. PMID: 6436590
35. Simar, L., Wilson, W.P.: Sensitivity analysis of efficiency scores: how to bootstrap in nonparametric frontier models. Manag. Sci. **44**(1), 49–61 (1998)
36. Torabipour, A., Najarzadeh, M., Arab, M., Farzianpour, F., Ghasemzadeh, R.: Hospitals productivity measurement using data envelopment analysis technique. Iran J. Public Health. **43**(11), 1576–81 (2014). PMID: 26060727; PMCID: PMC4449509
37. Ozcan, Y.A.: Performance measurement using data envelopment analysis (DEA). In: Health Care Benchmarking and Performance Evaluation, pp. 15–47. Springer, Cham (2014). https://doi.org/10.1007/978-1-4899-7472-3_2
38. Piubello Orsini, L., Leardini, C., Vernizzi, S., Campedelli, B.: Inefficiency of public hospitals: a multistage data envelopment analysis in an Italian region. BMC Health Serv. Res. **21**, 1–15 (2021). https://doi.org/10.1186/s12913-021-07276-5
39. O'Neill, L.: Multifactor efficiency in data envelopment analysis with an application to urban hospitals. Health Care Manag. Sci. **1**, 19–27 (1998)
40. Kohl, S., Schoenfelder, J., Fügener, A., Brunner, J.O.: The use of data envelopment analysis (DEA) in healthcare with a focus on hospitals. Health Care Manag. Sci. **22**, 245–286 (2019). https://doi.org/10.1007/s10729-018-9436-8
41. Siciliani, L.: Estimating technical efficiency in the hospital sector with panel data a comparison of parametric and non-parametric techniques. Appl. Health Econ. Health Policy **5**, 99–116 (2006). https://doi.org/10.2165/00148365-200605020-00004
42. Lari, M.S., Sefiddashti, S.E.: Measuring the efficiency of health systems: a case of mental health in middle east and North Africa countries. Iran. J. Public Health **50**, 1017–1027 (2021). https://doi.org/10.18502/ijph.v50i5.6119
43. Dimas, G., Goula, A., Soulis, S.: Productive performance and its components in Greek public hospitals. Oper. Res. **12**, 15–27 (2012). https://doi.org/10.1007/s12351-010-0082-2
44. Sultan, W.I.M., Crispim, J.: Measuring the efficiency of Palestinian public hospitals during 2010–2015: an application of a two-stage DEA method. BMC Health Serv. Res. **18**, 1–17(2018). https://doi.org/10.1186/s12913-018-3228-1

45. Hollingsworth, B.: The measurement of efficiency and productivity of health care delivery. Health Econ. **17**(10), 1107–1128 (2008). https://doi.org/10.1002/hec.1391. PMID: 18702091
46. O'Neill, L., Rauner, M., Heidenberger, K., Kraus, M.: A cross-national comparison and taxonomy of DEA-based hospital efficiency studies. Socioecon. Plann. Sci. **42**(3), 158–189 (2008). https://doi.org/10.1016/j.seps.2007.03.001
47. Paul, C.J.M., Johnson, W., Frengley, G.: Efficiency in New Zealand sheep and cattle farming: the impacts of regulatory Reéform. Rev. Econ. Stat. **82**, 325–337 (2000)
48. Dennis Aigner, D., Knox Lovell, C.A., Schmidt, P.: Formulation and estimation of stochastic frontier production function models. J. Econometr. **6**(1), 21–37 (1977). ISSN 0304-4076, https://doi.org/10.1016/0304-4076(77)90052-5
49. Meeusen, W., van Den Broeck, J.: Efficiency estimation from Cobb-Douglas production functions with composed error. Int. Econ. Rev. **18**, 435–444 (1977). https://doi.org/10.2307/2525757
50. Wheat, P., Stead, A.D., Greene, W.H.: Robust stochastic frontier analysis: a student's thalf normal model with application to highway maintenance costs in England. J. Prod. Anal. **51**, 21–38 (2019). https://doi.org/10.1007/s11123-018-0541-y
51. Chakraborty, K., Biswas, B., Lewis, W.C.: Technical efficiency in stochastic production frontier: a simultaneous equation approach. Econ. Res. Inst. Study Pap. 160 (1999)
52. Zhao, S.: Quantile estimation of stochastic frontier models with the normal-half normal specification: a cumulative distribution function approach (2021). https://ssrn.com/abstract=3877937, https://doi.org/10.2139/ssrn.3877937
53. Hlali, A.: Efficiency analysis with different models: the case of container ports. J. Marine Sci. Res. Dev. **8**, 250 (2018). https://doi.org/10.4172/2155-9910.1000250
54. Nguyen, H.T.: A closer look at stochastic frontier analysis in economics. Asian J. Econ. Bank. **4**(3), 3–28 (2020). https://doi.org/10.1108/AJEB07-2020-0032
55. Hollingsworth, B., Street, A.: The market for efficiency analysis of health care organisations. Health Econ. **15**, 1055–1059 (2006). https://doi.org/10.1002/hec.1169
56. Ruggiero, J.: A comparison of DEA and the stochastic frontier model using panel data. Int. Trans. Oper. Res. **14**, 259–266 (2007). https://doi.org/10.1111/j.1475-3995.2007.00585.x
57. Tsionas, M.G.: Optimal combinations of stochastic frontier and data envelopment analysis models. Eur. J. Oper. Res. **294**(2), 790–800 (2021)
58. Sun, M., Ye, Y., Zhang, G., Xue, Y., Shang, X.: Measuring the efficiency of public hospitals: a multistage data envelopment analysis in Fujian Province, China. Front. Public Health **11**, 1091811 (2023). https://doi.org/10.3389/fpubh.2023.1091811
59. Marschall, P., Flessa, S.: Efficiency of primary care in rural Burkina Faso. A two-stage DEA analysis. Health Econ. Rev. **1**, 5 (2011). https://doi.org/10.1186/2191-1991-1-5
60. Mohamadi, E., Kiani, M.M., Olyaeemanesh, A., Takian, A., Majdzadeh, R., Hosseinzadeh Lotfi, F., Sharafi, H., Sajadi, H.S., Goodarzi, Z., Noori, H.S.: Two-step estimation of the impact of contextual variables on technical efficiency of hospitals: the case study of public hospitals in Iran. Front. Public Health **6**(9), 785489 (2022). https://doi.org/10.3389/fpubh.2021.785489. PMID:35071166;PMCID:PMC8770937
61. Li, L., Dai, Q., Huang, H., et al.: Efficiency decomposition with shared inputs and outputs in two-stage DEA. J. Syst. Sci. Syst. Eng. **25**, 23–38 (2016). https://doi.org/10.1007/s11518016-5298-0
62. Cheng, Z.-H., Tao, H.-B., Cai, M., Lin, H.-F., Lin, X.-J., Shu, Q., Zhang, R.-N.: Using a two-stage data envelopment analysis to estimate the efficiency of county hospitals in China: a panel data study. Lancet **386**(Supplement 1), S64 (2015). ISSN 0140-6736. https://doi.org/10.1016/S0140-6736(15)00645-5
63. Leibenstein, H.: Allocative efficiency versus 'X-efficiency'. Am. Econ. Rev. **56**, 392–415 (1966)
64. Stigler, G.J.: The Xistence of X-efficiency. Am. Econ. Rev. **66**(1), 213–216 (1976). http://www.jstor.org/stable/1804963
65. Downs, A.: A theory of bureaucracy. Am. Econ. Rev. **55**(1/2), 439–446 (1965). http://www.jstor.org/stable/1816286

66. Chilingerian, J.A., Sherman, H.D.: Health-care applications: from hospitals to physicians, from productive efficiency to quality frontiers. In: Cooper, W., Seiford, L., Zhu, J. (eds.) Handbook on Data Envelopment Analysis. International Series in Operations Research & Management Science, vol. 164. Springer, Boston, MA (2011). https://doi.org/10.1007/978-1-4419-6151-8_16
67. Cislaghi, C., Marchi, M.: Indicators for assessment in health services. In: Crescenzi, F., Mignani, S. (eds.) Statistical Methods and Applications from a Historical Perspective. Studies in Theoretical and Applied Statistics. Springer, Cham (2014). https://doi.org/10.1007/978-3-319-05552-7_34
68. Cislaghi, C., Rizzo, M.G., Giuliani, F., Arena, V.: La struttura dei costi per livello di assistenza e per fattori produttivi nelle aziende sanitarie pubbliche. Mecosan: management ed economia sanitaria [The cost structure by level of care and by input in public health companies, Mecosan: management and health economics]: **89**, 1 (2014), 2384–8804 (Milano, Franco Angeli). http://digital.casalini.it/https://doi.org/10.3280/MESA2014-089006, Casalini id: 2956990

Steering Patient Flows: The Contribution of Quantification and Simulation to the Relevance of Care Pathways

Sarah Garidi and Auguste Rakotondranaivo

Abstract This study explores how flow quantification and simulations can improve the management of care pathways in a healthcare facility specialized in follow-up and rehabilitation care. It is based on an assessment of the current operation through the quantification of existing patient flows. Human and organizational constraints were identified to ensure a relevant stay in the facility. Subsequently, flow simulations conducted with the Flexim Healthcare® software allowed for an analysis of the system's functioning and the exploration of alternative optimization scenarios. The results of this work offer valuable perspectives for streamlining patient flows and optimizing the human resources required for care delivery, despite the identified limitations.

Keywords Patent flow · Care pathway · Relevance · Simulation · Quantification

Introduction

The evolution of the French healthcare system, characterized by a rapid shift towards outpatient care, is reshaping professional practices and transforming the care landscape into a multi-party and multidisciplinary structure. These changes underscore the growing need for coordination and a paradigm shift focused on care pathways [5]. In this context, the constant increase in healthcare demand, coupled with a mounting shortage of healthcare facilities, is compelling these institutions to explore more efficient management of human and material resources. Additionally, the financing of

S. Garidi
Université de Lorraine, Nancy, France

Direction of Belle-Isle and Robert Schuman Hospitals, Metz, France

S. Garidi
e-mail: sarah.garidi@univ-lorraine.fr

A. Rakotondranaivo (✉)
Université de Lorraine, ERPI, 54000 Nancy, France
e-mail: auguste.rakotondranaivo@univ-lorraine.fr

P. Landa et al. (eds.), *Operations Research and Artificial Intelligence in Healthcare Management*, Springer Proceedings in Mathematics & Statistics 506,
https://doi.org/10.1007/978-3-031-95659-1_6

healthcare facilities, now tied to measurable activities, highlights the need to optimize patient flow management as a means to reduce costs while ensuring the quality and safety of patient care.

The concept of care pathways is central to ongoing debates about strategies for healthcare system transformation. It is based on the principle of delivering "the right care, at the right time, in the right place, to the right patient." This approach goes beyond simple procedural rationalization; it encourages healthcare facilities to adopt systems inspired by the industrial sector to enhance resource efficiency [7].

Our goal is to further explore how the quantification and simulation of patient flows contribute to the effectiveness of care pathways in healthcare system organization. We propose employing these methods within a healthcare facility to support a project focused on improving patient care processes. This case is particularly compelling as it reflects experiments in the hospital sector utilizing methods and tools from the industrial sector—approaches that remain relatively unfamiliar to healthcare professionals [9].

1 The Relevance of Patient Care Pathways

At the end of the 1990s, the first definition of relevance of care was given by the Rand Corporation, which considers that care is relevant if provided when the margin between the expected benefits exceeds its expected negative consequences. In France several studies and reports reflect diversity in medical practices and show a variation in the care pathways provided, which are difficult to justify [7]. On this topic, the literature reports several decisive factors for the relevance of care [2]. They include:

- knowledge, beliefs and reasoning of professionals and patients;
- organisation of the system as well as incentives for certain activities;
- relations between the various stakeholders.

Also note that the advent of the relevance of care pathways refers to the literature on the concept of regulating the healthcare offer [1]. Within a hospital sector seeking to optimise resources based on a raft of reforms aiming to limit expenditure [6]. According to [8] the improvement of the relevance of care pathways seems to be a response to this goal. It may allow a facility to steer care towards efficient high-added value procedures focused on the patient, while improving the quality of care and reducing expenses. Several programmes have been implemented to promote the "right care" in the face of growing numbers of patients to be cared for and reduced numbers of healthcare professionals. A goal that has encouraged healthcare facilities to get involved in this subject, offering us a scientifically interesting research issue given its lack of exploration and the questions that it raises.

2 The Contribution of Flow Simulation

Simulation is one of the decision-making tools provided to designers and administrators of complex systems. Flow simulation involves designing a model of a real system in order to understand and anticipate how it behaves and thus improve its performance. The simulation models give a dynamic representation of an organisation to assess its performance, its re-sizing for experimenting with new steering strategies [3, 4] highlighted the goals of simulation:

- test solutions upstream before they are implemented;
- confirm sizing hypotheses;
- involve staff in analysis, optimisation of flows and the reorganisation strategy;
- facilitate support for change in ongoing improvement projects.

The model used in this study is a Discrete Event Simulation (DES). It analyzes patient flows while accounting for activity sequences, time constraints, and resource limitations in a hospital environment.

Several software tools can be used for flow simulation, including FlexSim®, Arena®, Promodel®, ExtendSim®, Anylogic®, Simio®, Repast®, and Simul8®. We have chosen the FlexSim® software because it offers two modelling environments: one for industrial flow modelling and another, called "Healthcare", for modelling patient flows in hospital environments. The other aforementioned software tools also support patient flow simulation but lack an environment specifically designed for this application.

3 Field of Investigation

The field of our study is a private healthcare facility which is part of the public hospital service. It belongs to an association for social and professional inclusion of people with disabilities. The facility offers rehabilitation and physiotherapy, and accommodates patients with varied pathologies in traumatology, orthopaedics, neurology and rheumatology. Patient care is offered with capacity of 60 day-hospital spots and 30 full hospitalisation beds. There are two types of patient care: Full Hospitalization (FH) and Day Hospitalization (DH). Day Hospitalization can take place in the morning or in the afternoon, hence the terms AM or PM. In 2021 patient care was heavily affected by the Covid-19 pandemic. The number of patients cared for in 2021 was 156 for Full hospitalisation (FH) and 407 for Day hospitalisation (DH), with 9,410 days in FH and 14,619 days in DH.

4 Issue and Goals

4.1 Issue in the Field

Patient care is provided by a multi-disciplinary team. Each patient is admitted for a stay which must meet several criteria which include in particular a number of procedures necessary to validate each day of care. Admissions management is assigned mainly to an admission committee made up of the following: four doctors, a healthcare executive and a rehabilitation executive. For 2021 overall, 1,132 requests were examined by the committee and only 823 requests were granted. The main grounds for rejection were the lack of places (51%), patients that do not meet the criteria set by the facility (42%) or who are outside the geographic area (7%). In 2021, for a total of 654 external consultations performed by doctors from the centre, 188 consultations led to admission to FH or DH. These elements reflect an extended waiting list whose repercussions may be non-negligible on patient flows. On this subject we see growing exasperation on the part of doctors, executives and professionals due to hospital stays deemed to be irrelevant, and with good reason, with treatment limited to one or two procedures per day instead of the recommended three procedures (in 2019, 17% of Hospital stays did not include 3 procedures per day). This situation is due to a flow management issue, with a lack of coordination between the required departments and the number of patients to be cared for. The facility thus finds itself overcrowded with patients who could be treated by non-hospital healthcare professionals. The facility thus finds itself overcrowded with patients who could be treated by non-hospital healthcare professionals. In addition, the Covid-19 pandemic upset the organisation of out-patient treatment, initially scheduled for a full day from 9:00 am to 4:00 pm, and now permitted as a half-day (9:00 am to 12:00 pm and 1:00 pm to 4:00 pm). Beyond reviewing the relevance of admissions, the problem experienced is that of rationalising technical platforms in terms of human resources to ensure the management of patient flows generated. The fair distribution of care staff is currently a major concern for the facility.

Given this situation, quantification and simulation of the existing flows and of the desired flows are recommended to improve the relevance of patient care pathways within the facility, due to the exponential increase in admission requests. The aim of this effort is twofold, namely to simulate the current operation of the facility using 2021 data, and then to build a projection of the optimum operation to be set up for the future. The secondary aim of this work is to identify the resources needed within the teams.

4.2 Scientific Issue

The new process management problems in the healthcare sector are reminiscent of those of the industrial sector and encourage development of the use of the tools and methods from this sector to provide answers to hospital administrators and help them manage their facility. Use of simulation in the hospital sector has developed gradually, as shown by the study of [11], who used simulation to help size the number of beds, or the study of [10], who used flow simulation to optimise steering to minimise average hospital stays. It appears to be a decision-making assistance tool to help confirm one-off solutions. Our case is based on the combination of quantification and simulation of patient flows within a healthcare facility for continuing and rehabilitation care, with the aim of rationalising the human resources needed to ensure that hospital stays are relevant.

5 Description of the Project Steps

The first step involves creating an overview of the facility's current operation in its flow management. This requires understanding the organisation of the multi-disciplinary team involved with the patient, identification of the different types of patient pathway (DH and FH) and criteria for relevance of pathways (staff implemented, number of procedures performed).

We conducted 11 semi-directive interviews according to an interview guide created with professional and academic experts. A doctor, a healthcare executive, a rehabilitation executive, three physiotherapists, two occupational therapists, two calisthenics coaches, and a nurse were interviewed. The questions focused on their practices, quantitative estimates of their activities, and the difficulties encountered on a daily basis. The questions were positively welcomed in all departments and in many cases other members of the team added to the responses of the interviewee. Therefore there is reliability in terms of the quality of responses.

However, it was difficult for most of the people interviewed to estimate the time spent on each task of the day. In fact, there was great variability according to patients and days, and it was difficult to estimate an average per day.

Then our analysis focused on patient flow from January 2021 to December 2021, a database giving the following over 52 weeks: patients treated; their pathology; the type of treatment; half-day (morning or afternoon) or full day (morning and afternoon); professionals involved and lastly the treatment procedures: physiotherapy, occupational therapy, callisthenics.

The second step of work is flow simulation using the FlexSim Healthcare® software in several steps, which we will detail in the results section.

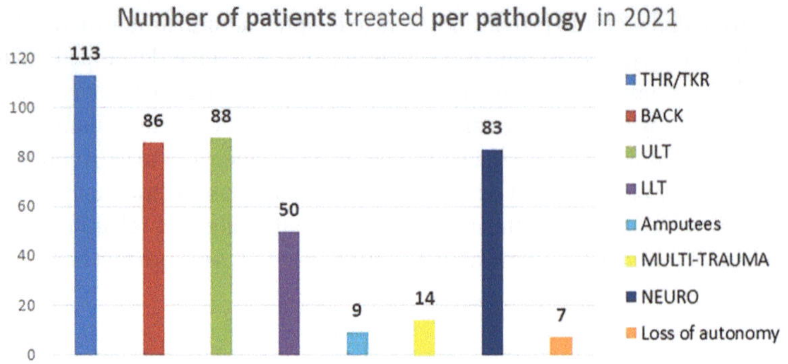

Fig. 1 Characteristics of the pathological profiles of patients

6 Results and Discussions

6.1 Quantification of Patient Pathways Types

This section gives an extract of the results on a total of 13 indicators analysed.

The results in the figures are derived from the establishment's database but are not simulated (Fig. 1).

The number of patients treated per pathology for 450 patients is broken down as follows: 113 patients had a total hip or knee replacement (THR/TKR), 86 patients had a back problem (Back), 88 patients were suffering from upper limb trauma (ULT) and 83 patients from neurological disorders (NEURO) (Fig. 2).

The analysis reveals a large number of patients not meeting the two therapists per day of care threshold for patients in day hospital. These stays where only one professional intervenes probe the relevance of admission of these patients and represent an area for improvement for the facility, which must offer multi-disciplinary care.

6.2 Quantification of Patient Flows

We see a gradual increase in the number of patients who from January to September were mainly in half-day treatment. Starting in September, there were a few full-day treatments. For the same technical platform, it appears that the number of morning treatments is higher than the number of afternoon treatments, which confirms the drive by the French government and reflects the impact of the Covid-19 pandemic which prioritised half-day treatments (Fig. 3).

A reorganization would be beneficial by redistributing part of these care activities to the afternoon. Simulation scenarios aimed at optimizing human resources within the facility are necessary. Resorting to outpatient care in community healthcare settings could also serve as an alternative.

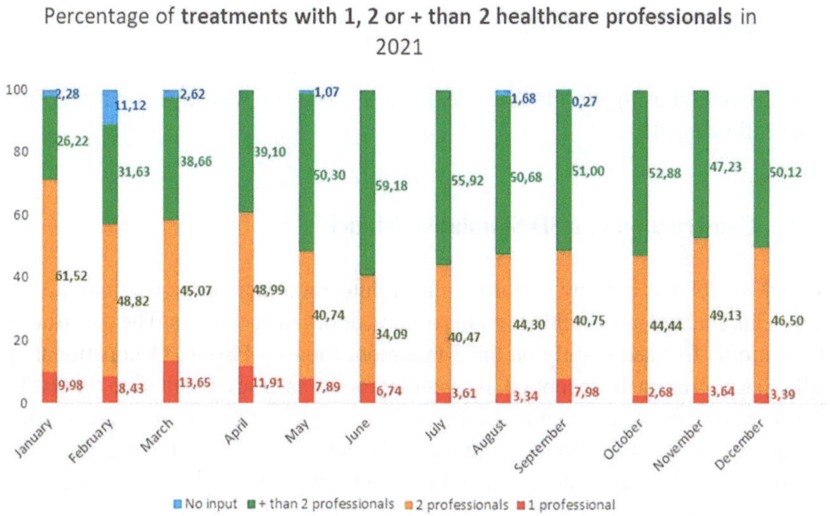

Fig. 2 Number of professionals involved in care

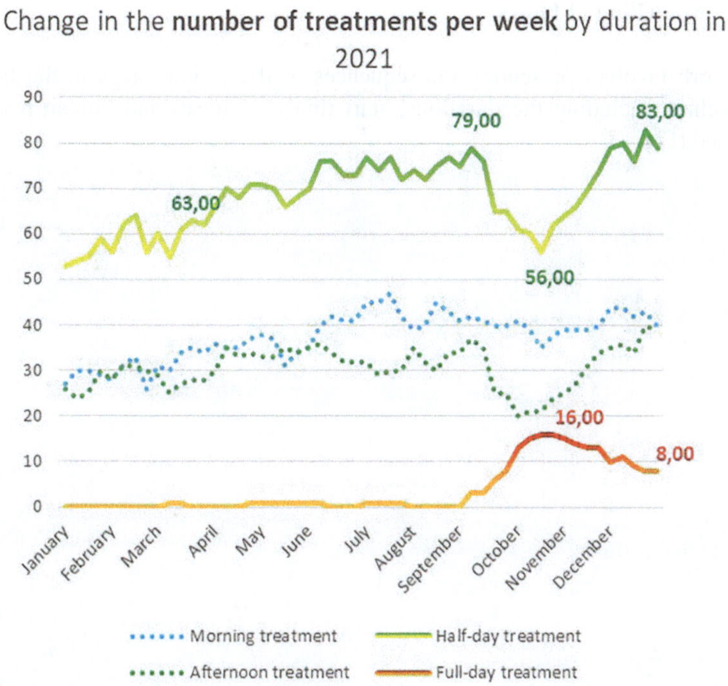

Fig. 3 Quantification of DH patient pathways

6.3 *Simulation of Flows*

Flow simulation using the FlexSim Healthcare® software was carried out according to the following steps.

6.3.1 Construction of a 3D Simulation Model

The 3D model was built by importing the architectural map of the site into the software. This enabled us to build the walls, offices, doors and corridors. The construction of the model focused mainly on the 3 treatment rooms—Physio, Occupational and Calli—as well as on the reception, the waiting rooms and the consultation rooms. The administrative areas, canteen and other sectors were not shown, because although they are essential to the smooth operation of the centre, they are not part of the patient care pathway. The care equipment and tools and the staff were added to the model after observations in the field.

6.3.2 Modelling of Flows

This work involves presenting the sequences of the various steps in the form of a flowchart, including the durations, start times, premises and human resources allocated (Fig. 4).

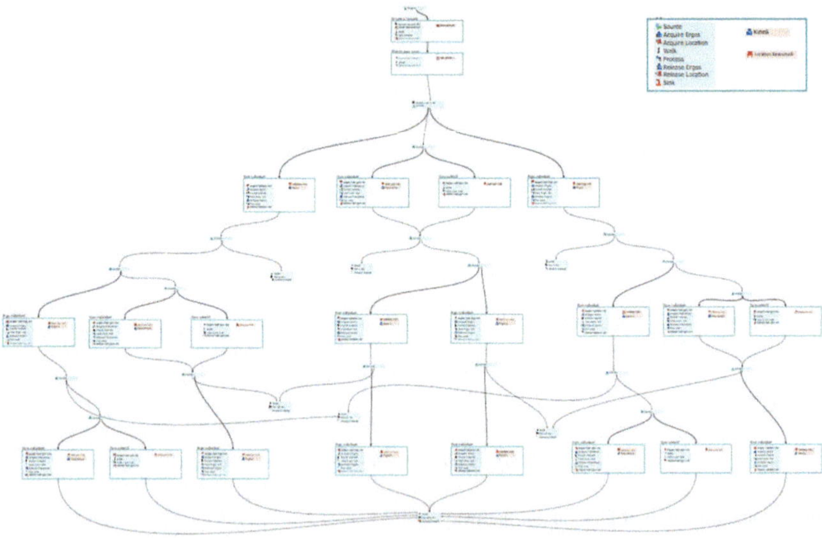

Fig. 4 Flow modelling flow chart

This work enables us to identify the various patient pathways. New patients must go through an admission and consultation phase before they are able to begin their treatment. This is the longest pathway. The second option is that of the patient who is already admitted to the centre and is returning to continue treatment. This patient goes directly from "Arrival" to "Awaiting treatment". Most patients follow this circuit. There are also pathway variations depending on the type and number of procedures to be performed.

A member of staff is assigned to each care activity. The availability of these staff varies throughout the day depending on the number of patients admitted to the centre, but also according to their schedule and related tasks to be performed throughout the day. To make the simulation more realistic, a schedule taking into account meal breaks, among other things, was included in the simulation. Additional related activities were also added, requiring simulation staff to spend a certain amount of time writing reports when not dealing with patients.

6.3.3 Launch of Simulation

This phase consists of four steps:

- Visualization of activity workflows with real data introduced
- Visualization of dashboards based on the real data introduced
- Experimentation to achieve a set objective
- Optimization to achieve a set objective.

Figure 5 provides an overview of the simulation of activity workflows. We can observe staff and patients moving according to the sequence of activities and the queues. It is possible to view the queue at the end of the day.

Depending on the needs, dashboards can be generated to display metrics such as the average waiting time before the first act, the daily evolution of the number of patients, the average staff occupancy rate, and the chronological occupancy of the staff (Fig. 6).

We obtained information on treatment time for the patient in the centre, which for example is 2.8 h on average for 3 procedures, the average wait time between the patient's arrival at the centre and the first procedure, which is 7 1/2 min on average, along with the status of the staff. Certain trends can be identified. For example, occupational therapy staff spend considerable time carrying out related tasks such as writing reports in the patient file, unlike sports instructors, who are more frequently in the field providing treatment procedures. These scoreboards can also be used to find out staff's free time.

Experimentation involves testing various resource allocation scenarios selected by the simulation operator based on a chosen objective. Figure 7 shows results with the goal of optimizing waiting times.

We observed the waiting times by testing the variation in the number of physiotherapists (kine), with four occupational therapists (ergo) and four gymnastics coaches (gym).

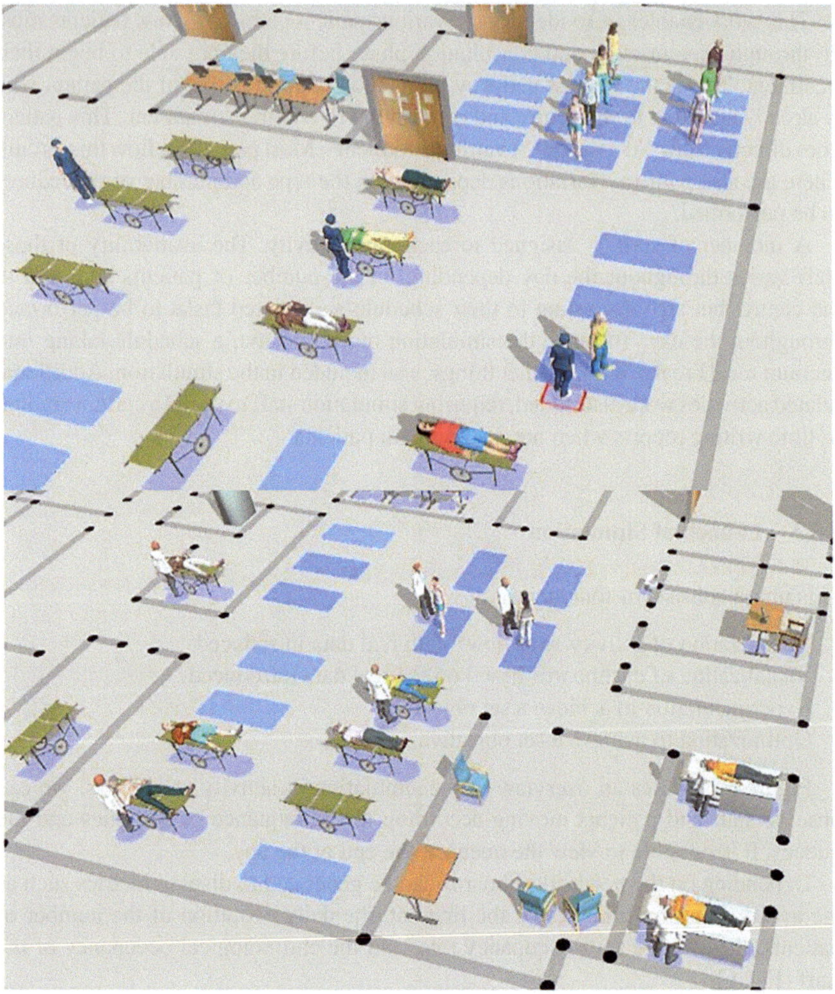

Fig. 5 Overview of the activity workflow with FlexSim Healthcare®

Optimization enables the execution of all scenarios to automatically achieve the best results using OptQuest, the optimization engine developed by OptTek Systems. This engine employs a set of algorithms, including metaheuristic optimization, evolutionary algorithms, tabu search, and scatter search. Figure 8 illustrates the optimization results. To eliminate waiting times, the following resource allocation would be required: 13 physiotherapists, six occupational therapists, nine calisthenics coaches, four doctors, and two nurses.

The simulation for half-day care cannot be considered due to the significant human resources required and the necessary organizational changes.

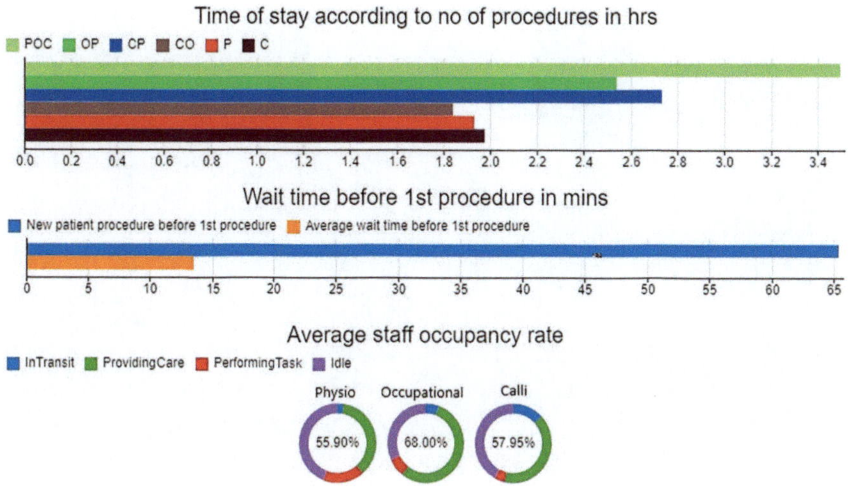

Fig. 6 Examples of dashboard overviews

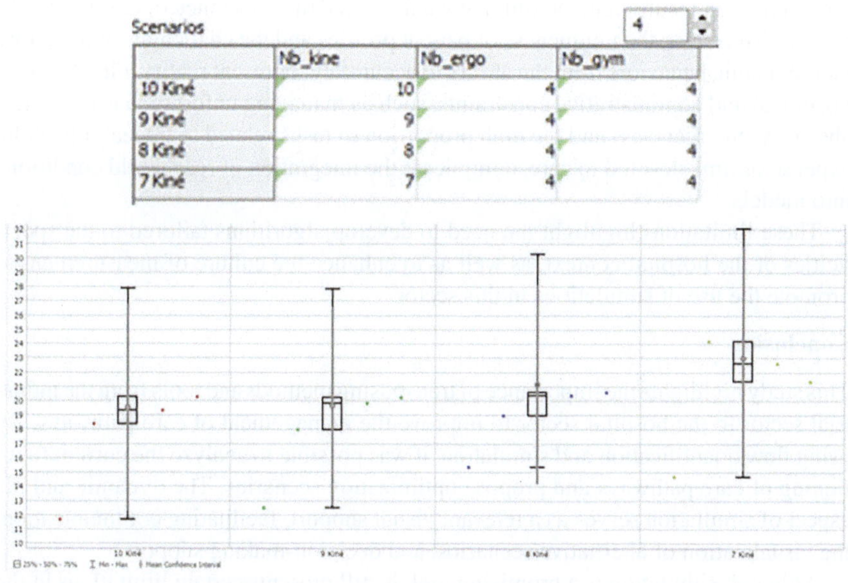

Fig. 7 Example of experimentation for waiting time optimization

3D simulation is a highly user-friendly communication tool that facilitates visualization, understanding, interactions, the establishment of a shared vision, and decision-making among stakeholders.

Although simulation offers numerous advantages, its application faces several limitations related to the specificities of the hospital sector. Data collection is often

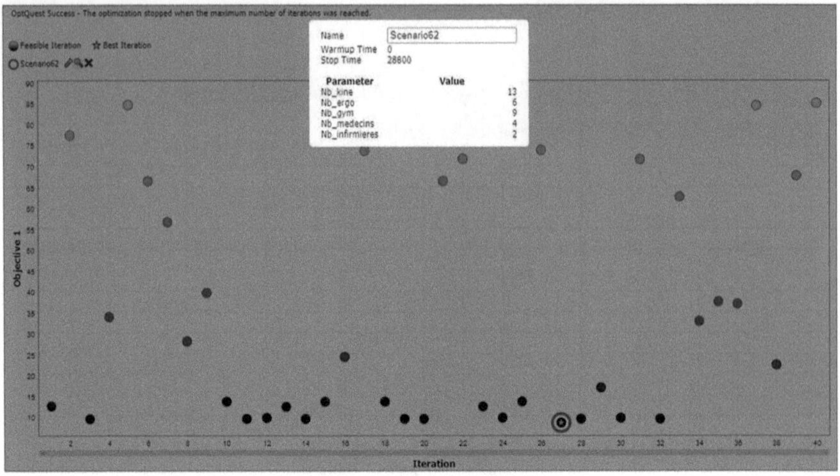

Fig. 8 Waiting time optimization scenario

hindered by an insufficient measurement culture and the reluctance of observed individuals. Moreover, the uniqueness of patient profiles and the challenges of modeling their dynamic behaviors limit the ability to accurately represent reality. Finally, organizational and administrative constraints, such as managing unforeseen events (staff absences, emergencies) and the high proportion of tasks related to traceability at the expense of time devoted to care, complicate the integration of real-world conditions into models.

These limitations highlight the need to develop algorithms tailored to the specificities of the hospital context, as well as to enhance the culture of measurement to promote the use of simulations in this sector.

Conclusion

This study highlights the importance of transposing methods and tools from the industrial sector to the hospital sector to improve the management of care pathways. By using flow quantification and simulation, it was possible to analyze the current functioning of care pathways and propose optimization scenarios. The dynamic and 3D aspect of simulation serves as a relevant visual support, facilitating communication, the visualization of alternative scenarios, and decision-making support.

Although simulation is a promising tool, it still presents certain limitations in the healthcare sector. Overcoming these challenges requires continuous improvement of modeling and simulation techniques, as well as a stronger culture of measurement and data analysis. It is a decision-making tool that should be more widely integrated into healthcare facilities. The ultimate goal is to offer decision-making tools to optimise the hospital logistics chain.

References

1. Abbott, K.W., Genschel, P., Snidal, D., Zangl, B. (eds.).: International Organizations as Orchestrators. Cambridge University Press (2015)
2. Baudelot, C., Caillé, Y., Godechot, O., Mercier, S.: Maladies rénales et inégalités sociales d'accès à la greffe en France [Kidney disease and social inequalities in access to transplantation in France]. Population **71**(1), 23–51 (2016)
3. Belaidi, A., Besombes, B., Guinet, A., Marcon, E.: Réorganisation d'un service d'urgences et aide au pilotage des flux de patients: Apport de la modélisation d'entreprise et de la simulation de flux [Reorganisation of an emergency department and assistance with patient flow management: The contribution of business modelling and flow simulation]. Logistique Manag. **15**(1), 61–73 (2007)
4. Compondu, C., Chaabane, S.: Optimisation et gestion des flux: apport de la simulation [Flow optimisation and management: the contribution of simulation]. In: 10ème Conférence francophone en Gestion et Ingénierie des systèmes Hospitaliers. Hybride. [10th Francophone Conference on Hospital Systems Management and Engineering. Hybrid] (2020)
5. Garidi, S.: L'impact des systèmes d'information hospitaliers sur la sécurisation du parcours de prise en charge du patient [The impact of hospital information systems on the security of the patient care process]. Ph.D. thesis, Université de Lorraine (2021)
6. Husson, J.: Le management hospitalier après la crise : changement de pratiques, changements de référentiels? Dans: *L'impact de la crise sur le management*, Dirigé par: M. Kalika. [Hospital management after the crisis: changing practices, changing frames of reference? In: Kalika, M. (ed.) The Impact of the Crisis on the Management]. Edition Management et Société (EMS) (2020)
7. Leclerc, A., Kaminski, M., Lang, T., Lang, T.: Inégaux face à la santé: du constat à l'action [Inequalities in health: from observation to action]. La Découverte, Paris; Michel, P., Grenier, C.: Le bon soin, au bon moment, au bon endroit, au bon patient, au bon coût [The right care, at the right time, in the right place, for the right patient, at the right cost]. Revue française des affaires sociales (3), 135–137 (2019)
8. Polton, D.: La pertinence : trop ou trop peu de soins ? [Relevance: too much or too little care?] Revue française des affaires sociales (3), 139–148 (2019)
9. Rakotondranaivo, A.: Lean Healthcare: retours d'expériences des établissements de santé en Lorraine in *Management par la Valeur et Lean six-Sigma. Une synergie pour plus de valeur dans les organisations de santé*. In: sous la direction de Grandhaye, J.-P., Husson, J. (eds.) [Lean Healthcare: feedback from healthcare establishments in Lorraine in Management par la Valeur et Lean six-Sigma. Une synergie pour plus de valeur dans les organisations de santé, Grandhaye, J.-P., Husson, J.]. Alternative, pp. 99–116 (2021)
10. Samaha, S., Wendy, S.: The use of simulation to reduce the length of stay in an emergency department. In: Proceedings of the 2003 Winter Simulation Conference. New Orleans, Louisiana, USA (2003)
11. Takakuwa, S., & Shiozaki, H.: Functional analysis for operating emergency department of a general hospital. In: Proceedings of the 2004 Winter Simulation Conference, no. 2, pp. 2003–2011 (2004)

Analysis of Risk Factors Associated with Chronic Obstructive Pulmonary Disease in Quebec

Balkissa Tonde and Maude Laberge

Abstract Chronic Obstructive Pulmonary Disease (COPD) is a major non-communicable disease responsible for millions of deaths annually worldwide. This study examines the risk factors associated with COPD in Quebec, using data from the 2017–2018 Canadian Community Health Survey (CCHS). We ran a logistic regression to analyze the association between a COPD diagnosis and various demographic, socioeconomic, clinical, and behavioral factors. Among the 15,080 participants included in the analysis, 5.8% (n = 874) were diagnosed with COPD. The results revealed significant positive associations with age, asthma, anxiety, smoking, and physical inactivity. Conversely, higher levels of education and income were negatively associated with the likelihood of having COPD.

Keywords COPD · Risk factors · Logistic regression · Canadian Community Health Survey · Quebec

B. Tonde
Department of Operations and Decision Systems, Université Laval, Quebec City, Canada
e-mail: balkissa.tonde.1@ulaval.ca

B. Tonde · M. Laberge
Centre de recherche du CHU de Québec, Université Laval, Quebec City, Canada

VITAM, Centre de recherche en santé durable – Université Laval, Quebec City, Canada

B. Tonde
Institut universitaire de cardiologie et de pneumologie de Québec – Université Laval, Quebec City, Canada

M. Laberge (✉)
Department of Social and Preventive Medicine, Faculty of Medicine, Université Laval, Quebec City, Canada
e-mail: maude.laberge@fmed.ulaval.ca

Centre de recherche du CISSS de Chaudière-Appalaches, Quebec, Canada

P. Landa et al. (eds.), *Operations Research and Artificial Intelligence in Healthcare Management*, Springer Proceedings in Mathematics & Statistics 506,
https://doi.org/10.1007/978-3-031-95659-1_7

1 Introduction

Quebec, like most other Canadian provinces, is facing a growing public health problem in the management of patients with Chronic Obstructive Pulmonary Disease (COPD). COPD is a progressive, non-reversible disease characterized by airway limitation, with significant morbidity and mortality implications. According to the World Health Organization (WHO), COPD is the third leading cause of death worldwide, responsible for more than 3 million deaths annually [1]. This disease is the leading cause of hospitalization in Quebec and the fourth leading cause of death nationwide [2]. Furthermore, the Quebec Lung Association (QLA) reports that COPD is the second leading cause of hospitalization among women after childbirth [3]. In 2022, an estimated 600,000 individuals lived with COPD in Quebec (population 8,8 million), exerting a substantial burden on the healthcare system and representing significant financial costs. COPD-related care costs account for over 6% of annual healthcare spending in Quebec [3]. Globally, COPD research emphasizes its multifactorial nature, including demographic, clinical, and socio-economic factors. International studies unanimously identify smoking as the primary risk factor, particularly chronic smoking [4, 5]. Exposure to second-hand smoke, air pollution, and occupational toxins also represent important risk factors, even affecting non-smokers [6–8]. Furthermore, several studies emphasize that advanced age increases the risk of COPD due to the natural decline in lung function and increased inflammation [2, 9]. Comorbidities such as asthma and cardiovascular diseases also exacerbate the risk of developing COPD [9–11]. Although socio-economic status is not always a direct predictor of COPD, its impact on access to healthcare and healthy lifestyles remains crucial [7]. In Canada, research has revealed a high prevalence of COPD among indigenous populations, and this high prevalence was attributed in part to exposure to smoking [12]. Thus, while the risk factors for COPD are widely shared globally, it is essential to consider regional specificities, both socio-economic and environmental.

The present study aims to analyze the association between demographic, clinical, and socio-economic risk factors and having a COPD diagnosis in Quebec.

2 Data and Methodology

2.1 Data

Our data come from the Canadian Community Health Survey—Annual Component (CCHS) conducted by Statistics Canada across the country during the 2017–2018 period. The CCHS is a cross-sectional sample survey conducted every two years to collect information on the health status, use of health services and health determinants of the population. The sampling method used for the CCHS is non-probabilistic, as participants are selected based on predefined criteria to ensure sufficient representation of key population groups and provinces.

The total sample size over the two years was 130,000 participants, distributed as follows: 120,000 participants from the population aged 18 or over and the remaining 10,000 representing the population aged 12–17. This sample is further distributed among the different provinces based on their respective populations, using a power allocation of 0.75. Individuals living on reserves, in remote areas, or in institutions, are excluded in the sampling. While this may slightly limit the generalizability of the results, the excluded groups represent a small fraction of the overall population (about 3%). The database contains 1,051 variables, and the unweighted response rate was 60.8%. Data collection was carried out using two Computer-Aided Engineering (CAE) applications, 75% by telephone interviews (CATI) and 23% by on-site interviews (CAPI). As the aim of the present study is to assess risk factors on the health status of COPD patients in Quebec, our study population is limited to respondents living in the province of Quebec. The choice of province was justified by the fact that, among Canadian provinces, Quebec has the highest prevalence of COPD, higher than the national prevalence (5.3 vs. 4.2%). People who did not answer the question about having had or not a COPD diagnosis were excluded. We decided to excluded people under 35 based on the evidence that the majority of people living with COPD are over 35 and that prevalence under 35 is very low [13, 14].

- *Dependent variable*

Given the objective of the analysis, the dependent variable "diagnosed with COPD" is identified by a binary variable that takes 0 if the individual reports that they have never been diagnosed with COPD and 1 if the individual reports having been diagnosed with COPD.

- *Independent variables*

In most empirical studies reviewed in the literature on this topic, several categories of risk factors associated with COPD are identified [4, 12, 13, 15], which we identify as follows:

- Demographic factors: These include age, gender, Aboriginal identity, and immigrant status. Age, measured in completed years, reflects the duration of an individual's life. Gender refers to the identity reported by the individual, categorized as man or woman. Aboriginal identity is a binary variable (1 = yes, 0 = no) and denotes individuals who identify as First Nations, Métis, Inuit, or Indian. Immigrant status is also a binary variable (1 = yes, 0 = no) and specifies whether an individual is an immigrant.
- Socioeconomic factors: level of education, and income category. We grouped the education level choices into three categories (Partial secondary, High school graduate, Postsecondary), representing the highest level of formal education attained by the individual. Income, classified into five levels, refers to the individual's monetary earnings or, in some cases, in-kind income over a one-year period.

- Health status factors: These include anxiety disorders, asthma. Anxiety disorders are identified as a binary variable (1 = yes, 0 = no) based on medical diagnoses of conditions such as depression, bipolar disorder, mania, or dysthymia.
- Asthma is a binary variable (1 = yes, 0 = no) indicating whether an individual has been diagnosed with the condition.
- Lifestyle factors: These include body mass index (BMI), physical activity, smoking habits, and exposure to second-hand smoke. Physical activity is measured as a binary variable (1 = yes, 0 = no) and refers to the individual's participation in sports activities over the past three months. BMI, defined as the ratio of weight in kilograms to height in meters squared, is divided into four categories: Underweight (BMI < 18), Normal weight ($18 \leq$ BMI < 25), Overweight ($25 \leq$ BMI < 30), and Obesity (BMI ≥ 30). Smoking habits are categorized based on the frequency of cigarette use (Never, Occasional, Every day). Second-hand smoke exposure is measured as a binary variable (1 = yes, 0 = no) and is determined by the presence of a family member smoking inside the home.

2.2 *Statistical Analysis*

In this study, univariate and bivariate descriptive analyses were first carried out to explore the distribution of the data and describe the relationship between the variable of interest and our explanatory variables. Given the qualitative nature of our indicators, the Chi-square test at the 5% threshold was used to determine the significance of the binary link between the dependent variable and the independent variables. Binary logit regression was then used to analyze the factors associated with COPD.

This approach was chosen because the explanation of a binary variable by a factor vector requires the construction of a probability model [16]. Among probabilistic models, logistic models are those that best illustrate the chance of occurrence of an event with two outcomes and allow detailed analysis of the presence or absence of a feature [13, 14]. All analyses were performed at the 5% significance level using Stata 18.0 software and RStudio 4.4.2.

3 Results

3.1 *Descriptive Analysis*

The shows the bivariate analysis between each explanatory variable and reporting a COPD diagnosis (the dependent variable). Chi-square tests reveal associations that are statistically significant (Table 1).

A total of 15,080 participants were included in the analysis, of whom 874 (5.80%) of the study population had chronic obstructive pulmonary disease (COPD), while

Table 1 Characteristics of the study population

Variables	With COPD n = 874 (5.80%)	Without COPD n = 14 206 (94.20%)	p-value
Participant Age Group			<0.001
35–44	33 (3.78%)	2,516 (17.71%)	
45–54	88 (10.07%)	2,416 (17.01%)	
55–64	232 (26.54%)	3,868 (27.23%)	
65–74	306 (35.01%)	3,442 (24.23%)	
75 and more	215 (24.60%)	1,964 (13.83%)	
Gender			0.001
Women	512 (58.58%)	7,524 (52.96%)	
Men	362 (41.42%)	6,682 (47.04%)	
Indigenous identity			<0.001
No	833 (95.31%)	13,831 (97.36%)	
Yes	41 (4.69%)	375 (2.64%)	
Immigration status			0.245
No	871 (99.66%)	14,111 (99.33%)	
Yes	3 (0.34%)	95 (0.67%)	
Level of education			<0.001
Partial secondary	321 (36.73%)	2,906 (20.46%)	
High school graduate	206 (23.57%)	2,720 (19.15%)	
Post-secondary	347 (39.70%)	8,580 (60.40%)	
Revenue			<0.001
Less than 20 000$	377 (43.14%)	3,278 (23.07%)	
20 000–39 999 $	283 (32.38%)	4,190 (29.49%)	
40 000–59 999 $	130 (14.87%)	3,035 (21.36%)	
60 000–79 999 $	45 (5.15%)	1,710 (12.04%)	
80 000 and more	39 (4.46%)	1,993 (14.03%)	
Physical activity			<0.001
No	579 (66.25%)	6,443 (45.35%)	
Yes	295 (33.75%)	7,763 (54.65%)	
Anxiety			<0.001
No	728 (83.3%)	13,161 (92.64%)	
Yes	146 (16.7%)	1,045 (7.36%)	
Asthma			<0.001
No	451 (51.6%)	13,231 (93.14%)	
Yes	423 (48.4%)	975 (6.86%)	
Type of smoker			<0.001
Never	598 (68.42%)	11,685 (82.25%)	

(continued)

Table 1 (continued)

Variables	With COPD n = 874 (5.80%)	Without COPD n = 14 206 (94.20%)	p-value
Occasional	36 (4.12%)	510 (3.59%)	
Every day	240 (27.46%)	2,011 (14.16%)	
Second-hand smoke			<0.001
No	677 (77.46%)	12,725 (89.57%)	
Yes	197 (22.54%)	1,481 (10.43%)	
BMI			
Underweight	13 (1.49%)	117 (0.82%)	<0.001
Normal weight	264 (30.21%)	4,461 (31.40%)	
Overweight	300 (34.32%)	5,528 (38.91%)	
Obesity	297 (33.98%)	4,100 (28.87%)	

P-value: Pearson's Chi-squared test; COPD: Chronic Obstructive Pulmonary Disease; BMI: Body Mass Index

14,206 (94.20%) did not. The age distribution differed significantly between participants with and without COPD p < 2.2e–16). The proportion of participants with COPD increased with age, with those aged 65 years and older accounting for 59.61% (n = 521) of cases. In contrast, participants without COPD were primarily between 35 and 64 years old, representing 61.95% (n = 8,800) of cases. The proportion of women was significantly higher in the COPD group (58.58%, n = 512) than in the group of respondents without COPD (52.96%, n = 7,524; p = 0.001). Similarly, there was a higher proportion of Indigenous people in the COPD group (4.69%, n = 41) compared to the non-COPD group (2.64%, n = 375; p = 0.000). Conversely, no significant difference was observed regarding immigration status between the two groups (p = 0.245), with nearly all participants, with or without COPD, being non-immigrants (99.66% vs. 99.33%).

Significant differences were observed in the distribution of education levels between the two groups (p < 2.2e–16). Participants with COPD reported lower levels of education (partial secondary education: 36.73%, n = 321 and high school graduates: 23.57%, n = 206), whereas those without COPD were predominantly postsecondary graduates (60.40%, n = 8,580). Similarly, annual income distribution also differed significantly between the groups (p < 2.2e–16). Participants with COPD tended to report lower incomes, with 43.14% earning less than $20,000 annually compared to 23.07% of those without COPD. Conversely, higher incomes of $80,000 or more were less common in the COPD group (4.46%) than in the non-COPD group (14.03%). Regarding physical activity, participants with COPD were significantly less likely to engage in regular physical activity (33.75%) compared to those without COPD (54.65%; p < 2.2e–16).

The results also show a higher prevalence of anxiety among participants with COPD (16.7%) compared to those without COPD (7.36%; p < 2.2e–16). There was also a strong association between COPD and asthma, with 48.4% of participants with COPD reporting a concurrent diagnosis of asthma, compared to only 6.86% in the non-COPD group ($p < 2.2e{-}16$). A majority of participants with COPD (66.25%) reported not participating in physical activity. Furthermore, smoking habits differed significantly between the groups ($p < 2.2e{-}16$). Participants with COPD were less likely to report never having smoked (68.42%) compared to those without COPD (82.25%), while the proportion of daily smokers was higher in the COPD group (27.46%) than in the non-COPD group (14.16%). Exposure to second-hand smoke was also more common among participants with COPD (22.54%) than among those without COPD (10.43%; $p < 2.2e{-}16$). The distribution of body mass index (BMI) categories differed significantly between the two groups ($p = 0.007$). Participants with COPD were significantly less likely to have a normal weight (30.21%) compared to those without COPD (31.40%). Similarly, the proportion of participants who were overweight was lower in the COPD group (34.32%) than in the non-COPD group (38.91%). However, a substantial proportion of COPD were classified as obese (33.98%), with a prevalence higher than that observed in the non-COPD group (28.87%). Additionally, the proportion of underweight individuals was slightly higher in the COPD group (1.49%) compared to the non-COPD group (0.82%).

3.2 Logistic Regression

The binary logistic regression analysis (Table 2) identified several factors associated with COPD. The model shows a McFadden pseudo-R^2 of 0.237, indicating satisfactory goodness of fit [17]. The area under the ROC curve reveals good predictive performance, with an area under the curve (AUC) is 84% (see Appendix Fig. 1), reflecting good discriminatory ability of the model [18].

The results reveal a significant association between participants age and COPD. Compared to the 35–44 age group, participants aged 45–54 have an Odds Ratio (OR) of 2.44 (95% CI: 1.61–3.78, $p < 0.001$), and this association becomes more pronounced for participants aged 75 and older (OR = 10.1, 95% CI: 6.77–15.4, $p < 0.001$). Regarding gender, although men have a slightly higher risk of developing COPD than women, this association is not significant (OR = 1.10, 95% CI: 0.94–1.29, $p = 0.2$). No significant associations were observed for Aboriginal identity (OR = 1.33, 95% CI: 0.90–1.93, $p = 0.14$) or immigration status (OR = 1.59, 95% CI: 0.53–7.02, $p = 0.5$).

However, significant associations were noted with education level and income. Participants with post-secondary education have a negative association with COPD (OR = 0.80, 95% CI: 0.67–0.97, $p = 0.026$) compared to those with partial secondary education. Similarly, higher income is associated with a reduced likelihood of COPD (OR = 0.44, 95% CI: 0.30–0.62, $p < 0.001$) for incomes of $80,000 or more compared to those with incomes below $20,000.

Other variables also show positive associations with COPD, including the presence of asthma (OR = 13.0, 95% CI: 11.0–15.2, $p < 0.001$), lack of physical activity

Table 2 Results of the binary logistic regression model examining the association between risk factors and COPD

Characteristic	OR[a]	95% CI[a]	p-value
Participant age group			
35–44	–	–	
45–54	2.44	1.61, 3.78	<0.001
55–64	4.57	3.14, 6.86	<0.001
65–74	7.49	5.15, 11.2	<0.001
75 and more	10.1	6.77, 15.4	<0.001
Gender			
Women	–	–	
Men	1.10	0.94, 1.29	0.2
Indigenous identity			
No	–	–	
Yes	1.33	0.90, 1.93	0.14
Immigration status			
No	–	–	
Yes	1.59	0.53, 7.02	0.5
Level of education			
Partial secondary	–	–	
High school graduate	1.12	0.91, 1.38	0.3
Post-secondary	0.80	0.67, 0.97	0.026
Revenue			
Less than 20 000$	–	–	
20 000–39 999 $	0.77	0.64, 0.92	0.005
40 000–59 999 $	0.69	0.54, 0.87	0.002
60 000–79 999 $	0.54	0.38, 0.75	<0.001
Physical activity			
Yes	–	–	
No	1.72	1.46, 2.02	<0.001
Asthma			
No	–	–	
Yes	13.0	11.0, 15.2	<0.001
Anxiety			
No	–	–	
Yes	1.88	1.49, 2.35	<0.001
Type of smoker			
Never	–	–	
Occasional	1.62	1.07, 2.38	0.018
Everyday	1.83	1.44, 2.32	<0.001
Second-hand smoke			

(continued)

Table 2 (continued)

Characteristic	OR[a]	95% CI[a]	p-value
No	–	–	
Yes	1.32	1.03, 1.70	0.026
BMI			
Normal weight	–	–	
Underweight	1.39	0.68, 2.61	0.3
Overweight	0.90	0.74, 1.08	0.3
Obesity	0.94	0.77, 1.15	0.6

[a] OR = Odds Ratio, CI = Confidence Interval
BMI: Body Mass Index
N = 15,080
pseudo-$R^2 = 0.237$
LROC = 84

(OR = 1.72, 95% CI: 1.46–2.02, $p < 0.001$), and anxiety (OR = 1.88, 95% CI: 1.49–2.35, $p < 0.001$).

Additionally, regular smokers have a significant positive association (OR = 1.83, 95% CI: 1.44–2.32, $p < 0.001$) compared to non-smokers, as does exposure to second-hand smoke (OR = 1.32, 95% CI: 1.03–1.70, $p = 0.026$). No significant associations were observed for the different categories of body mass index (BMI).

4 Discussion

The binary logistic regression analysis identified several significant associations between COPD and demographic, socio-economic, clinical, and behavioral variables. These associations characterize the direction and strength of the relationships but do not establish causality due to the cross-sectional nature of the data.

Age is significantly and positively associated with the odds of having in Quebec. The results show that, compared to individuals aged 35–44 years, those in older age groups are more likely to be diagnosed with COPD. This observation can be attributed to the natural decline in lung function with age, which increases the risk of inflammation; this age-related decline resembles the physiological impact of COPD. These findings are consistent with previous studies reporting a higher prevalence of COPD among individuals over 60 years of age compared to younger age groups [7, 19]. While the literature reports a higher prevalence of COPD in men [4, 7], we did not observe a significant effect of gender. However, the literature reporting higher prevalence of COPD in men also attribute it to more frequent smoking behaviors [4, 7], which we control for in our analyses.

The results reveal negative associations between COPD and some socioeconomic variables. Higher education and higher income are associated with a lower likelihood of COPD. These findings align with previous research suggesting that higher education and income levels are associated with reduced exposure to harmful environmental or occupational factors and greater health literacy [20, 21] that reduce the risk of developing COPD.

Several positive associations were identified with clinical and behavioral variables. Regular smoking is positively associated with having COPD, as is exposure to second-hand smoke. These findings reinforce established evidence identifying active and passive smoking as major factors associated with COPD [8, 22, 23]. Furthermore, the absence of physical activity is positively associated with COPD. This association may reflect a vicious cycle where respiratory limitations reduce physical activity, which in turn exacerbates symptoms and decreases patients' quality of life [24, 25]. Unlike some previous studies suggesting a potential link between obesity and reduced lung function [13, 24, 25], we found no significant association between BMI and COPD. Further analyses are needed to explore this relationship in other contexts or populations.

In terms of clinical risks, the positive association between anxiety and COPD that we found could reflect a potentially bidirectional relationship, where COPD could exacerbate anxiety due to functional limitations and psychological distress, while respiratory related anxiety may worsen respiratory symptoms [26, 27]. The presence of asthma is strongly associated with COPD, confirming symptomatic and pathophysiological overlaps between asthma and COPD, as noted in prior studies [27, 28].

This study has several limitations. First, the cross-sectional nature of the data does not allow for causal relationships between the studied variables and COPD, limiting conclusions on underlying mechanisms. Additionally, COPD diagnosis is based on self-reports by participants without spirometry confirmation, which could introduce measurement bias due to potential underreporting or overreporting of cases. Furthermore, as the study sample consists exclusively of participants from the Quebec population, the findings may not be generalizable to other geographical or cultural contexts. Lastly, the use of the AIC criterion for model selection could have introduced the risk of overfitting, potentially affecting the robustness and validity of the conclusions. These limitations underscore the need for further research with longitudinal data and objective diagnostic measures.

5 Conclusion

This study examined the risk factors for COPD in Quebec using a logit model and data from the 2017–2018 "Canadian Community Health Survey-Annual Component (CCHS)." The results identify several significant associations between COPD and demographic, socioeconomic, clinical, and behavioral variables. Positive associations with age, asthma, anxiety, smoking, and lack of physical activity, as well as negative associations with higher education levels and income, highlight important avenues for understanding COPD. These findings align with previous research [7, 19, 20, 26] while emphasizing the need for future studies using longitudinal data to explore causality and strengthen the foundation for COPD prevention and management strategies.

Appendix

Figure 1.

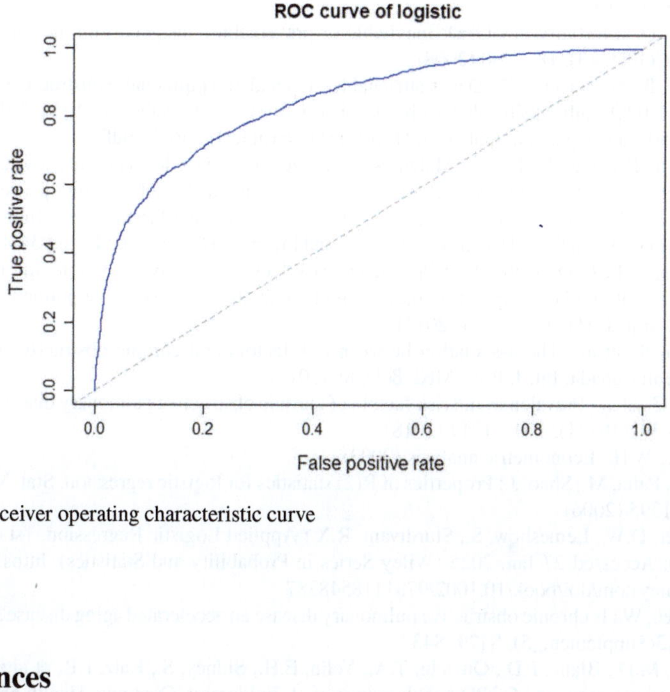

Fig. 1 Receiver operating characteristic curve

References

1. WHO.: Chronic obstructive pulmonary disease (COPD) [Internet]. Accessed 2025 Jan. 12. https://www.who.int/news-room/fact-sheets/detail/chronic-obstructive-pulmonary-disease-(copd)
2. Leung, C., Bourbeau, J., Sin, D.D., Aaron, S.D., FitzGerald, J.M., Maltais, F., et al.: The prevalence of Chronic Obstructive Pulmonary Disease (COPD) and the heterogeneity of risk factors in the Canadian population: results from the Canadian Obstructive Lung Disease (COLD) Study. Int. J. Chron. Obstruct. Pulmon. Dis. **16**, 305–320 (2021)
3. Association pulmonaire du Québec [Internet]. Accessed 5 Jan. 2025. MPOC, Emphysème et Bronchite. https://poumonquebec.ca/en/maladies/copd/
4. Celli, B.R., Halbert, R.J., Nordyke, R.J., Schau, B.: Airway obstruction in never smokers: results from the Third National Health and Nutrition Examination Survey. Am. J. Med. **118**(12), 1364–1372 (2005)
5. Chen, P., Li, Y., Wu, D., Liu, F., Cao, C.: Secondhand smoke exposure and the risk of chronic obstructive pulmonary disease: a systematic review and meta-analysis. Int. J. Chron. Obstruct. Pulmon. Dis. **18**, 1067–1076 (2023)

6. Wang, C., Xu, J., Yang, L., Xu, Y., Zhang, X., Bai, C., et al.: Prevalence and risk factors of chronic obstructive pulmonary disease in China (the China Pulmonary Health [CPH] study): a national cross-sectional study. Lancet **391**(10131), 1706–1717 (2018)
7. Chen, J., Yin, Y., Zhang, Y., Lin, X., Chen, T., Yang, Z., et al.: Chronic obstructive pulmonary disease prevalence and associated risk factors in adults aged 40 years and older in Southeast China: a cross-sectional study during 2019–2020. Int. J. Chron. Obstruct. Pulmon. Dis. **17**(17), 2317–2328 (2022)
8. Chen, H.C., Wu, C.F., Chong, I.W., Wu, M.T.: Exposure to cooking oil fumes and chronic bronchitis in nonsmoking women aged 40 years and over: a health-care based study. BMC Public Health **13**(18), 246 (2018)
9. Berry, C.E., Wise, R.A.: Mortality in COPD: causes, risk factors, and prevention. COPD **7**(5), 375–382 (2010)
10. Halpin, D.: Mortality in COPD: Inevitable or preventable? Insights from the cardiovascular arena. COPD **5**(3), 187–200 (2008)
11. Shirley, B., Navaneelan, T.: Décès attribuables à la maladie pulmonaire obstructive chronique, 1950 à 2011 [Deaths attributable to chronic obstructive pulmonary disease, 1950–2011]. https://www150.statcan.gc.ca/n1/pub/82-624-x/2015001/article/14246-fra.pdf
12. Bruce, S., Riediger, N., Lix, L.: Maladies chroniques et facteurs de risque chez les membres des Premières Nations, les Inuits et les Métis du Nord canadien. Maladies chroniques et blessures au Canada 2014 Nov [Chronic diseases and risk factors among First Nations, Inuit and Métis people in northern Canada. Chronic Diseases and Injuries in Canada 2014 Nov] **34**(4), 229–237
13. Vozoris, N.T., O'Donnell, D.E.: Prevalence, risk factors, activity limitation, and health care utilization of an obese population-based sample with chronic obstructive pulmonary disease. Can. Respir. J. **19**(3), e18–e24 (2012)
14. Osman, S., et al.: The association between risk factors and chronic obstructive pulmonary disease in Canada. Int. J. Prev. Med. **8**(1), 86 (2017)
15. Wang, C., et al.: Prevalence and risk factors of chronic obstructive pulmonary disease in China. Lancet **391**(10131), 1706–1717 (2018)
16. Greene, W.H.: Econometric analysis (2003)
17. Hu, B., Palta, M., Shao, J.: Properties of R(2) statistics for logistic regression. Stat. Med. **25**(8), 1383–1395 (2006)
18. Hosmer, D.W., Lemeshow, S., Sturdivant, R.X.: Applied Logistic Regression, 1st edn. Wiley (2013). Accessed 27 Jan. 2025 (Wiley Series in Probability and Statistics). https://onlinelibrary.wiley.com/doi/book/10.1002/9781118548387
19. MacNee, W.: Is chronic obstructive pulmonary disease an accelerated aging disease? Ann. ATS 2016 **13**(Supplement_5), S429–S437
20. Eisner, M.D., Blanc, P.D., Omachi, T.A., Yelin, E.H., Sidney, S., Katz, P.P., et al.: Socioeconomic status, race, and COPD health outcomes. J. Epidemiol. Commun. Health **65**(1), 26–34 (2011)
21. Lutter, J.I., Jörres, R.A., Welte, T., Watz, H., Waschki, B., Alter, P., et al.: Impact of education on COPD severity and all-cause mortality in lifetime never-smokers and longtime ex-smokers: results of the COSYCONET cohort. Int. J. Chron. Obstruct. Pulmon. Dis. **15**, 2787–2798 (2020)
22. Eisner, M.D., Anthonisen, N., Coultas, D., Kuenzli, N., Perez-Padilla, R., Postma, D., et al.: An Official American Thoracic Society public policy statement: novel risk factors and the global burden of chronic obstructive pulmonary disease. Am. J. Respir. Crit. Care Med. **182**(5), 693–718 (2010)
23. Blanc, P.D., Iribarren, C., Trupin, L., Earnest, G., Katz, P.P., Balmes, J., et al.: Occupational exposures and the risk of COPD: dusty trades revisited. Thorax **64**(1), 6–12 (2009)
24. Hanson, C.T.L.: Obesity and chronic obstructive pulmonary disease: recent knowledge and future directions. Curr. Opin. Pulm. Med. **23**(2), 149–153 (2017)
25. Verberne, L.D.M., et al.: Overweight in patients with chronic obstructive pulmonary disease needs more attention. NPJ. Primary Care Respir. Med. **27**, 63 (2017)
26. Hill, K., et al.: Anxiety and depression in end-stage COPD. Eur. Respir. J. **31**(3), 667–677 (2008)

27. Marcon, A., Locatelli, F., Dharmage, S.C., Svanes, C., Heinrich, J., Leynaert, B., et al.: The coexistence of asthma and COPD: risk factors, clinical history, and lung function trajectories. Eur. Respir. J. **58**(5) (2021)
28. Silva, G.E., Sherrill, D.L., Guerra, S., Barbee, R.A.: Asthma as a risk factor for COPD in a longitudinal study. Chest **126**(1), 59–65 (2004)

Application of Segmentation Methods in Health Care Services Planning and Delivery

Matthew T. Haren, Jean-Baptiste Gartner, André Côté, and Catherine Paquet

Abstract Segmentation is a well-known marketing technique used to identify homogenous groups of consumers to better respond to their needs and preferences. The method aligns with the concept of patient-centricity in health care and has already been applied in some contexts. This chapter provides an overview of existing applications of segmentation to improve the quality of health care services provided to individuals along the health continuum. The literature reviewed highlights applications of segmentation for population health management, risk stratification and personalized care purposes. Segmentation was either expert- or data-driven or a combination of the two. Data-driven approaches were often based on administrative data available from electronic health records and claims data, but the need to consider a more comprehensive set of health-related factors, such as social and behavioral determinants of health and patients' experience measures was highlighted. A

M. T. Haren · J.-B. Gartner · A. Côté · C. Paquet (✉)
Faculty of Business Administration, Laval University, Quebec City, QC, Canada
e-mail: catherine.paquet@fsa.ulaval.ca

Health Services Management Research Centre, Laval University, Quebec City, QC, Canada

M. T. Haren
e-mail: matthew.haren@fsa.ulaval.ca

J.-B. Gartner
e-mail: jean-baptiste.gartner.1@ulaval.ca

A. Côté
e-mail: andre.cote@fsa.ulaval.ca

J.-B. Gartner · A. Côté
Research Centre of the University Institute of Cardio-Pneumology of Quebec, Quebec City, QC, Canada

VITAM, Centre for Sustainable Health Research, Laval University, Quebec City, QC, Canada

J.-B. Gartner · A. Côté · C. Paquet
Research Centre of University Hospital of Quebec, Laval University, Quebec City, QC, Canada

J.-B. Gartner · A. Côté
CISSS of Chaudière-Appalaches Research Centre, Laval University, Quebec City, QC, Canada

P. Landa et al. (eds.), *Operations Research and Artificial Intelligence in Healthcare Management*, Springer Proceedings in Mathematics & Statistics 506,
https://doi.org/10.1007/978-3-031-95659-1_8

lack of evidence demonstrating how applications of segmentation approaches can lead to better tailoring of health services and improve the quality of care provided was noted and should be addressed in future research and applications.

Keywords Segmentation · Health care · Population health management

1 Introduction

The ever-increasing prevalence of chronic conditions and the ageing of populations challenge health system capacities in many parts of the world. These trends give rise to concerns about the quality of care that systems can deliver, the resulting patient and population health outcomes and the economic impact of delivering care to populations through these systems.

In 2001, the Institute of Medicine (IOM) spawned an emphasis on the quality of health care systems being measured in terms of patient-centricity (i.e., meeting patient's preferences and desires) as well as safety, effectiveness, efficiency, timeliness and equitability of health care delivery [1]. This has evolved to a global vision for person-focused health systems supported by health information technologies, patient engagement in all aspects of care and coordination among care teams [1, 2].

One approach to ensuring the consistent provision of the best quality care is with the standardization of evidence-based care by clinical practice guidelines (CPGs). The adherence to CPGs can be improved by integration with digital information technologies to standardize patient care pathways and automate clinical decision-making [3]. CPG implementation can increase the quality of care through enhanced timeliness and effectiveness of care processes, patient safety, patient satisfaction and resource efficiency [4, 5]. However, despite striving to incorporate patient perspectives in their development [6], CPGs do not always apply equally to all patients [7].

Two contemporary concepts in patient-centered care are mass customization and precision medicine. The first "emphasizes the need to respond to the needs and preferences of the consumer, providing goods and services at or near mass production prices" [8], therefore seeking to achieve an optimal balance between personalization and standardization whilst minimizing the budget implications of individualized care. The first key element of this approach to care design is consumer segmentation analysis [8]. The concept of precision medicine also focuses on the idea of patient stratification, with the so-called novel taxonomy being derived from analysis of large-scale data incorporating clinical, lifestyle, genetic and biomarker data. Konig and colleagues sought to advance the definition of precision medicine and propose that: (1) it is a process that includes a number of feedback loops, there is no steady end-point where, finally, precise medical care is provided to patients; (2) the cycle implies that there are ongoing efforts to become ever more precise; and (3) finer and more accurate stratifications of patients can be interim results of the overall process, which is captured by the term "stratified medicine" [9]. Thus, no matter the concept one is compelled to apply, the centerpiece of the process is appropriate patient segmentation analysis.

In the healthcare context, Arnold and colleagues state that "the ultimate goal of patient segmentation models should be to inform clinical care and system-level care planning (p. e76)" [10]. Segmentation in this context entails grouping individuals sharing similar characteristics or needs (e.g. clinical, demographic, behavioral, psychosocial) with the intent to offer these segments customized care, based on combinations of health care interventions or strategies that best meet their needs or to target intervention towards specific patient segments with greater needs [11–13].

This chapter seeks to provide a narrative review on the use of segmentation in health care and to map its use in different healthcare contexts in terms of purpose, methods, data types and sources, as well as the resulting segments, the managerial response and outcomes associated with the segmentation. In the following two sections, we outline the methodology used for this review and discuss key characteristics of applications of segmentation in health care. We conclude by highlighting key challenges and opportunities that emerge from the integration of evidence as well as implications for research, health care management and practice.

2 Methods

A narrative review approach informed by a systematic literature search was used to synthesize the literature. This approach was selected as it provides an overview of a specific topic, raising issues that are usually neglected and encouraging further research on the subject [14]. Within this, we integrate a synthesis of evidence bounded in scope by key characteristics of segmentation namely, purpose, health care context, methods, data types and sources, resulting segments, managerial response to segmentation, and outcomes of the response considering the seven IOM quality indicators: patient-centricity, cost savings, safety, effectiveness, efficiency, timeliness, and equitability [1].

2.1 *Search Strategy and Article Selection*

This narrative review is anchored into a broader systematic search and review aiming to determine how segmentation approaches are used in health care services design and delivery. Seven databases covering a range of fields related to medicine and business and google scholar were searched on 10 March 2023 using terms related to (1) segmentation, and (2) health care. As part of this screening process, relevant literature reviews were identified (systematic and non-systematic, n = 14) and retained for inclusion in this narrative review along with relevant primary research articles from the broader search that passed through abstract screening.

2.2 Synthesis

The following key segmentation characteristics were extracted by analyzing the content of the selected articles.

Purpose or rationale underlying the application of the various segmentation frameworks.

Health system context categorised according to three levels (*macro level*, representing populations for which health care systems, associated systems, infrastructures and policies are designed, *meso level*, representing health care catchment areas or regions where health care services are designed, delivered and coordinated, and *micro level*, where individual health care organizations develop and manage their service and program offerings and interface directly with patients).

Methods used to derive segments, such as expert-driven, data-driven, or mixed [15], as well as specific statistical methods.

Data types and sources that contributed to the segmentation analysis.

Resulting segments emerging from the applications of segmentation.

Managerial responses describing actions taken (actual or expected) by stakeholders in response to applying the segmentation approach within their jurisdiction.

Outcomes associated with the implementation of segmentation strategies related to the seven IOM domains of healthcare quality (patient-centricity, cost savings, safety, effectiveness, efficiency, timeliness, and equitability of care).

Information extracted under each characteristic was summarized narratively with illustrative examples identified from the reviews or the larger systematic review.

3 Segmentation: Applications in Health Care

We provide in this section an overview of key characteristics of the applications of segmentation in health care contexts. These applications varied in terms of the targeted population, health care context, and purposes. Although many relied on similar data sources (e.g., Electronic Health Records (EHRs)), a range of relevant data types and sources were identified, which were used by experts and/or analysts to uncover relevant segments. These different segmentation attributes are summarized in Fig. 1 and described in detail below.

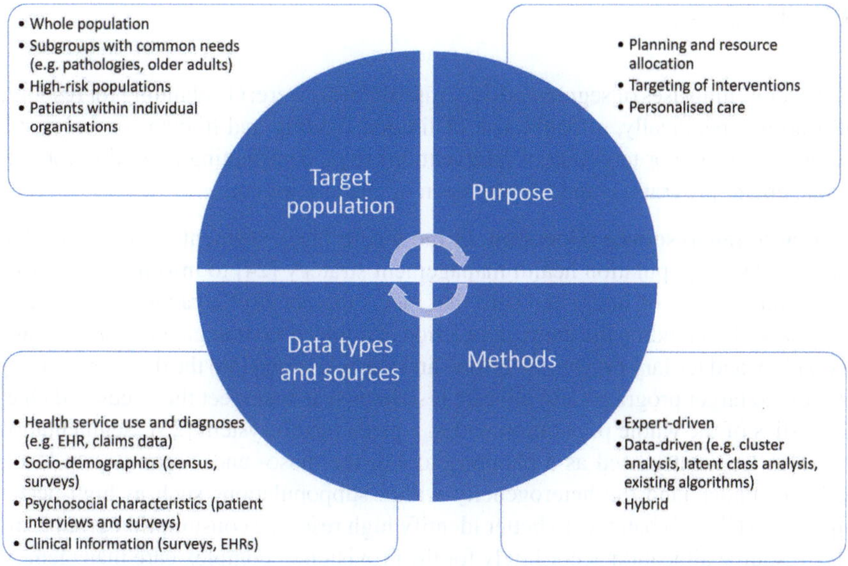

Fig. 1 Overview of characteristics of current applications of segmentation in health care

3.1 Health Care Context and Targeted Populations

Many applications of segmentation were found at the macro-level, where whole populations are studied to identify the needs of all individuals along the health continuum. The populations were defined based on either geography (e.g., State or regions) associated with entire health systems or enrollment into health insurance programs (e.g., Medicare). The concept of using segmentation at this level to better target healthcare resources to the sub-populations that are likely to benefit most is not new. One of the seminal works in the field was the Bridges to Health Model in 2007 [16], which was one of the first examples of applying segmentation at the population level to manage healthcare needs. This gave rise to different applications of the model and the creation of other models that similarly segmented populations according to logical expert-derived groups with broadly similar care needs. Examples include the Lombardy segmentation scheme [17]; British Columbia Health System Matrix [18, 19]; and the Ministry of Health (Singapore) Segmentation Framework [20].

Examples of applications were also observed at lower levels such as health service catchments (meso-level) or service organizations themselves (micro-level). At these levels, the subpopulations studied included individuals who already had an encounter with the health system (meso-level) or with a specific health institution (micro-level). Applications included patients receiving specific services (e.g. home-based rehabilitation services) [21], with specific diagnoses (e.g., Type 2 diabetes) [22], or representing specific populations (e.g., older adults) [23].

3.2 Purposes

The overarching uses of segmentation across all levels were: (1) planning for resource allocation, specifically, effective use of limited funding and human resources; (2) guiding provision or targeting of interventions (e.g., determining eligibility for care management programs); and (3) provision of customized care.

Planning and resource allocation At the macro level, segmentation was used as part of a larger population health management strategy [24] to inform the development and delivery of integrated care that meets the needs of a range of population segments. By including the entire population, it allowed to strategically plan primary, secondary and tertiary prevention efforts and was a key step into the decision-making process to target programs and allocate resources that best meet the needs and characteristics of the whole population within a given health system [25]. Segmentation was also frequently used as a planning tool at the meso- and micro-system levels to better understand the heterogeneity within subpopulations such as high-needs, high-cost (HNHC) patients to better identify high resource consumption groups and plan resource allocation accordingly for the provision of complex care management programs (CMPs) to those most likely to derive benefit [25, 26]. Other planning-related purposes for segmentation at these levels included creating efficient models of demand-driven or person-centered (as opposed to organization centered) care [27], improving care integration and developing effective integrated healthcare interventions [21, 28], and optimizing healthcare utilization, specifically reducing length and number of hospitalizations [25].

Targeting of interventions was another common purpose behind the application of segmentation strategies. This took the form of identifying subpopulations with greater needs or more likely to benefit from a given intervention with the intent to target specific resources towards these individuals. This type of application was the most common use of segmentation in meso- and micro-level contexts. For instance, a review by Jean-Baptiste and colleagues showed segmentation applications at these levels were used mostly to refer patients to CMPs [26]. For greater detail on the application of these approaches, see Sects. 3.3 Methods and 3.4 Data types and sources.

Customization of care. By identifying groups with homogeneous needs and characteristics, segmentation is presented as the first element of a 'mass customization' health care strategy [8], which aims to provide individually designed products or services through flexible processes allowing high volumes at reasonable costs [29, 30]. It was also considered as integral to personalized or precision medicine, which classifies individuals into subpopulations based on susceptibility to a particular disease or their response to a specific treatment [31]. Although precision medicine is often associated with physiological markers such as specific genetic profiles, it was noted that patients' individual needs, beliefs, behaviors, values and circumstances were sometimes considered in the conceptualization of precision medicine

[32]. One example of application of segmentation for personalization or customization purposes included micromarketing: a one-on-one approach where healthcare providers customize their marketing strategy to reach individual customers (usually through technology platforms). The use of Upfront Healthcare's proprietary (psychographic) segmentation method is another example which is used to target patients with hyper-relevant messages designed to trigger action such as scheduling an appointment for a screening test, or self-monitoring reminders [33, 34]. Other examples included seeking improved therapeutic outcomes for patients through segmentation to establish a patient's probability of having a therapeutic benefit from a specific drug or therapeutic regimen or determining treatment tailoring, specifically informing drug choice or development of targeted agents [32].

3.3 Methods

The literature provided examples of both empirical (data-driven) and theoretical (expert-driven) approaches. Most commonly, empirical approaches used latent class analysis (LCA), factor mixture models (FMM) or more traditional cluster analysis (hierarchical and/or k-means) methods to determine segments based on selected input variables (see Sect. 3.4 Data types and sources). These analyses were often preceded by data-mining steps to determine the input variables (data indicators), especially when using service utilization or claims-based data [17].

Other data-driven approaches common to all system levels were predictive risk modelling and risk stratification [35]. Predictive analytics based on statistical and machine learning techniques were used to predict the risk of adverse outcomes [35], that could be used to assign individual risk scores. Similarly, the use of existing grouping systems such as Clinical Risk Groups (3M) [36] and Adjusted Clinical Groups (John's Hopkins) [37] which are based on broad clusters of diagnoses, age and sex were common in all levels [26, 38]. A critical review of such risk prediction and segmentation models concluded that there was a lack of comprehensive models that integrate data from multiple sources (rather than solely using billing data) for application to whole populations [35].

At the meso- and micro-levels, these approaches were sometimes used in isolation [39, 40], integrated in a broader segmentation approach [41, 42], or combined with expert clinical judgement (a hybrid approach), as in the numerous examples of selecting HNHC patients for CMPs such as those by Pacific Business Group on Health and Partners HealthCare [26]. In this context, a common practice was for clinicians to review algorithm-generated lists of potential high-risk patients within their practice and select the patients most appropriate for the CMP [36, 43]. The clinician decision-making allowed the consideration of psychosocial aspects of the patients situation [44] and hence enriched the results of risk prediction models. This hybrid approach has been recognized as best practice for selecting patients for intensive outpatient care programs (IOCPs) [26, 36].

3.4 Data Types and Sources

Applications across all contexts reported segmentation models that used medical diagnoses and hospital and health service utilization data, commonly from electronic health records or claims data. These seemed readily available at all levels which may partly explain their widespread use. Socio-demographic data, clinical and functional assessment data from administrative sources or surveys were also commonly used in segmentation models across all health care levels, but to a lesser extent. For instance, Kaiser Permanente members aged 65 years and over and identified as having "advanced illness" based on complex or multiple chronic conditions or geriatric syndromes were further segmented with cluster and latent class analyses using 20 patient-reported items from the assessment, including health status, psychosocial factors, mood symptoms, health behaviors, basic and instrumental activities of daily living [23]. Similar examples were observed in other providers regarding care for older people [21, 45].

Common between the meso and micro levels was the use of medical claims data and clinical judgement, particularly applied in the context of selecting patients for CMPs as discussed above. In these contexts, clinicians made their selections based on not only clinical need (or risk prediction) (e.g., disease severity or multiple comorbidities), but also patients' predisposing (e.g., health literacy or navigation challenges, physical vulnerabilities, insight regarding their health) and enabling characteristics (e.g., social and home environment, coping skills, financial resources), existing linkages with the health system and whether other clinicians were already meeting a patient's care needs [44].

Present only in segmentation applications from the micro levels were more person-centered indicators such as patient activation, health motivation, consideration of future consequences, and preference-based indicators such as expectations related to medical expertise, personalized service, quality and price consciousness, needs, beliefs, values, wishes and aspects of a patient's environment and circumstances [26, 33, 34]. Also present only in the micro segment was the use of physiology-based "-omics" data (e.g., genomics, metabolomics) to determine treatment course in personalized medicine [32].

3.5 Resulting Segments and Managerial Responses

The nature and number of segments varied greatly across applications and depended on the inclusion criteria, input variables, data sources and modelling approaches [10]. In a review of health care needs-based population segmentation tools, Chong and colleagues [38] identified common segment themes with distinctive health care needs. These themes included segments related to the following groupings: healthy, acute illness, maternal and infant health, minor chronic disease, moderate chronic disease frailty, major chronic illness, cancer, mental illness, and end-of-life. These segments were mostly derived from medical, health care utilization, functional and demographic variables. These segments could then be used to inform resource allocation and strategies that consider both health care and prevention efforts tailored to the segment's needs, although limited examples of such tailoring were found [16, 17, 19].

Examples from within the meso and micro levels were mostly demonstrating allocation of patients to existing programs based on segmentation of high-risk or high-need patients. These examples commonly considered categorizations that distinguished patients with repeated hospitalizations and ED visits, chronic condition severity and prevalence, patients in transitional care, with advanced illness and older patients with disabilities [10, 26]. The resulting segments at these levels were mostly used to allocate particular management programs or resources (e.g., care manager coordination, education, social worker, home visits), with some exceptions of applications leading to innovative customizations. These included new program design elements targeting specific segments such as the tailoring of care interventions in a general medical practice and the development of new modular care options by a multidisciplinary task force [27], development of an integrated care package of services by implementing tailored care models for each segment [46], and segment-specific care management strategies [36]. Another example was the transformation of a regional managed care organization that used an expert-driven segmentation approach (Hewner's Complexedex) [47, 48] to identify gaps in the care continuum which were addressed through innovative program design targeting those under-served segments [38]. Finally, segmentation methods applied to individuals with a specific condition allowed the identification of distinct phenotypes that may benefit from different care trajectories [49–52], although illustrations of how segmentation results were used for tailoring were also sparse.

Although not common, a few examples of segments obtained when considering individuals' experience and psychosocial needs were found at the meso and micro levels. For instance, a Dutch study [27] reported the use of segmentation to improve the delivery of person-centered care provided to older adults using data reflecting the individuals' experience and perceptions regarding a holistic representation of their biopsychosocial needs. The resulting segments included groups characterized by feeling vital, experiencing difficulties with psychosocial coping, having physical and mobility complaints, having difficulties across multiple domains, and feeling extremely frail. These segments were considered useful to provide a more comprehensive set of triage variables during clinical encounters and to inform demand-driven allocation of resources by policy makers and care providers [27, 38].

3.6 Outcomes

Overall, limited information was provided on the outcomes of the application of segmentation. Notable exceptions include the use of the British Columbia Health System Matrix at the level of a provincial health system which led to improvements in all IOM quality indicators: focused attention on the care for people with chronic conditions (safety, timeliness, effectiveness) and on the need for care in the community (equitability, timeliness, efficiency) that would improve quality of life (effectiveness), raised the profile of prevention activities (timeliness, effectiveness, efficiency, cost savings); and allowed people to remain in their homes for longer (effectiveness), delaying entry into residential care (effectiveness, cost saving) [19, 38]. In the application of the Complexedex [47], the design of new programs in transitional care which resulted from the segmentation were found to be effective in smoothing the transition back into the community and preventing avoidable (re-)hospitalizations (timeliness, effectiveness, cost savings) [38, 48]. A Dutch application of a demand-driven, person-centered segmentation for older adults led to the development of new modular care options targeting specific segments, which enhanced efficiency in terms of coordination effort per client [27, 38]. In addition to documented outcomes from programs, some authors [32] interviewed a range of stakeholders, including members of patient associations, academics, clinicians, economists, representatives of pharmaceutical industries, payers and providers, on their perceived motivation for patient segmentation. Most common answers were improvement of outcomes with respect to effectiveness and efficacy (effectiveness), optimization of side effect profiles (safety), avoiding waste of resources and overtreatment (cost savings and safety), improved clinical outcomes and cost-effectiveness.

4 Challenges and Opportunities

Despite clear applications and expected benefits for the use of segmentation in health care contexts, a few challenges and opportunities were identified.

4.1 Electronic Health Records System

The majority of applications of segmentation used data extracted from electronic health records and claims data. This supposes that health care organizations already have in place well-designed and comprehensive electronic health record systems, allowing triangulation of patient information from various sources, which may not necessarily be the case [38]. An alternative to using electronic health records is the use of healthcare needs assessment tools, which may be available at micro levels, but less so for population health management purposes.

4.2 Social Determinants of Health

Many authors noted that the emphasis on clinical records provide a limited picture of patient needs and many called for a broader consideration of the social determinants of health, including psychosocial, behavioral, environmental and economic information [8, 26, 35, 53], which have been shown to have a considerable impact on population health outcomes [54, 55]. This echoes other calls or initiatives to formally consider the social determinants of health in clinical practice to improve health equity and patient-centered care [56–59]. In particular, the consideration of equity measures such as material and social deprivation measures into segmentation models, be it at the individual- or ecological levels was seen as critical to ensure equity in service planning and provision [24]. With the exception of some socio-demographic factors, these data are often not systematically collected and often captured through interactions with different health professionals, which may or may not be entered into the electronic health records. Future opportunities for research and practice exist to identify how such information may be already collected and could be captured systematically, efficiently and in a standardized manner to inform segmentation efforts and clinical practice [26]. In addition to data gathered in the context of clinical encounters, patient surveys, government or community-based health surveys, geospatial or environmental data, patient-generated data such as those obtained from electronic devices or web usage or industry-generated data on purchasing patterns (e.g., food purchases) could also be used for a richer consideration of factors contributing to individuals' health-related needs [35, 60].

4.3 Patient-Centricity

Relatively few examples of segmentation integrated information on patients' perspectives, including their motivations and preferences, even though segmentation was presented as a tool to improve patient-centered care. Although this may be explained by the difficulty to collect and access such information, recent global trends in monitoring of patient-reported experience measures (PREMS) [61] and developments in the application of natural language processing of patient surveys [62], might lead to greater integration of patients' experiences and perspectives in the future [62].

4.4 Experience with Analytics

Evidence from interviews with subject matter experts suggests that investment in analytics to identify complex patients was increasing in health care organizations 10 years ago, despite analytic models being limited in their effectiveness or lacking evidence of impact [53]. However, in addition to the limitations of data availability and quality, a lack of experience with using analytics tools and novel data types, including by providers and coordinators, was as key challenge for healthcare organizations [53]. This extended to the limited and immature integration of predictive model outputs into clinical workflows [53]. This suggests that building capability in these areas, at least at the time of this study (circa 2015), was emerging as a priority. There appears to be a lack of research describing the contemporary technical capabilities and experience required within the healthcare management workforce to conduct and use analytic models for patient segmentation.

4.5 Greater Evidence of Impact on Care Pathways

Application of consumer segmentation across all tiers of the healthcare system has not yet reached its potential of tailoring care pathway interventions to segments across the full healthcare continuum. For example, Rudin and colleagues found that most examples of segmentation analysis to identify complex patients did not extend to identifying subsets who could be helped by an intervention, or to match subgroups to specific interventions [53]. Except for the specific application of healthcare communication strategies, where patient segmentation has resulted in communication strategies customized and directed to specific patient segments [33, 34], few studies describe intentional post-segmentation design or tailoring of care pathway interventions specific to derived segments, with notable exceptions mentioned in Sect. 3.5 [27, 36, 38, 46]. More studies are required to document how empirically derived segments are used to tailor health care resources and care pathways and their impact on quality of care and costs [8, 10, 26].

5 Conclusion

This chapter outlines why, how, where and for whom segmentation approaches have been applied to improve health care services and ultimately population health. Although not exhaustive, the evidence reviewed has showed that segmentation has the potential to help policymakers and health care providers to design, adapt and improve health care programs to ensure the health needs of entire populations and subpopulations are addressed. A range of data indicators were considered relevant to derive insightful segments that could inform the delivery of patient-centered care, but most applications were restricted to readily available data such as health service utilization and diagnoses. Future applications and research should focus on: (1) the collection, integration and use of data indicators reflecting a broad spectrum of data sources related to psychosocial, behavioral, and experiential factors; and (2) developing an evidence base for how the application of segmentation approaches can lead to better tailoring of health services and improvement in the quality of care provided to the population.

Acknowledgements The authors thank Frédéric Bergeron, Bibliothèque-Direction des services-conseils, Université Laval, Québec, QC, for his expertise in developing and conducting the systematic search strategy.

References

1. Wolfe, A.: Institute of medicine report: crossing the quality chasm: a new health care system for the 21st century. Policy Polit. Nurs. Pract. **2**, 233–235 (2001). https://doi.org/10.1177/152715440100200312
2. National Academies of Sciences, Engineering, and Medicine: Crossing the Global Quality Chasm: Improving Health Care Worldwide. The National Academies Press, Washington, DC (2018)
3. Kwok, R., Dinh, M., Dinh, D., Chu, M.: Improving adherence to asthma clinical guidelines and discharge documentation from emergency departments: implementation of a dynamic and integrated electronic decision support system. Emerg. Med. Australas. **21**, 31–37 (2009). https://doi.org/10.1111/j.1742-6723.2008.01149.x
4. Hinchey, P.R., Myers, J.B., Lewis, R., De Maio, V.J., Reyer, E., Licatese, D., Zalkin, J., Snyder, G.: Improved out-of-hospital cardiac arrest survival after the sequential implementation of 2005 AHA guidelines for compressions, ventilations, and induced hypothermia: the Wake County experience. Ann. Emerg. Med. **56**, 348–357 (2010). https://doi.org/10.1016/j.annemergmed.2010.01.036
5. Mittal, V., Darnell, C., Walsh, B., Mehta, A., Badawy, M., Morse, R., Pop, R., Tidwell, J., Sheehan, M., McDermott, S., Cannon, C., Kahn, J.: Inpatient bronchiolitis guideline implementation and resource utilization. Pediatrics **133**, e730–737 (2014). https://doi.org/10.1542/peds.2013-2881
6. Gagliardi, A.R., Brouwers, M.C., Palda, V.A., Lemieux-Charles, L., Grimshaw, J.M.: How can we improve guideline use? A conceptual framework of implementability. Implement. Sci. **6**, 26 (2011). https://doi.org/10.1186/1748-5908-6-26
7. Kastner, M., Bhattacharyya, O., Hayden, L., Makarski, J., Estey, E., Durocher, L., Chatterjee, A., Perrier, L., Graham, I.D., Straus, S.E., Zwarenstein, M., Brouwers, M.: Guideline uptake is influenced by six implementability domains for creating and communicating guidelines: a realist review. J. Clin. Epidemiol. **68**, 498–509 (2015). https://doi.org/10.1016/j.jclinepi.2014.12.013
8. Minvielle, E., Fourcade, A., Ricketts, T., Waelli, M.: Current Developments in Delivering Customized Care: A Scoping Review. Springer (2021). https://doi.org/10.1186/s12913-021-06576-0
9. Konig, I.R., Fuchs, O., Hansen, G., von Mutius, E., Kopp, M.V.: What is precision medicine? Eur. Respir. J. **50**, 12 (2017). https://doi.org/10.1183/13993003.00391-2017
10. Arnold, J., Thorpe, J., Mains-Mason, J., Rosland, A.M.: Empiric segmentation of high-risk patients: a structured literature review. Am. J. Manag. Care **28**(2), e69 (2022)
11. Keleher, H.: Population health planning for health equity. Aust. J. Prim. Health **17**, 327–333 (2011)
12. Yan, S., Kwan, Y., Tan, C., Thumboo, J., Low, L.: A systematic review of the clinical application of data-driven population segmentation analysis. BMC Med. Res. Methodol. **18** (2018). https://doi.org/10.1186/s12874-018-0584-9
13. Schoen, C., Collins, S.R.: The big five health insurers' membership and revenue trends: implications for public policy. Health Aff. **36**, 2185–2194 (2017). https://doi.org/10.1377/hlthaff.2017.0858
14. Nambiema, A., Fouquet, J., Guilloteau, J., Descatha, A.: La revue systématique et autres types de revue de la littérature : qu'est-ce que c'est, quand, comment, pourquoi ? Archives des

Maladies Professionnelles et de l'Environnement [Systematic reviews and other types of literature review: what are they, when, how and why? Arch. Occup. Environ. Dis.] **82**, 539–552 (2021). https://doi.org/10.1016/j.admp.2021.03.004
15. Low, L., Yan, S., Kwan, Y., Tan, C., Thumboo, J.: Assessing the validity of a data driven segmentation approach: a 4 year longitudinal study of healthcare utilization and mortality. PLoS ONE [Electronic Resource] **13**, e0195243 (2018). https://doi.org/10.1371/journal.pone.0195243
16. Lynn, J., Straube, B., Bell, K., Jencks, S., Kambic, R.: Using population segmentation to provide better health care for all: the "bridges to health" model. Milbank Q. **85**, 185–208 (2007). https://doi.org/10.1111/j.1468-0009.2007.00483.x
17. Madotto, F., Riva, M.A., Fornari, C., Scalonem, L., Cianipichini, R., Bonazzi, C., Mantovani, L.G., Cesana, G.: Administrative databases as a tool for identifying healthcare demand and costs in an over-one million population. Epidemiol. Biostat. Public Health **10**, 11 (2013). https://doi.org/10.2427/8840
18. Briggs, T., Burd, M., Fransoo, R.: Identifying high users of healthcare in British Columbia, Alberta and Manitoba. Healthcarepapers **14**, 31–36; discussion 58 (2014)
19. Health Sector Planning and Innovation Division: Understanding the Health Care Needs of the British Columbia Population Through Population Segmentation. British Columbia Ministry of Health (2015)
20. Low, L.L., Kwan, Y.H., Liu, N., Jing, X., Low, E.C.T., Thumboo, J.: Evaluation of a practical expert defined approach to patient population segmentation: a case study in Singapore. BMC Health Serv. Res. **17**, 771 (2017). https://doi.org/10.1186/s12913-017-2736-8
21. Lafortune, L., Béland, F., Bergman, H., Ankri, J.: Health state profiles and service utilization in community-living elderly. Med. Care **47**, 286–294 (2009)
22. Seng, J.J.B., Monteiro, A.Y., Kwan, Y.H., Zainudin, S.B., Tan, C.S., Thumboo, J., Low, L.L.: Population segmentation of type 2 diabetes mellitus patients and its clinical applications—A scoping review. BMC Med. Res. Methodol. **21**, 49 (2021). https://doi.org/10.1186/s12874-021-01209-w
23. Bayliss, E.A., Ellis, J.L., Powers, J.D., Gozansky, W., Zeng, C.: Using self-reported data to segment older adult populations with complex care needs. EGEMS (Wash DC). **7**, 12 (2019). https://doi.org/10.5334/egems.275
24. Kadu, M., Ma, X., Pagalan, L., Rosella, L.C., Wodchis, W.P.: A Review of Population Segmentation Tools for Population Health Management: Applicability for Ontario Health Teams (2021)
25. Yoon, S., Goh, H., Kwan, Y., Thumboo, J., Low, L.: Identifying optimal indicators and purposes of population segmentation through engagement of key stakeholders: a qualitative study. Health Res. Policy Syst. 1**8** (2020). https://doi.org/10.1186/s12961-019-0519-x
26. Jean-Baptiste, D., O'Malley, A., Shah, T.: Population segmentation and targeting of health care resources: findings from a literature review. Math. Policy Res. (2017)
27. Eissens van der Laan, M.R., van Offenbeek, M.A.G., Broekhuis, H., Slaets, J.P.J.: A person-centred segmentation study in elderly care: towards efficient demand-driven care. Social Sci. Med. **113**, 68–76 (2014). https://doi.org/10.1016/j.socscimed.2014.05.012
28. Zhou, Y., Wong, W., Li, H.: Improving care for older adults: a model to segment the senior population. Perm J. **18**, 18–21 (2014). https://doi.org/10.7812/TPP/14-005
29. Da Silveira, G., Borenstein, D., Fogliatto, F.S.: Mass customization: literature review and research directions. Int. J. Prod. Econ. **72**, 1–13 (2001). https://doi.org/10.1016/S0925-5273(00)00079-7
30. Kotha, S.: Mass customization: implementing the emerging paradigm for competitive advantage. Strateg. Manag. J. **16**, 21–42 (1995). https://doi.org/10.1002/smj.4250160916
31. National Research Council: Toward Precision Medicine: Building a Knowledge Network for Biomedical Research and a New Taxonomy of Disease. The National Academies Press, Washington, DC (2011)
32. Antonello Di, P., Sarkozy, F., Ryll, B., Siebert, U.: Personalized medicine in Europe: not yet personal enough? BMC Health Serv. Res. **17** (2017). https://doi.org/10.1186/s12913-017-2205-4

33. Upfront Healthcare: UpFront Healthcare. https://upfronthealthcare.com/. Last accessed 01 Oct 2023
34. Adeola, O., Ehira, D., Nworie, A: Segmentation, targeting, and positioning in healthcare. In: Health Service Marketing Management in Africa, pp. 45–55. Productivity Press (2019)
35. Jeffery, A.D., Hewner, S., Pruinelli, L., Lekan, D., Lee, M., Gao, G., Holbrook, L., Sylvia, M.: Risk prediction and segmentation models used in the United States for assessing risk in whole populations: a critical literature review with implications for nurses' role in population health management. JAMIA Open **2**(1), 205–214 (2019)
36. Johnson, T.L., Brewer, D., Estacio, R., Vlasimsky, T.: Augmenting predictive modeling tools with clinical insights for care coordination program design and implementation. eGEMS (Gener. Evid. Methods Improve Patient Outcomes) **3**, 1–20 (2015). https://doi.org/10.13063/2327-9214.1181
37. Weiner, J.P., Starfield, B.H., Steinwachs, D.M., Mumford, L.M.: Development and application of a population-oriented measure of ambulatory care case-mix. Med. Care **29** (1991)
38. Chong, J.L., Lim, K.K., Matchar, D.B.: Population Segmentation Based on Healthcare Needs: A Systematic Review. Springer (2019). https://doi.org/10.1186/s13643-019-1105-6
39. Sancho-Mestre, C., Vivas-Consuelo, D., Alvis-Estrada, L., Romero, M., Usó-Talamantes, R., Caballer-Tarazona, V.: Pharmaceutical cost and multimorbidity with type 2 diabetes mellitus using electronic health record data. BMC Health Serv. Res. **16**, 394 (2016). https://doi.org/10.1186/s12913-016-1649-2
40. Shen, Y.: Applying the 3M all patient refined diagnosis related groups grouper to measure inpatient severity in the VA. Med. Care **41**, II103–II110 (2003)
41. Buja, A., Claus, M., Perin, L., Rivera, M., Corti, M.C., Avossa, F., Schievano, E., Rigon, S., Toffanin, R., Baldo, V., Boccuzzo, G.: Multimorbidity patterns in high-need, high-cost elderly patients. PLoS ONE **13**, 1–15 (2018). https://doi.org/10.1371/journal.pone.0208875
42. Buja, A., Rivera, M., Soattin, M., Corti, M.C., Avossa, F., Schievano, E., Rigon, S., Baldo, V., Boccuzzo, G., Damiani, G., Ebell, M.H.: Impactibility model for population health management in high-cost elderly heart failure patients: a capture method using the ACG system. Popul. Health Manag. **22**, 495–502 (2019). https://doi.org/10.1089/pop.2018.0190
43. Vogeli, C., Spirt, J., Brand, R., Hsu, J., Mohta, N., Hong, C., Weil, E., Ferris, T.G.: Implementing a hybrid approach to select patients for care management: variations across practices. Am. J. Manag. Care **22**, 358–365 (2016)
44. Haime, V., Hong, C., Mandel, L., Mohta, N., Iezzoni, L.I., Ferris, T.G., Vogeli, C.: Clinician considerations when selecting high-risk patients for care management. Am. J. Manag. Care **21**, e576–e582 (2015)
45. Armstrong, J.J., Zhu, M., Hirdes, J.P., Stolee, P.: K-means cluster analysis of rehabilitation service users in the home health care system of Ontario: examining the heterogeneity of a complex geriatric population. Arch. Phys. Med. Rehabil. **93**, 2198–2205 (2012). https://doi.org/10.1016/j.apmr.2012.05.026
46. Vuik, S., Mayer, E., Darzi, A.: Patient segmentation analysis offers significant benefits for integrated care and support. Health Aff. **35**, 769–775 (2016). https://doi.org/10.1377/hlthaff.2015.1311
47. Hewner, S., Seo, J.Y., Gothard, S.E., Johnson, B.J.: Aligning population-based care management with chronic disease complexity. Nurs. Outlook **62**, 250–258 (2014). https://doi.org/10.1016/j.outlook.2014.03.003
48. Hewner, S., Casucci, S., Sullivan, S., Mistretta, F., Xue, Y., Johnson, B., Pratt, R., Lin, L., Fox, C.: Integrating social determinants of health into primary care clinical and informational workflow during care transitions. EGEMS (Wash DC). **5**, 2 (2017). https://doi.org/10.13063/2327-9214.1282
49. Weatherall, M., Travers, J., Shirtcliffe, P.M., Marsh, S.E., Williams, M.V., Nowitz, M.R., Aldington, S., Beasley, R.: Distinct clinical phenotypes of airways disease defined by cluster analysis. Eur. Respir. J. **34**, 812–818 (2009). https://doi.org/10.1183/09031936.00174408
50. Ernande, L., Audureau, E., Jellis, C.L., Bergerot, C., Henegar, C., Sawaki, D., Czibik, G., Volpi, C., Canoui-Poitrine, F., Thibault, H., Ternacle, J., Moulin, P., Marwick, T.H., Derumeaux, G.:

Clinical implications of echocardiographic phenotypes of patients with diabetes mellitus. J. Am. Coll. Cardiol. **70**, 1704–1716 (2017). https://doi.org/10.1016/j.jacc.2017.07.792
51. Nunes, S., Ribeiro, L., Lobo, C., Cunha-Vaz, J.: Three different phenotypes of mild nonproliferative diabetic retinopathy with different risks for development of clinically significant macular edema. Invest. Ophthalmol. Vis. Sci. **54**, 4595–4604 (2013). https://doi.org/10.1167/iovs.13-11895
52. Boudier, A., Curjuric, I., Basagaña, X., Hazgui, H., Anto, J.M., Bousquet, J., Bridevaux, P.O., Dupuis-Lozeron, E., Garcia-Aymerich, J., Heinrich, J., Janson, C., Künzli, N., Leynaert, B., de Marco, R., Rochat, T., Schindler, C., Varraso, R., Pin, I., Probst-Hensch, N., Sunyer, J., Kauffmann, F., Siroux, V.: Ten-year follow-up of cluster-based asthma phenotypes in adults. A pooled analysis of three cohorts. Am. J. Respir. Crit. Care Med. **188**, 550–560 (2013). https://doi.org/10.1164/rccm.201301-0156OC
53. Rudin, R.S., Gidengil, C.A., Predmore, Z., Schneider, E.C., Sorace, J., Hornstein, R.: Identifying and coordinating care for complex patients: findings from the leading edge of analytics and health information technology. Rand Health Q. **6**, 2 (2017)
54. Alegría, M., NeMoyer, A., Falgàs Bagué, I., Wang, Y., Alvarez, K.: Social determinants of mental health: where we are and where we need to go. Curr. Psychiatry Rep. **20**, 95 (2018). https://doi.org/10.1007/s11920-018-0969-9
55. Powell-Wiley, T.M., Baumer, Y., Baah, F.O., Baez, A.S., Farmer, N., Mahlobo, C.T., Pita, M.A., Potharaju, K.A., Tamura, K., Wallen, G.R.: Social determinants of cardiovascular disease. Circ. Res. **130**, 782–799 (2022). https://doi.org/10.1161/CIRCRESAHA.121.319811
56. Andermann, A.: Taking action on the social determinants of health in clinical practice: a framework for health professionals. CMAJ **188**, E474–E483 (2016). https://doi.org/10.1503/cmaj.160177
57. Nowak, D.A., Mulligan, K.: Social prescribing. Can. Family Phys. **67**, 88–91 (2021). https://doi.org/10.46747/cfp.670288
58. Morse, D.F., Sandhu, S., Mulligan, K., Tierney, S., Polley, M., Giurca, B.C., Slade, S., Dias, S., Mahtani, K.R., Wells, L., Wang, H., Bo Zhao, Figueiredo, C.E.M.D., Meijs, J.J., Nam, H.K., Lee, K.H., Wallace, C., Elliott, M., Mendive, J.M., Robinson, D., Palo, M., Herrmann, W., Nielsen, R.Ø., Husk, K.: Global developments in social prescribing. BMJ Global Health. **7** (2022). https://doi.org/10.1136/bmjgh-2022-008524
59. Sullivan, S.S., Ledwin, K.M., Hewner, S.: A clinical classification framework for identifying persons with high social and medical needs: the COMPLEXedex-SDH. Nurs. Outlook **71**, 102044 (2023). https://doi.org/10.1016/j.outlook.2023.102044
60. Schulte, T., Bohnet-Joschko, S.: How can big data analytics support people-centred and integrated health services: a scoping review. Int. J. Integr. Care (IJIC) **22**, 1–18 (2022). https://doi.org/10.5334/ijic.5543
61. Jamieson Gilmore, K., Corazza, I., Coletta, L., Allin, S.: The uses of patient reported experience measures in health systems: a systematic narrative review. Health Policy **128**, 1–10 (2023). https://doi.org/10.1016/j.healthpol.2022.07.008
62. van Buchem, M.M., Neve, O.M., Kant, I.M.J., Steyerberg, E.W., Boosman, H., Hensen, E.F.: Analyzing patient experiences using natural language processing: development and validation of the artificial intelligence patient reported experience measure (AI-PREM). BMC Med. Inform. Decis. Mak. **22**, 183 (2022). https://doi.org/10.1186/s12911-022-01923-5

How Can We Better Take Person-Centered Needs into Account? The Integrated Care Trajectory Approach and Intersectoral Collaboration in Primary Care to Support People Living with Diabetes

Geraldine Layani

Abstract Chronic diseases are the leading cause of mortality in industrialized countries and diabetes is one of the most important systemic chronic diseases. The consequences of diabetes on physical and mental health, and the economic impact on Quebec's healthcare systems, are well documented. The organization of care by disease trajectory is a tool for optimizing the use of care and services in our healthcare system. However, the organization of care by disease trajectory does not always seem to correspond to people's needs and to the improvement of their health throughout their life course. Moreover, primary care and the community have a major role to play in the care of people with diabetes, as together they have the potential to better take into account the determinants of these people's health to optimize their follow-up. Indeed, living with a chronic disease is complex and requires a good understanding of the person's living environment. That's why collaboration between the healthcare sector and the community is a promising way of supporting people throughout their lives. The INMED-COMMUNITY trajectory has been developed and implemented since 2018 in a region near Montreal, Quebec, integrating a vision of care with the life course trajectory. This trajectory is promising and promotes an innovative approach to supporting people living with chronic diseases, described at the end of this chapter.

Keywords Life course health · Intersectoral collaboration · Primary care · Community · Chronic disease · Diabetes

G. Layani (✉)
University of Montreal, Montreal, QC, Canada
e-mail: geraldine.layani@umontreal.ca

P. Landa et al. (eds.), *Operations Research and Artificial Intelligence in Healthcare Management*, Springer Proceedings in Mathematics & Statistics 506,
https://doi.org/10.1007/978-3-031-95659-1_9

1 Introduction

Family doctors deal with patient care trajectories, which present several limitations for people living with chronic illnesses. These approaches to care are currently organized by disease trajectory, and generally take no account of the complexity of living with a chronic disease, nor of the resources available in the community to support these people throughout their lives [1–7]. Indeed, living with chronic health problems is demanding and requires the mobilization of many community resources, such as access to healthy food, adequate housing and a support network, to create social and physical environments conducive to health equity [8]. As a family doctor, I often felt at a loss, and as a primary care researcher, I was challenged by the findings in the literature on intersectoral collaboration in primary care [9–17]. The World Health Organization (WHO) has defined intersectoral collaboration for health as "actions undertaken by sectors outside the health sector, in collaboration with the health sector, on health outcomes or health equity, or on the determinants of health" [18]. This approach has the potential to mobilize resources in the community, create links with other sectors and collaborate with all caregivers interacting with the individual to better meet his or her needs [1, 19–22].

2 The Challenges of Current Interventions Organized by Care Trajectory for the Follow-Up of People Living with Diabetes

Chronic diseases are the leading cause of death in industrialized countries [23–28] and diabetes is one of the most important systemic chronic diseases [29–32]. The consequences of diabetes on physical and mental health, and the economic impact on Canadian healthcare systems, are well documented [33–38]. Care trajectories are instruments used by professionals to define the best processes that exist within the healthcare system for the management of particular patient populations based on the best evidence [26, 39–41]. However, this evidence-based approach does not necessarily incorporate an evidence-informed approach that takes into account each person's unique situation of living with diabetes [26, 41].

Despite research, individual health interventions organized by disease trajectory often have a suboptimal effect on health outcomes and quality of life for people living with diabetes [27]. In fact, to the best of our knowledge, disease-focused clinical interventions have no direct leverage on people's lives in the community [26]. On the one hand, these disease-focused clinical trajectories limit collaborative and integrated approaches to the care offered to these people in the community [26]. On the other hand, current disease-focused clinical interventions take little account of the person in his or her living environment and the issues related to housing, nutrition, access to local services, spaces and infrastructures enabling him or her to lead a physically active life, all of which are physical, social and economic factors contributing to the person's health [28, 31]. What's more, despite the potential of community-based health interventions, they have yet to prove their worth in improving the health of these people, and few interventions combine intersectoral action with traditional health system interventions [13].

So there is still much to be done to support people living with diabetes, to provide care in line with evidence-based guidelines [32] and to facilitate a person-centred approach to care, by adopting a new approach to care in partnership with the community [9, 36, 37].

3 The Contribution of Primary Care to the Care of People Living with Diabetes

Primary care is the backbone of any successful healthcare system. It ensures accessibility, continuity and coordination of care, meeting 80% of healthcare needs [38, 40]. It has been demonstrated that primary care teams are able to manage up to 90% of people with chronic diseases without access to specialized teams [41]. As Joanne Reeve and Marie-Dominique Beaulieu have already mentioned in the literature, family medicine has the potential to be the most competent specialty for supporting people living with chronic diseases, thanks to a strong understanding of the scientific approach and its limitations, since it consists in analyzing how knowledge derived from research on patient populations applies to each unique individual [26, 42].

In recent years, numerous applications have been developed to support people living with diabetes in monitoring their comorbidities or screening for diabetes-related complications, such as the home blood pressure measurement recommended by hypertension Canada and the screening for diabetic neuropathy recommended by Diabetes UK [43–46]. These applications promote the implementation of personalized care adapted to the living environments of people with diabetes [45, 47]. In addition, the COVID-19 pandemic has provided a favorable context for optimizing professional practices in primary care and proposing innovative approaches to care. Kiran et al., in particular, proposed recommendations for reorganizing in-person and teleconsultation care for people living with diabetes, in order to offer care that better responds to people living with diabetes. More specifically, these recommendations proposed optimizing access to relevant care according to patient needs and supporting the self-management and self-assessment essential to sustaining the empowerment of people living with diabetes [45, 47].

However, primary care needs to rethink its approaches to collaboration between healthcare professionals and community stakeholders, because it is not only by equipping professionals and patients, and intensifying the interventions of care teams, that primary care will be able to intervene on health inequalities, the main contributors to the rising prevalence and consequences of chronic disease [46]. Indeed, if we are to avoid the disease-based management silos of the 1980s, it is imperative that primary care professionals provide leadership to help design integrated chronic disease management care trajectories to better meet people's needs, contribute to the decompartmentalization of the healthcare system and foster a care approach that integrates the community into the care plans of people [26].

4 Promote a Person-Centred Approach to the "Life Course" of People Living with Chronic Diseases

Living with a chronic illness is complex and requires a good understanding of the person's living environment. Care trajectories are clinical tools that integrate evidence and best processes to deliver quality care but do not always take into account the patient's preferences and context [26, 47]. A person's health depends not only on the care they receive from healthcare professionals but also on their physical and socio-economic environment [48]. In fact, only 20% of the factors affecting a person's health concern the healthcare system, while 80% of factors are related to socio-economic, environmental and genetic issues [49]. For this reason, healthcare interventions focusing on the life course of people living with diabetes should be prioritized and considered essential by healthcare professionals to better support these people throughout their lives.

Indeed, life-course intervention research is an emerging discipline in health science. It combines the principles of intervention research with those of *Life Course Health Development (LCHD)* to improve the development of health over the lifetime of a person [50–52]. The *LCHD* model is *based on the* premise that health is an emergent set of developmental capacities that manifest and adapt throughout life [49–51]. Health development is a complex, non-linear process that takes place in multiple dimensions (time, place), at multiple levels (individual, family, society) and at different phases of life, with the aim of promoting resilience at each of these stages [51].

The *LCHD* model therefore goes far beyond traditional health interventions. This model enables the implementation of interventions that integrate not only the individual, but also his or her caregivers, family, network of professionals and community. This model has a much greater and faster impact on people's health, as has already been demonstrated in the follow-up of obesity [53] or mental health problems [54].

Taking into account the person in his or her living environment thus has the potential to gradually shift the focus from a disease-centred to a person-centred vision, with a better understanding of the complexity of living with a chronic disease such as diabetes. In addition, the adoption of the *LCHD* model has the potential to redefine the links developed by people living with diabetes with their caregivers, contributing to the decompartmentalization of care offered to people living with diabetes and giving people living with diabetes back the power to act on their disease.

With 80% of factors linked to socio-economic, environmental and genetic factors, healthcare professionals can no longer act alone to support people with chronic diseases, and collaboration with other sectors of society is essential to better support people throughout their life course [49].

5 The Potential of Intersectoral Collaboration in Primary Care to Better Meet Person-Centred Needs

Intersectoral collaboration in primary care is an innovative and promising approach that has great potential to create an inclusive care approach, based on bonding and partnership, to ultimately help people become empowered and engaged partners in the co-management of their chronic conditions [55–57]. This approach fosters interactions between people who are informed and active about their health condition, and healthcare providers who are prepared and proactive in supporting these people [58, 59].

Intersectoral collaboration is an approach to care that has the potential to better address people's health determinants and support a holistic and comprehensive approach to health [59]. Indeed, the determinants of a person's health encompass socio-economic, physical, genetic and health determinants, for which the healthcare system acts on only 25% of all determinants [60]. This is why collaborating with sectors other than the healthcare system, such as municipalities for housing, community organizations to combat food insecurity, or even schools to optimize health education, is essential and indispensable to better support people's health throughout their lives. In the context of chronic disease, a systemic approach that takes account of the social determinants of health through intersectoral integration can help individuals to become autonomous and committed partners in the co-management of their chronic disease [61–63].

Health networks around the world have emphasized the need to integrate chronic care across communities and health systems. The WHO recently described continuity and coordination of care based on community engagement and empowerment as global priorities for supporting integrated, people-centred health services for complex care needs [57]. Community-based approaches have also recently been put forward for the development of healthcare systems that reflect the values and needs of individuals and communities [64, 65]. Determining how, when and what community elements to integrate into care trajectories can be facilitated by linking strategies already established and used in the management of chronic diseases [13].

6 The Implementation of an Integrated Care Pathway Carried Out in Intersectoral Collaboration in Primary Care to Better Support the Life Course of People Living with Diabetes: INMED-COMMUNITY

The Interprofessional INterprofessional Management and Education in Diabetes care (INMED) care trajectory was developed in 2018 to improve diabetes care in two university family medicine (U-FMG) clinics in a large healthcare organization near Montreal in the province of Quebec (Canada). This trajectory is built around four axes of intervention: (a) continuing professional development, (b) ongoing patient education and community self-management support, (c) case management and follow-up by the interprofessional team, and (d) ongoing evaluation of the quality of diabetes care and services.

This trajectory was co-created by the co-principal investigators of the INMED project in partnership with stakeholders from both U-FMGs, based on best practice guidelines clinical for diabetes care [66, 67], as the organization of care and services for people living with diabetes no longer optimally met the needs of the population. As a result, managers, primary care and specialized clinicians, the executive director of a community organization dedicated to people living with diabetes, a community organizer and two patient partners collaborated to implement the INMED trajectory with the project's researchers, helping to redefine a person-centred approach to care since 2020. In addition to optimizing the coordination of clinical practices in primary care through a case management approach demonstrated in the literature to be effective in the follow-up of people living with complex clinical needs [67], the INMED trajectory has innovatively and promisingly integrated a community support group for patients and their families, in order to improve the progressive adaptation to diabetes and prevent diabetes-related distress for the person and their loved ones [66, 68]: INMED-COMMUNITY. This community support group facilitates access to resources and services in the community to provide complementary and innovative support to the care offered by healthcare professionals to people living with diabetes.

In the INMED-COMMUNITY trajectory, people are supported by a community organization, where patients are referred by their case manager to the community organization based on their needs and desired information on a range of resources required to optimize their diabetes care (nutritional, housing, social isolation, etc.). The community partner organization contacts the diabetic person referred by their case manager (family doctor or nurse) and shares with them the resources available in the community. Contact is then made at the individual's own pace, as he or she chooses the right moment to establish a link with the services available in the community. Finally, the community organization and the case manager provide follow-up feedback, so that the person living with diabetes feels supported by all the professionals involved in his or her care.

The INMED-COMMUNITY trajectory is currently being implemented, and the preliminary results of an evaluation of the trajectory's acceptability have demonstrated the vitality and relevance of this innovative collaborative approach to primary

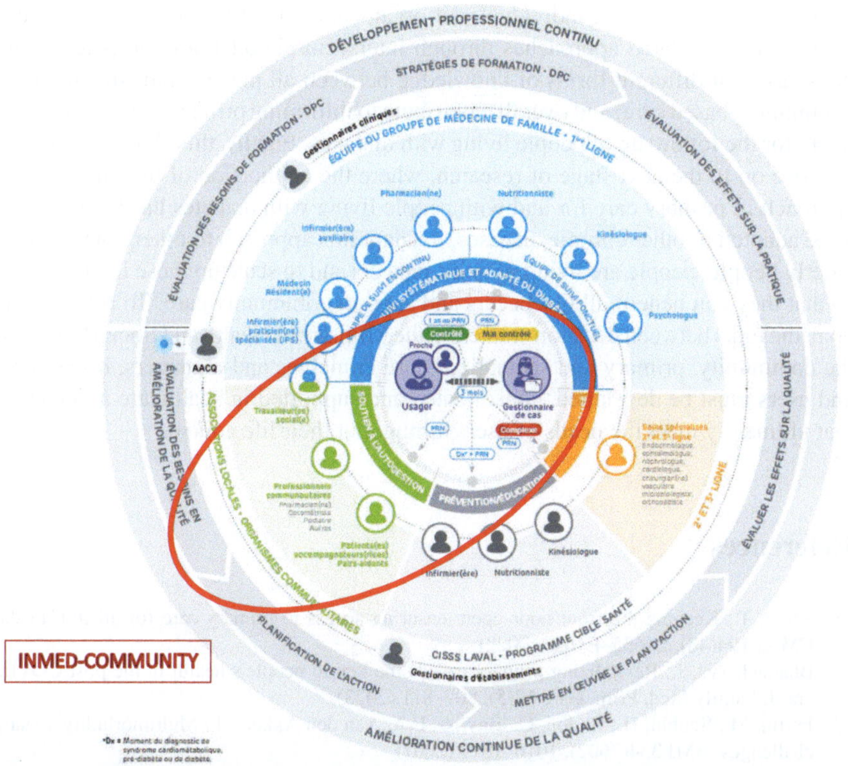

Fig. 1 The INterprofessional Management and Education in Diabetes care (INMED) care trajectory

care in this region of Quebec (Canada) to better meet the needs of these people. Two conditions for the implementation of this intersectoral intervention were identified: (1) the necessary presence of a "facilitator" to translate the understanding of the different sectors to all the actors involved in the SOINS Diabète trajectory; (2) the early identification and resolution of "controversies" essential to creating new links and a new standard environment for collaboration between actors from different sectors [69].

The next step is to adapt this social innovation in primary care to other chronic diseases and other regional contexts (Fig. 1).

7 Conclusion

In summary, this study provides a better understanding of the importance of advancing the state of knowledge on innovations in primary care, in particular on how to implement intersectoral primary care and generate effects at the microsystem level;

contribute to a change in individual and organizational culture by decompartmentalizing health-related approaches through intersectoral collaboration, potentiating the sharing of different forms of knowledge between all players and strengthening community-based care; and overall, contribute to informing primary care more effectively for the follow-up of people living with diabetes. Finally, this chapter allows us to move on to the next stage of research, where the application of the intersectoral approach in primary care for and with people living with diabetes has the potential to be adapted to other chronic diseases, to adapt this approach to other contexts (the elderly people, people are living with the cancer) and to scale up these interventions so that they can benefit all Quebecers and support community care. To achieve this goal, the links between decision-makers at the Ministry of Health and Social Services, the community, primary and specialized care clinicians and managers, researchers and users must be developed, consolidated and supported in healthcare approaches that ultimately meet the needs of users throughout their life course.

References

1. Kiran, T.: Keeping the front door open: ensuring access to primary care for all in Canada. CMAJ **194**(48), E1655–E1656 (2022)
2. Bhattacharya, J.: Revitalizing primary care is the key to people's health in the post-COVID era. J. Family Med. Prim. Care **12**(5), 807–811 (2023)
3. Fortin, M., Soubhi, H., Hudon, C., Bayliss, E.A., van den Akker, M.: Multimorbidity's many challenges. BMJ **334**(7602), 1016–1017 (2007)
4. Watt, G.: The inverse care law today. Lancet **360**(9328), 252–254 (2002)
5. Guthrie, B., Payne, K., Alderson, P., McMurdo, M.E., Mercer, S.W.: Adapting clinical guidelines to take account of multimorbidity. BMJ **345**, e6341 (2012)
6. Salive, M.E.: Multimorbidity in older adults. Epidemiol. Rev. **35**, 75–83 (2013)
7. Lehnert, T., Heider, D., Leicht, H., Heinrich, S., Corrieri, S., Luppa, M., et al.: Review: health care utilization and costs of elderly persons with multiple chronic conditions. Med. Care Res. Rev. **68**(4), 387–420 (2011)
8. Bauer, U.E., Briss, P.A., Goodman, R.A., Bowman, B.A.: Prevention of chronic disease in the 21st century: elimination of the leading preventable causes of premature death and disability in the USA. Lancet **384**(9937), 45–52 (2014)
9. World Health Organization: WHO Global Strategy on People-Centred and Integrated Health Services: Interim Report. World Health Organization, Geneva (2015)
10. Chiari, A.P.G., Senna, M.I.B., Gomes, V.E., Freire, M., Soares, A., Alves, C.R.L., et al.: Intersectoral collaboration to promote child development: the contributions of the actor-network theory. Qual. Health Res. **33**(5), 451–467 (2023)
11. Carron, T., Domeisen Benedetti, F., Fringer, A., Fierz, K., Peytremann-Bridevaux, I.: Integrated care models in Swiss primary care: an embedded multiple case study. J. Eval. Clin. Pract. (2023)
12. Kunihiro, S., da Silva Vernasque, J.R., da Silva, C., Santos, M.F.D., Cremasco, C.P., Gabriel Filho, L.R.A.: Intersectoral actions for the promotion and prevention of obesity, diabetes and hypertension in Brazilian cities: a systematic review and meta-analysis. Int. J. Environ. Res. Public Health **19**(20) (2022)
13. George, N.C., Radman, D., Zomahoun, H.T.V., Boivin, A., Ahmed, S.: Linkages between health systems and communities for chronic care: a scoping review protocol. BMJ Open **12**(8), e060430 (2022)

14. Allen, M.L., Salsberg, J., Knot, M., LeMaster, J.W., Felzien, M., Westfall, J.M., et al.: Engaging with communities, engaging with patients: amendment to the NAPCRG 1998 policy statement on responsible research with communities. Fam. Pract. **34**(3), 313–321 (2017)
15. Pinheiro, M.C., Moura, A., Bortolini, G.A., Coutinho, J.G., Rahal, L.D.S., Bandeira, L.M., et al.: Intersectoral approach to obesity prevention and control: the Brazilian experience from 2014 to 2018. Rev. Panam. Salud Publica **43**, e58 (2019)
16. Pratt, R., Gyllstrom, B., Gearin, K., Lange, C., Hahn, D., Baldwin, L.M., et al.: Identifying barriers to collaboration between primary care and public health: experiences at the local level. Public Health Rep. **133**(3), 311–317 (2018)
17. de Leeuw, E.: Engagement of sectors other than health in integrated health governance, policy, and action. Annu. Rev. Public Health **38**, 329–349 (2017)
18. World Health Organization, P.H.A.o.C.: Health Equity Through Intersectoral Action: An Analysis of 18 Country Case Studies [Internet]. World Health Organization, Geneva (2008)
19. Dahrouge, S., Gauthier, A.P., Durand, F., Lemonde, M., Saluja, K., Kendall, C., et al.: The feasibility of a primary care based navigation service to support access to health and social resources: the access to resources in the community (ARC) model. Int. J. Integr. Care **22**(4), 13 (2022)
20. World Health Organization: Continuity and coordination of care: a practice brief to support implementation of the who framework on integrated people-centred health services (2018)
21. Mullins, C.D., Wingate, L.T., Edwards, H.A., Tofade, T., Wutoh, A.: Transitioning from learning healthcare systems to learning health care communities. J. Comp. Eff. Res. **7**(6), 603–614 (2018)
22. Kuluski K, G.S.: Toward a person-centred learning health system: understanding value from the perspectives of patients and caregivers. Healthc. Pap. **18**, 36–46 (2019)
23. Agence de la santé publique du Canada: Vieillissement et maladies chroniques (2020)
24. Mbuya-Bienge, C.S.M., Fortin, M., Sirois, C.: Actes du Colloque – Multimorbidité : les enjeux liés à la surveillance populationnelle. Institut national de santé publique du Québec (2019)
25. Van der Aa, M.J., van den Broeke, J.R., Stronks, K., Plochg, T.: Patients with multimorbidity and their experiences with the healthcare process: a scoping review. J. Comorb. **7**(1), 11–21 (2017)
26. Beaulieu, M.D.: Trajectoire clinique: contribution unique de la médecine de famille. Can. Fam. Physician **59**(6), 706 (2013)
27. ElSayed, N.A., Aleppo, G., Aroda, V.R., Bannuru, R.R., Brown, F.M., Bruemmer, D., et al.: Improving care and promoting health in populations: standards of care in diabetes-2023. Diabetes Care **46**(Supple 1), S10–S18 (2023)
28. Christensen, D.: The health change trajectory model. An integrated model of health change. Adv. Nurs. Sci. **38**, 55–67 (2015)
29. Institut national de santé publique du Québec: Portrait du diabète dans la population québecoise âgeé d'un an et plus de 2001 à 2019 (2022)
30. World Health Organization: Obésité et surpoids. Aide-mémoire numéro 311 (2015)
31. Corbin, J.: The Corbin and Strauss chronic illness trajectory model: an update. Inquiry Nurs. Pract. Int. J. **12**, 33–41 (1998)
32. Committee, E., Guidelines, D.C.C.P.: Clinical practice guidelines for the prevention and management of diabetes in Canada. Can. J. Diabetes **42**, S1–S325 (2018)
33. World Health Organization: WHO acceleration plan to stop obesity (2023)
34. World Health Organization: Global health risks: mortality and burden of disease attributable to selected major risks (2009)
35. Public Health Agency of Canada: Twenty years of diabetes surveillance using the Canadian chronic disease surveillance system (2019)
36. Thornton, P.L., Kumanyika, S.K., Gregg, E.W., Araneta, M.R., Baskin, M.L., Chin, M.H., et al.: New research directions on disparities in obesity and type 2 diabetes. Ann. N. Y. Acad. Sci. **1461**(1), 5–24 (2020)
37. Ferreira, P.L., Morais, C., Pimenta, R., Ribeiro, I., Amorim, I., Alves, S.M.: Empowerment and knowledge as determinants for quality of life: a contribution to a better type 2 diabetes self-management. Int. J. Environ. Res. Public Health **20**(5) (2023)

38. Starfield, B.: Primary care: balancing health needs, services, and technology. Religion in America (1998)
39. Kitchiner, D., Davidson, C., Bundred, P.: Integrated care pathways: effective tools for continuous evaluation of clinical practice. J. Eval. Clin. Pract. **2**(1), 65–69 (1996)
40. Starfield, B.: Primary care: an increasingly important contributor to effectiveness, equity, and efficiency of health services. SESPAS report 2012. Gac. Sanit. **26**(Suppl 1), 20–26 (2012)
41. National Academies of Sciences, Engineering, and Medicine; Health and Medicine Division; Board on Health Care Services; Committee on Implementing High-Quality Primary Care, Robinson, S.K., Meisnere, M., Phillips, R.L., Jr., McCauley, L. (Eds.): Implementing High-Quality Primary Care: Rebuilding the Foundation of Health Care. National Academies Press (2021)
42. Reeve, J.: Protecting generalism: moving on from evidence-based medicine? Br. J. Gen. Pract. **60**(576), 521–523 (2010)
43. Collaboration for Leadership in Applied Health Research and Care Greater Manchester, British Hypertension Society: Home Blood Pressure Monitoring: Treatment Targets. British Hypertension Society, National Institute for Health Research, Leicester (2017). https://bihsoc.org/wp-content/uploads/2017/09/Clinic_and_home_treatment_targets.pdf
44. Diabetes UK: Touch the Toes Test. Diabetes UK, London (2012). https://diabetes-resources-production.s3-eu-west-1.amazonaws.com/diabetes-storage/migration/pdf/Touch-the-toes-test.0812.pdf
45. Kiran, T., Moonen, G., Bhattacharyya, O.K., Agarwal, P., Bajaj, H.S., Kim, J., Ivers, N.: Managing type 2 diabetes in primary care during COVID-19. Can. Family Phys. **66**(10), 745–747 (2020)
46. Contandriopoulos, D.P.M., Cockenpot, A., Duhoux, A., Jean, E.: Analytical typology of multiprofessional primary care models. BMC Family Pract. **19**, 44 (2018)
47. Cloninger, C.R.: Person-centered health promotion in chronic disease. Int. J. Pers. Cent. Med. **3**(1), 5–12 (2013)
48. Hudon, C., Dumont-Samson, O., Breton, M., Bourgueil, Y., Cohidon, C., Falcoff, H., et al.: How to better integrate social determinants of health into primary healthcare: various stakeholders' perspectives. Int. J. Environ. Res. Public Health **19**(23) (2022)
49. Lalonde, M.: Nouvelle perspective de la santé des Canadiens. Ministre de l'Approvisionnement et des Services du Canada, Ottawa, ON [A New Perspective on the Health of Canadians. Minister of Supply and Services Canada, Ottawa, ON] (1974). Retrieved from the Public Health Agency of Canada website: www.phac-aspc.gc.ca/ph-sp/pdf/perspect-fra.pdf
50. Halfon, N., Hochstein, M.: Life course health development: an integrated framework for developing health, policy, and research. Milbank Q. **80**(3), 433–479, iii (2002)
51. Halfon, N., Larson, K., Lu, M., Tullis, E., Russ, S.: Lifecourse health development: past, present and future. Matern. Child Health J. **18**(2), 344–365 (2014)
52. Halfon, N., Forrest, C.B., Lerner, R.M., Faustman, E.M., (eds.): Handbook of Life Course Health Development, pp. 19–43. Springer, Cham (2017)
53. Anderson, P.M., Butcher, K.F., Schanzenbach, D.W.: Understanding recent trends in childhood obesity in the United States. Econ. Hum. Biol. **34**, 16–25 (2019)
54. Ghandour, R.M., Sherman, L.J., Vladutiu, C.J., et al.: Prevalence and treatment of depression, anxiety, and conduct problems in US children. J. Pediatr. **206**, 256-267.e3 (2019)
55. Javanparast, S., Baum, F., Freeman, T., Ziersch, A., Henderson, J., Mackean, T.: Collaborative population health planning between Australian primary health care organisations and local government: lost opportunity. Aust. N. Z. J. Public Health **43**(1), 68–74 (2019)
56. Bloch, G., Rozmovits, L.: Implementing social interventions in primary care. CMAJ **193**(44), E1696–E1701 (2021)
57. World Health Organization: A vision of primary health care in the 21st century (2018)
58. Centers for Disease Control and Prevention: Community-Clinical Linkages for the Prevention and Control of Chronic Diseases: A Practitioner's Guide. Centers for Disease Control and Prevention, U.S. Department of Health and Human Services, Atlanta, GA (2016)

59. Hearld, L.R., Alexander, J.A., Wolf, L.J., Shi, Y.: The perceived importance of intersectoral collaboration by health care alliances. J. Commun. Psychol. **47**(4), 856–868 (2019)
60. Institut National de Santé Publique du Québec: Cadre conceptuel de la santé et de ses determinants [Conceptual Framework of Health and Its Determinants] (2010). ISBN: 978-2-550-59234-1
61. Delon, S., Mackinnon, B., Alberta Health CDM Advisory Committee: Alberta's systems approach to chronic disease management and prevention utilizing the expanded chronic care model. Healthc. Q. **13**, 98–104 (2009)
62. Hutchinson, S.L., Lauckner, H.: Recreation and collaboration within the expanded chronic care model: working towards social transformation. Health Promot. Int. **35**, 1531–1542 (2020)
63. Pulvirenti, M., McMillan, J., Empowerment, L.S.: Patient centred care and self-management. Health Expect. **17**, 303–310 (2014)
64. Kuluski, K., Guilcher, S.J.T.: Toward a person-centred learning health system: understanding value from the perspectives of patients and caregivers. Healthc. Pap. **18**, 36–46 (2019)
65. Mullins, C.D., Wingate La'Marcus, T., Edwards, H.A., et al.: Transitioning from learning healthcare systems to learning healthcare communities. J. Comp. Eff. Res. **7**, 603–614 (2018)
66. Clement, M., Filteau, P., Harvey, B., Jin, S., Laubscher, T., Mukerji, G., Sherifali, D., Committee, D.C.C.P.G.E.: Organization of diabetes care. Can. J. Diabetes **42**(1), S27–S35 (2018). https://doi.org/10.1016/j.jcjd.2017.10.005
67. Layani, G., Vachon, B., Duhoux, A., Lussier, M.T., Gil, J., Brault, I., Vanier, M.C., Rodrigues, I., Motulsky, A., Kaczorowski, J., David, P.M., Battaglini, A.: Structuring and organizing interprofessional healthcare in partnership with patients with diabetes: the INterprofessional Management and Education in Diabetes care (INMED) pathway. J. Interprof. Care **37**(2), 329–332 (2023). https://doi.org/10.1080/13561820.2022.2051452. Epub 2022 Apr 11. PMID: 35403546
68. Aziz, Z., Riddell, M.A., Absetz, P., Brand, M., Oldenburg, B., Australasian Peers for Progress Diabetes Project Investigators: Peer support to improve diabetes care: an implementation evaluation of the Australasian Peers for Progress Diabetes Program. BMC Public Health **18**(1), 262 (2018). https://doi.org/10.1186/s12889-018-5148-8
69. Layani, G., Tremblay, A., Lussier, M.T., Godbout, I., Bihan, H., Gosselin, C., Pierre, M., Motulsky, A., Brault, I., Rodrigues, I., Kaczorowski, J., Vanier, M.C., Yapi, S.M.: Cross-sector collaboration to improve access to community services for people living with diabetes: contributions from actor-network theory. Health Serv. Insights **17**, 11786329231222408 (2024). https://doi.org/10.1177/11786329231222408

Tools for Analyzing and Measuring the Performance of Care and Service Pathways

Lara Maillet, Isabelle Godbout, Anna Goudet, and Georges-Charles Thiebaut

Abstract Over the past thirty years, numerous calls have been made to promote the integration of health care and services in order to control dysfunctions in health care systems. The implementation of care and service pathways has been identified as an appropriate strategy to remedy these dysfunctions. In 2015, the government of Quebec (Canada) undertook a vast reorganization of the health and social services network, leading to significant changes in the governance of health care organizations. In this context, several organizations became interested in the principle of management by care and service pathways. To support teams aiming to implement this approach, tools were developed based on the expertise of a research team, a review of scientific and grey literature, consultation with an advisory committee, and practical experimentation with a pathway management organization. This chapter presents the components and functioning of the performance analysis model that was developed and proposes an example of the performance analysis carried out. This tool has the potential to support the teams involved in achieving better demographic and clinical outcomes, a better user experience and judicious use of resources.

Keywords Care and service pathways · Complexity · Management · Measurement of the performance · Health and social services network

L. Maillet (✉) · I. Godbout · A. Goudet · G.-C. Thiebaut
National School of Public Administration, Montréal, QC, Canada
e-mail: lara.maillet@enap.ca

I. Godbout
e-mail: isabelle.godbout@enap.ca

A. Goudet
e-mail: anna.goudet@enap.ca

G.-C. Thiebaut
e-mail: georges-charles.thiebaut@csbe.gouv.qc.ca

P. Landa et al. (eds.), *Operations Research and Artificial Intelligence in Healthcare Management*, Springer Proceedings in Mathematics & Statistics 506,
https://doi.org/10.1007/978-3-031-95659-1_10

1 Context of the Implementation of the Measurement of the Performance of Care and Service Pathways

Over the past thirty years, in Canada as elsewhere, numerous calls have been made to promote the integration of health care and services to control the dysfunctions of health systems. These dysfunctions are particularly characterized by the fragmentation of care, the inadequate use of human and material resources, and challenges related to access—ranging from difficulties in accessing care to inequitable access to services [1, 6, 8]. The establishment of care and service pathways (CSP) has been identified as an appropriate strategy to mitigate these dysfunctions.

Based on multidisciplinary work in both their design and their operation [2], the CSP aim to: (1) support the formalization of the sequencing of processes and care actions [21]; (2) promote shared decision-making within the organization [2]; (3) reduce variations in care; and (4) increase the quality of care in terms of relevance, execution and safety [2, 9]. CSP can take various forms, such as descriptions of real practices and tools to improve them, or more prescriptive strategies that are very detailed, or even, complex [9, 20, 22]. Although CSP may address diverse themes, they must be based on clearly identified inclusion and exclusion criteria [23]. Some CSP are grounded in real-world practices and evolve though continuous improvement loop or others are designed from an ideal and a more significant restructuring. However, any CSP requires the implementation of clinical and organizational integration processes within the organization [22] to support the improvement of the continuity, quality and efficiency of care [9].

In 2015, the government of Quebec (Canada) undertook a vast reorganization of its health and social services network (HSSN) by setting up integrated health and social service centers (HSSC). This reform was primarily aimed at promoting and simplifying access to services for the population, contributing to improving the quality and safety of care and increasing the efficiency and effectiveness of the network. The adoption of the Act to modify the organization and governance of the health and social services network (Bill 10) led to significant changes in the governance of health organizations in the province [16].

In this context, several health care organizations (HCOs) have shown interest in the principle of management through care and service pathways (MCSP) [4, 10] and have tried to implement it in their organization. In Quebec, during the period from 2015 to 2024, the HCOs were called to merge (university) health and social services centers ((U)HSSC). These organizations bring together local community service centers (CLSCs), hospital centers (CHs), residential and long-term care centers (RLTCCs), child and youth protection centers (CYPSs), rehabilitation centers (RCs), and other resources. Their responsibilities include planning and coordinating all health care and social services offered to the population in a territory, usually on a regional basis [15].

The Ministry of Health and Social Services of Quebec defines a CSP as an effective and efficient clinical path that allows the person to have quick access to services in a way coordinated between establishments or organizations that have a common responsibility for a clientele [17]. It is a complex intervention supporting mutual decision-making and the organization of predictable care for a defined group of patients, and a defined period [22]. CSP are therefore a method of integrating care and services based on multidisciplinary work and the use of evidence data, the objective of which is to improve coordination and communication between professionals and users.

MCSP, for its part, aims to continuously improve the performance of health establishments through greater integration of services and practices according to four principles: continuous improvement, partnerships, performance measurement by the choosing the right monitoring indicators and setting up matrix governance based on a bottom-up approach. It considers the complexity of the issues facing health systems, including accessibility, equity, performance of care and allocation of resources. It also represents a governance innovation that aims to increase the adaptability of HCOs to the needs of the population, in particular by improving the accessibility and continuity of care and services [13, 14].

To support the deployment of the MCSP, tools have been developed by a research team in collaboration with three HCOs and representatives of the Ministry of Health and Social Services. Tools aim to (1) support and accompany the HCOs in the continuous improvement of the offer of care and services of pathways and (2) to strengthen the analytical capacities of the actors of the pathway management bodies. More specifically, this toolkit supports decision-making to improve pathway performance by allowing a global and targeted analysis of the performance of a pathway to identify its critical areas, its root causes, and to determine actions and monitor its impact. This article presents the components and operation of the Performance Analysis Model (PAM) of care and service pathways that was developed. The article ends by showing an example of analysis of the performance of a pathway carried out by an HCO in collaboration with the research team.

2 Challenges of Performance Measurement and Analysis

Management through care and services pathways consists of bringing the various players in the HSSN, such as stakeholders and managers, partners, and users, to work together to improve continuity of care and services and the organization of the health and social services system. This type of management aims to meet the needs, and to achieve health and well-being results perceptible to the user and the population, within the limits of the capacity of the organization. It requires the involvement of actors in terms of governance and evaluation of services at the organization level as well as the recognition of the knowledge of each of the actors, including experiential knowledge of users and practitioners. This new form of management involves specific challenges and the adoption of a posture of responsibility shared by all the actors involved. Matrix management by pathway in fact adopts a perspective that is both hierarchical and transversal to the HCO, ranging from health promotion to rehabilitation or end-of-life support, including users and all partners.

The evaluation of the performance of a pathway must also support the implementation and monitoring of continuous improvement cycles of a pathway to offer better population and clinical results, a better user experience and the judicious use of resources. Measuring and analyzing performance thus also represents several challenges regarding to rational and contextualized decision-making. First, representative measures of the different dimensions of performance, stages and services offered in the pathway must be identified. Then, a framework to comprehensively analyze pathways and identify critical areas, root causes and actions to improve them must be developed. This framework must include population and territorial data to deploy pathways adapted to the territory and the needs of the target population. Finally, a process of use based on the deliberation and the crossing of professional, experiential and scientific knowledge must be developed to support the teams wishing to implement the MCSP. The PAM was developed to address these challenges.

3 Methodological and Theoretical Foundations of Performance Measurement

The tool developed here was designed by a research team associated with a university research institute in collaboration with representatives of HCOs and the Ministry of Health and Social Services [18]. The content developed here is based on the work and expertise of the members of the research team, reviews of the scientific and grey literature, consultations with an advisory committee that reviewed and commented the proposed model and an experiment with a pathway management body within HCOs.

The development of the PAM is based on an understanding of performance as a multidimensional construct, in which the relationships between its dimensions are crucial. The identification of the dimensions of performance, their nature and their relationships are based on systematic reviews of the scientific literature. This framework allows the various stakeholders to debate and develop a judgment on the essential and specific qualities of a CSP according to the interaction between performance dimensions and contextual dimensions [7].

The use of the PAM is based on a comprehensive and deliberative approach. This approach is at the heart of both the construction of the tool and its use to assess performance: experiential, professional and scientific knowledge are called upon to select and analyze performance indicators in relation to the needs of the target population and territory. The quantitative measurement of performance indicators is a first step, but it is not sufficient for a performance assessment that takes account of the context and enables the development of reasoned and justified actions to support continuous improvement. Indeed, this tool mobilizes different data sources. First, scientific data that represent the model and the nature of the relationships between the dimensions of performance. Next, quantitative data, like indicators measuring the

Table 1 Performance and contextual dimensions

	Performance dimensions	Contextual dimensions
Structures and resources	1. Viability	Characteristics of the territory, individuals and partners Equity
	2. Accessibility	
	3. Adjustment to the needs of the target population	
Process	4. Coordination and continuity	
	5. Appropriateness	
	6. Security	
	7. Humanism	
	8. Productivity	
Outcomes	9. Clinical and population efficacy	
	10. Efficiency	
	11. User experience	

various dimensions of performance. Finally, qualitative data based on users' experiential knowledge as well as the knowledge of professionals that make it possible to understand and judge the level of performance of the pathway.

The PAM of a pathway is composed of 11 performance dimensions and two contextual dimensions. The dimensions of performance are grouped into three categories: structures and resources, processes, and results. These dimensions are dynamic and influence each other. In the toolkit, the nature of this influence is identified: the dimensions by which the performance of each dimension is determined and those on which the dimension has an effect. Indeed, certain dimensions can influence a particular dimension. In this context, they are considered as determinants of this dimension. It is also possible that certain dimensions influence the level of performance of other dimensions and are therefore considered to have effects on them. Table 1 presents the dimensions of performance and the contextual dimensions. Figure 1 schematizes the PAM of a pathway. Finally, Fig. 2 presents the effects of the dimensions of performance. The interactions between each dimension are identified by a dot in the relevant cells.

4 Analysis and Performance Measurement Tools: A Device to Support Decision-Making

The tools developed here support justified and reasoned decision-making. They can be used to carry out three types of complementary analysis: type 1 analysis which consists of the global analysis of the performance of a pathway and identification of critical areas; type 2 analysis which constitutes root cause analysis of critical areas of a pathway; and type 3 analysis which represents the monitoring of the performance

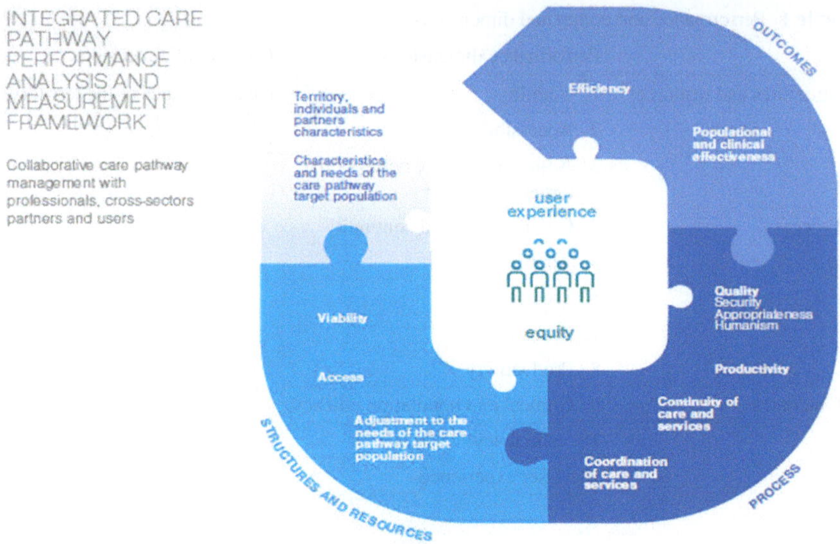

Fig. 1 Model for analyzing the performance of a care and service pathway. *Source* Thiebaut et al. [18]

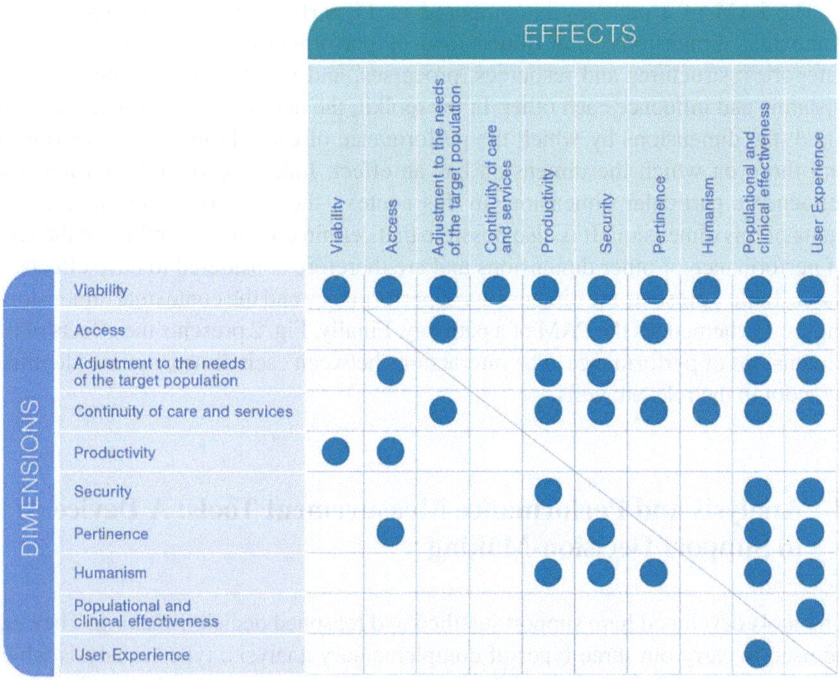

Fig. 2 Effects of performance dimensions. *Source* Thiebaut et al. [18]

of a pathway. Each analysis is structured in steps that achieve specific objectives. These analyses can be repeated multiple times to support continuous improvement cycles and are based on two processes. The first process crosses quantitative data (indicators), qualitative data (experiences of stakeholders, users, and professionals) and tools built from scientific knowledge that allows performance to be analyzed according to the dimensions of the model and their relationships. The second process consists of a reasoned debate between the actors working to improve performance. The objective is to make a judgment on the overall performance of the pathway, to identify the critical areas, and to make decisions on the actions to be taken to improve it.

The type 1 analysis is carried out in three steps: drawing up a portrait of the performance of the pathway, identifying the critical areas of the pathway and prioritizing these critical areas. This analysis should be conducted initially during the launch of a pathway to have an exhaustive portrait of the performance according to each dimension. A mapping of the existing care and services offer must be carried out before carrying out this analysis. The portrait of the pathway's performance is based on the measurement of each dimension of the PAM using indicators according to standards, and on the analysis of the relationships between the dimensions of performance according to a logic of determining factors and effects. Based on these data and a joint analysis by the actors responsible for the management of the pathway, it is possible to judge the performance of the pathway and to identify critical zones.

Type 2 analysis aims to identify and analyze the root causes of the critical areas identified, to support the identification and ensure the relevance of the actions to be implemented. This analysis is carried out in four stages: documentation of critical areas, identification of root causes and their prioritization and identification of continuous improvement actions while ensuring their relevance. It is based on a detailed examination of the critical areas identified and prioritized through the study of the determinants and their effects according to the PAM. A critical area corresponds to structures, processes, services, or interventions described in the PAM. It can be analyzed according to one or more dimensions of performance, the results of indicators and the experience of stakeholders, users and partners or problems. Like the type 1 analysis, the determination of the root causes and the actions for continuous improvement of the critical zone must result from a deliberation of the various actors participating in the management of the pathway. The objective here is to reach a consensus based on tools, quantitative and qualitative data, and their experiences. The critical areas are finally prioritized by the team according to the needs of the users, the feasibility of the actions to be implemented, and cost–benefit ratio.

Finally, the type 3 analysis aims to monitor the overall performance of the pathway and to assess the impact of the actions taken on the performance of the critical zone and the pathway. These two objectives are associated with types 1 and 2 analyses, the indicators selected to measure the dimensions of performance and the standards chosen for each indicator being reused at this stage. They will be used this time to monitor the overall performance of the pathway and to assess the impact of actions to improve the critical zone. This analysis is carried out in two stages: the construction of a dashboard and the monitoring of performance according to a monthly or quarterly interval.

5 Contents of the Toolkit

The toolkit includes three elements for analyzing and measuring the performance of a CSP: (1) the PAM and its glossary; (2) tools to support the analysis and measurement of performance, broken down into sheets for each of the performance and contextual dimensions, and two tables summarizing the links between the different performance dimensions; (3) a user guide proposing three types of complementary analysis that can be carried out with the tool. The PAM and its glossary define each dimension. This model is contextualized according to the different territories and populations for which the pathway is designed. The sheets for their part include the definition of the dimensions and the sub-dimensions that constitute it, examples of themes and indicators allowing the dimensions and their sub-dimensions to be measured, a figure summarizing the relationships between the dimensions and examples illustrating the nature of the relationships between the dimensions.

This toolkit is intended for managers and all those involved in clinical departments responsible for the implementation, piloting or management of a pathway. It is also intended for managers and support department workers who assist clinical departments in analyzing performance and selecting indicators and standards for monitoring. A short version has been made available for users, partners and stakeholders who need to quickly understand the main dimensions of the performance of a pathway, their interrelationships and how to measure them without going into details on the nature of these relationships.

6 Experimentation as a Prerequisite for Institutionalization

To test and validate the PAM, an analysis experiment of types 1 and 3 was carried out in a HCO. The pathway selected by the team focused on chronic obstructive pulmonary diseases (COPD). A complete continuous improvement cycle has been achieved. This exercise has resulted in a process of adapting tools and co-construction of a use methodology adapted to the organization. It aimed to convince the clinical and support directions responsible for the pathways to use it.

The analytical approach included various preliminary and structuring elements. First, the pathway was mapped out, including sequencing services and interventions, coordination mechanisms, stakeholders involved, and clinical tools. Then, the evidence data useful to support the analysis and the guidelines to construct an ideal pathway were identified. This was followed by the construction of the indicators adapted to the pathway. Finally, the identification and involvement of key actors were determined. Table 2 presents the crossing of data and knowledge produced by the team. Table 3 presents the indicators of the targeted COPD pathway.

Table 2 Combination of data and knowledge

	What	Why	How
Evidence data	• Guide to best clinical and organizational practices • Reference pathways • Quality standards	• Identify normative clinical and organizational benchmarks • Locate on the key elements by dimensions of performance and in stages of the pathway	• Summary of the main international quality guides and standards • Synthesis sheet by diagnosis
Popular and epidemiological data	• Health determinants • Prevalence and incidence rate • Mortality rate • Partner services offer	• Know the needs of the target population by territory • Have an epidemiological portrait • Identify target population	• Extraction from databases • Analysis of risk factors and the target population
Performance indicators	• Indicators classified according to the dimensions of performance and steps in the pathway	• Analyze the performance of the pathway by dimensions and relationships • Identify the dimensions whose performance is considered worrying	• Identify the indicators of the pathway according to the dimensions • Extract internal and external data • Identify targets for standards
Experiential and professional knowledge	Knowledge and experiences of: • Users and caregiver • Stakeholders and managers	• Share knowledge and experiences • Contextualize the data and the pathway • Identify the clinical and organizational challenges of the pathway	• Cross-referencing evidence, population data and performance indicators, based on professional and experiential knowledge and context
Ultimate results	• Portrait of the pathway performance (steps and dimensions) • Identification, operational description, and prioritization of critical zones of the pathway • Identification of root causes and improvement actions • Pathway dashboard		

Table 3 Indicators of the COPD pathway

Dimensions	Indicators
Characteristics of the target population of the pathway, and of the territory of individuals and partners	• Adjusted proportion of regular smokers and occasional smokers aged 15 and over, by local health network (LHN) [12, 19] • Index of social and material deprivation by LHN and age group • Number and proportion of users with COPD by age group and LHN • Offer of Community Services (support group) for people by LHN
Viability/innovation	• Knowledge and integration of guidelines
Accessibility	• Waiting time on the COPD teaching and monitoring program • Waiting time for access to pulmonary rehabilitation programs • Access to palliative care for users with COPD
Adjustment to the needs of the target population	• Number of people diagnosed each year for each LHN • Proportion of the smoker population participating in a program to quit smoking [11, 12, 19] • Rate of COPD people registered with a family physician (FP) having made at least one visit with their FP [12] • Rate of users with COPD having participated and completed the training in self-management associated with COPD • User rate with moderate to severe COPD symptoms that have received services from the pulmonary rehabilitation program
Continuity/Coordination	• Adjusted proportion of COPD people registered with a FP having made at least one visit to their FP within 21 days of the date of release of a hospitalization [3, 5] • Adjusted proportion of people with COPD having made at least one visit to the emergency and who return there within 7 days of this visit to the emergency [16, 17]

(continued)

Table 3 (continued)

Dimensions	Indicators
Appropriateness	• Rate of people diagnosed with a COPD for a year which received a complete test of their pulmonary functions and a Spirometry test [11, 19] • COPD levels that have received at least one long-lasting bronchodilator prescription [12] • Rate of persons with COPD having received at least one Corticosteroids in inhalation without having received, in the same year, at least one prescription from a long-lasting bronchodilator [12, 19] • User rate reaches COPD for which an action plan has been established including self-management and management of drug prescriptions
Humanism	• Assiduity rate on the self-management program
Clinical efficiency	• Proportion of people with COPD having at least had a hospitalization in short-term care [12] • Proportion of people with COPD having at least had hospitalization and who were readmitted to the hospital within 30 days of the release date of the previous hospitalization [12, 19] • Rate of users with COPD which are followed, and which are presented to the priority emergency [11, 19]
Popular efficiency	• Impact rate of users with COPD by age group, gender and LHN [11]
Equity	• Indicators of ventilated accessibility, relevance, and efficiency according to the stratification factors (place of residence, gender, index of social and material disadvantage)

7 Conclusion

The Performance Analysis Model presented in this chapter aims to support the decision-making of the actors concerned by care and service pathways (managers, clinicians, users, intersectoral stakeholders). The originality of this toolkit lies in its operational nature and its ability to analyze trajectory performance longitudinally in relation to the needs of the target population and the characteristics of the territory. The use of this toolkit is based on a deliberative and comprehensive approach that enables critical areas and their root causes to be identified, so that continuous improvement actions targeting them can be developed collectively.

However, this toolkit also has a few limitations. On the one hand, because it is intended to be complete and to reflect the complexity of management by care and service pathways, the actors involved may find it difficult to assimilate and use this tool without the support of the research team. On the other hand, it implies being able to rely on precise, up-to-date data once the indicators have been identified for analysis. Yet this still poses challenges in health and social service organizations today.

This tool nevertheless has the potential to support the teams concerned in achieving better demographic and clinical outcomes, a better user experience and a judicious use of resources, in line with the population-based responsibility of health and social service organizations.

References

1. Ackerman, F.K., III.: The movement toward vertically integrated regional health systems. Health Care Manag. Rev. **17**(3), 81–88 (1992)
2. Allen, D., Gillen, E., Rixson, L.: Systematic review of the effectiveness of integrated care pathways: what works, for whom, in which circumstances? Int. J. Evid. Based Healthc. **7**(2), 61–74 (2009). https://doi.org/10.1111/j.1744-1609.2009.00127.x
3. Bourbeau, J., et al.: Énoncé de position de la SCT : mise à jour de la pharmacothérapie chez les patients ayant une MPOC [CTS position statement: drug therapy update for patients with COPD]. Revue Canadienne des soins respiratoires et critiques et de la médecine du sommeil [Can. J. Respir. Crit. Care Sleep Med.] (2019)
4. Bragato, L., Jacobs, K.: Care pathways: the road to better health services? J. Health Organ. Manag. **17**(3), 164–180 (2003). https://doi.org/10.1108/14777260310480721
5. Çolak, Y., Afzal, S., Nordestgaard, B.G., Vestbo, J., Lange, P.: Prognosis of asymptomatic and symptomatic, undiagnosed COPD in the general population in Denmark: a prospective cohort study. Lancet Respir. Med. **5**(5), 426–434 (2017)
6. Commission d'étude sur les services de santé et les services sociaux (CESSSS): Les solutions émergentes [Emerging Solutions]. Gouvernement du Québec (2000)
7. Contandriopoulos, A.P., Champagne, F.: Mesurer la performance: Les grands éléments théoriques à la disposition des décideurs et chercheurs. Séminaire du MSSS « les mesures de performance : Un outil pour assurer la pérennité des systèmes de santé et des services sociaux [Measuring performance: the main theoretical elements available to decision-makers and researchers. MSSS Seminar "Performance Measurement: A Tool for Ensuring the Sustainability of Health and Social Services Systems] (2011)
8. Contandriopoulos, A.P., Denis, J.L., Touati, N., Rodriguez, R.: Intégration des soins: dimensions et mise en œuvre. Ruptures, revue transdisciplinaire en santé [Integration of care: dimensions and implementation. Ruptures Transdiscipl. Health J.] **8**(2), 38–52 (2001)
9. De Bleser, L., Depreitiere, R., De Waele, K., Vanhaecht, K., Vlayen, J., Sermeus, W.: Defining pathways. J. Nurs. Manag. **14**(7), 553–563 (2006). https://doi.org/10.1111/j.1365-2934.2006.00702.x
10. Ellis Brian, W.: The care pathway: a tool to enhance clinical governance. Br. J. Clin. Gov. **4**(2), 61–72 (1999). https://doi.org/10.1108/14664109910306820
11. Health Quality Ontario: Quality Standard. Chronic Obstructive Pulmonary Disease Care in the Community for Adults. Measurement Guide (2018)
12. INESSS: Regard sur les parcours de soins et de services des personnes atteintes de la maladie pulmonaire obstructive chronique (MPOC) [A look at care and service pathways for people with chronic obstructive pulmonary disease (COPD)]. COMPAS+ (2019)

13. Maillet, L., Thiebaut, G.-C., Touati, N., Champagne, G.: L'expérience des trajectoires de soins et des services de santé au Québec : l'animation comme levier de gouvernance collaborative et intersectorielle. In: Bazinet, A., Christian, B., Michèle, C. (eds.) La collaboration interorganisationnelle : Conditions, retombées et perspectives en contexte public [The experience of care pathways and health services in Quebec: facilitation as a lever for collaborative and intersectoral governance. In: Bazinet, A., Christian, B., Michèle, C. (eds.) Interorganizational Collaboration: Conditions, Impacts, and Perspectives in the Public Sector]. PUQ, pp. 131–157 (2021)
14. Moore, M., Hartley, J.: Innovations in governance. Public Manag. Rev. **10**(1), 3–20 (2008). https://doi.org/10.1080/14719030701763161
15. MSSS: Plan d'accès aux services pour les personnes ayant une déficience. Gouvernement du Québec, Québec. [Access Plan to Services for Persons with Disabilities. Government of Quebec, Quebec.] (2008)
16. MSSS: Projet de loi n° 10 Loi modifiant l'organisation et la gouvernance du réseau de la santé et des services sociaux notamment par l'abolition des agences régionales. Gouvernement du Québec, Québec. [Bill No. 10: An Act to Modify the Organization and Governance of the Health and Social Services Network, in Particular by Abolishing the Regional Agencies. Government of Quebec, Quebec.] (2014)
17. MSSS: Le système de santé et de services sociaux au Québec. Gouvernement du Québec [The Health and Social Services System in Quebec. Government of Quebec.] (2017). https://publications.msss.gouv.qc.ca/msss/fichiers/2017/17-731-01WF.pdf
18. Thiebaut, G.C., Lavoie, C., Labrecque-Pégoraro, S., Maillet, L.: Pour des trajectoires de soins et de services performantes : un outillage pour l'analyse et la mesure. Institut universitaire de première ligne en santé et services sociaux, Centre intégré universitaire de santé et services sociaux de l'Estrie-Centre hospitalier universitaire de Sherbrooke. [For Effective Care and Service Pathways: Tools for Analysis and Measurement. University Institute for Primary Health and Social Services, Integrated University Health and Social Services Centre of Estrie—Sherbrooke University Hospital Centre.] (2020)
19. Tyrrell, L.: Bringing About Change in COPD Care—white Paper (Ser. Ihe Report). Institute of Health Economics (2016)
20. Vanhaecht, K., De Witte, K., Sermeus, W.: The impact of clinical pathways on the organization of care processes (2007)
21. Vanhaecht, K., De Witte, K., Panella, M., Sermeus, W.: Do pathways lead to better organized care processes? J. Eval. Clin. Pract. **15**(5), 782–788 (2009). https://doi.org/10.1111/j.1365-2753.2008.01068.x
22. Vanhaecht, K., Ovretveit, J., Elliott, M.J., Sermeus, W., Ellershaw, J., Panella, M.: Have we drawn the wrong conclusions about the value of care pathways? Is a Cochrane review appropriate? Eval. Health Prof. **35**(1), 28–42 (2012). https://doi.org/10.1177/0163278711408293
23. World Health Organization—Europe: Primary Health Care (2016). https://www.who.int/health-topics/primary-health-care#tab=tab_1

An Overview on Adopting Clinical Pathways in Primary Care: A Literature Review

Jean-Denis Lalonde and Paolo Landa

Abstract Primary care is considered an essential service within the public healthcare system because it is responsible for offering continuity of care, patient-centeredness, coordination of care, prevention, health promotion, and patient autonomy. ** Clinicians are increasingly interested in utilizing clinical pathways to improve primary care quality and service delivery, providing more efficient use of available resources. ** At the secondary care level, clinical pathways are regularly used to ensure adequate management of care for a specific population to receive appropriate and timely care in an institution. It would be interesting to know if this process could have the same benefits within primary care. This literature review aims to screen the scientific literature on whether there have been studies able to address the application of clinical pathways in primary care. After screening both titles and abstracts, 26 papers were selected among 5,807 articles found. After the application of inclusion criteria for this literature review, 10 articles were selected. The results indicate the benefits and the limitation of using clinical pathways. However, the lack of resources in primary care and the resistance to change may limit the adoption of CPs.

Keywords Primary care · Clinical pathways · Health care system · Health care management · Evidence-based management

J.-D. Lalonde (✉) · P. Landa
Operations and Decision Systems Department, Laval University, Québec City, QC, Canada
e-mail: jean-denis.lalonde.1@ulaval.ca

P. Landa
e-mail: paolo.landa@fsa.ulaval.ca; paolo.landa@cirrelt.ca; paolo.landa@crchudequebec.ulaval.ca

P. Landa
Interuniversity Research Centre on Enterprise, Networks, Logistics and Transport (CIRRELT), Laval University, Québec City, QC, Canada

Oral Ecology Research Group, Laval University, Québec City, QC, Canada

Population Health and Optimal Health Practices, Hospital Research Center of Quebec, (CRCHUQ), Laval University, Québec City, QC, Canada

P. Landa et al. (eds.), *Operations Research and Artificial Intelligence in Healthcare Management*, Springer Proceedings in Mathematics & Statistics 506,
https://doi.org/10.1007/978-3-031-95659-1_11

1 Introduction

1.1 Primary Health Care Services

The continuous evolution of healthcare systems, the increase in population needs, and service demands are causing challenges globally for public and privately funded healthcare. To meet these challenges, health system research has developed tools and solutions to efficiently meet both patient and health stakeholders' needs. Health care is a complex system and it is a hard challenge to meet needs and efficiency where there are budget constraints typically regulated by the government in publicly funded health systems. Healthcare systems have three main service levels: primary care, secondary care, and tertiary care. Primary care is defined by the US Institute of Medicine as "*the provision of integrated, accessible health care services by clinicians who are accountable for addressing a large majority of personal health care needs, developing a sustained partnership with patients, and practicing in the context of family and community*" [1]. The primary care (PC) services include the patient first-contact with the healthcare system, accessibility, continuity, comprehension, and coordination of person-focused care [2]. Unlike primary care, secondary care consists of specialized care provided on an outpatient or inpatient basis. They take place following a referral from primary care. Finally, tertiary care refers to highly specialized services in outpatient and inpatient settings or within a facility dedicated to performing specific investigations using advanced medical treatments [3].

PC aims to optimize population health and reduce disparities. It ensures that all community members can have access to services despite socioeconomic determinants of health. Five main functions are identified in PC: (i) First contact accessibility creates an entry point for and optimizes access to health services; (ii) Continuity which promotes the development of long-term personal relationships between the patient and the health provider; (iii) Comprehensiveness that ensures to provide a diverse range of promotive, protective, preventive, curative, rehabilitative, and palliative services; (iv) Coordination that is responsible to organize services and care across levels of the health system and over time; and (v) People-centered care ensures the education and support needed to people and maximizes the autonomy in people's care [1].

Primary care is a very important component of the system as it addresses the health needs of patients at the community level, integrates care, prevents disease, and promotes wellness and education. In the international literature was demonstrated that overall healthcare expenditures can be decreased through primary care while improving population health and access [4]. Primary care aims to efficiently and effectively distribute health and well-being by focusing on the health needs and preferences of individuals and communities. Through its initiatives, the continuum of health becomes a key consideration for adopting accessible resources in community environments.

It has been well demonstrated by the international community that primary care improves access to health services and reduces the number of emergency room visits.

Primary care reduces the negative impact of poor economic conditions on the health of a population [5–9]. The benefits provided impact the private healthcare system, as more appropriate access to healthcare services reduces costs and increases benefits for both patients and healthcare insurance. An example of this would include the economic benefit resulting from increased workforce participation and productivity, leading to less absenteeism among workers [10]. In addition, primary care principles support education that can be used to improve population lifestyle habits such as the adoption of healthy nutrition in daily life. This leads to the prevention of obesity and improving the quality of nutrition among children [11]. Thus, primary care can intervene at the behavioral level where there are social inequalities in health access or health deprivation. Social inequalities refer to a difference in health and service access between individuals according to social and economic factors or criteria of differentiation. This problem is due to a poor distribution of resources within the population [12]. To ensure equitable access to primary care for the entire population (or to the largest part of it), there should be a larger ratio of general practitioners within the population [13].

The emphasis in primary care is also focused on community-based services, ensuring access to health systems in rural or remote areas and disadvantaged populations, leading to more favorable health outcomes [4]. A recent health research initiative that supports improved health outcomes is based on CP.

CPs utilization is an effective way to provide patient care, as it is consistent with the values, needs, and desires of patients. It supports clinicians to involve patients in discussions and decisions. CPs utilization improves health outcomes, and patient satisfaction, and reduces health costs [14]. In an Italian study conducted in 2018, researchers studied CPs utilization during acute ischemic stroke cases, eliciting an overall positive effect on patient management and service efficiency. The results were owing to the standardized application of time-dependent protocols and multidisciplinary/integrated care implementation. The authors reported that all acute stroke CP steps were optimized, increasing prompt and adequate interventions and possibly affecting stroke patient outcomes. This impacted outcomes such as the readmission rate of the patients, which was reduced with respect to previous periods [15].

The objective of this study is to provide an overview of the application of CPs within the organization of primary care services, together with the analysis of both the benefits and limitations of its implementation and application. The development of this analysis has the following structure: the main concepts of the topic and the characteristics of both the primary care sector and CPs are introduced in Sect. 1, then a literature review aimed at analyzing the use of CPs in primary care is presented in Sect. 2. The results from the analysis of the literature together with the benefits and limitations of the implementation of CPs in primary care are reported in Sect. 3, then conclusions and future research are discussed in Sect. 4.

1.2 Clinical Pathways and Its Application

A recent study defines CPs broadly as a "*long-term and complex managerial intervention adopting a systemic approach, for a well-defined group of patients who journey across the entire continuum of care, from prevention and screening to recovery or palliative care. This intervention:*

- *Prioritizes the centricity of patients and caregivers by analyzing the patient experience through their needs and expectations, taking into account the need for information, education, engagement and involvement and integrates the patient relationship as a fundamental need.*
- *Supports the roles of professional actors involved in the care pathway by developing adherence to the patient-centered care approach; working on interdisciplinarity through the development of skills, both technical and above all relational; the clarification of roles and responsibilities; and by taking into account the experience of professionals both in understanding the organizational constraints and their well-being at work;*
- *Integrates a process of care approach through the modeling and improvement of the care pathway by continuously integrating the latest knowledge and information to support clinical decision-making and by defining feedback loops to continuously improve clinical and non-clinical process supported by operation management contained within process improvement methodology approaches;*
- *Embeds coordination structures through: the implementation of best practices and the translation of guidelines into daily practice; the support of information continuity through the integration of services at the systemic level; the implementation of knowledge management along the care continuum; and the identification of leaders at each step of the care pathway; and the identification of leaders at each step of the care pathway;*
- *Adapts to the contexts of both the physical and social structures by integrating the human, material, economics and financial resource constraints, as well as the social dynamics of power and trust relationships;*
- *Is supported by information systems and data management enabled by digitalization, which ensure the flow of information within the right context at the right time and place, and allows the continuous integration of the latest knowledge into the care flow and the management of accessible data in real time to monitor and evaluate variances in practices and outcomes;*
- *Promotes the development of a learning health system to support the care pathway*[14]."

There are several other definitions of CPs in the international literature. One definition described CPs as a set of tools used to guide evidence-based healthcare, capable of translating clinical practice guideline recommendations into clinical processes of care within the unique culture and environment of a healthcare institution. A CP was implemented as a structured multidisciplinary care plan with the following characteristics: (i) used to translate guidelines or evidence into local structures; (ii) details the steps in a course of treatment or care in a plan, pathway, algorithm, guideline, protocol or other "inventory of actions"; and (iii) aims to standardize care or a specific clinical problem, procedure or episode of healthcare in a specific population [16].

2 Materials and Methods

Currently, there is a limited number of studies in the international literature analyzing the use of CPs at the primary healthcare level. However, there is a large literature based on CPs use in secondary care and acute care settings (e.g., management of older adult inpatients with malnutrition) [17–21].

A piloted search on databases (PubMed and ancestral searching) was performed in February 2023 using the following keywords and search terms ("clinical pathways" AND "primary care" OR "health care" OR "healthcare"). The final selection of the most recent and relevant articles was defined by authors (PL, JDL). Inclusion criteria included only peer-reviewed articles; the primary language of the articles had to be English or French and analyzed the primary care CPs use. The article could be issued by any country and the publication had to in the years 2000–2023. The articles were selected following inclusion criteria that considered the benefits of CPs utilization, any positive points shown by the different articles; content found in the various articles; and link with primary care.

An article was excluded if it: was grey literature; did not discuss CPs use in primary care; was not in the English or French language; did not discuss primary care; or did not focus on health-related issues. A dedicated extraction form was developed to report data from the articles using the following information: title, authors, year of publication, country where the study was conducted, the CP type, benefits of adopting CPs reported in the study, limitations of using CPs reported in the study, and details on the CP.

Among the 5,807 articles found, only 26 articles were selected after the screening of both titles and abstracts. After the full-text reading and analysis, ten articles were found to meet the inclusion criteria for this literature review.

3 Results

The search strategy provided 10 articles where the adoption of CPs was reported in primary care. More than half of the studies were published after 2020 (n = 7) [22–29], while only three studies were published in the first decade of the twenty-first century. This indicates an increased interest in this topic over the last ten years [29–31]. Eight studies focused on North American countries (Canada and the United States), while the remaining studies (n = 2) were conducted in European countries [24, 31].

Only six studies adopted qualitative methods, while four studies adopted quantitative methods. No mixed-methods studies were included in this literature review. The types of disease pathways reported in the included articles varied, as CPs are versatile and can be applied to many health areas. CPs for the following disease processes/ body systems were reported in the included articles: spine [25], pelvic floor [25], hip and knee [25], prostate assessment [25], stroke [25], wound care[25], fertility care[25], non-alcoholic fatty liver disease [30], hospital admission prevention [31], patient management and organization [32], kidney disease [26], mental health [27], COVID-19 [22, 27], pediatric asthma [28] and chronic gout [29].

3.1 How CPs May Contribute to Healthcare Quality

The implementation of CPs in primary care reduces hospital readmission and complication rates; improves patient management and flow; promotes appropriate organizational and clinical health care; and enhances service quality [15]. CPs program implementation led to stability in care delivery, optimized accessibility, quality, sustainability and cost-effectiveness of care [33]. Moreover, the WHO (2020) encourages countries to focus their quality improvement policies on the holistic continuum of care and emphasizes the need to improve CPs. WHO also supports a focus on outcomes that matter to the patient from clinical, quality of life and health system experience perspectives.

CPs are now promoted in government health policy reports, as in NHS, and their use is still increasing [34]. There is a growing focus on evidence-based practice and improved quality of care in health care systems. Some countries as Belgium and Germany, are increasing the development and implementation of CPs [34]. The European Pathways Association (EPA) is the world's largest CP professional organization and it supports the development, implementation, and evaluation of CP in Europe [34]. If CPs are implemented successfully, they may have an impact on health care macro-variation phenomena (e.g., length of stay and patient based on pathways indicators) and in performance based on micro-variation (e.g., variations in diagnostic and therapeutic prescriptions and protocol implementation indicators). CPs implementation improves outcomes by providing a mechanism to coordinate care, reduce fragmentation, and lower healthcare costs without reducing the quality of patient care [35].

Primary care providers such as nurses, pharmacists, and physicians who provide direct patient care are adequately positioned to save lives and prevent hospitalizations. The utilization of CPs can help to identify the patients at risk of disease and to manage them by providing a roadmap for sustainable and feasible primary care such as suicide prevention [36]. Considering these characteristics, CPs are associated with improved patient outcomes, and improved organizational indicators, and play an important role in patient safety [22]. Quality improvement in health care is required to: (1) align clinical practice with guideline recommendations in order to provide high-quality care within an institution; (2) reduce variations in clinical practice, thereby maximizing patient outcomes/ clinical efficiency; (3) promote safe, evidence-based care by providing locally oriented recommendations for the management of a specific condition, disease, and specific healthcare needs [17].

CPs are often developed by multi-professional teams composed partly of physicians, nurses, social workers, and administrators who are responsible for safe patient care. Benefits resulting from CP implementation include sharing information to strengthen the learning processes within an organization; supporting professionals to understand their roles and responsibilities; and improving clinical integration of system flow throughout the healthcare system [35].

3.2 Implementation of CPs

CPs were found to improve care coordination, strengthen care organization, and enhance patient follow-up in a Belgian study [31]. Researchers in this study recommended ongoing evaluation of CPs use. Further to this, Kanwal et al. [25] reported on the work that was conducted by the American Gastroenterological Association's multidisciplinary panel of experts who created primary care CPs to screen, diagnose, and treat non-alcoholic fatty liver disease. The authors of this study supported the use of evidence-based primary care CPs for this specific health challenge as they stated it makes patient care more timely, accessible, and standardized. Access to care was also discussed by European researchers who studied the use of primary care CPs during the COVID-19 pandemic [22]. The use of the CPs supported detection and case management for patients in 30 European countries. This review identified inequalities in access to care. The researchers recommended a common agreement in Europe for future pandemics [22].

COVID-19 was the subject of another article where a Canadian health zone in one province used integrated CPs to share patient information between their primary care networks and their central system to keep patients in the community and out of acute care [27]. Their research suggests these types of CPs have the potential to improve primary care and reduce hospital visits. In addition to a reduction in hospital visits, Rotter et al. [35] found that hospital complications could be reduced with the implementation of CPs.

Lack of CP buy-in, sustainability planning, and utilization were noteworthy findings of the current review. Groot et al. [24]. explored the lack of CPs uptake by family physicians in one Canadian province. In their article, researchers reported on several facilitators and barriers to CPs utilization. Overall, Groot et al. [24] stated that there is a desire from the family physicians in their study to support CPs development for health challenges where a multidisciplinary team approach is required (e.g., mental health). Another Canadian study explored the facilitators and barriers that primary care practitioners experienced while implementing primary care CPs for pediatric asthma [28]. Researchers in this study found that pediatric asthma CPs would be successfully used if primary care practitioners supported the use of the CPs, could understand their role, and had a sustainability plan in place. In a study exploring primary care CPs current use, interest, and perceived usability, researchers found that there is a high interest in using CPs but low utilization [29].

The findings of this review indicate that CPs, once developed, do not require a lot of maintenance and if used in primary care, could provide vital care. In a Canadian study, researchers found that using a CP for chronic kidney disease led to higher rates of testing to monitor the disease and more medication treatment used [31]. Researchers in this study found that CPs did not require a lot of resources or maintenance time once the CP was created and used. In addition to this, a suicide assessment CP was developed by Ayer et al. [36] for use with adult patients in a primary care setting. Researchers in this study discussed how many suicide decedents accessed primary care prior to their suicide, making this type of CP vital for use in primary care.

3.3 *Benefits of CPs*

Many benefits of CPs were identified in the studies. CPs are primarily developed to assemble relevant information for clinicians from a variety of practices to improve the overall care processes within primary care. Kanwai et al. [25] discussed that CP creation by an expert multidisciplinary team was beneficial for collecting all available data and assembling it in an easily accessible format relevant to clinicians from a variety of practices, including frontline providers. The CP in this study was adapted to manage patients with non-alcoholic fatty liver disease in primary care. There was careful explanation in each step of the CP to screen, diagnose, and treat the patient. The results of this study showed an improvement in the quality of healthcare delivery which is crucial to addressing the often-inconsistent care processes characterizing current approaches to care (e.g., for non-alcoholic fatty liver disease).

A similar outcome was observed for a different pathology, chronic kidney disease [31], where the application of a CPs led to a significant improvement in albumin-creatinine ratio testing. These findings may contribute to improving some aspects of the medical management of chronic kidney disease. The application of CPs to mental health was presented by Ayer et al. [36]. CPs were used to identify and effectively manage patients at risk of suicide, providing a roadmap for sustainable and feasible suicide prevention. The CPs represented a flexible tool for primary care that could be adapted to meet the needs of individual primary care workflows. For example, this CP could be used by other comprehensive suicide prevention frameworks to assist their screening efforts. Alternatively, the CP could be used by practices focusing more narrowly on managing patients who screen positive for suicide risk. In [30] the benefits of primary care were the reduction in in-hospital complications, an improved health outcome for patients, and improved documentation exchanged between GPs and hospital physicians. In addition, the study shows a significant reduction in hospital length of stay and a decrease in hospital costs/charges as there was more appropriate access to the resources, which could result of a better organization of care. This aspect is supported by Vanhaecht, et al. [31] which shows

CPs have a positive impact on the organization of care processes because it represents a method to achieve a result. A pathway is a tool for empowering clinicians and resources dimensions of care and between the requirements of both clinician autonomy and transparent accountability. In [28], it is explained that CPs have the potential to connect patients to specialists or other resources as required. CPs provide clear and rapid information in a rapidly changing context and have the potential to reduce acute care visits. The findings [29] show that the implementation of CPs in primary care would be welcomed par clinicians. CPs give Guideline-informed about the disease management and provide helpful tools and resources. According to the study [29], it could be explained by the fact that Pathways improves accuracy and confidence in answering written clinical questions.

3.4 Challenges of CPs

The adoption of CPs represents still a challenge in primary healthcare settings. This is given by several factors such as culture, innovation and technology, management, and organization. Usually, there is a lack of education and training for primary care providers, there are also administration barriers including lack of time, staff or facility or limited human resources availability.

A study reported that there was time-consuming paperwork when utilizing CPs. However, in healthcare organizations, there is an ongoing development based on Electronic Data and paperless activities and documents. It was observed that knowledge is continuing to evolve and the recommendation may change accordingly over time, forcing the revision of CPs each time is needed. Another study evidences the underestimation of costs for the implementation of CPs. It was mentioned that CPs require a minimum of resources and time to maintain them established. Another constraint is that CPs require a lot of workload and time and this can be a barrier to achieving optimal care. It was mentioned above there was a reduction in in-hospital complications but it has no evidence of differences between the number of readmissions to hospital or in-hospital mortality. It was mentioned there was a decrease in hospital costs/charges but it wasn't mentioned if the lower hospital costs contributed to a cost shifting to another health sector. Most studies used small sample sizes and there was a risk of selection bias because the surveys might have been completed by the participants most interested in CPs.

There is another study [31] used the Care Process Self Evaluation Tool (CPSET) to evaluate the care organization processes. The CPSET is an instrument for evaluating the care management process from the point of view of a multidisciplinary team. Based on the realistic evaluation paradigm, the CPSET is a self-evaluation instrument for measuring the perceptions of the team members. However, it is a difficult task to generalize the CPSET tool and its results because CPSET scores and outcome indicators have to be analyzed to determine if there is a relationship between subjective perceptions and objective outcomes. A suicide assessment CP in primary care was developed by Ayer et al. [36] for adult patients but this tool presents several limitations as it hasn't been tested through research. Another limitation of this tool isn't universal. It needs to be adapted to the clinical settings where it will be used and it can be difficult to interpret the results.

4 Discussion and Conclusions

After the analysis of the literature, we can note that the adoption of CPs in primary care is quite limited. Many conditions may limit the adoption of CPs such as the availability of resources (primary care vs secondary care) or culture (resistance to change especially in primary care). However, each of the articles herein analyzed reported the adoption of CPs approach to several typologies of diseases (e.g., chronic kidney disease or liver disease). This means that CPs are flexible and can adapt to any type of clinical process or disease management. The studies included indicating also that there is still improvement in terms of CPs in primary care, whereas in secondary care there are fewer resources and a negative approach to a change culture.

In addition, the presence of a hierarchical structural organization and many stakeholders may represent a factor that increases the adoption of CPs, and these characteristics are present in secondary care and missing in primary care. The challenges remain to understand how these improvements can be introduced and the impact in terms of public health. In secondary care, there is large evidence that CPs can improve outcomes such as 30-day inpatient hospital readmission rate or inpatient hospital mortality. This means that more studies need to be done to verify the impact of the implementation of CPs in primary care.

It would be important to know if the application of CPs in primary care could suit any public or private healthcare system. Given the limited studies analyzed and the limited application of CPs in primary care [17], more work to be done and a more in-depth investigation on the subject will assess the evidence of CPs. The objective of this study consists of providing an overview of the subject treated in a limited number of articles. The study also aimed to see the possible barriers to deal with when there is the introduction of innovation at the management level within primary care. As reported before, there are many benefits to the implementation of CPs such as better organization of care as well as better connection with specialist doctors when required. However, some limitations have been described such as the lack of time and resources needed for the CP introduction and implementation. A systematic literature review together with a meta-analysis will provide an analytic investigation on the subject and may confirm the results herein reported.

References

1. Donaldson, M.S., Yordy, K.D., Lohr, K.N., et al.: Institute of Medicine (US) Committee on the Future of Primary Care. Primary Care: America's Health in a New Era, 416 pp. National

Academies Press, Washington (DC) (1996). https://www.ncbi.nlm.nih.gov/books/NBK232631/
2. WHO: Primary Care. World Health Organization (2023). https://www.who.int/teams/integrated-health-services/clinical-services-and-systems/primary-care. Last accessed 17 May 2023
3. WHO. Care Process Levels in Dementia Care Coordination [Primary/Secondary/Tertiary]. World Health Organization (2023). https://www.who.int/data/gho/indicator-metadata-registry/imr-details/5063
4. WHO: A Vision for Primary Health Care in the 21st Century. In: WHO, UNICEF. (eds.), pp. 1–64. Geneva (2018)
5. Shi, L.: The Impact of Primary Care: A Focused Review, p. 22. Hindawi Publishing Corporation Scientifica (2012)
6. Liedes-Kauppila, M., Heikkinen, A.-M., Rahkonen, O., Lehto, M., Mustonen, K., Raina, M., Kauppila, T.: Development of the use of primary health care emergency departments after interventions aimed at decreasing overcrowding: a longitudinal follow-up study. BMC Emerg. Med. **22**(1), 1–9 (2022)
7. Jones, A., Bronskill, S.E., Schumacher, C., Seow, H., Feeny, D., Costa, A.-P.: Effect of access to after-hours primary care on the association between home nursing visits and same-day emergency department use. Ann. Fam. Med. **18**(5), 406–412 (2020)
8. Pinchbeck, E.W.: Convenient primary care and emergency hospital utilisation. J. Health Econ. (2019)
9. Whittaker, W., Anselmi, L., Kristensen, S.R., Lau, Y.S., Bailey, S., Bower, P., Checkland, K., Elvey, R., Rothwell, K., Stokes, J., Hodgson, D.: Associations between extending access to primary care and emergency department visits: a difference-in-differences analysis. PLoS Med. **13**(9), 1–19 (2016)
10. WHO: Building the Economic Case for Primary Health Care: A Scoping Review, pp. 1–40. World Health Organization, Geneva (2018)
11. Bourgueil, Y., Jusot, F., Leleu, H. : Comment les soins primaires peuvent-ils contribuer à réduire les inégalités de santé? [How can primary care help to reduce health inequalities?] IRDES **179**, 8 (2012)
12. Aïach, P., Leclerc, D., Fassin, H., Grandjean, M., Kaminski, M., Lang, T.: De la mesure des inégalités : enjeux sociopolitiques et théoriques, pp. 81–91. [Measuring Inequalities: Socio-political and Theoretical Issues.] La Découverte/INSERM (2000)
13. Starfield, B., Shi, L., Macinki, J.: Contribution of primary care to health systems and health. Milbank Q. **83**(3), 457–502 (2005)
14. Gartner, J.B., Abasse, K.-S., Bergeron, F., et al.: Definition and conceptualization of the patient-centered care pathway, a proposed integrative framework for consensus: a concept analysis and systematic review. BMC Health Serv. Res. **22**(1), 1–24 (2022)
15. De Belvis, A., et al.: Ischemic stroke: CPW impact. Int. J. Health Care Qual. Assur. **32**(3), 588–598 (2019)
16. Aspland, E., Gartner, D., Harper, P.: Clinical pathway modelling: a literature review. Health Syst. **10**(1), 1–23 (2019)
17. Rotter, T., et al.: Clinical pathway as a quality strategy. Health Policy Ser. **53** (2019)
18. Chakravarty, P.D., Ton, T., Scott, A., Doherty, C., Douglas, C.M., Montgomery, J.: Outpatient secondary care pathways for head and neck cancer referral result in patient delays for cancer treatment. Ann. R. Coll. Surg. Engl. **105**(4), 352–356 (2023)
19. Levell, N.J.: NHS outpatient secondary care: a time of challenges and opportunities. Future Healthc. J. **9**(2), 106–112 (2022)
20. Bourne, R.S., Baqir, W., Onatade, R.: Pharmacist independent prescribing in secondary care: opportunities and challenges. Int. J. Clin. Pharm. **38**(1), 1–6 (2016)
21. Button, K., Morgan, F., Hodgson, H., Weightman, A.L., Jones, S.: Musculoskeletal care pathways for adults with hip and knee pain at the interface between primary and secondary care: protocol for a systematic review. Syst. Rev. **5**(1), 128 (2016)
22. Rotter, T., Baatenburg de Jong, R., Lacko, S.E., Ronellenfitsch, U., Kinsman, L.: Clinical pathways as a quality strategy. Eur. Observ. Health Syst. Policies (53) (2019)

23. Ares-Blanco, S., et al.: CPW of Covid-19 patients in primary health care in 30 European countries: Eurodata study. Eur. J. Gen. Pract. **29**(2), 1–13 (2023)
24. Groot, G., Ollegasagrem, S., et al.: Facilitators and barriers to clinical pathway uptake and utilization among primary care providers in Saskatchewan—a qualitative study. Clin. Invest. Med. **45**(2), E1–9 (2022)
25. Kanwal, F., Shubrook, J.-H., Adam, L.-A., et al.: Clinical care pathway for the risk stratification and management of patients with nonalcoholic fatty liver disease. Gastroenterology **161**(5), 1657–1669 (2021)
26. Ayer, L., Horowitz, L.-M., Colpe, L., et al.: Clinical pathway for suicide risk screening in adult primary care settings: special recommendations. J. Acad. Consult. Liaison Psychiatry **63**(5), 497–510 (2022)
27. Aghajafari, F., Hansen, B., McBrien, K., et al.: The primary care COVID-19 integrated pathway: a rapid response to health and social impacts of COVID-19. BMC Prim. Care **23**(1), 333 (2022)
28. Sharpe, H., Potestio, M., Cave, A., Johnson, D.-W., Scott, S.-D.: Facilitators and barriers to the implementation of the Primary Care Asthma Paediatric Pathway: a qualitative analysis. BMJ Open **12**(5), 1–8 (2022)
29. Toy, J.-M., Drechsler, A., Waters, R.-C.: Clinical pathways for primary care: current use, interest and perceived usability. J. Am. Med. Inform. Assoc. **25**(7), 901–906 (2018)
30. Rotter, T., Kinsman, L., James, E., et al.: Clinical pathways: effects on professional practice, patient outcomes, length of stay and hospital costs. Cochrane Database Syst. Rev. **22**(3), 1–22 (2010)
31. Vanhaecht, K., Whitte, K.-D., Panella, M., Sermeus, W.: Do pathways lead to better organized care processes? J. Eval. Clin. Pract. **15**(5), 782–788 (2009)
32. Donald, M., Smekal, M.-D., Elliott, M.-J., et al.: Online clinical pathway for chronic kidney disease management in primary care: a retrospective cohort study. BMC Nephol. **22**(332), 1–11 (2021)
33. Bergin, R.J., Whitfield, K., White, V., et al.: Optimal care pathways: a national policy to improve quality of cancer care and address inequalities in cancer outcomes. J. Cancer Policy (25) (2020)
34. Busse, R., Klazinga, N., Panteli, D., Quentin, W.: Improving healthcare quality in Europe: Characteristics, effectiveness and implementation of different strategies. Eur. Observ. Health Syst. (2019)
35. Panella, M., et al.: Reducing clinical variations with CPWs: do pathways work? Int. J. Qual. Health Care **15**(6), 509–521 (2003)
36. Ayer, L., et al.: CPW for suicide risk screening in adult primary care settings: special recommendations. J. Acad. Consult. Liaison Psychiatry (63), 497–510 (2022)

An Ailing Healthcare Organization

Marie-Eve Dufour, Julie Dextras-Gauthier, Gaëlle Falcon, Marie-Hélène Gilbert, and Pierre-Sébastien Fournier

Abstract Organizations in the healthcare sector are faced with the challenges of reducing costs, improving service quality and increasing work demands. The context of workforce shortages highlights the urgent need for action to ensure access to quality healthcare and services. The World Health Organization estimates that there is a shortage of nearly 6 million healthcare professionals worldwide. In May 2022, 8,700 full-time positions were vacant in the Quebec healthcare network. This situation calls for effective attraction, retention and loyalty strategies to attract and retain the necessary qualified personnel. Among the levers outlined in this chapter, the importance of equity, diversity and inclusion in personnel management is discussed. By fostering an inclusive environment, the organization benefits from access to a wider pool of skills, meets the expectations of under-represented groups and promotes cohesion with users. Retention of workers aged 55 and over is also highlighted as an important issue, notably by adapting their working conditions and recognizing their contributions. Organizations also benefit from tackling work overload, a source of stress and burnout, through sustainable prevention, involving good management, identification of risk factors and implementation of concrete actions. Finally, as key players in the implementation of these levers, managers, through their leadership and management practices, play a key role in promoting the attraction, retention and loyalty of human resources. It is therefore essential to ensure their well-being, so

M.-E. Dufour (✉) · J. Dextras-Gauthier · G. Falcon · M.-H. Gilbert · P.-S. Fournier
Faculty of Business Administration, Laval University, Quebec City, Canada
e-mail: Marie-Eve.Dufour@fsa.ulaval.ca

J. Dextras-Gauthier
e-mail: Julie.Dextras-Gauthier@fsa.ulaval.ca

G. Falcon
e-mail: gaelle.falcon@fsa.ulaval.ca

M.-H. Gilbert
e-mail: Marie-Helene.Gilbert@fsa.ulaval.ca

P.-S. Fournier
e-mail: Pierre-Sebastien.Fournier@fsa.ulaval.ca

P. Landa et al. (eds.), *Operations Research and Artificial Intelligence in Healthcare Management*, Springer Proceedings in Mathematics & Statistics 506,
https://doi.org/10.1007/978-3-031-95659-1_12

that they are in a position to adopt the behaviors needed to ensure the organization's longevity.

Keywords Health · Attraction · Retention · Loyalty

1 Introduction

Over the past three decades, public sector organizations have had to cope with the implementation of government policies aimed at reducing costs, while at the same time having to continue improving the quality of services offered to the population. At the same time, the work environment in public organizations, and more specifically in the healthcare sector, has seen an increase in work-related demands. In addition, the current labor shortage in Quebec's Health and Social Services Network, accentuated by the COVID-19 crisis, highlights the urgent need to act to preserve and improve access to safe healthcare and services for the population. In May 2022, 8700 full-time care positions were vacant in the Quebec network [1]. At the same time, nearly one in five healthcare workers was absent from work due to physical and/or psychological health problems [2]. Between 2020 and 2030, the demand for workers in this sector is expected to grow by 16% [3]. The shortage of healthcare professionals is not a problem specific to Quebec [4]. Worldwide, according to the World Health Organization, the shortage of healthcare professionals is estimated at nearly 6 million people [5], with some regions more affected than others in terms of difficulties attracting and retaining labor, such as rural areas [6]. In the specific context of Quebec, a Canadian province characterized by a pronounced aging of its population and increased demand for healthcare services and care [1], it is important for establishments to be able to count on sufficient, but above all committed and healthy, staff. Yet the challenges are many: difficult working conditions, task transformation and increasing workloads are just some of the factors adding to the already high pressure on staff and facility management. Various provincial measures have been put in place to alleviate the situation, including the use of placement agencies, mandatory overtime, and increased compensation for overtime hours worked [1]. While these measures may be effective in the short term, they are, for the most part, temporary and sub-optimal, as they do not address the causes of the difficulties experienced by Quebec's Health and Social Services Network staff [7]. Not to mention the fact that most of these measures are aimed at just one category of employees: caregiving staff, who, although of vital importance, would not be able to work without the contribution of all Quebec's Health and Social Services Network job categories, including the managers who are on hand to supervise and support them. However, the recent mass departures of managers and employees are exacerbating the exhaustion of those who remain. The current scarcity of manpower is making it even more difficult for healthcare establishments to fulfill their main mission: to offer a positive, pleasant and high-quality user experience, while guaranteeing health and social services based on proximity and continuity. This chapter looks at various issues associated with this problem, and the levers that healthcare organizations can use to stand out in today's job market. It focuses on the importance of understanding the aspect of retention with a view to attracting human resources.

2 Attraction, Retention, Loyalty: The Importance of Knowing Where to Start

Whether in the healthcare sector or elsewhere, the issue of staff shortages needs to be addressed in the right way. It is at the forefront of organizational, social, governmental and academic priorities and discourse. There is much talk of a labor shortage, i.e., a significant lack of employees resulting in an imbalance between employment needs and the availability of current or potential personnel on the job market. The healthcare sector, like many other economic sectors, is experiencing a situation of labor scarcity, meaning that employees are very hard to find, which is more a reflection of the pre- and post-pandemic situation.

Talking about workforce imbalance in organizations is not, however, a recent topic. As far back as 2015–2016, statistics from de province of Quebec showed that the labor market was heading towards a critical situation, caused by various factors such as the aging of the population or the immigration strategy [8]. Most organizations are focusing on improving their attractiveness in order to redress the often quantitative imbalance affecting their human resources. There's no doubt that this is a quicker solution in the short term. But is it the only way to ensure organizational sustainability and performance? In a context where the balance of power is currently in the hands of both candidates and employees, we need to think again.

Attraction and retention are part of the recruitment process, with attraction being the objective and retention the element on which it depends (Fig. 1). More specifically, attraction is defined as "an individual's positive attitude towards an organization he or she perceives as a potential employer" [9]. Indeed, the labor market is full of unemployed individuals. The average unemployment rate in the province of Quebec in 2022 was 4.3% [10]. In this case, the problem lies in the fact that the individuals available do not have the skills required to fill the positions to be filled. On the other hand, 2016 census data show a significant percentage of healthcare graduates who have made the decision not to work in the sector, estimating that there are probably more than 250,000 adults with an underutilized level of healthcare education, primarily in nursing, health aides and health and medical administration/management services. Among adults with underutilized health education in 2016, 62% were in the 20–34 age group. Skill atrophy should therefore be relatively low among these recent graduates, making them a potential source of healthcare labor [11].

Retention, on the other hand, is the process that encourages employees to stay with the organization [9]. It is frequently contrasted with turnover, which represents its opposite. For an organization, the average cost associated with voluntary turnover ranges from 30 to 150% of annual salary. For management positions, it can even

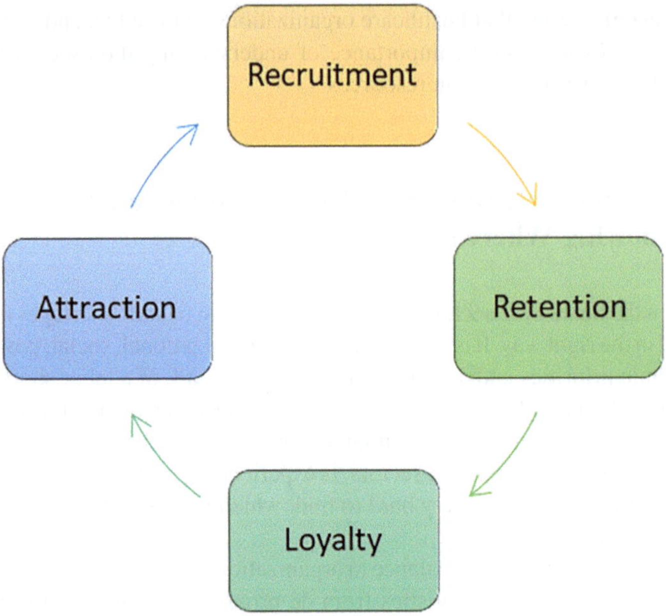

Fig. 1 The attraction-retention-loyalty cycle

exceed 200% [12]. In this context, and given the challenges of attracting and retaining staff, it's in an organization's interest to start by retaining its employees, or even building their loyalty, before hiring new ones. Otherwise, there is a high risk of perpetuating the cycle of labor turnover and having to deal with the repercussions of labor scarcity, such as limiting the organization's growth or reducing the quality of goods or services offered [13].

The final element in the cycle described in Fig. 1 is retention. It's clear that the concepts of retention and loyalty are used interchangeably. However, there is a nuance, as explained by Paillé [14] through the theory of social exchange [15]. According to this view, retention is associated with loyalty. Thus, retention occurs when the organization adopts a short-term perspective, focused on economic exchange. In fact, retention is about understanding why employees leave the organization. Loyalty is a proactive process of long-term anticipation. Its aim is to get employees to stay. It involves understanding what to do to keep employees. Building employee loyalty means fostering long-term commitment.

3 Employer Branding and Employee Experience: An Asset for Health and Social Services Network?

The concept of employer branding is based on the principle that the benefits of working and building a career within an organization should be promoted to both applicants and employees [16]. Employer branding thus has a dual effect: helping to attract potential candidates, but also retaining employees by reminding them of the benefits of being part of the organization [17]. The healthcare sector is no exception, and must also capitalize on employer branding, although not in a sector-specific way, as each establishment benefits from developing its own brand image. That said, employer branding must always be the result of strategic thinking at HR level, but also of an HR marketing approach [18]. Employer branding should reflect the employee experience and even help to improve it, while serving the organization's attraction objectives. For an organization, it's important to have a good understanding of its main attraction factors, i.e. the strengths of the organization that can be externally valued to attract candidates, such as total compensation or non-monetary factors like recognition [19]. But that's not all: it's necessary to ensure that the employee experience on offer is fully consistent with the employer brand promise. Creating consistency begins with training managers to understand the essence of employer branding and how it affects the way they do their jobs. They are on the front line, acting as the interface between employees and the organization [20]. In this respect, employer brand depends on the way managers deliver the employee experience. Managers are therefore key players in the implementation of employer brand and employee experience. Employer branding also requires a review of the various human resources management processes to ensure that they are consistent with the employer brand value proposition. It is also important to make employer branding a unifying organizational project. Employees and future candidates alike need to live the proposed experience in every interaction they have with the organization. Employer branding is therefore not just an attraction tool for recruiters, it is a strategic orientation to which all the organization's stakeholders must adhere [21]. Employer branding is not the exclusive responsibility of the human resources department; it must be supported by senior management and expressed by all the organization's stakeholders. The process of developing and implementing an employer brand is therefore central to harmonizing the organization's practices while helping to attract and retain employees, with the aim of creating value for the organization.

4 Equity, Diversity and Inclusion: Aiming for Integration and Learning

Today, attraction, retention and loyalty involve managing equity, diversity and inclusion (EDI), defined as the development and implementation of "coordinated actions and interventions with the aim of creating an environment that will enable all people

[…] to reach their full potential while pursuing the organization's objectives" [22]. It represents an important lever, since it provides access to a wider pool of skills, contributes to the employer brand, meets the expectations of certain historically discriminated groups and of society in general, and enables the issues of all to be considered, regardless of the individual characteristics or groups with which one identifies. In the healthcare sector, EDI management also plays a role in cohesion with users, who are better able to identify with the resources offering them services.

Diversity management in the healthcare sector is all the more paramount when we consider that the share of immigrants in the jobs of nursing aides, orderlies and patient service associates is 26.1% in Quebec, compared with 14.7% in all other occupations according to the 2016 census. This overrepresentation of immigrants in jobs in the sector is even greater for visible minority immigrants and women [23].

That said, all organizations appear to be fertile ground for the emergence of obstacles, inequities and discrimination against certain individuals working within them [22]. According to the theories of similarity-attraction, identity and social categorization, individuals tend to be attracted to people who are similar to them and, conversely, distrust those who are different or belong to other social groups [24] [25]. In today's context, EDI actions are essential.

EDI can be grouped into three approaches, each underpinned by a different rationale [26]. The first approach is based on equity of access and non-discrimination. It is based on a logic of compliance with legislative frameworks and assumes the principle of assimilation. The second approach recognizes and values diversity as a competitive advantage and a means of differentiation from other organizations in the sector. It is based on a business strategy of accepting and valuing differences, particularly with a view to responding to increasingly diverse users. The third approach, the one that should be favored, is based on a vision of integrating diversity as a source of efficiency and learning, considering the advantages induced by diverse teams in terms of the quality of decisions taken, creativity and performance. These three approaches can be complementary in organizations and evolve over time as the organization matures. That said, EDI intervention requires targeting biases and obstacles at institutional, social (Fig. 2), organizational (Fig. 3) and individual levels (Fig. 4), in order to develop a positive diversity climate [27] that reconciles equity, inclusion of all and organizational performance.

5 Attracting and Retaining Workers Aged 55 and over: What Are the Levers for Action?

In province of Quebec, the aging of the population has been underway for several decades, and there are not enough young people to fully replace workers who leave the job market [29]. This is therefore an important issue for organizations in both the public and private sectors, but also for workers aged 55 and over, as some of them want to remain in employment, but cannot find the working conditions they want to

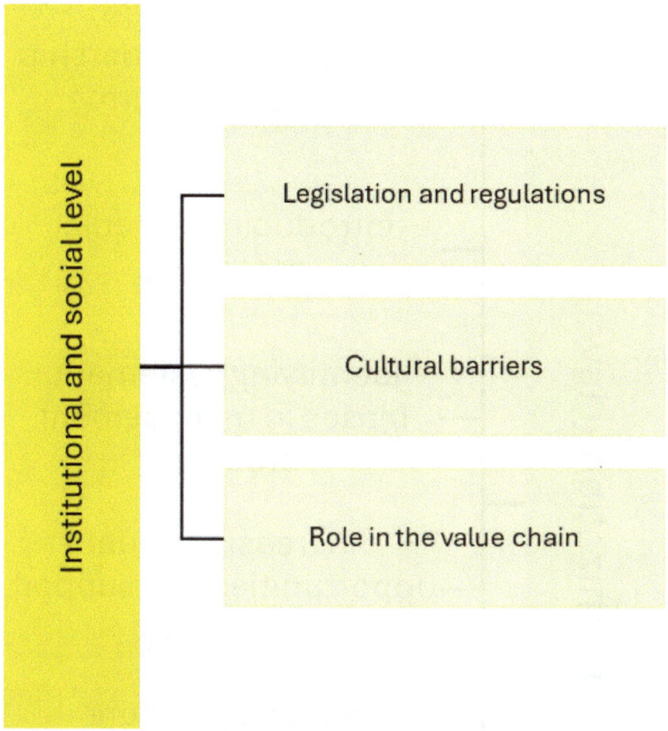

Fig. 2 Institutional and social level of intervention in EDI [28]

do so. In fact, it has to be said that workers aged 55 and over are part of the solution to labor scarcity. In fact, the OECD [30] has been calling for the employability of these workers for several years now.

In the province of Quebec, the situation in the healthcare sector dates back to the 1990s, when the government, in an effort to rationalize the workforce, made advantageous early retirement offers, characterized by lower actuarial penalties and a lower minimum retirement age [31]. For instance, in 1997, 4,000 nurses left the healthcare sector. In the public sector, 37,000 retirements were recorded, compared with a forecast of 15,000 [32]. A 2014 study of retirees from the healthcare sector showed that 55.2% of retiring respondents subsequently returned to work or attempted to do so, on average 9.56 months after officially leaving the job market [33]. In the same vein, three decades later, the aim is more of prolonging working life, by retiring later or taking a transitional job, than of encouraging early retirement.

That said, there are a number of reasons why workers aged 55 and over may leave their jobs at a relatively early stage, often as early as age 60. The reasons cited include: an enviable financial situation (especially in the public sector), a caring role, having grandchildren, mental overload (especially in the public sector) and physical overload and drudgery [34]. Reasons for not returning to work after retirement are

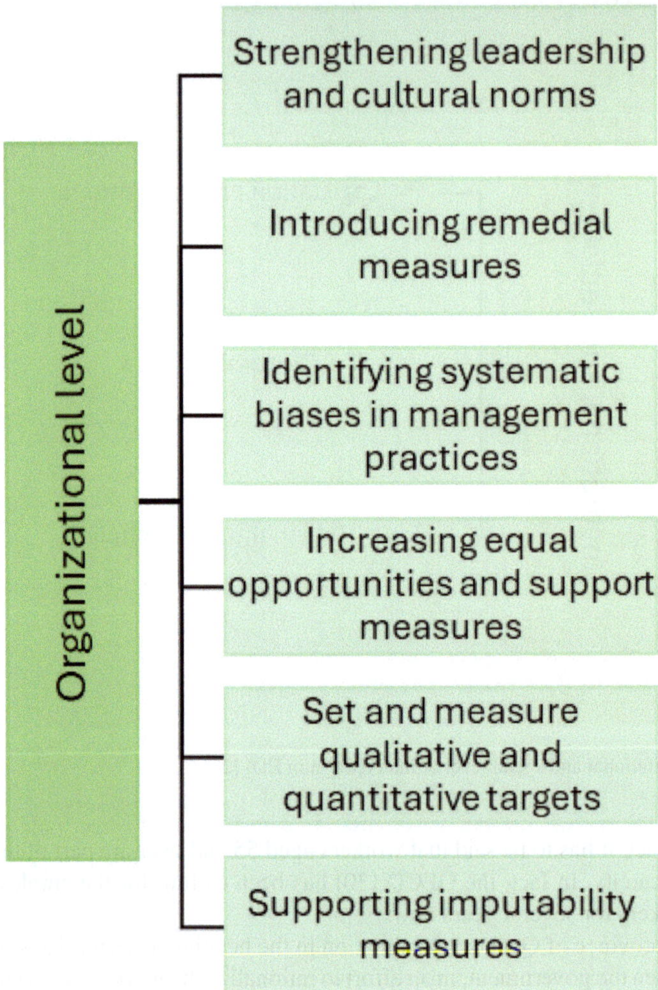

Fig. 3 Organizational level of intervention in EDI [28]

similar, including: poor health, work overload and fatigue, spousal retirement, and enviable pensions and incomes [35].

In fact, it's much easier to keep people employed in an organization, than to bring them back once they've retired. Retaining workers aged 55 and over is in line with the trend towards later participation in the labour market, already well underway over the past twenty years. The participation rate is increasing with rising levels of education, improved job quality, more jobs in the service sector, and the rising participation rate of women in all age groups [35]. For many workers aged 55 and over, a reduction in working hours would be one of the most important retention factors [35]. Other factors are also cited, such as recognition for work accomplished, reduced workload,

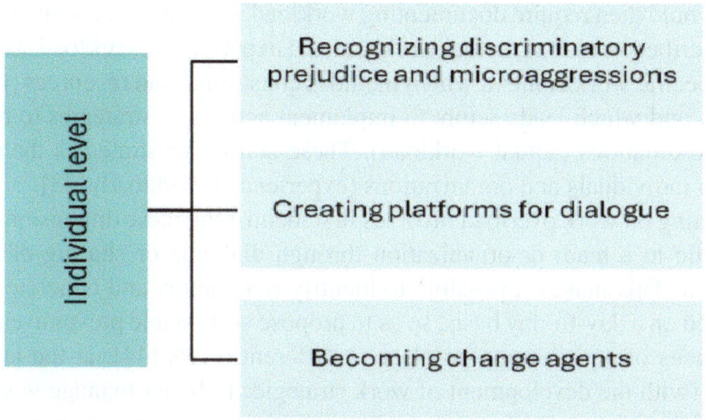

Fig. 4 Individual level of intervention in EDI [28]

remuneration adapted to their situation and the opportunity to pass on their expertise and knowledge [34]. And so, to attract and retain workers aged 55 and over, it's essential to make jobs attractive. This means modifying working conditions, such as shorter working hours, longer vacations, a 4-day week or part-time work. Recognition and knowledge transfer are also important factors in retention and loyalty.

6 Sustainable Workload Prevention: A Key Retention Factor

During the pandemic and even today, work overload remains the main reason cited for burnout and stress [36]. Several factors have been put forward to explain this phenomenon of work overload, such as the fact that everything is now urgent, the non-respect of so-called normal working hours, the amplitude of working days (starting earlier, finishing later), the continuous alternation of work and family with no downtime, the increased time spent in meetings, social isolation and constant connectivity [36]. The consequences of this overload on individuals and organizations are manifold. For example, it is said to be associated with an increase in risk-taking at work [37], musculoskeletal disorders [38], sleep disorders and chronic fatigue [39]. In addition, workload is associated with an increase in withdrawal behaviors, such as absenteeism, presenteeism and turnover [40]. It is therefore essential that organizations tackle this issue head-on.

However, the challenges are many, and it is still difficult to clearly define the nature of the workload problem and the means to be deployed to tackle it. These challenges are partly due to the lack of consensus on the nature of workload, its antecedents and consequences. Sometimes, workload is considered in terms of feelings of overwhelm or psychological demand [41], while in other contexts it is assessed in terms of performance in the execution of a given task [42]. Understanding and acting on work overload would then require documenting workload in its entirety along three dimensions: prescribed workload, actual workload and experienced workload. Workload is part of a specific work context, which includes constraints and resources (prescribed workload), and which leads actors to implement actions or strategies to respond to these work situations (actual workload). These actions or strategies then generate impacts on individuals and organizations (experienced workload) [43].

Intervening on work overload involves first identifying these dimensions of workload specific to a team or organization through dialogue or sharing of situations encountered. This makes it possible to identify risk factors and concrete problems encountered on a day-to-day basis, so as to propose sustainable preventive measures. These courses of action can take place at different levels [44]: at the level of the individual (with the development of work strategies to better manage workload), at the level of the group (with better social support from colleagues to better distribute responsibilities but above all to help each other), at the level of the manager (with a manager who gets involved and intervenes to properly identify priorities and by providing appropriate resources to his or her team) and finally, at the level of the organization itself (with mechanisms to review rules and procedures, to review deadlines and to provide adequate resources particularly in terms of technology).

On this point, the literature nonetheless indicates that there are protective factors, and this is particularly the case for the manager, who plays a key role in the effective prevention of occupational health and safety [45]. The manager plays two main roles: the more structuring one where he or she guides and directs tasks, and the one where he or she supports his or her teams and the individuals who make them up [45]. These two main roles enable him, in particular, to distribute the workload according to the situations encountered in his team.

Faced with the problems created by work overload, organizations are faced with two choices: to be in crisis management mode, or to be in sustainable workload prevention mode. In crisis management mode, immediate action is taken to respond to a critical situation for an individual or a team. The actions are aimed at calming the situation in the short term, to help get through the crisis. However, very often in this management mode, there is no real in-depth discussion of the workload, so the solutions provided are only temporary.

As part of a sustainable approach to workload prevention, a process of invention is planned based on the reality of work in the organizational context. Based on this approach, it is possible to propose concrete avenues for preventive action, since the day-to-day constraints to be overcome will have been identified, as well as the resources available (in terms of quality and quantity) to overcome these constraints. For organizations, intervening on workload is an essential element in retaining workers within their organization.

However, assessing workload is not just a question of quantity and time. In fact, workload is a complex issue that requires an in-depth prevention approach in the same way as other occupational health and safety risk factors. The literature clearly shows that certain organizational factors play an important role in the feeling of work overload, including work intensification and the accumulation of organizational changes [46]. Thus, the acceleration in the pace of work combined with the effects of labor shortages in the Health and Social Services Network is making it increasingly difficult to match the objectives set for workers with the work demands they must meet and the resources available to them. Faced with ever more numerous and complex work demands, but also with diminishing resources, the mantra of "doing more with less" no longer holds true, as workers become increasingly exhausted [47]. The urgent need to act to manage workloads in a preventive and sustainable way is more than important, it's essential.

7 Leadership and the Quality of the Relationship with the Supervisor: A Factor in Attracting and Retaining Staff

As an integral part of the employee experience, which refers to the employee's overall, real-life experience at work [48, 49], managers are an important factor in retention and loyalty [50]. Representing a concrete and visible link between employees and senior management, managers are standard-bearers for organizational values and mission. In addition to ensuring the quality of the care and services offered within their facilities, managers of the Health and Social Services Network establishments are also powerful referents for their employees. Indeed, through their management practices, managers can, among other things, weigh down or lessen the effect of psychosocial risk factors in the work environment (e.g. workload) on their employees [51, 52], while contributing to, or detracting from, the establishment of a psychologically safe work climate [53]. In the field of work in general and in healthcare in particular, studies highlight the benefits of positive leadership practices for employee functioning [54, 55]. However, to ensure that we maximize the benefits that positive leadership can have on employee well-being, we must first ensure that managers themselves are psychologically and physically healthy [56]. Indeed, some studies have shown that, over time, managers suffering from psychological health problems at work exercised weaker transformational leadership and higher laissez-faire leadership [57]. In recent years, the health and working conditions of managers themselves have deteriorated [58]. Indeed, several studies report stressful working conditions and a high turnover rate among managers in the healthcare network [59]. As managers themselves face a number of constraints that can affect their well-being and their ability to adopt good management practices [58], organizations need to intervene on these constraints to reduce them. Indeed, since managers play a key role in fostering a good experience for employees, increasing their motivation, well-being and intention to stay employed, organizations have no choice but to concern themselves with the psychological health of their managers.

In conclusion, organizations in the healthcare sector are currently suffering from a major workforce crisis. The next generation is in short supply, a significant number of employees are on sick leave, and qualified personnel are leaving the network. It is therefore urgent that measures be put in place to revitalize the healthcare network, which has been severely impacted in recent years. This chapter highlights possible solutions aimed at attracting, retaining and developing the loyalty of the human resources at the heart of these organizations, because it is now urgent to take care of those who, on a daily basis, look after the health of the population.

References

1. Ministère de la Santé et des Services Sociaux (MSSS) du Québec. Plan pour mettre en œuvre les changements nécessaires en santé. Direction des communications du ministère de la Santé et des Services sociaux, Québec (2022) [Quebec Ministry of Health and Social Services (MSSS). Plan to Implement the Necessary Changes in Health Care. Communications Branch of the Ministry of Health and Social Services, Quebec (2022)]. https://publications.msss.gouv.qc.ca/msss/document003355/?&date=DESC#:~:text=Le%20Plan%20pour%20mettre%20en,prise%20en%20charge%20des%20patients. Last accessed 12 Aug 2023
2. Dubois, C.-A., Bentein, K., Marchand, A., Prud'homme, A., Borgès Da Silva, R., Fournier, M.: Les problèmes de santé physiques et mentale au travail dans le réseau de la santé : comprendre les causes et y remédier [Physical and Mental Health Issues at Work in the Health Network: Understanding the Causes and Addressing Them] (2022RP-114, CIRANO) (2022)
3. Randstad. Healthcare Job Trends That Will Change How You Hire. 10 janvier 2023. https://www.randstad.ca/employers/workplace-insights/job-market-in-canada/job-market-trends-in-healthcare/
4. Wu, Q., Zhao, L., Ye, X.C.: Shortage of healthcare professionals in China. BMJ **354** (2016)
5. Chaib, F., Reddy, S., Ellot, R., Driscoll, D.: WHO and Partners Call for Urgent Investment in Nurses. Organisation mondiale de la santé (2020). https://www.who.int/news/item/07-04-2020-who-and-partners-call-for-urgentinvestmentin-nurses
6. Møller, N., Berthelsen, C., Hølge-Hazelton, B.: Driving for the unique opportunity for work: a qualitative study of nurses' motivation to commute to work. J. Manag. Psychol. **37**(3), 279–293 (2022)
7. Carleton, N., Reichert, C., Stelnicki, A.: Nurses' Mental Health and Well-Being: COVID-19 Impacts. Can. J. Nurs. Res. **52**(3), 237–239 (2020)
8. Venne, J.-F.: Pénurie de main-d'œuvre : La catastrophe annoncée. Gestion (2022) [Labor Shortage: The Foretold Disaster. Gestion (2022)]. https://www.revuegestion.ca/penurie-de-main-douvre-la-catastrophe-annoncee. Last accessed 12 Aug 2023
9. St-Onge, S., Guerrero, S., Haines, V., Audet, M.: Relever les défis de la gestion des ressources humaines [Meeting the Challenges of Human Resource Management], 3rd ed. Chenelière Éducation Inc., Montréal (2009)
10. Institut de la Statistique du Québec. Résultats de l'Enquête sur la population active pour le Québec au mois de décembre 2022 (2022) [Quebec Institute of Statistics. Results of the Labour Force Survey for Quebec for December 2022 (2022)]. https://statistique.quebec.ca/fr/communique/resultats-enquete-population-active-quebec-decembre-2022
11. Statistique Canada. Recensement de la population de 2016 (2021) [Statistics Canada. 2016 Population Census (2021)]. https://www12.statcan.gc.ca/census-recensement/2016/dp-pd/index-fra.cfm
12. Pelletier, E., Dubois, D., Morin, D.: Comment attirer et fidéliser des employés [How to Attract and Retain Employees]. Les Éditions Transcontinental, Montréal (2022)
13. Bouchard, I.: How to Adapt to the Labour Shortage Situation: Hiring Difficulties Are Not Going Away. Business Development Bank of Canada (2023). https://www.bdc.ca/en/about/analysis-research/labour-shortage
14. Paillé, P.: La fidélisation des ressources humaines: Approches conceptuelles et recherches empiriques [Employee Retention: Conceptual Approaches and Empirical Research]. PUL, Québec (2011)

15. Somogyvari, G.: But Wait Before You Go…The Effect of Psychological Contract Breach on Employee Commitment Targets and Retention. Thèse de doctorat, Université Laval (2022)
16. Cascio, W.F., Graham, B.Z.: New strategic role for HR: leading the employer-branding process. Org. Manag. J. **13**(4), 182–192 (2016)
17. Lievens, F.: Employer branding in the Belgian Army: the importance of instrumental and symbolic beliefs for potential applicants, actual applicants, and military employees. Human Resour. Manag. **46**(1), 51–69 (2007)
18. Tumasjan, A., Kunze, F., Bruch, H., Welpw, I.S.: Linking employer branding orientation and firm performance: testing a dual mediation route of recruitment efficiency and positive affective climate. Hum. Resour. Manag. **59**(1), 83–99 (2020)
19. Saini, G.K., Rai, P., Chaudhary, M.K.: What do best employer surveys reveal about employer branding and intention to apply? J. Brand Manag. **21**(2), 95–111 (2014)
20. Alnıaçık, E., Alnıaçık, Ü.: Identifying dimensions of attractiveness in employer branding: effects of age, gender, and current employment status. Procedia Soc. Behav. Sci. **58**(8), 1336–1343 (2012)
21. Martin, G., Gollan, P.J., Grigg, K.: Is there a bigger and better future for employer branding? Facing up to innovation, corporate reputations and wicked problems in SHRM. Int. J. Human Resour. Manag. **22**(17), 3618–3637 (2011)
22. Saba, T., Dolan, S.L.: La gestion des ressources humaines : Pour des milieux de travail plus durables, humains et performants [Human Resource Management: Towards More Sustainable, Humane, and High-Performing Workplaces], 6th ed. Pearson, Montréal (2021)
23. Statistique Canada. Recensement de la population de 2016 (2021). [Statistics Canada. 2016 Population Census (2021).] https://www12.statcan.gc.ca/census-recensement/2016/dp-pd/index-fra.cfm
24. Byrne, D.E.: The Attraction Paradigm. Academic Press, New York (1971)
25. Tajfel, H., Turner, J.: The social identity theory of intergroup behavior. In: Worchel, D., Austin, W.G. (eds.) Psychology of Intergroup Relations, pp. 7–24. Nelson-Hall, Chicago (1986)
26. Ely, R.J., Thomas, D.A.: Cultural diversity at work: the effects of diversity perspectives on work group processes and outcomes. Adm. Sci. Q. **46**(2), 229–273 (2001)
27. Cachat-Rosset, G., Klarsfeld, A., Carillo, K.: Exploring the impact of diversity climate on individual work role performance: a novel approach. Eur. Manag. Rev. **19**(2), 248–262 (2022)
28. Saba, T., Chicha, M.-T., Dufour, M.-E., Cachat-Rosset, G., Balleste-ros Leiva, F.: L'équité, la diversité et l'inclusion dans la fonc-tion publique du Québec, Rapport de recherche, Centre d'expertise en gestion des ressources humaines, Secrétariat du Conseil du trésor, Gouvernement du Québec (2023) [Equity, Diversity, and Inclusion in the Quebec Public Service, Research Report, Center of Expertise in Human Resource Management, Secretariat of the Treasury Board, Government of Quebec (2023)]
29. Gouvernement du Québec, Institut de la statistique du Québec: Perspectives démographiques du Québec et des régions, 2016–2066 (2019) [Government of Quebec, Quebec Institute of Statistics: Demographic Projections for Quebec and Its Regions, 2016–2066 (2019)]
30. OECD: Aging and Employment Policies. OECD, Paris (2006)
31. Saba, T.: Promoting active aging: the canadian experience of bridge employment. In: Alcover, C.M., Topa Cantisano, G., Depolo, M., Fraccaroli, F., Parry, E. (eds.) Research Handbook in Bridge Employment, pp. 216–235. Routledge, London (2014)
32. Lessard, D.: Mises à la retraite massives: L'objectif de l'État a-t-il été atteint? [Mass Retirements: Has the Government's Objective Been Achieved?] (2010). http://www.lapresse.ca/actualites/dossiers/la-presse-est-a-vous/201010/23/01-4335428-mises-a-la-retraite-massives-lobjectif-de-letat-a-t-il-ete-atteint.php. Last accessed 20 Nov 2015
33. Dufour, M.-E.., Saba, T., Desborough, Z.: Retraite et retour au travail dans le secteur des services de santé : Rapport de recherche (2016)
34. Tremblay, D.-G.: Comment attirer et fidéliser la main-d'œuvre d'expérience : quelques propositions pour les employeurs. Rapport de recherche sur les pratiques des entreprises à l'endroit de la main-d'œuvre d'expérience. Rapport de recherche diffusé par la LCNA et l'Université TÉLUQ [How to Attract and Retain Experienced Workers: Some Proposals for Employers.

Research Report on Business Practices Regarding Experienced Workers. Research Report Published by the LCNA and TÉLUQ University]. Montréal (2022)

35. Tremblay, D.-G.: Attirer et retenir la main-d'œuvre expérimentée; la situation au Québec. Rapport de recherche sur les aspirations des travailleurs d'expérience et les pratiques des entreprises, Montréal : Comité consultatif 45+ et Université TÉLUQ (2022) [Attracting and Retaining Experienced Workers: The Situation in Quebec. Research Report on the Aspirations of Experienced Workers and Business Practices, Montreal: Advisory Committee 45+ and TÉLUQ University (2022)]
36. Moss, J.: Beyond Burned Out. Harvard Business Review (2021)
37. Man, S.S., Chan, A.H.S., Wong, H.M.: Risk-taking behaviors of Hong Kong construction workers—a thematic study. Saf. Sci. **98**, 25–36 (2017)
38. Sprigg, C.A., Stride, C.B., Wall, T.D., Holman, D.J., Smith, P.R.: Work characteristics, musculoskeletal disorders and the mediating role of the psychological strain: a study of call center employees. J. Appl. Psychol. **92**(5), 1456–1466 (2007)
39. Liu, H., Fan, J., Fu, Y., Liu, F.: Intrinsic motivation as a mediator of the relationship between organizational support and quantitative workload and work-related fatigue. Human Factors Ergon. Manuf. Serv. Ind. **28**(3), 154–162 (2018)
40. Rjbhandary, S., Basu, K.: Working conditions of nurses and absenteeism: is there a relationship? An empirical analysis using national survey of the work and health of nurses. Health Policy **97**(2–3), 152–159 (2010)
41. Karasek, Jr., R.A.: Job demands, job decision latitude, and mental strain: implications for job redesign. Admin. Sci. Q. 285–308 (1979)
42. Matthews, G., Wohleber, R.W., Lin, J.: Stress, skilled performance, and expertise: overload and beyond. In: Ward, P., Schraagen, J., Gore, J., Roth, E. (eds.) The Oxford Handbook of Expertise, pp. 490–527. Oxford University Press (2019)
43. Fournier, P.S., Montreuil, S., Villa, J.: Contribution à un modèle explicatif de la charge de travail : Le cas du service à la clientèle. Relations Industrielles/Industrial Relations [Contribution to an explanatory model of workload: the case of customer service. Relations Industrielles/ Ind. Relat.] **68**(1), 46–70 (2013)
44. Nielsen, K., Nielsen, M.B., Ogbonnaya, C., Känsälä, M., Saari, E., Isaksson, K.: Workplace resources to improve both employee well-being and performance: a systematic review and meta-analysis. Work Stress. **31**, 101–120 (2017)
45. Willis, S., Clarke, S., O'Connor, E.: Contextualizing leadership: transformational leadership and management-by-exception-active in safety-critical contexts. J. Occup. Organ. Psychol. **90**(3), 281–305 (2017)
46. Evans, S.: HRM and front line managers: the influence of role stress. Int. J. Human Resour. Manag. **28**(22), 3128–3148 (2017)
47. Campbell, M., Gavett, G.: What covid-19 has done to our well-being, in 12 charts. Harv. Bus. Rev. **10** (2021)
48. Morgan, J.: The Employee Experience Advantage: How to Win the War for Talent by Giving Employees the Workspaces They Want, the Tools They Need, and a Culture They Can Celebrate. Wiley (2017)
49. Plaskoff, J.: Employee experience: the new human resource management approach. Strateg. HR Rev. **16**, 136–141 (2017)
50. Dussault, J., St-Jacques, S.: Renforcer le leadership de proximité : synthèse des connaissances [Strengthening Frontline Leadership: Knowledge Summary]. UETMISSS, CIUSSS de la Capitale-Nationale (2019)
51. Chénard, C., Mantha-Bélisle, M.-M., Vézina, M.: Intervenir sur les risques psychosociaux du travail : leviers et stratégies de mobilisation [Addressing Psychosocial Risks at Work: Levers and Mobilization Strategies]. INSPQ (2018)
52. St-Hilaire, F., Gilbert, M.H., Lefebvre, R.: Managerial practices to reduce psychosocial risk exposure: a competency-based approach. Can. J. Admin. Sci./Revue Canadienne des Sciences de l'Administration **35**(4), 535–550 (2018)

53. Parent-Lamarche, A., Biron, C.: When bosses are burned out: psychological safety climate and its effect on managerial quality. Int. J. Stress. Manag. **29**(3), 219–228 (2022)
54. Broetje, S., Jenny, G.J., Bauer, G.F.: The key job demands and resources of nursing staff: an integrative review of reviews. Front. Psychol. **11**, 84 (2020)
55. Gill, C., Gardner, W., Claeys, J., Vangronsvelt, K.: Using theory on authentic leadership to build a strong human resource management system. Hum. Resour. Manag. Rev. **28**(3), 304–318 (2018)
56. Nielsen, M.B., Skogstad, A., Gjerstad, J., Einarsen, S.V.: Are transformational and laissez-faire leadership related to state anxiety among subordinates? A two-wave prospective study of forward and reverse associations. Work Stress. **33**(2), 137–155 (2019)
57. Dellve, L., Eriksson, A.: Health-promoting managerial work: a theoretical framework for a leadership program that supports knowledge and capability to craft sustainable work practices in daily practice and during organizational change. Societies **7**(2), 12 (2017)
58. Corbière, M., Mazaniello-Chézol, M., Bastien, M.F., Geoffrion, S., Briand, C., Lavoie-Tremblay, M., Tanguay, P.: Enjeux et solutions en santé mentale et travail: le point de vue des gestionnaires d'une grande organisation de santé. Santé mentale au Québec [Issues and solutions in mental health and work: the perspective of managers in a large health organization. Mental Health Quebec] **45**(1), 147–181 (2020)
59. Gilbert, M.H., Dextras-Gauthier, J., Fournier, P.S., Côté, A., Auclair, I., Knani, M.: Organizational constraints as root causes of role conflict: the situation of physician-managers and their responses. J. Health Organ. Manag. **33**(2), 204–220 (2019)

Healthcare Experiences of Elderly Patients and Managers' Reactions to Video Testimonies

Marie-Soleil Hardy, Laurie-Ann Bergeron-Drolet, Denise Corbeil, and Isabelle Côté

Abstract **Introduction**: The involvement of citizen/patient partners is increasingly essential in health care research and in the management of health organizations. Capturing the perspective of citizen/patient partners allows better targeting of their needs and expectations in research projects, in teaching health professionals, and in organizational or clinical decision-making in health and social services networks. However, the involvement of older people in reflections on care trajectories is a challenge given the different characteristics associated with aging (age, mobility, neurocognitive disorders, comorbidities, frailty, etc.). **Objective**: To expose the voices of elderly patients with respect to their care trajectories in the Quebec context and to elicit managers' reactions to their testimonies. **Methodology**: With the help of citizen partners, the coordinating team of a workshop presented at the Summer School in Health Services Management of the Faculty of Administrative Sciences (Université Laval, Québec, Canada) 2022, recruited nine elderly people who were living at home or in a residence for autonomous elderly to discuss their experiences in the health care system. Through semi-structured interviews, their testimonies were videotaped and presented to health care managers during a workshop. **Results**: The testimonies exposed issues and their appreciation of health and social services under the themes of the ability to meet their needs and expectations, coordination and care trajectory, home help services and potential improvements. **Discussion**: The testimonies of these elderly patients are particularly touching and informative. Although the data cannot be generalized, they can serve as an exploratory basis for reflection on improving health care and social services for the elderly population by ensuring that their needs are at the heart of our priorities.

M.-S. Hardy (✉)
Faculty of Nursing Sciences, Université Laval, Quebec City, Canada
e-mail: marie-soleil.hardy@fsi.ulaval.ca

L.-A. Bergeron-Drolet
Department of Social and Preventive Medicine, Université Laval, Quebec City, Canada

M.-S. Hardy · L.-A. Bergeron-Drolet · D. Corbeil · I. Côté
Vitam - Centre de recherche en santé durable, Quebec City, Canada

P. Landa et al. (eds.), *Operations Research and Artificial Intelligence in Healthcare Management*, Springer Proceedings in Mathematics & Statistics 506,
https://doi.org/10.1007/978-3-031-95659-1_13

Keywords Patient partner · Elderly · Care trajectory · Patient experience

1 Introduction

Understanding citizen/patients' experiences of care, both positive and negative, their perspectives on what worked well and what could be improved, is increasingly useful for health care and social services systems. Their voice helps to focus on their expectations and priority needs, which can provide useful solutions to persistent organizational problems.

The elderly are high users of health care and social services. People over the age of 65 account for approximately 45% of hospital days in Europe and America [1, 2, 3]. Also, this age group is growing faster than the allocated funds needed for care [4]. This clientele is associated with poor health outcomes in the short term (hospital morbidity, hospital-acquired infections, falls, and pressure sores) and longer term (increased likelihood of hospital readmission, reduced quality of life, and increased levels of dependency [5, 6]. In addition, fundamental care, commonly referred to as basic care, is very frequently neglected with this assistance-requiring clientele [7] especially when resources are low [8, 9].

Despite many recommendations for improving health care and social services for the elderly [4], outcomes do not get better over time. Thus, capturing the perspective of older citizen/patient partners allows us to better target their needs and expectations in their different care trajectories. A better understanding of their priority needs and expectations can lead to better planning and organization of care that can, in turn, lead to better outcomes for both the individuals and the health care system [10, 11]. However, involving the elderly in reflections on the organisation of the health care and social services is a challenge given the different characteristics associated with aging (age, mobility, neurocognitive disorders, comorbidities, frailty, etc.). Indeed, in addition to the physical and psychological effects of participating in focus groups and the necessary travel, ethical challenges often limit their representation in discussions on improving health care and social services. To enhance engagement, Bobard et al. [11] suggest creating a supportive environment as a strategy, such as meeting citizen/patient partners in their homes and fostering a positive atmosphere that promotes mutual respect and collaboration.

This manuscript aims to expose the voices of the elderly on their health care and social services trajectories in the province of Quebec and offers an overview of the reactions of managers involved in clinical and administrative decisions in health care institutions and social services.

2 Methodology

2.1 Context of the Workshop

In the context of the Summer School in Health Services Management of the Faculty of Administration of Laval University (Quebec, Canada), professors, master and doctoral students as well as citizen partners formed a team to organize an awareness workshop on the perspective of the elderly using the health care and social services in the region. This event brings together managers in the health and social services field from both the public and private sectors in Quebec and France. In order to hear the voice of elderly and to facilitate their participation, a citizen partner generously offered to meet them in their living environment.

2.2 Process and Strategies Used to Meet with Elderly

An interview guide was developed and validated by all team members (Appendix 1). Simple, concise questions, worded at a literacy level appropriate for the target population were developed on five themes: (1) Isolation of the elderly, (2) Relationships with health professionals, (3) Healthcare accessibility, (4) Advice for managers, (5) Artificial intelligence and technologies in healthcare. The team identified main questions for each theme and sub-questions to accommodate the volubility of the participants. To make the participants comfortable, a few random questions about their lives, well-being, or daily lives were asked before the interviews began. Participants were invited to express themselves freely. Their speech was never rushed by the interviewer. The interviewer only tried to reframe the conversation towards the predetermined themes while letting the participants develop their thoughts fully. The participants were extremely generous with their time and were able to receive good listening skills from the interviewer. The interviews were approximately 30 min in length to avoid causing physical or psychological fatigue in the participants. The interviews were filmed by a member of the research team in order to diffuse them at the workshop. An inductive approach was used to analyze the interviews [12]. Each interview was independently watched by two members of the team to identify key learnings. They then present all the samples to the research team to reach a consensus and validate the themes. Video samples were reorganized in inductive themes: (1) Ability to meet needs and expectations, (2) Coordination and trajectory of care services, (3) Suggested improvements.

The characteristics of the interviewer and her approach were very important in gathering meaningful data. The citizen partner who conducted the interviews is herself of a certain age, has lived through experiences of health and illness in the health and social services network and has also worked as a resource person for the elderly. This strategy of using a person who shares similar characteristics to the people we met is intended to be effective. Older people may fear, refuse or hold back their words if they are interviewed by a much younger person, researcher, health professional or manager. The interviewer must also have an attitude of openness to the other person, be gentle, welcoming, put herself at the same level as the older person and speak slowly. In addition, the participants recruited knew the citizen partner well since she regularly visited them to provide support with domestic tasks or emotional support. The interviewer therefore had a bond of trust with the participants, which facilitated the exchange and their participation.

Finally, it was easier to meet the elderly participants in their own environment. In addition to avoiding a trip, which can require a lot of effort for the elderly person and cause fatigue and physical effects, this strategy facilitates the expression of the persons feelings.

2.3 Characteristics of the Elderly Participants

Nine elderly people, living in their own homes or in retirement homes, agreed to participate in a semi-structured interview and to be filmed. The citizen partner was asked to recruit a heterogeneous sample of elderly to represent different needs and perspectives. The participants came from different socio-economic classes, lived in different living environments and had different health conditions. They all signed an information and consent form prior to their participation.

2.4 Characteristics of the Participant Managers at the Workshop

At the Summer School in Health Services Management of the Faculty of Administration, 43 managers participated in a day dedicated to the basic concepts and foundations of participation and integration of citizens/patient partners in organizational and decision-making committees in the health sector. These French-speaking managers came from various healthcare institutions in Quebec and France.

During the workshop, managers were invited to react and discuss after each video presented. Professor Hardy and two citizen partners facilitated the discussions. The next section presents a summary of each video, as well as the reactions of the participating managers and an overview of the discussions.

3 Results: Summary of Videos and Managers' Reactions

In the first video on the theme of "The capacity to respond to the needs and expectations of the elderly", seniors talked about their experiences in the health care and social services system. What they mainly reported was the lack of attention to their needs, especially their need to be listened to and accompanied both morally and physically. A strong desire for professionals to use a more holistic approach adapted to the elderly person and his or her personal situation was heard. According to them, this holistic approach could also contribute to alleviating the feeling of isolation experienced. Some of the comments also showed a dehumanization of care that translated into hygiene care schedules that are disrespectful of the patients' rhythm, and a rigidity in the supply and routine of home care.

Managers were touched by these interviews because they provide a window into details related to personal care experiences that lack personalization and person-centered care. Although the majority of health care facilities and social networks claim that humanistic values and person-centred care are embedded in their facility vision, managers too often find themselves removed from the actual experiences of the patients and families who use their services. They do not have a realistic idea of care, one that is marked by real experiences and emotions. This short video was an opportunity to get closer to the reality of the elderly and to see the importance of being interested in their needs in order to better understand, guide and care for them. Finally, some managers expressed their lack of solutions. Faced with the current challenges, the shortage of peoplepower and resources amplified by the pandemic, realistic solutions that can be put in place quickly are difficult to establish. Recognizing the need to do things differently, to revisit the vision of productivity so that time devoted to the patient is valued, must be prioritized.

The second video dealt with the theme of "Coordination and care trajectory". In the different situations presented, the elderly emphasized the confusion they felt when accessing health care and social services depending on their current condition. The fragmentation of care and the hyper specialization of medicine were often ill suited to the comprehensive management of comorbidities in the elderly. However, we also hear their recognition when they feel accompanied and listened to by health professionals. Difficulties in accessing health care and effective coordination of care trajectories are current problems that affect older populations in Canada as much as in Europe. Access to care and continuity of care are also a challenge. The elderly recounted experiencing uncertainty in the face of a new health episode. The number and complexity of different information received by a wide range of stakeholders made them very anxious. As proposed by one participant, they need a health professional they can trust to accompany them throughout their episode of care. Interventions adapted to the characteristics of their illnesses, aging and their priorities are desired.

The managers present noted the desire of the elderly to be better informed about what is being done in the various settings throughout their care trajectory. All agreed that it should not be up to the patient or their family members to find the "front door" to the system when they need to access care and services. In sum, participants recognized that valuing the voice of the older person could be a real catalyst for change to reverse current paradigms. Recognizing the intelligence and resilience of the elderly can certainly help managers find solutions to improve coordination and care pathways.

The third video showed different realities of home care services. We could hear different situations of the elderly still living in their homes and others who are in apartments. What stood out the most from the testimonies was the need for self-determination and independence. Indeed, they clearly stated their desire to remain as long as possible in their residence, which is in line with the objectives of maintaining frail elderly people in their homes. Some of them feared being separated if they moved to a nursing home because they do not always have the power to choose which department or which residence they can move to. Often, it depends on their healthcare needs. However, faced with their various needs for help and support, there is a lack of resources to meet them. Also, the steps to be taken to ensure that services are put in place are complex. Often, they have no choice but to consider moving.

The various managers present mentioned that services exist in the community, but that they are variable. In their opinion, what seems to be the most problematic is the lack of knowledge of homecare services available to the elderly. Coordination and getting the right care and services in place in a timely manner were also challenges. Better coordination and support to take the steps to choose and implement the right services at the right time could certainly allow the elderly to feel accompanied, reassured and avoid other problems. In addition, the characteristics of older people mean that changes related to their health and aging make it difficult for them to deal with the various community organizations and to manage the implementation of services on their own can be a source of anxiety for the older person. This can even limit the use of these services.

In the final video, the elderly interviewed suggested improvements they would like to see in the health care and social services system. The testimonies were full of hope which created a tangible sense of positivity and affirmation in the workshop with managers. Improvements in the coordination of care, the human and personalized approach of health professionals, listening, support, but above all, the wish to be treated as a whole person and not just as a disease was mentioned. Older people also stressed the need to break down silos and practices to facilitate access to care and make care trajectories more fluid. A common testimony was having multiple specialists to listen to and feeling lost and confused with all the recommendations.

The managers were amazed to hear the accuracy of the elderly patients comments and the analytical capacity that emanated from their suggestions. In short, this last vignette reinforced the need not only to be open to the perceptions of the elderly and to listen to them, but also to make them essential collaborators in the improvement of tomorrow's health care and social services.

4 Discussion

The testimonies of the elderly and the reactions of the managers are in line with the real problems of the care system and the current research.

Testimonies of the dehumanization of care and a partial response to their needs are consistent with current concerns in nursing. Fundamental care involves actions on the part of the nurse that respect and focus on a person's essential needs to ensure their physical and psychosocial wellbeing. These needs are met by developing a positive and trusting relationship with the person being cared for as well as their family/carers [13]. Feo and Kitson [14] noted that there are significant gaps in the provision of basic care for both physical and psychosocial needs, affecting the safety of older adults and leading to adverse health outcomes and poor care experiences.

In the same sense that the elderly and managers have mentioned, many authors have pointed out different problems related to the coordination and continuity of care. The fragmentation of care processes, unsuccessful transition of care, problems related to lack of information or communication breakdowns between caregivers are just a few examples documented in the literature and for which we know the negative impacts on the population [15–17]. Finally, the desire of the elderly to maintain their autonomy and to remain at home as long as possible characterizes this population. Many contemporary health care systems are aiming for a broader range of home care services in order to keep this clientele as independent as possible in their own homes. However, various issues in the provision of services remain current.

5 Conclusion

Giving voice to the elderly by inviting their testimonies about their health experiences and avenues for improvement can certainly provide answers and points of improvement that had not been considered previously by managers and organizations. Their suggestions were mostly simple and efficient. Their testimonies touched our values and practices. Particular attention must be paid to the testimonies of the elderly patient population to better meet their needs. In the face of an aging population and the growing health care and social service needs of this patient segment, visiting them and hearing their stories can certainly help to unlock innovative solutions to the problems that can no longer be sustained. In the fine details of these testimonies, there are inevitably concrete, humane and effective solutions that need to be heard.

Appendix 1

Questions—Health Care Needs and Services for Elderly

Isolation	Are there times when you feel alone or less involved when interacting with health care professionals?
	– What support services would you like to have during your care or during your daily life (support from a psychology professional…), If in a nursing home: Did you feel well accompanied and supported during your stay? – In your opinion, what are the strategies to break the isolation? – Do you think it would be good to implement changes to mitigate the effect of isolation during your care and promote better social ties (e.g., mobilize technology to facilitate maintaining contact with family members, avoid "opaque" rooms to have more open spaces where other patients could be visible, give patients the opportunity to converse with each other via loudspeakers or other technological tools for hygiene precautions, entertainment programs, etc.)
Relationships with health professionnals	Do you feel listened to by the professionals? Do you have any examples of situations?
	– Were you satisfied with the time between communicating a need and when it was met? – Do you feel important when you are in contact with health care professionals? – What do you think are some strategies and ways to break the isolation? – What tips would you suggest to make you feel more important in a situation with other professionals?
Health care access	What difficulties do you encounter in making an appointment or accessing a health care or services?
	– What was the longest wait time to access your care? And what service was it for? How would you have liked this situation to be handled? – Did you find it difficult to find the relevant information to know where to go for your care/ or understand the different options available to you? – In general, what improvements do you think could be made in public care for the elderly? – Do you feel valued in your appointment with a care professional or in your visit to a health care facility? – Have you been hospitalized? If so, were you offered a suitable service for your return home? How did you find this experience? How was your return home after your hospitalization? (e.g. did you get the help you needed at the right time?) – What would you suggest to improve your stay here? – Were you able to communicate your needs freely during your stay?

(continued)

(continued)

Advice	Today you are being recorded to present this vignette to managers, so what would be the advice/tips you would like to pass on to them so that they can meet your needs and those of the elderly in general?
AI and technologies	(Optional) How do you feel about using technology to access care?
	– Are you comfortable with the collection of personal data to improve health services through artificial intelligence techniques? Do you think it infringes on your privacy? – Would you be comfortable with the use of technologies such as Artificial Intelligence to improve the quality of your stay (e.g. early detection of ailments, intelligent analysis of symptoms, etc.)

References

1. Imison, C., Poteliakhoff, E., Thompson, J.: Older people and emergency bed use: exploring variation (2012). https://www.kingsfund.org.uk/sites/default/files/field/field_publication_file/older-people-and-emergency-bed-use-aug-2012.pdf
2. The Health Foundation. Emergency hospital admissions in England. Which may be avoidable and how? (2018). https://www.health.org.uk/publications/emergency-hospital-admissions-in-england-which-may-be-avoidable-and-how
3. Ministère de la Santé et des Services sociaux du Québec. Approche adaptée à la personne âgée en milieu hospitalier: Cadre de référence (Publication no 10-830-03W) (2011). https://publications.msss.gouv.qc.ca/msss/fichiers/2010/10-830-03.pdf
4. Nguyen, Q.D., Goulden, R., Zhang, S.: Rapport épidémiologique en soutien aux travaux de la Commissaire à la santé et au bien-être du Québec sur l'évaluation de la performance des soins et des services dans les milieux de vie pour ainés lors de la première vague de la COVID-19 [Enligne]. [Epidemiological Report Supporting the Work of the Commissioner of Health and Well-being of Quebec on the Evaluation of the Performance of Care and Services in Living Environments for Seniors during the First Wave of COVID-19 [Online]]Québec: Québec BeAnd; Janvier 2022 2021. https://www.csbe.gouv.qc.ca/fileadmin/www/2021/Rapportpr%C3%A9liminaire_Mandat/CSBE-Rapport_pr%C3%A9liminaire_MandatSp%C3%A9cial.pdf. Last accessed 29 Mar 2022.
5. Cunha, A.I.L., Veronese, N., de Melo Borges, S., Ricci, N.A.: Frailty as a predictor of adverse outcomes in hospitalized older adults: a systematic review and meta-analysis. Ageing Res. Rev. **56**, 100960 (2019). https://doi.org/10.1016/j.arr.2019.100960
6. Keeble, E., Roberts, H.C., Williams, C.D., Van Oppen, J., Conroy, S.P.: Outcomes of hospital admissions among frail older people: a 2-year cohort study. Br. J. Gen. Pract. **69**(685), e555–e560 (2019). https://doi.org/10.3399/bjgp19X704621
7. Bagnasco, A., Dasso, N., Rossi, S., Galanti, C., Varone, G., Catania, G., Zanini, M., Aleo, G., Watson, R., Hayter, M., Sasso, L.: Unmet nursing care needs on medical and surgical wards: a scoping review of patients' perspectives. J. Clin. Nurs. **29**(3–4), 347–369 (2019). https://doi.org/10.1111/jocn.15089
8. Aiken, L.H., Sloane, D.M., Bruyneel, L., Van den Heede, K., Griffiths, P., Busse, R., Diomidous, M., Kinnunen, J., Kozka, M., Lesaffre, E., McHugh, M.D., Moreno-Casbas, M.T., Rafferty, A.M., Schwendimann, R., Scott, P.A., Tishelman, C., van Achterberg, T., Sermeus, W.: For the RN4CAST consortium, RN4CAST Consortium and RN4CAST consortium. Nurse staffing and education and hospital mortality in nine European countries: a retrospective observational

study. The Lancet (British edition), **383**(9931), 1824–1830 (2014). https://doi.org/10.1016/S0140-6736(13)62631-8
9. Blackman, I., Henderson, J., Weger, K., Willis, E.: Causal links associated with missed residential aged care. J. Nurs. Manag. **28**, 1909–1917 (2020). https://doi.org/10.1111/jonm.12889
10. Bokhour, B.G., Fix, G.M., Mueller, N.M., Barker, A.M., Lavela, S.L., Hill, J.N., Solomon, J.L., Lukas, C.V.: How can healthcare organizations implement patient-centered care? Examining a large-scale cultural transformation. BMC Health Serv. Res. **18**(1), 168 (2018). https://doi.org/10.1186/s12913-018-2949-5
11. Bombard, Y., Baker, G.R., Orlando, E., Fancott, C., Bhatia, P., Casalino, S., Onate, K., Denis, J.L., Pomey, M.P.: Engaging patients to improve quality of care: a systematic review. Implement. Sci.: IS **13**(1), 98 (2018). https://doi.org/10.1186/s13012-018-0784-z
12. Williams, M., Moser, T.:. The art of coding and thematic exploration in qualitative research. Int. Manag. Rev. **15**(1), 45–55,71–72 (2019). https://acces.bibl.ulaval.ca/login?. https://www.proquest.com/scholarly-journals/art-coding-thematic-exploration-qualitative/docview/2210886420/se-2
13. Feo, R., Rasmussen, P., Wiechula, R., Conroy, T., Kitson, A.: Developing effective and caring nurse-patient relationships. Nurs. Stand. **31**(28), 54–63 (2017). https://doi.org/10.7748/ns.2017.e10735
14. Feo, R., Kitson, A.: Promoting patient-centred fundamental care in acute healthcare systems. Int. J. Nurs. Stud. **57**, 1–11 (2016). https://doi.org/10.1016/j.ijnurstu.2016.01.006
15. Dyer, S.M., Suen, J., Williams, H., Inacio, M.C., Harvey, G., Roder, D., Wesselingh, S., Kellie, A., Crotty, M., Caughey, G.E.: Impact of relational continuity of primary care in aged care: a systematic review. BMC Geriatr. **22**(1), 579 (2022). https://doi.org/10.1186/s12877-022-03131-2
16. Groenvynck, L., Fakha, A., de Boer, B., Hamers, J.P.H., van Achterberg, T., van Rossum, E., Verbeek, H.: Interventions to improve the transition from home to a nursing home: a scoping review. Gerontologist **62**(7), e369–e383 (2022). https://doi.org/10.1093/geront/gnab036
17. Morkisch, N., Upegui-Arango, L.D., Cardona, M.I., van den Heuvel, D., Rimmele, M., Sieber, C.C., Freiberger, E.: Components of the transitional care model (TCM) to reduce readmission in geriatric patients: a systematic review. BMC Geriatr. **20**(1), 345 (2020). https://doi.org/10.1186/s12877-020-01747-w

Contributions of Value Management and Colour Abacuses for Improving the Daily Lives of Patients and Their Caregivers

Auguste Rakotondranaivo and Jean-Pierre Grandhaye

Abstract The regional project proposed by the French Red Cross aims to improve the daily lives of cancer patients and of their caregivers. The first statistical part, based on an in-depth survey via questionnaire among 515 patients and 468 caregivers, was used as a springboard for our additional study. It deals with the same subject using the Value Management approach. The functional analysis, a key element of this approach, examined patients, their caregivers and the various stakeholders that we involved through two focus groups. Five meetings were held to identify and confirm information from the focus group discussions. These meetings were facilitated using an approach that we will present, and which was used to build the necessary consensus to develop suitable solutions within this complex context. The findings highlight the challenges faced in daily life, particularly the need for information, psychological support, and coordination among the involved stakeholders. Consensus was reached on initiatives such as the creation of a "caregiver's guide" and improving collaboration between healthcare professionals and community organizations. This approach, combining quantitative and qualitative methods, offers promising avenues to enhance the support provided to individuals with chronic illnesses in other contexts.

Keywords Colour abacuses · Functional analysis · Value management · Daily life

---

A. Rakotondranaivo (✉)
Université de Lorraine ERPI, 54000 Nancy, France
e-mail: auguste.rakotondranaivo@univ-lorraine.fr

J.-P. Grandhaye
AFAV Lorraine, Nancy, France
e-mail: grandhaye-ent@vafop.eu

P. Landa et al. (eds.), *Operations Research and Artificial Intelligence in Healthcare Management*, Springer Proceedings in Mathematics & Statistics 506,
https://doi.org/10.1007/978-3-031-95659-1_14

Table 1 Elements of the statistical survey on patients and caregivers

	Patients—n = 515	Caregivers—n = 468
Men/Women	40%/60%	47%/53%
Average age	63 years old (21 to 91)	59 years old (19 to 90)
Urban habitat	50%	47%
Family situation (couple)	73%	83%
Level of education	67% completed high school	67% completed high school

1 Introduction

1.1 Statistical Study Prior to the Project

The study of the daily lives of cancer patients and of their caregivers is part of the healthcare field, with all the complexity of its context, the parties involved and the many challenges [1]. Our work is proposed by department no. 54 of the French Red Cross and supplements a vast survey conducted among 515 cancer patients and 468 caregivers. Two specific questionnaires of 10 and 11 pages respectively, with a total of around 200 questions, were administered. These questionnaires were developed, administered and handled by clinical medicine experts and evaluators (Table 1).

In the short term, the goal is to identify the difficulties and needs experienced on a daily basis by cancer patients at their initial onboarding, when they relapse or when the disease progresses, as well as during the post-therapy follow-up phase, until two years after the initial diagnosis or diagnosis of relapse.

In the medium term, it's a question of implementing improvement actions based on data collected, emphasising training, coordination and strengthening connections between existing support systems.

1.2 Value Approach to the Daily Lives of Patients and Their Caregivers

Our contribution involves interpreting the first statistical results, interviewing stakeholders and developing scenarios for value creation by offering concrete solutions. The various actions will be carried out over a short period of three months.

It is a rich topic and our contribution may prove relevant. However, the fact that an in-depth statistical survey in the field is ending at the same time is tricky to manage, so we have identified three pre-requisites.

1. Having strategic, tactical and operational contacts suited to the subject, in particular health professionals from the Nancy CHU (university hospital) and from the regional oncology network ONCOLOR. They will be contacted along with the caregiver associations and institutional partners from the city.

2. Encouraging interaction between the project customers, patients, their caregivers or representatives, and stakeholders such as health professionals, associations and city services. This interaction will be achieved through two focus groups.
3. Approaching the subject from a functional standpoint, i.e. thinking about function before seeking solutions. The Functional Analysis used within the meaning of the standard is known by a few participants.

2 Tools and Methods Proposed

2.1 Focus Groups

The focus groups are platforms for communication aiming to qualitatively collect subjective information such as opinions, motivations, images or representations relating to a project for the development or improvement of a system (product, process, organisation, etc.). Sometimes referred to as consumer meetings, focus groups have participants who share their ideas, openly or secretly, and talk about representations currently in development.

To represent and then characterise the complexity of the context of the topic to be addressed with its target, two focus groups were created. The participants of focus group 1 are institutional representatives from the city, the ARS (regional health agency), the oncology network ONCOLOR, with a total of 10 participants. Focus group 2 features users, patient associations and health professionals, with a total of 9 participants. We organised two meetings of around two hours per group, as well as a plenary session to identify common proposals.

How the Focus Groups Work

Before the first meeting the participants all received the patient questionnaire and the caregiver questionnaire. The focus group meetings began with a reminder of the objectives and of the information from the first statistical analyses.

Organisation of Focus Groups

After a review of the objectives and the schedule, we presented some information from an initial sorting of the returned questionnaires. Figure 1 illustrates the organization of the focus groups, detailing the key steps and main discussions.

Meeting 1: Quick, targeted review of the questionnaires and of the initial results, functional proposals and discussion on the goals and action plans to understand the rationale.

Meeting 2: Review of the action plans related to the questionnaires, proposed terms of action with the resources considered.

Meeting 3: Summary of goals, rationale, action plans, resources, proposed ranking with rationale and consistent methods.

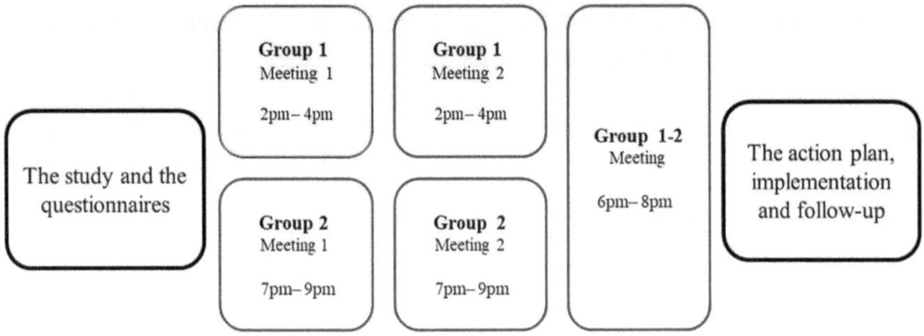

Fig. 1 Organisation of focus group meetings

Well thought out feedback on discussions during each meeting was established with items for the coloured abacuses. The questionnaire results served as a report and a springboard for discussion at the next meeting.

2.2 Functional Approach to the Project

This approach comes from the Value Analysis approach standardised [2, 3] at the European level and used in industrial companies and in organisations mainly in the health and social sector. Figure 2 illustrates the approach to functional analysis.

In the overall value management approach, we will specifically use the functional analysis with the external environments and the functional tree [4, 5]. The colour abacuses will supplement the consensus in the focus groups.

2.3 Colour Abacuses: A Method for Empowering Focus Groups

Colour voting provides a shared language using colour-coding (Fig. 3) to organise group work or work in a network of participants [6, 7]. An app facilitates use since it lets you interview participants, collect results and analyse them [8].

This method uses items that are brief statements on which participants “announce their colour”. This produces a raw data matrix.

Instead of simple vote collection, this method is an instrument for dialogue and clarification of positions. We can address points of consensus and disagreement that become visible, to release collective intelligence. The matSrix of items (Fig. 2) classifies items according to their degree of consensus, whether they are favourable or unfavourable [9].

It was agreed to carry out well thought out feedback on the discussions that took place in each meeting. The colour abacus method will use items or proposals from the

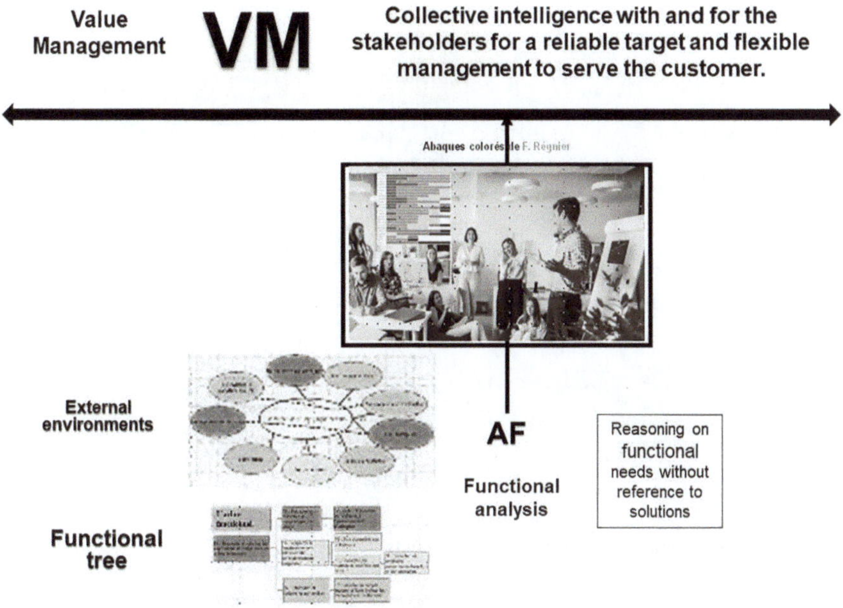

Fig. 2 Structure of the VM methodological tools proposed

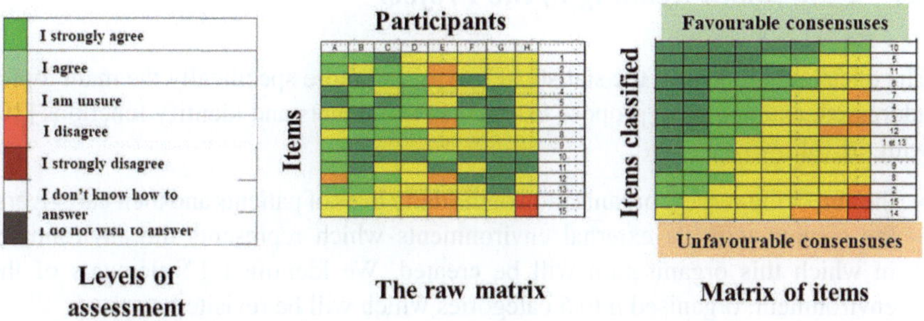

Fig. 3 Colour abacuses: levels of assessment, raw matrix and item matrix

discussions between participants during the meeting. The feedback with the colour abacuses will serve as a springboard for the next meeting.

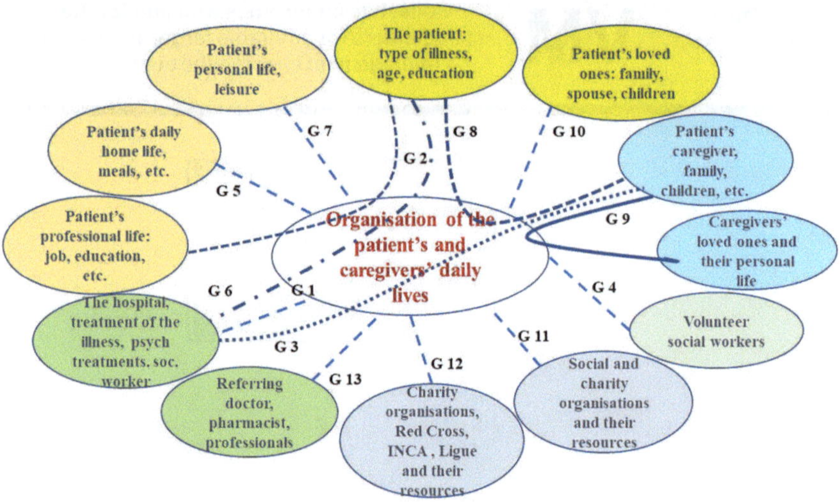

Fig. 4 Functional analysis of external environments

3 Implementation of the Project and Results

3.1 Functional Reading of the Project

The questionnaires from the statistical survey and more specifically the main topics addressed, enabled us to propose external environments and identify functions [10] with the following:

- the aim of the survey: organisation of the daily lives of patients and their caregivers.
- the context with its external environments which represents the environment in which this organisation will be created. We identified 12 elements of the environment, organised into 5 categories which will be revisited.
- 13 functioning or function objectives (Fig. 4).

These various functional objectives are then structured into a functional tree (Fig. 5) which gives an idea of the possible functioning [11].

3.2 Focus Group: Organisation of Meetings and Results

In this part we will present the organisation of discussions during meetings and the results of the colour abacus questionnaires.

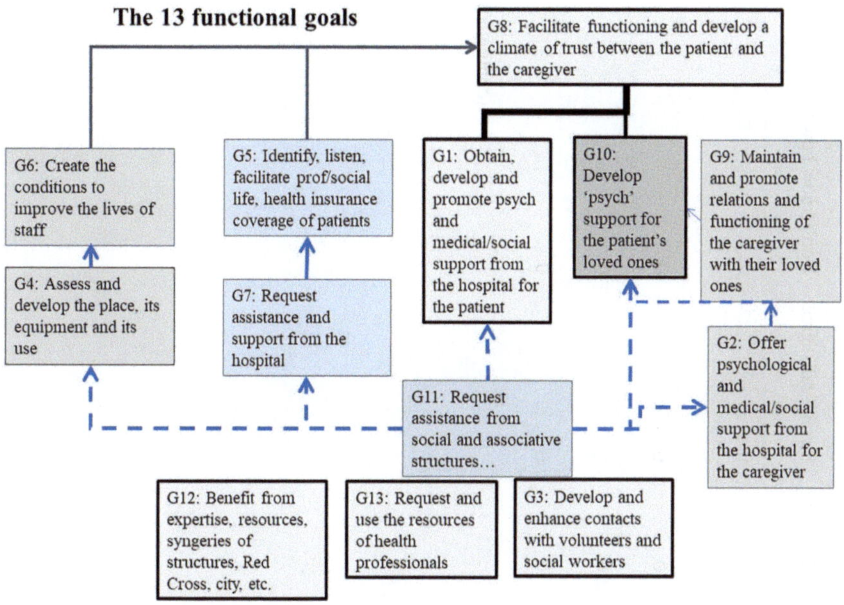

Fig. 5 A functional reading of the daily lives of patients and their caregivers

Discussions During Meeting 1 of Group 1

After focusing the debate on the patient and the caregiver, emphasising daily life rather than the illness, the group addressed the following points:

- the notion of emergency situations, not just in medial terms.
- the options for support for the caregiver, in particular listening to the patient.
- an increasing desire for contact with others, the principle of "helpful neighbour".

These discussions led us to draft a list of 15 items for participants. These items constituted the content of the colour abacus questionnaire.

The feedback from questionnaires administered between meetings 1 and 2 served as a report on the points addressed in meeting 1, and above all as a guide to identify the key points, whether they are the subject of consensus or disagreement [12]. The table below shows an extract of the classification of 15 items in decreasing order of consensus (Table 2).

Discussions During Meeting 1 of Group 2

We addressed the caregiver, their role and their tasks. The caregiver must assist with material, social and medical needs concerning the patient, despite their own constraints and limits. We also addressed the role of health professionals, particularly dispensary pharmacists, in terms of listening to patients concerning their daily lives and relations between the patient and their caregiver(s).

Table 2 Extract from the classification of items proposed to group 1

Classification of items proposed in group 1 after meeting 1	Strongly agree	Some-what agree	Not sure	Disagree	Strongly disagree	Don't know how to respond
8. It is important to organize a real professional and clear network around the Caregiver	7	2	1	0	0	0
3. The Patient's return home is an event requiring support	6	3	1	0	0	0
6. The minimum expertise for a volunteer caregiver must be identified	6	3	1	0	0	0
2. The proposals of the Focus Group will involve the Patient's daily life at home	5	5	0	0	0	0

(continued)

Table 2 (continued)

Classification of items proposed in group 1 after meeting 1	Strongly agree	Some-what agree	Not sure	Disagree	Strongly disagree	Don't know how to respond
14. The referring doctor is a major resource for managing 'alerts' from the Patient	5	4	1	0	0	0
12. Many resources exist, what's lacking is a suitable network adapted to each situation	4	4	0	1	1	0

We also addressed the role of health professionals, particularly dispensary pharmacists, in terms of listening to patients concerning their daily lives and relations between the patient and their caregiver(s).

The colour abacuses between meetings 1 and 2 served as a report, and above all a guide to identifying the key points, whether they are the subject of consensus or disagreement (Table 3).

Discussions During Meeting 2 of Group 1

Coaching, as a contact or support person, could be an essential resource as part of a support structure for caregivers, aiming to meet needs expressed or alert situations connected to the patient's care. Supervision of volunteers and training of caregivers in medical issues do not present any specific difficulties. It is essential to take into account the uniqueness and thus the specificity of requests, whether they concern material, psychological support or both.

Discussions During Meeting 2 of Group 2

Group 2 discussed how the caregiver operates and specifically their worries. Therefore it would seem useful to offer a "guide" to the caregiver, allowing them to plan ahead and to take a step back in certain tricky or complex situations. This would be a new profession for the person acting as this "guide", and a psychological aspect would be needed for listening and understanding. The person should have a practical and pragmatic attitude to respond simply and effectively to questions identified.

The patient is generally assumed to be well-informed about their illness and their medical treatment. For problems concerning daily life, the existing proposals do not address the patient's specific situation or the many problems faced when they leave hospital. Non-hospital health professionals such as doctors, pharmacists and nurses are valuable resources for facilitating the daily lives of patients and detecting moments of fragility.

Discussions During Meeting 3 of All Groups

This third focus group meeting involved all participants from focus group 1 and 2 and aimed to map out consensual solutions and implement them.

The work of meeting 2 of groups 1 and 2 showed a certain convergence of proposals. 13 items were identified and then submitted for the participant's assessment. The abbreviated form of the item will be used for reading the detailed analysis (Table 4).

The items proposed add to or converge with the topics discussed in meeting 2. Certain points were clarified or supplemented:

- Concerning the vocabulary, terms such as social workers, referring caregiver, support workers, best practices and coordination of support workers, were explained.
- The tricky issue of information and training was addressed.

Table 3 Extract from the classification of items proposed to group 2

Classification of items group 2 meeting 1	Strongly agree	Some-what agree	Not sure	Disagree	Strongly disagree	Don't know how to respond
1. When facilitating the Focus Group, the Patient must be the focus of our discussions	5	4	0	0	0	0
11. The Caregiver must be supported so that they can identify and ask the right questions	5	3	1	0	0	0
8. It is important to involve all resources: paid providers, associations, volunteers, etc	4	3	2	0	0	0
12. Many resources exist, what's lacking is a suitable network adapted to each situation	3	5	1	0	0	0
13. The referring doctor is a major resource for managing 'alerts' from the Patient	3	2	4	0	0	0
3. The specific nature of Patients' cases may mean we don't find general solutions	3	2	2	2	0	0
15. Implementation of the recommendations could have human or financial limits	2	6	1	0	0	0

Table 4 Abbreviated form of 13 items for meeting 3

1—Patient info	The patient is informed on the information and medical decisions concerning them
2—PV have knowledge	The patient has all the information to decide by themselves on the referring doctor's intervention
3—TS have knowledge	Health professionals have a good overview of the patient daily live
4—PV have resources	Health professionals can operate effectively within the patient daily live
5—TS have resources	There are many useful existing solutions to answer patient' questions
6—Tools exist	The are many useful existing solution, we need to find the right one
7—Access tools	The current status of solutions leaves some gaps where suitable proposals must be made
8—Coord needed	There are many useful existing solutions to answer caregivers' questions on their assignments
9—Coord and AR	There are already many supports, we need to work on their appeal, quality and accessibility
10 – AA Training	Depending of the type of problem experienced by the patient, several caregivers many intervene in a coordinated manner
11—AA support	Accessible 'referring Caregivers' should be considered in order to capitalise
12—Network meth	The 'Referring 'Caregivers' must have specific skills and/or training
13—Evaluation	Developments (technological, societal) must be taken into account

- The role of non-hospital medical professionals, particularly as regards the information that they may provide and the possibilities of being involved in the daily lives of patients and caregivers, was clarified.

We administered a questionnaire using colour abacuses, and 17 people responded:

- 12 health professionals (dispensary pharmacists, hospital pharmacists, doctors, executives, nurses), 2 institutional participants (ARS and city), 3 representatives (neighbourhood life, social worker, paramedic).
- The respondents used the range of choices of colour abacuses: from strongly agree to don't know how to respond.

The tables below give an overview of the data processing.

This matrix gives an overview of a strong consensus on 13 items, 1 participant is very much opposed to the proposals (5 out of 13), and 2 others do not wish to respond (3 and 5 proposals out of 13). Lastly, the matrix of items gives a classification of the items according to consensus in terms of acceptance of the item independently of the participant (Figs. 6 and 7).

It is this last matrix that served as a guide for facilitating the discussions during meeting 3 of the focus group.

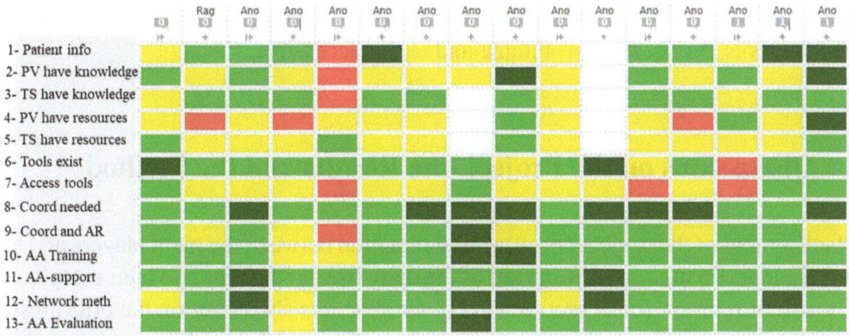

Fig. 6 Matrix of the most consensual items

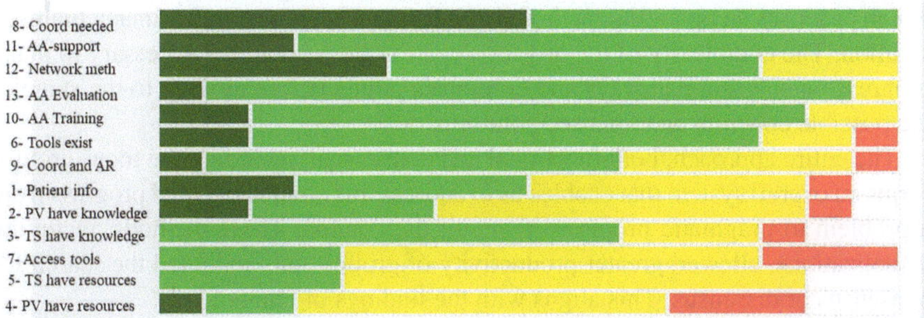

Fig. 7 Matrix of items meeting 3

The 3 items numbered 8, 11 and 12 garnered strong consensus. They deal with support workers, a term that needs clarification. Even though the term was clarified with the questionnaire "support workers are volunteers and as such different from paid caregivers", it remains too vague for the participants in meeting 3.

The items numbered 1, 6 and 9 enable us to work more in-depth on the notions of referring caregiver and information. Patients are often well-informed, but there may be exceptions, since some patients may refuse to hear information about medical decisions. The referring caregiver, also known as resource caregiver, should have documentary resources and connections with associations. It is important to establish what could be called the "Basic kit" to provide the right information at the right time and to the right person (whether this is the patient, the caregiver or the support persons). This role of resource referring caregiver may be filled by a local individual, such as a person at the level of the city or the municipality, acting as a go-between in a specific geographic area. Their profile could be similar to that of a social worker.

The items led us to address the role of non-hospital medical professionals that have interesting and relevant information about the daily lives of patients and their caregivers (item 2), but have few resources to act (item 4). This observation is similar for social workers (item 3 and 5). The responses to item 7 confirm the observation that the tools are not always suitable and easily accessible.

4 Discussions on the Project, the Results and the Method

Management of the project encouraged interaction between the main players and the stakeholders on the complex subject of the daily lives of patients and their caregivers. The use of relevant focus groups and colour abacuses shed light on the priorities of each focus group, then offered consensus for action at the final meeting.

The consensus points achieved at the plenary meeting united the parties involved in finding appropriate solution pathways.

These solution pathways are a logical continuation of the functional approach, which proposes an operating method in the form of functions, rather than a finalised solution. The complexity of the project's context shows that it is necessary to make progress on solution pathways and consensus points before moving to the stage of the possible concrete and finalised solutions.

The entire approach, both functional and consensual, including the focus groups, forms an overall system that enables us to address this complexity, and progress from a problem to pragmatic proposals that suit the context. These methods, including visualizations, allowed greater productivity of groups and facilitated the search for consensus or dissensus. This aligns with the findings of Dimara [13].

The solutions are not limited to isolated recommendations but provide a coherent framework to address the complexity of patients' and caregivers' needs. For example, creating a dedicated guide for caregivers and establishing a local support network were identified as consensus priorities.

The complexity of the context was also addressed through a comprehensive statistical analysis. This analysis consolidated the progress made during focus groups by providing robust quantitative data on the needs and priorities of patients and caregivers. The statistics enriched the understanding of critical pain points and validated the proposed solutions. This underscores the importance of a complementary approach combining both quantitative and qualitative analyses.

Finally, the integration of stakeholders into the functional and consensus-driven process transformed an initially complex issue into pragmatic proposals tailored to the local context.

5 Conclusion

Our work offers an innovative approach to improving the quality of life of cancer patients and their caregivers. Combining a methodology based on value management, focus groups featuring stakeholders and the use of colour abacuses, we were able to address the complexity of daily life in a comprehensive way. The results obtained helped us identify consensus points and put forward appropriate ideas for action. These solution pathways, coming from the participants themselves, offer a concrete perspective for meeting the specific needs of patients and their caregivers. This approach, combining quantitative and qualitative methods, offers promising avenues to enhance the support provided to individuals with chronic illnesses in other contexts [14].

References

1. Chow, R., Mathews, J.J., Cheng, E.Y., Lo, S., Wong, J., Alam, S., Hannon, B., Rodin, G., Nissim, R., Hales, S., Kavalieratos, D., Quinn, K.L., Tomlinson, G., Zimmermann, C.: Interventions to improve outcomes for caregivers of patients with advanced cancer: a meta-analysis. J. Natl. Cancer Inst. **115**(8), 896–908 (2023). https://doi.org/10.1093/jnci/djad075
2. AFNOR.: Value management, EN 12973:2020 (2020)
3. AFNOR.: Value management. Function analysis: basic charateristics, requirements and guidance for implementation, EN 17952:2024 (2024)
4. Thiry, M.: Combining value and project management into an effective programme management model. Int. J. Project Manag. **20**(3), 221–227 (2002)
5. Thiry, M.: Value management practice. Project Management Institute: Newton Square Pennsylvania, ISBN9781880410141, p.112 (2009)
6. Godet, M.: Scenarios and strategic management, Butterworth, Ed. Economica (1987)
7. Godet, M.: L'Abaque de Régnier, de l'Anticipation à l'Action, Manuel de Prospective et de Stratégie [Régnier's Abacus, from Anticipation to Action, Manual of Foresight and Strategy], pp. 158–161. Dunod, Paris (1991)
8. Linstone, H.A., Turrof, M.: The Delphi method, techniques and applications. Addison wesley publishing, Reading (1975)
9. Riemens, J., Lemieux, A., Lamouri, S., Garnier, L.: A Delphi-Régnier study addressing the challenges of textile recycling in Europe for the fashion and apparel industry. Sustainability **3**(21), 1–30 (2021). https://doi.org/10.3390/su132111700
10. Grandhaye J.P., Husson J.: Value analysis and security process in a Bank (2022). https://valuef oreurope.com. Last accessed 17 Sept 2022
11. Martinsuo, M., Killen, C.P.: Value management in project portfolios: identifying and assessing strategic value. Manag. J. **45**(5), 56–70 (2014). https://doi.org/10.1002/pmj.21452
12. Rocha M., Oliveira E., Guimaraes, I.: Stakeholders perception of recruitment criteria: a Régnier's abacus approach of market valued skills. Universidade Católica Portuguesa (Porto) in its series Management Working Papers de Gestão (2010)
13. Dimara, D., Stasko, J.: A critical reflection on visualization research: where do decision making tasks hide? IEEE Trans. Visual Comput. Graphics **28**(1), 1128–1138 (2022). https://doi.org/10.1109/TVCG.2021.3114813
14. Tierney, N.W.: Value management in healthcare how to establish a value management office to support value-based outcomes in healthcare. 2nd Ed, p. 336. https://doi.org/10.4324/978100 3493556

Collective Analysis of Work to Increase the Amount of Time Spent with Patients. A Case Study Looking at the Value of Activities Using the Lean Approach

Noura Zaghmouri and Julien Husson

Abstract For several years now, healthcare professionals have expressed their frustration at the increasing number of administrative and logistical tasks that take them away from patients' bedsides, where their work is most meaningful. In March 2022, the French Senate published a report on the state of hospitals and the healthcare system in France. Faced with a "never-ending crisis" (Speech by Emmanuel Macron, presentation of the National Health Plan, 6 January 2023.) and a feeling of loss of purpose widely expressed by healthcare professionals, "we need to put patient care back at the heart of the hospital professions, which are too far removed from it because they do not have enough time to devote to it" (Commission of Inquiry Report No. 587 (2021–2022), Volume I, published on 29 March 2022.). Lean, a method of reorganising processes that focuses on customer-perceived value, would appear to be a promising solution to the situation described above. Based on the following research question: "How can collective analysis of work during lean healthcare implementation contribute to increase the amount of time spent with patients?", we will explore ways of analysing the activities carried out by healthcare professionals in order to increase the amount of time devoted to care. Our research is based in the geriatric ward of a hospital group. For a number of years, this ward has faced major organisational difficulties that have led to occupational burnout. The results show the potential for refocusing healthcare activities and limiting non-value added tasks, based on an analysis of the tasks performed by professionals in the field.

Keywords Hospital · Work analysis · Value of care · Lean healthcare

---

N. Zaghmouri (✉)
Reims Champagne-Ardenne University, Reims, France
e-mail: noura.zaghmouri@univ-reims.fr

J. Husson
Lorraine University, Nancy, France

P. Landa et al. (eds.), *Operations Research and Artificial Intelligence in Healthcare Management*, Springer Proceedings in Mathematics & Statistics 506,
https://doi.org/10.1007/978-3-031-95659-1_15

1 Lean Healthcare, a Work Analysis Focusing on the Added Value of Tasks

1.1 Lean Management

The term Lean was first introduced in 1988 by Krafcik, a researcher at the Massachusetts Institute of Technology (MIT), to define the method associated with the success of the Japanese production system Toyota Product System (TPS), which was developed within the Toyota industry in the 1950s [1]. The TPS aims to eliminate various types of waste throughout the value stream, based on one of its key principles, Just-in-Time [2]. Taïchi Ohno, the founder of TPS, identified three components of waste: Muda (non-value added tasks), Mura (variability) and Muri (excesses, overburdening professionals) [2, 3]. Furthermore, according to the TPS principles, workflows must be analysed collectively by professionals in the field, by introducing a managerial philosophy that promotes the development of skills [4].

Lean was formalised by transposing the TPS management philosophy. The approach is based on practices and tools taken from the TPS, but also on quality management theories [2, 5]. While the original concept of Lean was an anti-Taylorism revolution [6] that challenged notions of control within organisations, today's Lean has moved away from its original principles by reverting to a form of neo-Taylorism to become productive Lean aimed at reducing costs [6]. As a result, Lean could be seen as a cost-cutting method, associated with work intensification and with an impact on psycho-social risks [7]. This evolution of Lean has led to a variety of applications of the approach and divergences within the Lean community [8–10].

For the purposes of this study, we consider the Lean approach according to its original principles, which lead to a socio-technical vision of work [8], and approach it as an organisational model built around an organisational culture that supports learning, managerial principles that encourage the commitment of professionals, and methods that aim to organise activities around the value perceived by the customer (customer-perceived value) [3, 11].

1.2 Lean Healthcare, a Promising Management Philosophy for Hospitals

After observing the positive results obtained in various sectors, Lean Management was introduced into the healthcare sector to become Lean Healthcare, defined as a method of reorganising processes with a focus on the value perceived by the patient [12]. It can be seen as a management response to the desire to control resources while limiting waste, which in this case is considered in its entirety. Hospitals in the US and UK have been recommending its use since 2002, following a number of successful trials [13]. There are also several examples in the literature that highlight the results of the approach in terms of quality of care, waiting times and financial outcomes [12–15].

However, despite being implemented in a number of hospitals in Europe, Asia and America, the results of Lean Healthcare are still difficult to generalise [13]. Critics also point out that the application is often limited to tools and rarely focuses on the value perceived by the patient [16–18].

1.3 The Value Stream, a Key Element in Implementing the Lean Approach

Implementing the Lean approach is part of a series of steps aimed at perfecting the value stream [3]:

1. Define the value
2. Identify the value chain
3. Make the remaining steps in the value stream flow by eliminating all non-value added activities
4. Use a demand-driven system that only produces goods or services requested by the customer
5. Aim for perfection

When value is defined by the customer [3], it can be difficult to focus on it, given the productivity and average length of stay targets imposed by changes in funding methods, resulting in less time spent in care [19, 20]. As a result, administrative tasks have multiplied to the detriment of time spent with patients, even though this appears to be a source of added value of activities and an important factor in attracting and retaining healthcare professionals [21, 22]. A recent report by the French Senate entitled "La situation de l'hôpital et le système de santé en France" (The state of hospitals and the healthcare system in France)[1] highlights the need to restore the amount of time spent caring for patients, particularly in light of the declining attractiveness of the healthcare professions and the shortage of resources and skills, which means that better use needs to be made of them. But healthcare activities do not always seem to focus on value-added activities. They do, however, appear to be a lever for creating a sense of purpose and attractiveness for healthcare professionals, who are essential resources in the value stream [23].

[1] Commission of Inquiry Report No. 587 (2021–2022), Volume I, published on 29 March 2022.

Table 1 Interviews conducted

Position	Length of the interview (min)
Managing director	87
Continuous improvement manager	74
Lean specialist	68
Nursing manager	37
Nurse 1	66
Nurse 2	48
Nurse 3	51
Nurse 4	38
Director of nursing	35
Process coordinator	55
Doctor, medical director	54

2 A Question for Empirical Research

Rethinking the value stream using the Lean approach could be one way of addressing the shortage of human resources and the associated attractiveness issues. Here we question the ability of Lean to improve patient-defined value while meeting the expectations of healthcare professionals who want to spend more time with patients, and pose the following research question: "How can collective analysis of work during lean healthcare implementation contribute to increase the amount of time spent with patients?".

Our research is based on a French hospital group with over 300 doctors and almost 2,250 employees. The hospital group's management is committed to value-based strategic positioning and management approach (Annual Report 2020). Since 2019 and following the recruitment of a Managing Director who is strongly committed to a continuous improvement approach, management has developed a ***Lean*** approach.

The aim of our research is to identify the ways in which the concept of value is analysed during the implementation of *Lean Healthcare*. This research was conducted during a Kaizen[2] project in a geriatric ward with high levels of staff absenteeism and occupational burnout.

We adopted a qualitative approach [24] and used a triangulation of data sources, combining semi-structured interviews with personnel involved in implementing the *Lean* approach, observation periods documented in a logbook, and documentary analysis tracking the implementation. Participants were selected according to a theoretical sampling strategy designed to capture the experiences of the facility's managers and professionals involved in the continuous improvement project (Table 1). Additionally, patients who had been hospitalized during the project period were interviewed.

[2] Kaizen is Japanese for continuous improvement.

The interview guides were based on the themes of value and participation in work analysis and were adapted to the interviewees. The transcribed interviews were then subjected to a multi-theme coding process. For the purpose of coding the collected data, NVivo software was utilized to conduct a thematic content analysis. An open coding approach was implemented, combining top-down coding from the theoretical framework and bottom-up coding from the field, in order to approach the process of data condensation from a comprehensive perspective. Consequently, certain categories of analysis were defined a priori based on the literature, while others emerged during the data coding process. The second stage of coding entails linking the first-order codes to elucidate the main recurrences in the analysis. This constitutes the axial coding phase, leading to the formalization of categories. In the third phase, the accumulation of these categories facilitates the emergence of themes, which synthesize the key ideas in the data and provide a comprehensive understanding of the mechanisms under study. The various coding stages contribute to structuring the collected data, fostering progressive conceptualization.

3 The Added Value of Time, at the Centre of the Collective Analysis of Work

3.1 Time Spent with Patients, Shared Added Value for Managers, Patients and Professionals in the Field

The interviews elucidate the complexity inherent in the concept of value within healthcare activities, revealing distinct perceptions among various stakeholder categories. Nevertheless, the individuals interviewed—patients, healthcare professionals, and members of management—collectively expressed a shared perception of care, articulated through various perspectives: optimal resource allocation, minimization of waste, and ultimately, enhancement of activity value. Patients, professionals, and management alike perceive nursing time as a significant contributor to the value of care.

The Value Perceived by Management

The hospital group's strategy[3] demonstrates its management's determination to mobilise resources effectively and involve all employees in a collective effort to prevent accidents, lost opportunities, waste and poor quality as part of a safety culture. The hospital group's management is particularly attentive to human resources, the pillars of its sustainability, especially in a context of staff shortages: "*our activity depends largely on human resources, bed closures, department closures,*etc.*"* (Managing Director). In this sense, they are an essential resource in the value stream

[3] The hospital group's 2018–2023 strategic plan.

and must be carefully organised to increase the value perceived by patients by responding to their needs and meeting their expectations.

The Value Perceived by the Patient

In collaboration with the quality department, short surveys have been introduced to identify patients' expectations based on the question *"What is most important to you when you are admitted to hospital?"* Those conducting the surveys are positioned at key points where patients pass through, such as the entrance hall, and ask the patients questions. Patients stressed the importance of receiving clear and transparent information about their state of health and of being able to talk freely with health professionals about their fears etc. "*Not seeing anyone*" can be anxiety-provoking for patients. Thus, the time taken by professionals to be with them is appreciated.

The Value Perceived by Healthcare Professionals

Interviews with nurses highlighted how important it was for them to be close to patients:

> *"We no longer have time to talk to patients, and that's really frustrating"* (Nurse)
> *"We spend most of our time filling in forms, that's not what I signed up for"* (Nurse)

They believe that the added value of their work is the time they spend with patients.

3.2 *Implementing the Lean Approach*

Management's ambition is to improve the performance of its activities while focusing on the patient. With this in mind, it made a strategic decision to implement *Lean Healthcare* and set up a Continuous Improvement Team, made up of Lean specialists dedicated to innovation and continuous improvement. Short-term Lean projects, known as Kaizen projects, are implemented with the aim of achieving rapid improvements, thereby creating "*team acceptance*" (*Lean* specialist). A multidisciplinary team has been set up for each of them, consisting of department managers, professionals in the field and *Lean* specialists. A rigorous methodology was applied, combining a census and an analysis of the data in the ward, which allowed us to objectively identify the organisational difficulties. Improvement measures are then decided on collectively. The *Lean* specialist insists on his role in providing methodological support: "*We bring a methodology and we do it with the people who work on the ward*" (*Lean* specialist). In this way, the *Lean* approach is established in conjunction with a formalised patient-centred strategy and careful use of resources.

3.3 *The Kaizen Project*

The improvement project presented was carried out in an acute geriatric ward over a period of eight days. Concerned about the level of occupational burnout among its healthcare professionals, the management asked the Continuous Improvement Team to intervene.

Preparing the Kaizen Project

After setting up a project team consisting of 2 *Lean* specialists, the ward manager, 4 nurses and a doctor from the ward, an assessment was carried out based on the perceptions of the professionals. The project team found:

- A struggling ward and teams under constant stress;
- A lack of time for patients;
- An excessive workload for all personnel;
- A change in the nature of the tasks required of nurses;
- A vague definition of roles and responsibilities;
- A lack of time to participate in projects and continuous improvement efforts.

Defining an Added Value Indicator

It was then necessary to define an indicator that best reflects the value of the work of healthcare professionals: *"looking after the patient"*, *"being close to patients"* or *"caring for patients"*.

An indicator was jointly developed to measure the time spent with patients, which is synonymous with the added value of the healthcare activity. This indicator is called PATIENT FACE TIME and is expressed in two ways:

- Patient Face Time (as a percentage), which represents the proportion of working hours that a healthcare professional spends face-to-face with patients during an 8-h shift;
- Patient Face Time (in minutes), which is the amount of time a patient spends face-to-face with a healthcare professional over a 24-h period.

Planning the Kaizen Project

The Kaizen project was planned in the following stages (Table 2):

Table 2 Stages of the Kaizen project

D1	D2	D3	D4	D5	D6	D7	D8
Data collection					Data analysis and mapping the existing organisation	Defining the future organisation	Finalising the future organisation with the supporting departments and evaluating the results

- Data collection—collected from the ward over a period of five days. The aim was to measure patient face time and to identify and quantify the tasks performed;
- Data analysis and organisation mapping. At this stage, healthcare professionals categorise tasks by consensus according to whether they believe they add value or not (value added or non-value added);
- Defining the future organisation—with the aim of identifying solutions to reduce the amount of time spent on non-value added tasks in order to increase the amount of time spent on value added tasks;
- Finalising the proposed organisation—aligning it with the supporting departments and assessing the benefits and efforts involved. This involved quantifying the benefits and costs of implementation and drawing up an implementation plan.

Data Collection

The data was collected in the geriatric ward over a period of five days. The Lean specialists followed the healthcare professionals as they went about their work, day and night. They transcribed all the tasks carried out by the nurses, who accepted their presence: "*We're happy that they're showing an interest in our problems, that they're coming to see what's going on in the ward, what difficulties we're experiencing*" (nurse).

Data Analysis and Mapping the Existing Organisation

The collected data was then collated by the Lean specialists. The tasks identified were categorised (Fig. 1) and variability described over time (Fig. 2), revealing a high degree of variability in the work as well as numerous task interruptions, including those related to receiving telephone calls.

The tasks were discussed with the healthcare professionals in order to distinguish between value-added tasks, which contribute to patient care, and non-value

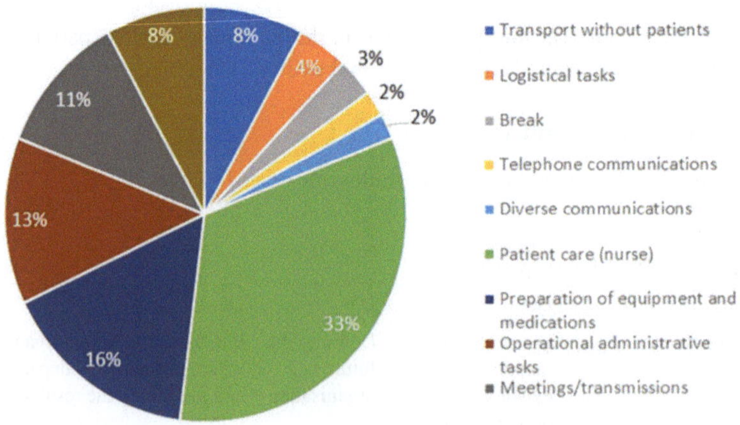

Fig. 1 Average distribution of tasks performed by a nurse at a workstation

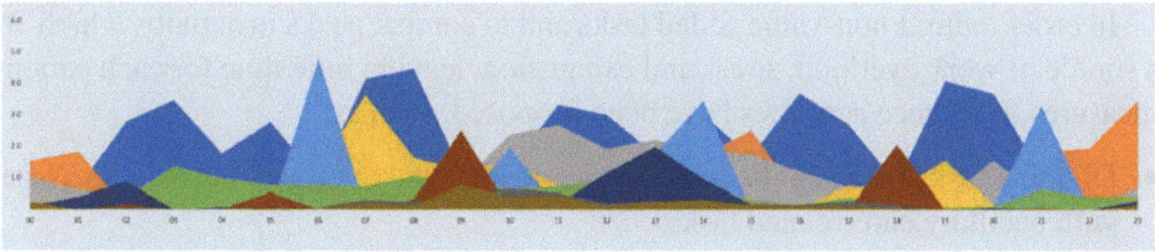

Fig. 2 Timeline by type of task (average)

added tasks. This led to some heated discussions before a consensus was reached, as illustrated by the *Lean* specialist's report:

> *"And when they enter products into stock, is that a caring task or a non-caring task? And then they have to fold the boxes. We asked ourselves all these questions, task by task, in great detail. We had to go down to a really precise level of detail to be able to identify all these little actions. And there are so many of them"* (Lean specialist).

The data collected enabled us to estimate patient face time at **36 min/patient**. This means that over the course of a day, a patient spends 36 min face-to-face with a nurse.

It is also apparent that **38% of the tasks performed were considered to be non-value added tasks**.

The analysis identified numerous stress factors, including repeated interruptions to tasks and tasks that could be carried out by other personnel (Fig. 3).

Defining the Future Organisation and Proposed Action Plan

The desired future situation is then formalised and the members of the Continuous Improvement Team step aside to give the floor to the professionals in the field.

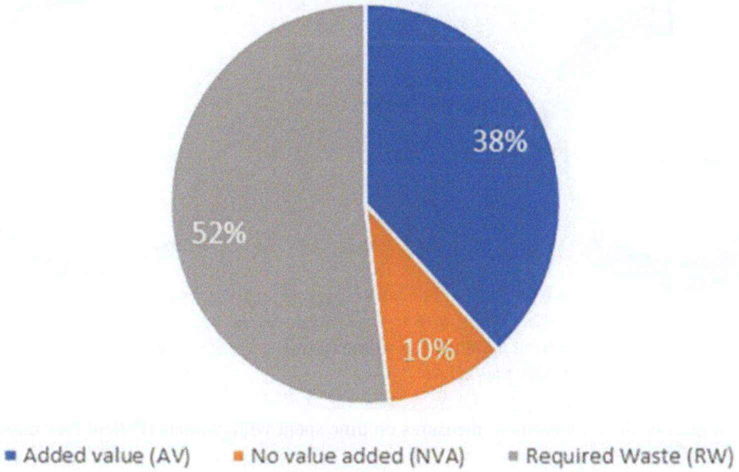

Fig. 3 Distribution of value-added and non-value added tasks

In order to limit non-value added tasks and to combat peaks in activity, which are a source of work overload, stress and exhaustion, leaving little time for each patient, measures to balance activities have been proposed, such as:

- Dividing tasks between the nurse in charge and the "Springer" nurse, who assists with ancillary care-related tasks;
- Changing the communication structure to avoid repeating information, etc.
- Moving doctors' visits;
- Changing patients' mealtimes;
- Changing break times;
- Respecting patients' sleeping patterns.

These measures were collectively determined by the project team and then submitted to management for approval. Their implementation, led by the Continuous Improvement Team, requires support from the management:

> *"The management helped us a lot with the changes. They had to communicate a great deal, especially with the doctors. Some of them weren't ready to accept the changes right away."* (Continuous Improvement Manager).

The Results of the Kaizen Project

The impact of these evaluation measures was assessed 60 days after their implementation (Fig. 4). Patient face time increased by 24% (or 13 min per patient).

The collective analysis has therefore led to a significant increase in time spent with patients.

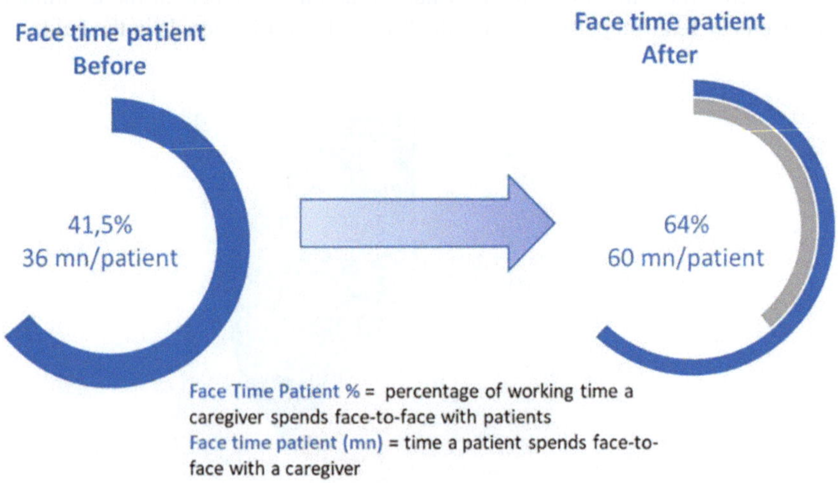

Fig. 4 Impact of the improvement measures on time spent with patients (Patient face time)

4 Conclusion

The collective analysis of work facilitates the development of a consensus regarding the concept of care value, taking into account the multiplicity of perceptions. Beyond individual interests, time spent with patients emerges as a central element in the collective interest and added value of care activities. This consensus establishes a foundation for a collective approach aimed at enhancing the value chain in service of added value, specifically healthcare professionals. The methodology employed provides a detailed description and quantification of the tasks performed. The subsequent analysis necessitates a consensus to assess the value of the work and identify tasks considered to be of no added value. It leads to a shared objectification of task value and enables the critical examination of practices, work organization, and individual roles. Furthermore, the support of lean experts proves to be a significant asset, providing both expertise in the approach and analysis of work, as well as a degree of impartiality in the face of a plurality of professionals with divergent interests.

By contributing to the creation of value in the content of the work of healthcare professionals, Lean becomes a lever for quality of life in the workplace, defined as "a balanced compromise between technical, managerial, organisational and social logics, which is constructed above all by discussing the reality of work in all its dimensions (organisation, content, conditions and results)" (Agence nationale pour l'amélioration des conditions de travail, ANACT—National Agency for the Improvement of Working Conditions). The Lean approach leads us to rethink the different dimensions of work: how work is organised, the conditions and content of the work, and the value created by the work [25, 26]

Despite the contributions of the research presented, it is worth pointing out its limitations, which are mainly related to the methodology, i.e. a case study. Indeed, the unique nature of the study limits the scope of the results. It would therefore be worthwhile repeating this study.

References

1. Krafcik, J.F.: Triumph of the lean production system. MIT Sloan Manag. Rev. **30**(1), 41 (1988)
2. Liker, J.K.: Le modèle Toyota: 14 principes qui feront la réussite de votre entreprise (The Toyota model: 14 principles that will make your business a success). Pearson Education France (2008)
3. Ohno, T.: Toyota production system: Beyond large-scale production. CRC Press, Boca Raton (1988)
4. Womack, J., Jones, D.: Système Lean: Penser l'entreprise au plus juste (Lean System: Thinking lean in business). Pearson, Paris (2007)
5. Hohmann, C.: Lean Management: Outils, méthodes, retours d'expériences, questions/réponses (Lean Management: Tools, methods, feedback and Q&A). Editions Eyrolles (2012)
6. Lorino, P.: Pragmatism and organization studies. Oxford University Press (2018)
7. Detchessahar, M.: Management et santé (management and healthcare). Rev. Française Gest. (Fr. Manag. Rev.) **214**(5), 65–68 (2011)

8. Lorino, P.: La fuite managériale devant la complexité: l'exemple historique du "Lean Management" (The managerial escape from complexity: the historical example of "Lean Management") (2014)
9. Bamber, G.J., Stanton, P., Bartram, T., Ballardie, R.: Human resource management, lean processes and outcomes for employees: towards a research agenda. Int. J. Hum. Resour. Manag. **25**(21), 2881–2891 (2014)
10. Hasle, P.: Lean production—an evaluation of the possibilities for an employee supportive Lean practice. Hum. Factors Ergon. Manuf. Serv. Ind. **24**(1), 40–53 (2014)
11. Liker, J.K., Ross, K.: The Toyota way to service excellence: lean transformation in service organizations: lean transformation in service organizations. McGraw Hill Professional (2016)
12. Trilling, L., Pellet, B., Delacroix, S., Fleury, H.C., Marcon, E.: Retour d'expérience sur la mise en place du Lean dans un centre de Radiothérapie (Feedback on implementing Lean in a radiation therapy centre). In: Conférence Francophone Gestion et Ingénierie des Systèmes Hospitaliers (In French-speaking Conference on Hospital Systems Management and Engineering), p. 8 (2010)
13. D'Andreamatteo, A., Lanni, L., Lega, F., Sargiacomo, M.: Lean in healthcare: a comprehensive review. Health Policy **119**(9), 1197–1209 (2015)
14. Shortell, S.M., Blodgett, J.C., Rundall, T.G., Henke, R.M., Reponen, E.: Lean Management and hospital performance: adoption vs. implementation. Jt. Comm. J. Qual. Patient Saf. **47**(5), 296–305 (2021)
15. Tlapa, D., Zepeda-Lugo, C.A., Tortorella, G.L., Baez-Lopez, Y.A., Limon-Romero, J., Alvarado-Iniesta, A., Rodriguez-Borbon, M.I.: Effects of lean healthcare on patient flow: a systematic review. Value in Health **23**(2), 260–273 (2020)
16. Radnor, Z.J., Holweg, M., Waring, J.: Lean in healthcare: the unfilled promise? Soc Sci Med **74**(3), 364–371 (2012)
17. Larman, C., Vodde, B.: Lean primer. Version **1**, 1–46 (2009)
18. Ballé, M., Beauvallet, G.: Le management lean (lean management). Pearson Education France, Paris (2013)
19. Barrier, J., Georges-Tarragano, C., Saccoman, B., Pierru, F., Astre, H.: Le temps, une dimension indispensable du soin (Time, an essential aspect of care). In: Claire Georges-Tarragano ed., Soigner (l')humain: Manifeste pour un juste soin au juste coût (Caring for people: Manifesto for fair care at a fair cost). Rennes: EHESP Press, pp. 95–110 (2015). https://rbu.univ-reims.fr:2088/10.3917/ehesp.georg.2015.01.0095
20. Dumond, J.-P.: La grande transformation hospitalière (The great hospital transformation). Millau: Seli Arslan (2021)
21. Michot, F., Launois, B., Bertrand, D., Bringer, J., Degos, L., Olie, J.P., Thuillez, C.: Report 19–02. L'hôpital public en crise: origines et propositions (Public hospitals in crisis: origins and proposals). Bulletin de l'Académie Nationale de Médecine (Bulletin of the National Academy of Medicine), **203**(3–4), 109–121 (2019)
22. Riet, Z.: Relever le défi de l'attractivité pour l'hôpital public (Meeting the challenge of making public hospitals more attractive). Les Tribunes de la santé (The Healthcare Forums) **2**, 77–84 (2023)
23. Porter, P.: "ME." Competitive Advantage, Creating and Sustaining Superior Performance "the free press, New York, pp.110–112 (1985)
24. Yin, R.K.: Validity and generalization in future case study evaluations. Evaluation **19**(3), 321–332 (2013)
25. Ballé, M., Jones, D., Chaize, J., Fiume, O.: La stratégie Lean: Créer un avantage compétitif, libérer l'innovation, assurer une croissance durable en développant les personnes (The Lean strategy: creating competitive advantage, unleashing innovation and ensuring sustainable growth through people development). Editions Eyrolles (2018)
26. Foropon, C., Landry, S.: Le déploiement du Lean à l'hôpital Saint-Boniface: L'importance du leadership transformationnel (implementing the lean approach at Saint-Boniface hospital: the importance of transformational leadership). Gestion (Management) **39**(3), 107–115 (2014)

Towards the Development of a Conceptual Framework Adapted to the Specific Needs of Healthcare and Social Services Establishments for a Sustainable Transition of Their Supply Chain

André Côté, Mohamed Hakim Raki, and Jean-Baptiste Gartner

Abstract The Covid-19 crisis has highlighted the vulnerability of healthcare establishments' supply chains, highlighting their dependence on a globalised chain that is primarily focused on economic aspects rather than the essential criteria of robustness and sustainability. It is becoming imperative for healthcare establishments to adapt their strategies so as to transcend the current approach focused primarily on efficiency and cost reduction, in favour of an intelligent, integrated supply chain. This must encourage the sharing of information while promoting proactive environmental and social initiatives. This article is the first stage in a research programme designed to provide managers of healthcare institutions with theoretical, methodological and empirical tools to help them in their quest to transition their supply chain towards sustainable development. It also aims to propose reliable and robust measurement

A. Côté (✉) · M. H. Raki · J.-B. Gartner
Department of Management, Faculty of Business Administration, Laval University, Quebec City, QC, Canada
e-mail: andre.cote@fsa.ulaval.ca

Research Center in Health Services Management, Laval University, Quebec City, QC, Canada

Research Center of the University Institute of Cardio-Pneumology of Quebec, Quebec City, Canada

M. H. Raki
e-mail: mohamed-hakim.raki@fsa.ulaval.ca

J.-B. Gartner
e-mail: jean-baptiste.gartner.1@ulaval.ca

A. Côté · J.-B. Gartner
VITAM, Research Center for Sustainable Health, Laval University, Quebec City, QC, Canada

Research Center of the University Hospital of Quebec, Laval University, Quebec City, QC, Canada

CISSS of Chaudière-Appalaches Research Centre, Laval University, Quebec City, QC, Canada

P. Landa et al. (eds.), *Operations Research and Artificial Intelligence in Healthcare Management*, Springer Proceedings in Mathematics & Statistics 506,
https://doi.org/10.1007/978-3-031-95659-1_16

methods and tools for determining the economic (minimisation of supply, production, storage and transport costs), environmental (reduction of waste, rationalisation of waste, reduction of GHG emissions, etc.) and social (working conditions and patient satisfaction) benefits arising from the sustainable transition of the supply chain. To do this, we used a narrative literature review. The literature review enabled us to identify nine key elements which, a priori, favour a sustainable supply chain transition in healthcare establishments. We grouped these key elements into major themes, namely the perspective of sustainable development, the prerequisites for a sustainable transition, best practices for a sustainable transition, the performance resulting from the transition, and the learning healthcare systems approach, including the precepts of communicative action. Despite the scarcity of literature on this theme, this study has enabled us to identify key elements, analyse their interactions and highlight existing gaps. These discoveries will guide future research in this field.

Keywords Supply chain · Sustainable transformation · Environmental performance · Learning health systems

1 Background

The Covid-19 crisis highlighted the vulnerability of the healthcare supply chain, highlighting its dependence on a globalized chain focused primarily on economic aspects, to the detriment of the essential criteria of robustness and sustainability. The impact of this vulnerability was particularly noticeable in the supply chain, especially for masks, medicines, and vaccines. Recurrent structural reforms and budget restrictions have exacerbated these weaknesses [1].

The current fragility of the supply chain is not limited to the Covid-19 health crisis we're facing. International institutions, such as the United Nations Environment Programme (UNEP), point to the likelihood of other, potentially more serious, impending health crises. By way of illustration, the Bank of America predicts that disruptions comparable to Covid-19 could occur every five years on average [2], directly affecting the supply chain of healthcare establishments.

It is becoming imperative for healthcare establishments to adapt their strategies so as to transcend the current approach focused primarily on efficiency and cost reduction, in favor of an intelligent, integrated supply chain. This must encourage information sharing while promoting proactive environmental and social initiatives [3, 4]. This need is even more pressing in the current context, where healthcare establishments face the challenge of maintaining efficient, equitable and sustainable delivery of health and social services in an increasingly uncertain environment. The origins of these challenges are multiple, encompassing growing demand due to an aging population, a shortage of manpower, significant increases in logistical costs, not to mention the environmental consequences inherent in climate change.

Against this backdrop, many establishments aspire to radically transform their practices. Yet most approach this transformation with a limited understanding of the issues and impacts inherent to the healthcare sector. In fact, there is a gap in logistics management skills among healthcare facility managers [5]. It is important to emphasize the specificity of the healthcare supply chain, characterized by specific requirements in terms of quality of care, patient safety, medical supply, and hazardous waste management. Any failure in this system can have serious, even fatal, consequences for patient health or cause considerable environmental damage [6]. However, specific research into logistics in the healthcare sector is still lacking [7]. It would therefore be imprudent to simply extrapolate knowledge from the industrial sector to fill this gap. We can draw on it for the development of our conceptual framework, but the need to produce new knowledge in the field of logistics within ESSS healthcare facilities is both relevant and necessary [6].

This article is the first step in a research program designed to provide healthcare facility managers with theoretical, methodological, and empirical tools to help them make the transition to a sustainable supply chain. It also aims to propose reliable and robust measurement methods and tools to determine the economic (minimization of procurement, production, warehousing, and transport costs), environmental (reduction of waste, rationalization of waste, reduction of GHG emissions, etc.) and social (working conditions and patient satisfaction) benefits arising from sustainable supply chain transition. In this first article, based on a review of the scientific literature, we seek to identify the key elements for the development of an optimized conceptual framework, adapted to the specific needs of health and social service establishments, for the sustainable transition of their supply chain.

2 Methods

To do this, we used a conventional "narrative" literature review. This method enables us to update our knowledge of a given subject and aims to identify relevant publications through a review of the literature that is not necessarily systematic or exhaustive. This type of review provides an overview of a specific topic, raising issues that are usually neglected and encouraging further research into the subject. It should be noted, however, that this type of review is not a summary from which conclusions can be drawn on the whole body of evidence, unlike the systematic literature review, whose aim is to produce a more reliable review by considering all relevant data.

3 Results

In its generic sense, the sustainable supply chain is defined by actions that take account of social, economic, and environmental concerns in supply chain management [7]. It covers all phases of a product's life cycle, from the extraction of raw materials, through the design, production, and distribution phases, to the use of the product by consumers and its disposal at the end of the life cycle [6–8]. In

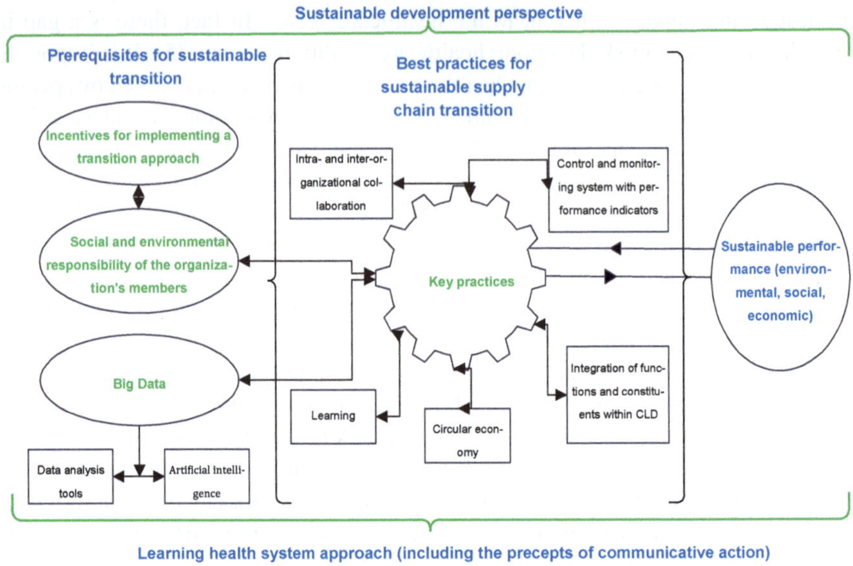

Fig. 1 Towards the development of a conceptual framework adapted to the specific needs of healthcare and social services establishments for a sustainable transition of their supply chain

healthcare, the supply chain covers patient flows, bed management, waste, laundry, catering, supplies and medical devices. Activities referring to purchasing and supply management, internal and external transport, storage, production, and all medical care activities are also linked to the supply chain [7, 9, 10].

The literature review enabled us to identify nine (9) key elements that, a priori, favor a sustainable transition of the supply chain in healthcare facilities. We have grouped these key elements into broad themes: the perspective of sustainable development, the prerequisites for a sustainable transition, best practices for a sustainable transition, the performances resulting from the transition, and the approach to learning healthcare systems, including the precepts of communicative action. We elaborate on each of these themes in the following paragraphs and present the model that emerges from this work (Fig. 1).

3.1 *The Perspective of Sustainable Development*

The distinctive feature of the conceptual model we wish to develop is to propose a supply chain transition that integrates the three major dimensions of sustainable development: economic, social, and environmental performance. We endorse the definition of sustainable development as meeting the needs of the present without compromising the ability of future generations to meet their own needs. Sustainable development is based on a long-term vision that considers the inseparable nature of the environmental, social and economic dimensions of development activities. The sustainable development approach also advocates the adoption of a circular organization model, a perspective that is in line with work on the learning healthcare system [11]. Proposed in 2007 by the Institute of Medicine (now National Academy of Medicine) during the course of a series of workshops [12], this model has generated much enthusiasm in North America and worldwide. Learning healthcare systems were defined as systems where 'science, informatics, incentives, and culture are aligned for continuous improvement, innovation, and equity—with best practices and discovery seamlessly embedded in the delivery process, individuals and families as active participants in all elements, and new knowledge generated as an integral by-product of the delivery experience' [13]. According to Friedman and colleagues [14], learning healthcare systems aim to generate new data from real-life processes, create knowledge from these data and then feed knowledge back into practice, thus generating a continuous learning cycle. As for her, the sustainable development perspective has received very little attention in the literature on logistics management in healthcare facilities. There is a wealth of literature on supply chains, but very little on all the functions of a logistics chain, i.e. warehousing, transport between and within healthcare facilities, and product distribution to target clienteles [15]. What's more, most of the work in the literature is set in the context of manufacturing industries, such as mining, automotive, paper, leather, telecommunications, manufacturing, tanning and construction [15]. As for service companies, often described as "silent destroyers of the environment" [16], they receive curiously little attention in the literature, despite their significant impact. Healthcare establishments are intensive consumers of energy and water, and massive producers of household and infectious waste [15].

3.2 *Prerequisites for a Sustainable Supply Chain*

Several writings highlight the contribution of digital tools for analyzing massive data (Data Lake) and artificial intelligence on the integration of sustainable logistics practices within healthcare facilities [7, 10, 17]. These innovative technologies improve information processing capacity, make decision-making more efficient, streamline chain exchanges and consequently simplify intra- and inter-organizational collaboration [6] Another interesting element to highlight is the contribution of these technologies to the process of integrating the various logistics functions within healthcare establishments [7, 17].

Sustainable transition also requires a profound sense of social and environmental responsibility on the part of the members of healthcare establishments. This approach is rooted in an awareness of the repercussions of their decisions and actions on society and the environment. To be fully committed, social and environmental concerns must be integrated into management processes (such as planning, evaluation and reporting) and day-to-day activities, such as the production of goods and services, purchasing and communication. The goal is to promote ethical and transparent behavior, aligned with the principles of sustainable development [18].

Management plays a crucial role in this transformation. Senior management's determination to steer the organizational culture towards an ecologically responsible approach is an essential linchpin of any responsible commitment [19]. In the industrial sector, for example, it has been established that for this transition to succeed, management must demonstrate leadership, maintain open communication with its staff and emphasize the benefits of a sustainable transition [20]. This translates concretely into developing a clear strategy, funding environmental projects, and promoting practices aligned with the principles of sustainable development [15].

Still in the industrial sector, the drive towards a sustainable transition is strongly influenced by incentives such as the Regulatory and Normative Framework, internal policies, and economic optimization. Environmental laws and regulations provide a regulatory and normative framework that acts as an essential constraint, pushing managers to adopt more environmentally friendly behaviors [15]. However, beyond these external obligations, internal guidelines such as compensation policies, management objectives and financial performance measurement systems also play a crucial role in steering organizations towards an ecological transition. In addition, economic optimization, notably the desire to reduce costs and ensure better supply chain integration, emerges as another major incentive for these companies [15].

3.3 Best Practices for Sustainable Supply Chain Transition

The literature prioritizes the need to develop exemplary logistics practices contextualized to the facility's reality; note that we consider exemplary practices to be those that result from expert judgment following an exhaustive analysis of the literature [21, 22]. Three properties characterize an interaction system from which logistics practices emerge: modes of action requiring a particular technology, interaction routines and goals to which stakeholders adhere [23]. In the service sector, the sustainable management practices adopted can be classified into three main types: organizational and planning practices, communication practices and operational practices [24, 25]. Referring to the literature from the industrial sector—due to the limited literature related to healthcare facilities—it is possible for us to identify five best practices for a sustainable supply chain transition in healthcare. These practices are: learning, inter-organizational collaboration, the control and monitoring system via performance indicators, the integration of internal supply chain processes, and the circular economy. We address each of these themes in the following paragraphs.

The literature also reveals a worrying gap in managers' competence vis-à-vis sustainable logistics strategies. Many remain ambivalent or uninformed about the methodical incorporation of sustainability practices within their supply chains, let alone the potential benefits derived from these practices [26]. This inadequacy, in the current context of ecological imperatives, calls for rigorous educational intervention.

Recent studies suggest the introduction of training programs specifically designed to strengthen the understanding and implementation of sustainable logistics. These programs, while tailored to the specifics of supply chain managers, should also encompass all stakeholders involved, to ensure cross-functional operational coherence [27].

Raising awareness and mobilizing staff around environmental concerns requires a nuanced pedagogical approach. It is imperative to employ innovative and tailored teaching methods, aimed at increasing not only technical skills, but also ecological awareness [20]. With this in mind, more recent research highlights the merits of digital learning. Seen as a forward-thinking pedagogical tool, it could serve as a catalyst for strengthening interdisciplinary collaboration, while instilling sustainability principles within the supply chain [7].

The learning healthcare systems approach, by way of illustration, advocates inclusive management of healthcare facilities. It suggests considering the cross-cutting interactions and potential impacts of products and services throughout their life cycle. This systemic perspective is reinforced by the notion of the circular economy, which seeks to maximize synergies and beneficial interactions between various players in an economic sector [28].

So, when faced with the daunting challenges of sustainability, it's clear that these challenges are systemic in nature. Proposed solutions must therefore be systemic, not piecemeal. Ideally, they should be developed jointly by a range of organizations working in coalition. The essence of these solutions lies in integrated co-construction, where different organizations work together to develop robust strategies to meet the complex demands of sustainability [29].

The implementation of a rigorous monitoring and control system is just as essential when it comes to the transition to a sustainable supply chain. Using performance indicators is strategic for promptly identifying areas requiring improvement, such as bottlenecks, while evaluating progress at each stage of implementation. It's crucial to remember that these indicators go beyond environmental performance and also encompass socio-economic considerations.

The framework for assessing sustainable health systems developed by Buffoli et al. [30] is proving to be a relevant reference tool. This framework distinguishes indicators into three major domains: economic, environmental, and social. These domains distinguish and categorize indicators along three major axes: economic, environmental, and social. These axes are then broken down into 14 specific constructs, where each construct is defined and interpreted through 4 to 5 distinct indicators. In addition, this methodology offers a holistic perspective on evaluation, enabling the final score to be adjusted according to the theoretical weighting of each indicator, thus guaranteeing accurate and appropriate measurement.

Alarmingly, many companies are not equipped with appropriate tools to assess their social and environmental performance [31]. This deficiency fuels persistent ambiguity regarding the tangible benefits of sustainable logistics, and even more so, its actual realization [26, 31]. Certain facets of environmental performance, such as green purchasing, green products, and reverse logistics, can be closely linked to the standards set by standards like ISO 14001. In conclusion, it should be noted that these performance measures not only serve to ensure compliance, but they can also highlight the concrete or perceived benefits arising from investments in environmentally responsible initiatives [15].

The integration of processes within a supply chain is fundamental to ensuring harmony and coherence between the different functional areas of a company, thus contributing to the complete integration of the supply chain. This integration is even more crucial in complex logistics systems, such as hospital chains. According to Bentahar and Benzidia [10], this complexity stems from the plurality of activities—whether core or support—the diversity of flows, whether physical or informational, and the high number of actors involved. Indeed, healthcare establishments encompass a wide variety of flows, such as those relating to patients, medication, linen, catering, and waste. A further difficulty lies in the fact that the actors working within these institutions often have a limited understanding of the activities taking place in other functional units [17].

Some work suggests that an organization's sustainable performance is intrinsically linked to the effective integration of its operations management [32]. However, it should be noted that empirical evidence demonstrating the increase in sustainable performance via optimal integration of supply chain processes is still limited. As part of our research, we propose that robust internal integration should encompass the entirety of HSSC processes, including both managerial and medical activities. Such integration would provide a platform for effective cross-functional collaboration within the HSSCs, strengthening their involvement in sustainability-related decisions and fostering the adoption of shared goals.

3.4 The Learning Health Systems (LHS) Approach as a Vector for Transition

In The Learning Health Systems (LHS) approach is seen as a logical progression from evidence-based medicine [33]. Its aim is to stimulate the creation and integration of knowledge into both organizational, administrative, and clinical practices [14]. The fundamental principles of this approach encompass: (1) the active involvement of users and the organization, (2) the real-time gathering, analysis, and sharing of relevant data according to various expertise, (3) the generation of real-time evidence, (4) the implementation of decision-making systems, (5) the harmonization of mechanisms relating to governance, funding and the conduct of educational activities, (6) the promotion of a culture focused on learning and improvement, and (7) the strengthening of adequate skills, particularly for the implementation of best practices [11, 34].

This approach is strongly encouraged by renowned entities such as the World Health Organization, aiming to stimulate the transformation of healthcare systems on a national scale. With specific reference to the healthcare facility supply chain, the SSA approach facilitates interdisciplinary collaboration [35], merging management sciences, logistics, evaluative sciences, data science and clinical sciences. As such, this innovative paradigm is relevant to areas of transformation of various hospital flows such as those related to patients, medication, linen, catering, and waste or at a macroscopic scale of a healthcare system, to drive improvement and mutation of practices to address clinical, logistical, social, economic, and environmental challenges.

This vision calls for the joint involvement of users, managers, decision-makers, and researchers, with the aim of gaining a comprehensive and in-depth perception of the issues driving healthcare facilities to innovate their logistics methods. In short, it's a holistic and integrated research paradigm, focused on user needs, innovation, testing, evaluation and, more broadly, knowledge translation. This collaborative approach contributes to a better understanding of the needs of target groups, emphasizing knowledge discovery and translation, with the aim of rapidly maximizing the benefits of research and evidence-based practice [22].

3.5 Communicative Action

The Learning Health Systems (LHS) approach focuses primarily on promoting organizational learning, but its primary aim is to encourage stakeholders to embrace the organization's objectives. It is intrinsically marked by a strategic focus on efficiency and control. This strategy values individual potential as a cognitive actor capable of constructing an understanding of the world by mobilizing processes of conscious reflection. Much of this approach is based on individual learning, where each individual processes and interprets information based on past experience [23].

However, Norman et al. [36] emphasize the importance of incorporating communicative action to bring about real change in operational practices. In contrast to a purely strategic and individual vision, communicative acting, as conceptualized by Habermas, aims to create a mutual understanding of a situation or phenomenon through dialogue and collective action. This perspective not only perceives reality as objectively defined, but also integrates the social and subjective dimensions of reality [37]. Organizational learning is thus enriched by considering individuals' intersubjective relations and their relationship to the world, enabling openness to other perspectives and encouraging intersubjectivity, fundamental to mutual understanding in the "lived world" [38]. With reference to our previous work, we postulate that the LHS approach, combined with Habermas's communicative acting, can facilitate a sustainable transition in logistics within healthcare establishments.

Figure 1 presents a model of the key elements for developing a framework adapted to health and social services establishments. This model aims to achieve a sustainable transition of their supply chain and is based on an initial literature review.

4 Conclusion

Through a narrative literature review, we established the current state of knowledge concerning sustainable supply chain transition within the health and social care sector, a topic still under-represented in the literature. Despite the scarcity of literature on this topic, this study enabled us to identify key elements, analyze their interactions and highlight existing gaps. These discoveries can thus guide future research in this field.

The use of a less rigorous approach in terms of methodological criteria could explain the low volume of articles identified on sustainable supply chain transition in healthcare facilities. As a continuation of our work, we plan to conduct a systematic literature review to take stock of current knowledge. The guiding question of this review will be: what key elements (concepts, dimensions, etc.), methods and tools are most relevant to facilitating a sustainable transition in healthcare facilities? We will take a close look at various themes, including prerequisites, challenges, best practices, successful and unsuccessful interventions, as well as assessment and monitoring methods and tools specifically related to economic, social and environmental transition.

The knowledge acquired through the systematic literature review will enrich our conceptual framework, specifically adapted to healthcare and social services establishments. This will guide a sustainable transition of their supply chain and enable us to suggest relevant methods and tools for its implementation and operationalization.

References

1. Bentahar, O., Benzidia, S., Husson J.: Enjeux de la logistique et du supply chain management de la santé. Management and Avenir Santé. [Issues in Health Logistics and Supply Chain Management. Management and Future Health] **1**, 7–11 (2022). https://doi.org/10.3917/mavs.009.0007
2. Bank of America. Global Equity Strategy: The USD 1 trillion cost of remaking chaîne logistiques: Significant but not prohibitive. In: BofA Securities (2020). https://ctmfile.com/story/the-us1-trillion-cost-of-remaking-supply-chains
3. McMahon, M., Nadigel, J., Thompson, E., Glazier, R.H.: Informing Canada's health system response to COVID-19: priorities for health services and policy research. Healthcare Policy **16**(1), 112–124 (2020). https://doi.org/10.12927/hcpol.2020.26249
4. Lin, M., Beliavsky, A., Katz, K., et al.: What can early Canadian experience screening for COVID-19 teach us about how to prepare for a pandemic? CMAJ **192**(12), E314–E318 (2020). https://doi.org/10.1503/cmaj.200305
5. Beaulieu, M., Bentahar, O., Benzidia, S.: The evolution of healthcare logistics: the Canadian experience. J. Appl. Bus. Econ. **22**(14), 196 (2020). https://doi.org/10.33423/jabe.v22i14.3977
6. Jæger, B., Menebo, M.M., Upadhyay, A.: Identification of environmental supply chain bottlenecks: a case study of the Ethiopian healthcare supply chain. Manag. Environ. Qual.: Int. J. **32**(6), 1233–1254 (2021). https://doi.org/10.1108/MEQ-12-2019-0277
7. Benzidia, S., Makaoui, N., Bentahar, O.: The impact of big data analytics and artificial intelligence on green supply chain process integration and hospital environmental performance.

Technol. Forecast. Soc. Chang. **165**, 120557 (2021). https://doi.org/10.1016/j.techfore.2020.120557
8. Walker, H., Di Sisto, L., McBain, D.: Drivers and barriers to environmental supply chain management practices: lessons from the public and private sectors. J. Purch. Supply Manag. **14**(1), 69–85 (2008). https://doi.org/10.1016/j.pursup.2008.01.007
9. Feibert, D.C., Jacobsen, P.: Measuring process performance within healthcare logistics-a decision tool for selecting track and trace technologies. Acad. Strateg. Manag. J. **14**(1), 33–57 (2015)
10. Bentahar, O., Benzidia, S.: Supply chain management de la santé. [Health Supply Chain Management] Éditions EMS, Caen (2019)
11. Menear, M., Blanchette, M.A., Demers-Payette, O., Roy, D.: A framework for value-creating learning health systems. Health Res Policy Syst. **17**(1), 1–13 (2019). https://doi.org/10.1186/s12961-019-0477-3
12. Olsen, L., Aisner, D., McGinnis, J.M.: The learning healthcare system: workshop summary. National Academies Press (US), Washington (DC) (2007)
13. Institute of Medicine.: Roundtable on value and science-driven health care: the learning health system and its innovation Collaboratives: update report. National Academies Press (US), Washington (DC) (2011)
14. Friedman, C.P., Allee, N.J., Delaney, B.C., et al.: The science of learning health systems: foundations for a new journal. Learn Health Syst. **1**(1), e10020 (2017). https://doi.org/10.1002/lrh2.10020
15. Bentahar, O., Benzidia, S., Bourlakis, M.: A green supply chain taxonomy in healthcare: critical factors for a proactive approach. Int. J. Logist. Manag. **34**(1), 60–83 (2023). https://doi.org/10.1108/IJLM-04-2021-0240
16. Molina-Azorín, J.F., Claver-Cortés, E., López-Gamero, M.D., Tarí, J.J.: Green management and financial performance: a literature review. Manag. Decis. **47**(7), 1080–1100 (2009). https://doi.org/10.1108/00251740910978313
17. Benzidia, S., Bentahar, O., Husson, J., Makaoui, N.: Big data analytics capability in healthcare operations and supply chain management: the role of green process innovation. Ann. Oper. Res. **333**, 1077–1101 (2023). https://doi.org/10.1007/s10479-022-05157-6
18. Ministère de la Santé et des Services Sociaux du Québec. Sustainable Development: Development Strategy 2023–2028 (2023). https://www.quebec.ca/en/government/policies-orientations/sustainable-development
19. Baumgartner, R.J.: Organizational culture and leadership: preconditions for the development of a sustainable corporation. Sustain. Dev. **17**(2), 102–113 (2009). https://doi.org/10.1002/sd.405
20. Graves, L.M., Sarkis, J., Zhu, Q.: How transformational leadership and employee motivation combine to predict employee proenvironmental behaviors in China. J. Environ. Psychol. **35**, 81–91 (2013). https://doi.org/10.1016/j.jenvp.2013.05.002
21. Parmigiani, A., Howard-Grenville, J.: Routines revisited: exploring the capabilities and practice perspectives. Acad. Manag. Ann. **5**(1), 413–453 (2011). https://doi.org/10.5465/19416520.2011.589143
22. Gartner, J.B., Abasse, K.S., Bergeron, F., Landa, P., Lemaire, C., Côté, A.: Definition and conceptualization of the patient-centered care pathway, a proposed integrative framework for consensus: a Concept analysis and systematic review. BMC Health Serv. Res. **22**(1), 1–24 (2022). https://doi.org/10.1186/s12913-022-07960-0
23. Côté, A., Demers, C., Seguin, F.: La transformation des pratiques cliniques, une perspective interactionniste. [The Transformation of Clinical Practices: An Interactionist Perspective.] Management International (Montréal) **12**(1), 91–101 (2008). https://doi.org/10.59876/a-psz7-84sr
24. González-Benito, J., González-Benito, Ó.: A review of determinant factors of environmental proactivity. Bus. Strateg. Environ. **15**(2), 87–102 (2006). https://doi.org/10.1002/bse.450
25. Migdadi, Y.K.A.A., Omari, A.A.: Identifying the best practices in green operations strategy of hospitals. Benchmarking: Int. J. **26**(4), 1106–1131 (2019). https://doi.org/10.1108/BIJ-09-2017-0242

26. Govindan, K., Seuring, S., Zhu, Q., Azevedo, S.G.: Accelerating the transition towards sustainability dynamics into supply chain relationship management and governance structures. J. Clean. Prod. **112**, 1813–1823 (2016). https://doi.org/10.1016/j.jclepro.2015.11.084
27. Zhu, Q., Feng, Y., Choi, S.B.: The role of customer relational governance in environmental and economic performance improvement through green supply chain management. J. Clean. Prod. **155**, 46–53 (2017). https://doi.org/10.1016/j.jclepro.2016.02.124
28. Calisto Friant, M., Lakerveld, D., Vermeulen, W.J., Salomone, R.: Transition to a sustainable circular plastics economy in the Netherlands: discourse and policy analysis. Sustainability **14**(1), 190 (2021). https://doi.org/10.3390/su14010190
29. Gümüsay, A.A., Marti, E., Trittin-Ulbrich, H., Wickert, C.: How organizing matters for societal grand challenges. In: Organizing for Societal Grand Challenges. Emerald Publishing Limited, Bingley (2022)
30. Buffoli, M., Capolongo, S., Bottero, M., Cavagliato, E., Speranza, S., Volpatti, L.: Sustainable healthcare: how to assess and improve healthcare structures' sustainability. Ann. Ig. **25**(5), 411–418 (2013). https://doi.org/10.7416/ai.2013.1942
31. Rauer, J., Kaufmann, L.: Mitigating external barriers to implementing green supply chain management: a grounded theory investigation of green-tech companies' rare earth metals supply chains. J. Supply Chain Manag. **51**(2), 65–88 (2015). https://doi.org/10.1111/jscm.12063
32. Shah, N., Soomro, B.A.: Internal green integration and environmental performance: the predictive power of proactive environmental strategy, greening the supplier, and environmental collaboration with the supplier. Bus. Strateg. Environ. **30**(2), 1333–1344 (2021). https://doi.org/10.1002/bse.2687
33. Friedman, C., Rubin, J., Brown, J., et al.: Toward a science of learning systems: a research agenda for the high-functioning learning health system. J. Am. Med. Inf. Assoc. **22**(1), 43–50 (2015). https://doi.org/10.1136/amiajnl-2014-002977
34. Institute of Medicine.: The learning health system and its innovation Collaboratives: update report, IOMOTN Academies
35. Forrest, C.B., Chesley, F.D., Jr., Tregear, M.L., Mistry, K.B.: Development of the learning health system researcher core competencies. Health Serv. Res. **53**(4), 2615–2632 (2018). https://doi.org/10.1111/1475-6773.12751
36. Norman, A.C., Fritzen, L., Fridh, M.L.: One lens missing? Clarifying the clinical microsystem framework with learning theories. Qual. Manag. Healthc. **22**(2), 126–136 (2013). https://doi.org/10.1097/QMH.0b013e31828c22e2
37. Côté, A., Beogo, I., Abasse, K.S., Laberge, M., Dogba, M.J., Dallaire, C.: The clinical microsystems approach: does it really work? A systematic review of organizational theories of health care practices. J. Am. Pharm. Assoc. **60**(6), e388–e410 (2020). https://doi.org/10.1016/j.japh.2020.06.013
38. Habermas, J.: The theory of communicative action: reason and the rationalization of society, vol 1. Beacon press, Boston (1984)

Why be a Manager When You're a Hospital Doctor? A Review of the Literature

André Côté, Boutheina Benharbit, Célia Lemaire, Frédéric Bergeron, and Jean-Baptiste Gartner

Abstract Developing management skills for physicians is important for healthcare organisations with the advent of clinical and administrative management. However, the identification of the factors that encourage their involvement in this process is patchy. This systematic review of the literature, including 26 studies selected using the PRISMA (Preferred Reporting Items for Systematic Reviews and Meta-Analyses) protocol, identifies factors facilitating/inhibiting physician involvement, expectations on the part of managers and avenues for improvement. The results reveal the factors determining doctors' motivation to take on a managerial role, the influence

A. Côté · B. Benharbit · C. Lemaire (✉) · J.-B. Gartner
Department of Management, Faculty of Business Administration, Laval University, Quebec City, QC, Canada
e-mail: celia.lemaire@univ-lyon3.fr

A. Côté
e-mail: andre.cote@fsa.ulaval.ca

J.-B. Gartner
e-mail: jean-baptiste.gartner.1@ulaval.ca

A. Côté · B. Benharbit · J.-B. Gartner
Health Services Management Research Center, Laval University, Quebec City, QC, Canada

A. Côté · J.-B. Gartner
Research Centre of the University Institute of Cardiology and Pneumology of Quebec, Quebec City, QC, Canada

VITAM, Centre for Sustainable Health Research, Laval University, Quebec City, QC, Canada

Centre of Research of University Hospital of Québec, Laval University, Quebec City, QC, Canada

CISSS of Chaudière-Appalaches Research Centre, Laval University, Quebec City, QC, Canada

C. Lemaire
Jean Moulin University, Lyon, France

French University Institute, Paris, France

F. Bergeron
Library-Advisory Services Department, Laval University, Quebec City, QC, Canada
e-mail: frederic.bergeron@bibl.ulaval.ca

P. Landa et al. (eds.), *Operations Research and Artificial Intelligence in Healthcare Management*, Springer Proceedings in Mathematics & Statistics 506,
https://doi.org/10.1007/978-3-031-95659-1_17

of organizational context and support, and avenues for process improvement. In addition, corrective measures are proposed to encourage physician involvement in the management of clinical activities, and the challenges associated are presented. These findings are of interest both for career management policies within healthcare organizations and for the academic training of physicians.

Keywords Physician-manager · Hybrid role · Systematic review

1 Background and Objectives

Hybridization between clinical and managerial domains [1–3] is a process that is not simply a juxtaposition of two different cultures, but the interweaving of values intrinsically linked to these two cultures where organizing becomes an integral part of professional work with an overlap of managerial and professional discourses [4–6]. Physician managers play a mediating role between managerial and clinical requirements [3, 7] facilitating communication and collaboration between the worlds of medicine and management. Despite the need to develop managerial skills suited to their dual roles, the hybridization process for doctors is hampered by the lack of administrative support offered by hospitals to clinical directors [3, 8].

Hospitals support this process, while there is a consensus on the relevance of involving physicians in the management of clinical activities. Indeed, involving physicians in management strengthens the essential link between strategic and operational concerns, enabling better-informed decision-making, particularly with regard to resource allocation [9], as well as the alignment of professional practice with organizational objectives [3]. Indeed, physician managers have every opportunity to ensure that the care models in place are effective, efficient and of the highest quality. Moreover, they have the opportunity to positively influence the strategic directions of the organization, to exercise this responsibility with benevolence and compassion, and to influence others to work together to achieve these changes [2, 10, 11].

This consensus on the desirability of combining expertise is based, however, on distinct references to the role of physician managers and associated models. Saxena et al. [12] describe 3 possible ways of configuring dyads, corresponding to the creation of a medical and nursing manager pair, namely "(1) the parallel model with shared overall responsibility for the whole, but with separate portfolio flows that do not overlap [...]. (2) the integrated model with shared overall responsibility, but where each partner in the dyad is individually responsible for each sub-role [...]. (3) the hybrid model is the one preferred by many because it allows individual expertise to be used and joint leadership to be developed, with well-defined responsibilities in both shared and individual areas".

What's more, senior management's expectations of the physician-managers are not explicitly expressed or documented, or do not necessarily correspond to the reality of the work expected of them. This lack of clarity regarding the definition of positions and the hierarchical responsibilities of each is a source of tension, according to medical managers [13].

Thus, the literature highlights the interest of certain doctors in developing managerial skills but does not focus on the motivating factors that encourage doctors to become involved in management, nor on the challenges of participation that may hold them back in their ambition (barriers, constraints, strategies that have an impact on doctors' involvement). We therefore felt it necessary to carry out a systematic literature review to identify the factors that facilitate or inhibit motivation to become a physician manager, the expectations of these professionals, and avenues for improvement.

2 Methodology

In order to identify the conditions facilitating or hindering physicians' involvement in the management of clinical activities within healthcare facilities, we conducted a systematic literature review. In addition, we followed the recommendations of the revised PRISMA (Preferred Reporting Items for Systematic Reviews and Meta-Analyses) protocol [14] to report selected literature. Eight database aggregations were consulted: Medline, Embase, CINAHL, Web of Science, PsycInfo, ABI/Inform, Academic Search Premier and MedRxiv. To guide the selection, we opted for the PCC mnemonic criteria (population, context, concept) proposed by the Joanna Briggs Institute [15]. The elements specified for the development of the PCC are as follows:

- Target population: physician-managers, managers and/or clinicians.
- Context: healthcare facilities in all geographical areas.
- Concept: involvement and commitment of physicians in management at institutional, organizational and operational levels.

The latest strategy was launched on 01 February 2022. Research articles were uploaded to Covidence software (version 2020). The team developed selection questions and forms for levels 1 (abstract) and 2 (full text) of the selection, based on the inclusion and exclusion criteria presented in Table 1.

Data coding was carried out by two independent coders, in the following stages:

- Inductive coding identified recurring themes and listed them in a table made available to all team members.
- Themes were re-evaluated throughout the extraction process, with a constant to-and-fro between the themes to be coded and the content of the articles.
- Validation of the themes was carried out by two senior researchers, following multiple discussions within the group of researchers.
- From the extracted data, a synthesis of each theme was produced, retaining the original citations to avoid the risk of altering the meaning. The extracts from the articles were numbered and arranged in chronological order to analyze the evolution of the themes addressed in the literature over the years, and to document

Table 1 Inclusion and exclusion criteria

Inclusion criteria	Exclusion criteria
Studies on:	Studies focusing on:
The motivating factors that encourage doctors to get involved in management, and the challenges to participation that can hold them back in their ambitions	Physician involvement at the operational level (physician–patient interaction) and at the macro level (institutional and organizational level)
Barriers, constraints and strategies affecting physician involvement	Issues and impacts of physician involvement in management processes on the organization
The studies to be included should describe the strategies put forward to involve physicians in the management processes of the healthcare organization (meso level), and the responses (impact and consequences) of these strategies on the behavior of the physicians involved	Performance evaluation; impact of physician involvement on organizational performance; studies to be included should outline the strategies put forward by the studies outlining the strategies
	Writing of the following nature: opinions, commentaries, dissertations and theses

the possible emergence of new themes (Table 2). The results of this systematic review reveal five major analytical themes, corresponding to numbers I to V in the table:

- Concrete nature of the role, work and responsibilities of medical chiefs within healthcare establishments (I)
- Factors that encourage or discourage doctors from getting involved in the management of their respective medical departments (II)
- Expectations and needs of medical directors and non-medical clinical directors with regard to the function of medical chief (III)
- Expectations and needs of medical chiefs in relation to the function of medical chief (IV)
- Suggested corrective measures to make the medical manager's task more efficient (V)

Table 2 Table summarizing theme extraction

Authors	Year	I				II		
		I.1	I.2A	I.2B	I.2C	II.1	II.2	II.3
Durán-Arenas et al. [16]	1992		X				X	X
Balderson and MacFadyen [17]	1994					X	X	
Buchanan et al. [18]	1997		X	X	X	X	X	X
Hearing et al. [19]	1999					X		
Callanan et al. [20]	2002				X	X	X	
Forbes et al. [13]	2004			X		X		X
Ham [21]	2008			X	X			
Fernandez and Fellow-Smith [22]	2011							
Snell et al. [11]	2011			X	X		X	
Dalmas [23]	2012						X	
Kaissi [24]	2014					X	X	X
Kreindler et al. [25]	2014							
Quinn and Perelli [26]	2016					X		
Macinati et al. [1]	2016	X			X	X	X	X
Lega and Sartirana [8]	2016	X	X		X	X	X	X
Roth et al. [27]	2016						X	X
Snell et al. [9]	2016			X	X	X		
Throgmorton et al. [10]	2016				X			
Skillman et al. [28]	2016							
Saxena et al. [12]	2018			X				
Perreira et al. [29]	2018						X	
Kirk et al. [30]	2019						X	
Giacomelli et al. [2]	2019	X			X	X		X
Sartirana [3]	2019	X	X		X			X
Saxena [31]	2021						X	
Prenestini et al. [7]	2021	X			X			

Authors	Year	III	IV	V				
				V.1A	V1B		V.2	V.3
					V.1B1	V.1B2		
Durán-Arenas et al. [16]	1992			X				X
Balderson and MacFadyen [17]	1994		X		X	X	X	
Buchanan et al. [18]	1997	X		X	X	X		
Hearing et al. [19]	1999		X		X	X	X	
Callanan et al. [20]	2002	X	X	X	X			
Forbes et al. [13]	2004		X	X		X	X	
Ham [21]	2008					X	X	X

(continued)

Table 2 (continued)

Authors	Year	III	IV	V				
				V.1A	V1B		V.2	V.3
					V.1B1	V.1B2		
Fernandez and Fellow-Smith [22]	2011				X	X	X	
Snell et al. [11]	2011		X	X	X			
Dalmas [23]	2012		X			X		X
Kaissi [24]	2014		X				X	X
Kreindler et al. [25]	2014			X				X
Quinn and Perelli [26]	2016			X				
Macinati et al. [1]	2016							
Lega and Sartirana [8]	2016					X	X	X
Roth et al. [27]	2016		X		X			X
Snell et al. [9]	2016				X	X		
Throgmorton et al. [10]	2016	X						
Skillman et al. [28]	2016							X
Saxena et al. [12]	2018			X				
Perreira et al. [29]	2018							X
Kirk et al. [30]	2019				X			X
Giacomelli et al. [2]	2019			X	X			
Sartirana [3]	2019			X				X
Saxena [31]	2021			X			X	X
Prenestini et al. [7]	2021			X				

3 Results

The Fig. 1. presents the article selection flow chart.

3.1 Factors Influencing Physician Involvement in the Management of Medical Activities

Physician involvement in the day-to-day management of clinical activities depends on a number of factors. Adequate organizational support, a clear definition of the role, autonomy, authority and appropriate resources are essential to facilitate physician-manager involvement in their role. Table 3 provides a summary of the factors favourable and unfavourable to physician involvement in the day-to-day management of clinical activities.

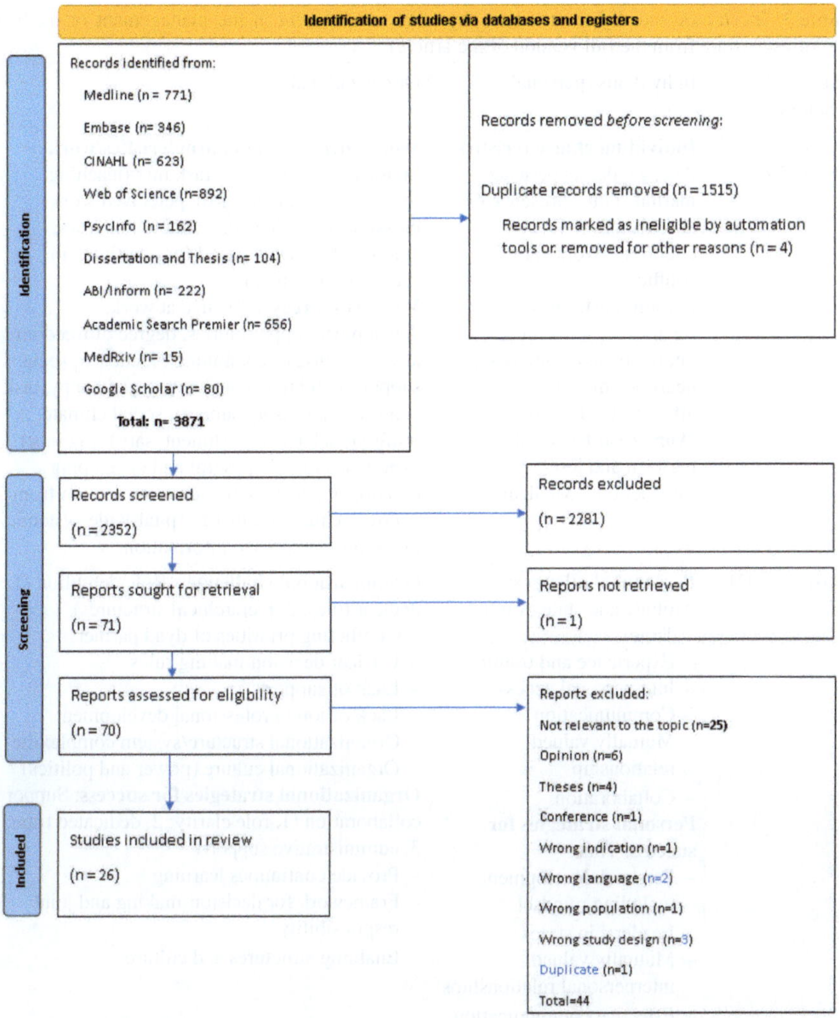

Fig. 1 PRISMA 2020 article selection flow chart [14]

The dichotomy between managers who are willing to get involved and those who show a certain reluctance to get involved in the management of their service and department remains present, both in terms of profiles and motivations.

Table 3 Incentives and disincentives to physician involvement in the management of medical activities (extract from the full version of the article)

Authors/ Factors	Individuals (personal)	Organizational
Perreira et al., 2018 [29]	**Individual characteristics**: Age, gender, experience, marital status, presence or absence of children—Work-family conflict **Personal attributes**: Resilience, self-efficacy, optimism, agreeableness, neuroticism and affectivity—Pessimism **Work results**: Ability to perform and job satisfaction—Medical errors	**Work environment characteristics/work factors**: Quality of life, task mix (teaching, research and patient care), perceived work pressure, work demands: amount of work, emotional demands, need for overtime, no access to information **Work resources**: Influence at work, development opportunities, degree of freedom at work, sense of community, feedback, social support, making people healthy and happy, task control, supervisory support, social climate, professional accomplishment, satisfying inner experience of being useful and developing organizational support such as protection from courtesy calls and other hospital-wide systemic measures—Access to information
Saxena, 2021 [31]	**Personal challenges**: Attitude and state of mind – Time – Experience and training – Interpersonal access – Communication – Mutually valued relationship – Collaboration **Personal strategies for success**: Time – Personal development, including mindset – Leadership styles – Mutually valued interpersonal relationships – Effective communication – Effective collaboration – Experience and training	**Organizational challenges**: Role definition (1. unclear roles; 2. hierarchical structures) – Conflicting priorities of dyad partners – Unclear decision-making rules – Lack of support – Lack of joint professional development – Organizational structure/system complexities – Organizational culture (power and politics) **Organizational strategies for success**: Support collaboration (1. role clarity; 2. dedicated time; 3. administrative support) – Provide continuous learning – Framework for decision-making and joint responsibility – Enabling structures and culture

3.2 *Expectations and Needs Expressed by Medical Managers*

Expectations of physician-managers include regular meetings, a less distant attitude, an effective and visible presence within the organization, sharing their experience and expertise, and exercising their authority in difficult situations [18]. Clinicians involved in management are also asked to impose restrictions on the provision of care and services to meet the organization's financial imperatives [20]. In addition, they are also asked to engage in teamwork, demonstrate communication skills [18], develop emotional intelligence and business acumen [10].

Physicians in charge of medical services and departments are first and foremost doctors, and as such demand a high degree of autonomy in their decisions and actions [20]. The need for organizational support is also mentioned in several studies. A support team including nurses and managers is also called for [18]. Finally, Saxena et al. [12] point out that support begins with clarification of the role, which must be both meaningful and strategic [17]. The function must not be merely symbolic, and the influence exerted must be significant and positive, enabling it to contribute directly to the hospital's success [11]. Physician-managers feel that their role cannot be strategic, and that their influence remains limited without formal recognition of it [11].

3.3 Ways to Improve Involvement

The literature suggests a number of corrective measures to encourage physician involvement in the management of clinical activities, and the challenges associated with this involvement. We have grouped them under three main headings:

- Structuring the physician-manager role and providing the necessary resources.
- Recruiting physicians with a natural aptitude for management.
- Establishing a culture that encourages the emergence of physician-managers.

By implementing these changes, organizations can contribute to the emergence of a new culture in which doctors are more willing to take on leadership roles and become actively involved in hospital management [8].

4 Conclusions

This literature review suggests a few avenues for future research.

The first would be to investigate the effects of role hybridization on physicians' long-term efficiency and well-being at work. The question of job benefits, and more specifically remuneration, could also be of interest. It would be counter-intuitive to expect doctors to tolerate a significant loss of earnings by accepting administrative responsibility. Traditionally, doctors' income has been a major stake in their status, and it would be interesting to investigate the extent to which accepting a hybrid role may or may not provide an intrinsic motivator that outweighs income. If not, what means could be put forward to compensate for the loss of income resulting from the workload imposed by the position of department head?

We could also question the merits of the hybrid status of physician-manager. We could, for example, experiment with and compare the managerial performance of a physician-manager with that of a manager who is familiar with healthcare services.

In other words, we could investigate how doctors trained in management would be more effective than managers trained in health services.

Acknowledgements The authors would like to thank Mrs Samar Koubeissy, Mrs Vivian Gomez, Mrs Chantale Simard and Mr Gildas Agbon for their significant contribution to this research. An extended and French version of this paper is available [32].

References

1. Macinati, M.S., Bozzi, S., Rizzo, M.G.: Budgetary participation and performance: the mediating effects of medical managers' job engagement and self-efficacy. Health Policy **120**(9), 1017–1028 (2016). https://doi.org/10.1016/j.healthpol.2016.08.005
2. Giacomelli, G., Ferré, F., Furlan, M., Nuti, S.: Involving hybrid professionals in top management decision-making: how managerial training can make the difference. Health Serv. Manage. Res. **32**(4), 168–179 (2019). https://doi.org/10.1177/0951484819844778
3. Sartirana, M.: Beyond hybrid professionals: evidence from the hospital sector. BMC Health Serv. Res. **19**, 634 (2019). https://doi.org/10.1186/s12913-019-4442-1
4. Noordegraaf, M.: Hybrid professionalism and beyond:(new) forms of public professionalism in changing organizational and societal contexts. J. Prof. Organ. **2**(2), 187–206 (2015). https://doi.org/10.1093/jpo/jov002
5. Olakivi, A., Niska, M.: Rethinking managerialism in professional work: from competing logics to overlapping discourses. J. Prof. Organ. **4**(1), 20–35 (2017). https://doi.org/10.1093/jpo/jow007
6. Pache, A.C., Santos, F.: Inside the hybrid organization: selective coupling as a response to competing institutional logics. Acad. Manag. J. **56**(4), 972–1001 (2013). https://doi.org/10.5465/amj.2011.0405
7. Prenestini, A., Sartirana, M., Lega, F.: Involving clinicians in management: assessing views of doctors and nurses on hybrid professionalism in clinical directorates. BMC Health Serv. Res. **21**(1), 1–11 (2021). https://doi.org/10.1186/s12913-021-06352-0
8. Lega, F., Sartirana, M.: Making doctors manage… but how? Recent developments in the Italian NHS. BMC Health Serv. Res. **16**(2), 65–72 (2016). https://doi.org/10.1186/s12913-016-1394-6
9. Snell, A.J., Dickson, G., Wirtzfeld, D., Van Aerde, J.: In their own words: describing Canadian physician leadership. Leadersh. Health Serv. **29**(3), 264–281 (2016). https://doi.org/10.1108/LHS-12-2015-0045
10. Throgmorton, C., Mitchell, T., Morley, T., Snyder, M.: Evaluating a physician leadership development program–a mixed methods approach. J. Health Organ. Manag. **30**(3), 390–407 (2016). https://doi.org/10.1108/JHOM-11-2014-0187
11. Snell, A.J., Briscoe, D., Dickson, G.: From the inside out: the engagement of physicians as leaders in health care settings. Qual. Health Res. **21**(7), 952–967 (2011). https://doi.org/10.1177/1049732311399780
12. Saxena, A., Davies, M., Philippon, D.: Structure of health-care dyad leadership: an organization's experience. Leadersh. Health Serv. **31**(2), 238–253 (2018). https://doi.org/10.1108/LHS-12-2017-0076
13. Forbes, T., Hallier, J., Kelly, L.: Doctors as managers: investors and reluctants in a dual role. Health Serv. Manag. Res. **17**(3), 167–176 (2004). https://doi.org/10.1258/0951484041485638
14. Page, M.J., McKenzie, J.E., Bossuyt, P.M. et al.: The PRISMA 2020 statement: an updated guideline for reporting systematic reviews. Bmj **372** (2021). https://doi.org/10.1136/bmj.n71
15. Aromataris, E., Munn, Z.: Joanna Briggs Institute reviewer's manual. The Joanna Briggs Institute, Adelaide (2017)

16. Durán-Arenas, L., Asfura, M.B., Mora, J.F.: The role of doctors as health care managers: an international perspective. Soc Sci Med **35**(4), 549–555 (1992). https://doi.org/10.1016/0277-9536(92)90348-T
17. Balderson, S., MacFadyen, U.: Management training for doctors: an in-house approach. J. Manag. Med. **8**(6), 17–19 (1994). https://doi.org/10.1108/02689239410073402
18. Buchanan, D., Jordan, S., Preston, D., Smith, A.: Doctor in the process the engagement of clinical directors in hospital management. J. Manag. Med. **11**(3), 132–156 (1997). https://doi.org/10.1108/02689239710177774
19. Hearing, S., Dent, T., Swann, J., Gunaratna, I., McLellan, I., Ikidde, U.: Maximizing the contribution doctors make to NHS management. Health Serv. Manag. Res. **12**(4), 227–231 (1999). https://doi.org/10.1177/095148489901200404
20. Callanan, I., McDermott, R., Buttimer, A.: Management issues in healthcare Involving Irish clinicians in hospital management roles–barriers to successful integration. Clin. Manag. **11**, 77–87 (2002)
21. Ham, C.: Doctors in leadership: learning from international experience. Int. J. Clin. Lead. **16**(1), 11–16 (2008)
22. Fernandez, V., Fellow-Smith, E.A.: Feedback on a specialty trainees management and leadership group. Int. J. Clin. Lead. **17**(1), 53 (2011)
23. Dalmas, M.: Involving clinicians in hospital management roles: towards a functional integrative approach. Int. J. Clin. Lead. **17**(3), 139 (2012)
24. Kaissi, A.: Enhancing physician engagement: an international perspective. Int. J. Health Serv. **44**(3), 567–592 (2014). https://doi.org/10.2190/HS.44.3.h
25. Kreindler, S.A., Larson, B.K., Wum, F.M., et al.: The rules of engagement: physician engagement strategies in intergroup contexts. J. Health Organ. Manag. **28**(1), 41–61 (2014). https://doi.org/10.1108/JHOM-02-2013-0024
26. Quinn, J.F., Perelli, S.: First and foremost, physicians: the clinical versus leadership identities of physician leaders. J. Health Organ. Manag. **30**(4), 711–728 (2016). https://doi.org/10.1108/JHOM-05-2015-0079
27. Roth, V.R., Theriault, A., Clement, C., Worthington, J.: Women physicians as healthcare leaders: a qualitative study. J. Health Organ. Manag. **30**(4), 648–665 (2016). https://doi.org/10.1108/JHOM-09-2014-0164
28. Skillman, M., Cross-Barnet, C., Singer, R.F., et al.: Physician engagement strategies in care coordination: findings from the centers for medicare and medicaid services' health care innovation awards program. Health Serv. Res. **52**(1), 291–312 (2017). https://doi.org/10.1111/1475-6773.12622
29. Perreira, T.A., Perrier, L., Prokopy, M.: Hospital physician engagement. Med. Care **56**(12), 969–975 (2018). https://doi.org/10.1097/MLR.0000000000000983
30. Kirk, V.G., Kania-Richmond, A., Chaput, K.: Executive coaching for leadership development: experience of academic physician leaders. Healthc. Q. (Tor. Ont) **22**(1), 54–59 (2019). https://doi.org/10.12927/hcq.2019.25835;
31. Saxena, A.: Challenges and success strategies for dyad leadership model in healthcare **34**(3), 137–148 (2020). https://doi.org/10.1177/0840470420961522
32. Côté, A., Benharbit, B., Lemaire, C., Gartner, J.-B., Bergeron, F., & Gilbert, M.-H.: Médecin ET gestionnaire: Une étude de portée ! Journal de gestion et d'économie de la santé, 3(3), 6–38 (2024). https://doi.org/10.54695/jdds.042.3.0006

Evolving Landscape of For-Profit Private Hospitals in France

Jean-Baptiste Capgras and Jean-Pierre Claveranne

Abstract This paper provides an in-depth analysis of the dynamic changes in France's for-profit private hospital sector from the 1980s to the present. It starts by exploring the sector's genesis, focusing on the initial developments that set the stage for subsequent transformations. A significant aspect of this evolution is the concentration phenomenon, which highlights how mergers and acquisitions reshaped the landscape, creating a more consolidated and competitive market. The paper delves into the impact of technological innovations, emphasizing how advancements in medical technology influenced the operations and strategies of private clinics. It also examines the shift towards more outpatient care and shorter hospital stays, a trend driven by efficiency goals and changing patient needs. A critical part of the analysis is the interplay between the state and private clinics. The study investigates how regulatory changes, particularly in tariffs, affected clinic activities, leading to strategic adaptations within the sector. The paper concludes by discussing the current dynamics of private hospitalization, including ongoing trends in mergers and acquisitions. This comprehensive study offers valuable insights into the changing face of France's private healthcare sector, highlighting key developments, challenges, and future directions.

Keywords Healthcare consolidation · Private hospital innovation · Outpatient care trends · Public–private healthcare dynamics

While in the collective imagination, public hospitals, and in particular university hospitals, are the archetypal form of healthcare provision, however the French hospital system is characterized by the important role played by private players in the healthcare sector. Of France's 3,000 healthcare establishments, 55% have private

J.-B. Capgras (✉)
IFROSS-CRDMS, Lyon 3 University, Lyon, France
e-mail: jean-baptiste.capgras@univ-lyon3.fr

J.-P. Claveranne
Lyon 3 University, Lyon, France

P. Landa et al. (eds.), *Operations Research and Artificial Intelligence in Healthcare Management*, Springer Proceedings in Mathematics & Statistics 506,
https://doi.org/10.1007/978-3-031-95659-1_18

status. Smaller overall than public hospitals, private establishments account for more than a third of full hospital bed capacity, and 45% of partial hospital bed capacity (ambulatory care) [1]. At the heart of this private offer, private for-profit hospitalization has been undergoing a restructuring process since the mid-2000s, which has intensified over the past five years and is set to continue. Today, it accounts for a third of all French hospitals (983 establishments), and covers the full range of hospital services.[1]

In a context marked by an aging population, an increase in chronic pathologies, and the concentration of populations in large cities and metropolises, public and private hospital structures are adapting and profoundly modifying their care offering, notably through the development of part-time hospitalization or home hospitalization, often resulting in a redesign of real estate. So, despite appearances, the clinic of the good Doctor X, his heirs and successors is no longer, or not quite, the same. When it "endures", it has sometimes forgotten its former name, no longer has its old address because its real estate has been transferred, but above all, in many cases, it has abandoned what characterized it and made it original: a business run by doctors for doctors.

This silent economic and legal metamorphosis, which in many cases has enabled the company to overcome difficult management challenges and resolve transmission problems or conflicts between doctors, has taken place within the broader context of the major upheaval that the world of healthcare, and more specifically the entire hospital sector, has been undergoing for the past 40 years.

The traditional clinic owned by a few associated doctors and housing few beds is a thing of the past. Since the early 1990s, the number of MSO clinics (Medicine, Surgery, Obstetrics) has halved, from 1,014 in 1992 to 478 in 2019.

These Brownian movements of vertical and horizontal concentration, as well as of cooperation, are part and parcel of other upheavals, in the sense of upheavals in the organization of something that needs to be briefly recalled if we are to understand the general framework of forces that have traversed the field of hospitalization.

The purpose of our paper is to explore the dynamics of private for-profit hospitalization during this period, understood as the study of things in their movement, a movement itself in relation to the forces that produce it, in turn producing causes and effects, with the aim of outlining the prospects heralded by this recompositing at national and international level.

This phenomenological research, conceived as a descriptive study of a set of phenomena, is based in particular on a "on the way" method of data collection linked to our immersion as actors/researchers within the hospital sector.

In the first part, entitled "Genesis", we will show how the observed concentration has its roots in two apparently distinct elements: the economic and legal nature of the clinic, confronted with the disruptions in medical practices. In the second part, we'll show how financial operators have taken advantage of the windfall in a sector made attractive by a number of factors.

---

[1] 478 acute and multidisciplinary care facilities, 334 follow-up care and rehabilitation facilities, 145 mental health facilities.

1 The Concentration Phenomenon: Unraveling the Core Complexities

Understanding the deconstruction and reconstruction of the sector means first of all bringing to light a multi-faceted intrigue in which strategies initially favorable to the stability of an organization turn against one of the pillars of the clinical entity, the operating company owned by a handful of doctors.

Unlike the public and private not-for-profit sectors, which bring together doctors, paramedics and other staff under a single banner to carry out their "healthcare work"[2], the for-profit healthcare establishment achieves this by offering a multitude of doctors, acting individually or in partnership, a "platform" from which to practice their art. This platform, broadly defined, is made up of two categories of elements:

- Medical equipment, devices and personnel involved in the diagnosis and treatment of patients;
- A set of services, or "processes", provided by the clinic (and/or by the group of clinics to which it belongs) to doctors on the basis of premises, staff, technical and IT equipment essential for doctors to practice their specialty, and for which the consideration due by the doctor to the clinic is called a fee.

This interweaving of structures, whose actions combine and recombine with each other on a daily basis as a function of the care and services provided to patients, constitutes what is commonly referred to as a clinic or, in administrative parlance, a private healthcare establishment, without drawing all the consequences on the obligations of each of the elements (Fig. 1).

1.1 The Basic element—the Legal Structure of the Private Clinic

In the beginning was "the clinic", whose name was that of one or more of the founding heirs [2]. It was set up on a simpler basis than the previous one, with two legal structures, one of a commercial nature dedicated to operations, and the other a civil structure carrying ownership of the real estate.

The credo of the original structure is a project implemented to develop a specific response to the needs of patients [3]: a facility run by doctors who are shareholders in the operating company and/or hold shares in the non-trading company that owns the premises, for shareholder doctors practicing their art in the clinic on an individual basis or grouped around a non-trading company.

[2] There are, however, rare exceptions in the not-for-profit sector, where doctors are paid on a fee-for-service basis, while the platform is run as an association, such as the Clinique Protestante in Lyon.

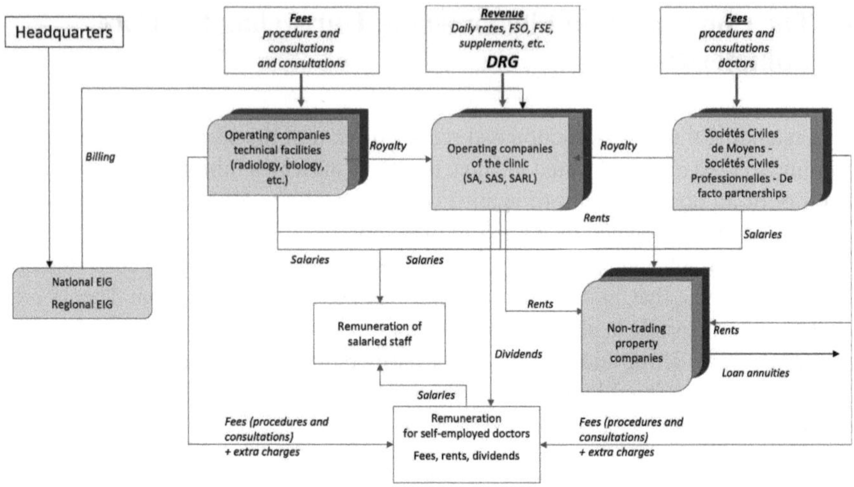

Fig. 1 The "clinic" in its economic interweaving

Long before the letter of the law, behind its apparent uniqueness, the clinic is a network organization, a virtual, organized structure of companies that combine their knowledge and/or skills in a close, mutually supportive collaboration, with the aim of realizing a single project.

Economically, this structure can be represented as a matrix in which the columns represent the various practitioners, and each row represents all the patients cared for by these practitioners.

This type of organization, which saves on transaction costs, offers the advantages of plasticity in the composition of the network (which can welcome or withdraw members), flexibility and the potential for innovation in the nature of activities.

1.2 The Business Model Associated with the Project

The clinic's network model is associated with an economic model that is relatively simple in principle: the remuneration linked to the hospitalization activity is made up of the financing of the[3] clinic on the one hand, and the remuneration of medical

[3] Prior to 2004 and the introduction of the Tarification à l'activité (T2A) system, the operating company's remuneration consisted of a daily rate based on historical tariffs negotiated by each establishment with the regional health insurance fund to which it belonged, to which lump-sum payments could be added (operating room lump-sum payment, safety and environment lump-sum payment, etc.). Since 2004, the operating company mainly receives a tariff set annually at national level for each stay (and no longer for each day), based on its automated classification in a Groupe homogène de séjours (GHS), depending mainly on the reason for hospitalization, any procedures performed, and the presence of comorbidities or comorbidity factors. In addition to the main fee,

acts for the practitioners on the other. The operating company pays rent to the SCI, and the practitioners pay a fee to the operating company.

A relatively simple legal structure and an economic model that associates each player with a remuneration: salaries for employees, fees paid by doctors to the operating clinic in return for services provided, rents paid according to usage to the non-trading company, a GHS and fees allocated by the social security system according to activity, make the clinic an apparently stable organization. This fee-based system, which is sufficiently robust to have adapted to the transition to Tarification à l'activité (T2A), will function smoothly overall, as long as the various players remain linked, each practitioner being a shareholder in both the operating company and/or the SCI.

The gradual concentration of clinics and the increase in their activity correlated with the arrival of a large number of doctors was to undermine this model, as a result of a dissociation in status between the doctors who owned the clinics and those who simply offered their know-how. Centrifugal forces will counteract the centripetal forces of the initial project. Here, as elsewhere, the devil is in the detail: a lack of remuneration for one of the agents, a questioning of the services provided within the structure, and the whole system (an organization by doctors for doctors) whose stability had successfully survived two centuries of history could be transformed into another system denying this originality.

2 Technological Breakthroughs and Their Impact on Private Clinics

From the 1980s onwards, three series of major innovations in medical practice led to major upheavals in the management of private clinics: radiology, the "New French Revolution" and anesthesia.

Radiology. The transition of medical imaging from an exploratory discipline focused on diagnosis to a discipline which, in an ever-increasing number of situations, carries out patient management including interventional and therapeutic activities, has revolutionized not only the organization of patient management, but also fields of specialization such as vascular or cardiac surgery [4].

The "new French revolution" [5]. In an article devoted to the dynamics of private hospitalization, we could do no less than give a special place to the fundamental role played by surgeon Philippe Mouret, founder of the Sauvegarde clinic in Lyon and author of the first laparoscopic cholecystectomy in Lyon in 1987, which revolutionized surgical management. The development of laparoscopy enabled the development of outpatient surgery and early rehabilitation, particularly in private clinics, thanks to an organization that is almost industrialized and, at the very least, meticulous.

ancillary funding may be added to finance certain implantable medical devices or "expensive" molecules.

Anesthesia. The development of anaesthesia has enabled surgery to take off, and as part of the general effort to reduce the impact of surgery on patients, it has made it possible to manage patients with increasingly severe co-morbidities. In the operating theatre, the anaesthetist has access to increasingly sophisticated technological aids to continue reducing the risks of this essential surgical procedure.

These innovations will support the development of our facilities and strengthen the positioning of our clinics in a number of specialties, where the potential offered by very short stays and outpatient hospitalization is greatest. Funding constraints and the strain placed on the original business model are accelerating the restructuring of clinics in search of increasing returns.

2.1 The Consequences of These Innovations

The development of outpatient activity leads to a pendulum swing, firstly in the clinics' favor, enabling them to increase their market share while reducing the length of their stays and therefore the turnover of their capital [6], and then more unfavorably, as the funding bodies retaliate by pointing out that the game is closed by the National Health Insurance Expenditure Target (ONDAM), and that any increase in activity leads to a reduction in rates.

The Shift Towards Outpatient Care: Reducing Hospital Stay Durations

The multiplication of surgical specialties at the heart of these innovations has led to a revolution in patient care and clinic organization. Over the years, the proportion of inpatient stays lasting several days has been reduced in favor of inpatient beds enabling patients to be cared for in less than 24 h, resulting in a considerable reduction in the average length of stay (ALOS) (Fig. 2).

After a significant decline over the previous 30 years, the relative stagnation of ALOS over the last 20 years in national and international statistics is only apparent. These statistics are in fact limited to full hospitalization, and in fact remain blind to the main development of the last 20 years, which is the growth in outpatient activity common to the entire sector, but more particularly driven by private for-profit establishments, which account for almost half of all short-stay outpatient activity. Over the last 10 years, the proportion of MSO activity carried out on an outpatient basis has risen from 46 to 57% in private for-profit establishments, and the ALOS calculated on the total activity in full and partial hospitalization has risen from 2.7 days to 2.1 days[4] (Fig. 3).

Technological developments, combined with advances in anaesthesia, are fostering the emergence of new segments, as demonstrated by the development of

[4] For full hospital stays alone, Drees reports an ALOS of 4.2 days in 2019 for private for-profit establishments. Our own calculations reintegrate all full and partial hospitalization activity (excluding sessions) based on a deliberately conservative scenario counting 1 day per outpatient stay, whereas it is more common to have outpatient hospitalizations of less than half a day.

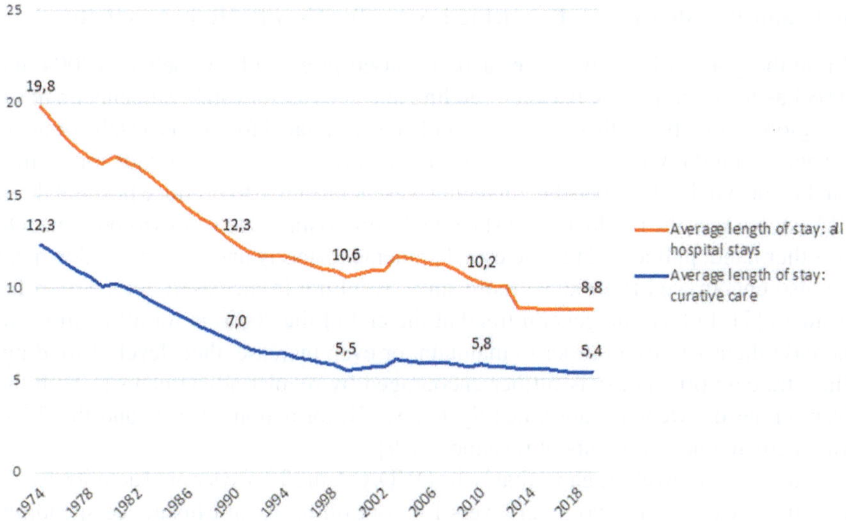

Fig. 2 Decrease in average length of stay (1974–2019)[5]

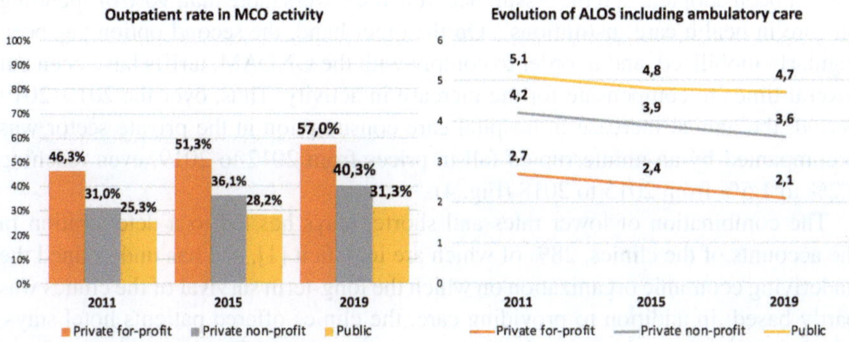

Fig. 3 Trends in ambulatory activity rates and ALOS including ambulatory activity (2011–2019)[6]

very short stays. These new activities are leading to the transformation of existing establishments, and even to the entry of new players specializing in ophthalmology, orthopedics, gastrology or urology. These new establishments provide hyperspecialized care 5 days a week, in real-estate structures strictly adapted to patients' needs, and with planned and optimized care. These new organizations, which benefit from the same rates as traditional clinics, generate highly profitable rates of return (operating income/sales), accentuated by the increase in sales per euro of capital invested and the leverage effect inherent in the difference between the economic rate of return and the cost of borrowing.

[5] *Source* OECD statistics.

[6] *Sources* SAE, Drees, ATIH. ALOS calculated by us from ATIH data.

State and Private Clinics: Balancing Lower Tariffs with Higher Activity

While the gradual introduction of activity-based pricing (T2A) between 2004 and 2008 has restored the link between funding and activity for establishments financed on a global grant basis, this link has never been eliminated for private establishments financed on a daily fee basis. However, the revolution is no less major for clinics. On the one hand, where per-day financing was an incentive to produce hospital days, T2A encourages the production of stays each comprising as few days as possible. On the other hand, public and private establishments formerly under global endowment are also encouraged to produce more stays, resulting in increased competition for business [7]. In fact, the general trend at the end of the 2000s is for all facilities to increase their activity in order to maintain, or even increase, their level of funding. This strategic orientation is further encouraged by regular adjustments to both the Programme de Médicalisation des Systèmes d'Information (PMSI) and the T2A, which create uncertainty about revenues [8, 9].

In the closed-envelope game that is the ONDAM, the T2A system of activity-based incentives leaves only two main levers for controlling Health Insurance spending: shifting part of the expenditure to other funders (supplementary health insurance schemes and patients), and reducing tariffs. For the time being, the first approach has not been adopted, and the Assurance Maladie covers more than 90% of spending on care in health care institutions.[7] On the other hand, the second option has been regularly mobilized, and in order to comply with the ONDAM, tariffs have been cut several times to compensate for the increase in activity. Thus, over the 2010–2019 period, the annual increase in hospital care consumption in the private sector was accompanied by an uninterrupted fall in prices from 2012 to 2019, even reaching 1.2% to 1.5% from 2015 to 2018 (Fig. 4).

The combination of lower rates and shorter stays has led to a deterioration in the accounts of the clinics, 28% of which are in deficit [1], and has undermined the underlying economic organization on which the long-term survival of the clinics was partly based: in addition to providing care, the clinics offered patients hotel stays, which generated rental income for the real estate company. The decline in lengths of stay is drying up part of the rental income of the non-trading company, whose real estate, oversized and ill-suited to the new treatments, costs more than it earns.

[7] However, in private, for-profit establishments, the majority of practitioners practice in sector 2, giving them the right to charge fees that are, by definition, not covered by health insurance. According to ATIH data, in 2018, 30% of the 15 million procedures performed by practitioners in private, for-profit healthcare establishments resulted in an average overcharge of 110% above the conventional tariff.

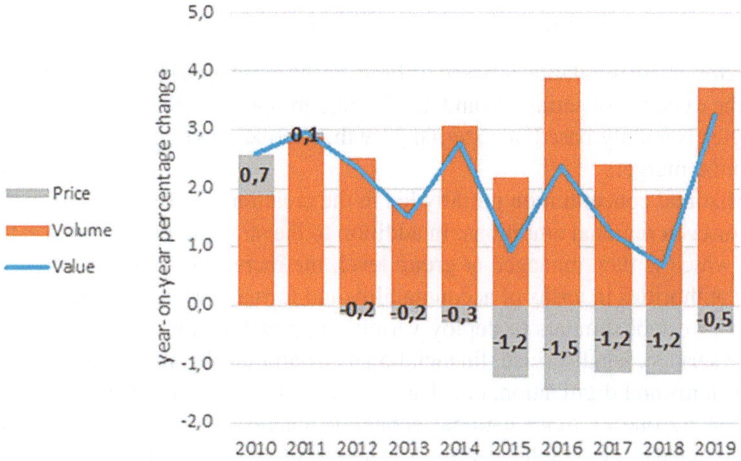

Fig. 4 Evolution of hospital care consumption in the private sector in value and price/volume breakdown (2010–2019) [10]

2.2 *Conclusion of the Narrative: Latest Trends in Private Hospitalization Dynamics*

Caught between falling tariffs and oversized real estate, clinics are faced with two difficulties: restoring their finances or investing to adapt their real estate. However, as mentioned *above*, the initial model has withered away, and investment in SCI and/or the operating company does not hold the same appeal for new generations of practitioners. Faced with this new situation, owner-practitioners have come up with various *scenarios* in an attempt to save their work tool:

- or share a number of services with other establishments, thereby generating synergies;
- or be absorbed by a regional or even national private group, by selling them the authorization they hold. Financial players then replace the practicing owners in the operating companies.

Since the mid-2000s, this trend has led to a major restructuring of the private hospital sector, with the emergence of regional, national and international groups whose growth has accelerated in recent years, driven by the attraction of the healthcare sector to financial groups from all over the world[8].

[8] In 2005, the top 3 groups (Générale de santé, Capio and Médi partenaires) accounted for 12% of MSO clinics, with cumulative sales of 1.9 billion euros. In 2020, the top 3 groups (Elsan, Ramsay Santé and Vivalto Santé) accounted for 43% of MSO clinics, with cumulative sales of 7.1 billion euros.

Mergers and Acquisitions: Key Drivers in the Current Era

In a sector where regulation is based on limiting the number of business authorizations [11], the dynamic of setting up and developing groups of establishments in search of synergies is mainly based on external growth, alternating or combining vertical and horizontal mergers.

Horizontal concentration initially led to the creation of several groups with territorial or even regional ambitions. In addition to the strategic policy of the establishment, which is then managed at group level, the increasing demands of the supervisory authorities in terms of accountability and formalization of organizations lead groups of establishments to deploy various support functions at head office level: quality service, legal service, financial analysis and management control, information systems and digitization, etc. The largest groups generally have these services provided by one or more national economic interest groupings (EIGs), possibly supplemented by geographical areas. The largest groups generally have these services provided by one or more national economic interest groupings (EIGs), possibly supplemented by EIGs for specific geographical areas. In addition to gains in efficiency and compliance, groups also seek to increase their negotiating power with all stakeholders, including public authorities.

The last decade has been marked by the search for greater synergies through vertical concentration along the care pathway. From the end of the 2000s, under pressure from the roll-out of the T2A, groups of MSO clinics sought to control their downstream activities by acquiring follow-up and rehabilitation care (SSR) establishments and home hospitalization (HAD) structures. The groups then expanded into the support functions of these sectors, investing in imaging, biology and, more recently, transport services. This movement of vertical concentration is far from complete, and today extends from the care pathway to the healthcare pathway, breaking down the historical boundaries between primary care and hospital care, and between the health, social and medico-social sectors.

The Attractiveness of the Healthcare Sector

In a world where capital circulates freely, several endogenous and exogenous factors explain the strong appeal of the French private hospital sector. Banks and property developers are investing in the sector, and a handful of financial groups are battling it out for leadership.

France's private hospital system offers three major endogenous advantages for investors: the outlook for demand driven by an ageing population, the fact that this demand is largely solvent thanks to a collectivized system, and the prospects for efficiency gains.

In terms of demand, between 2020 and 2030, the number of people aged 75 to 84—the age group with the highest proportion of hospital admissions—will increase by 49% in France, reaching 6.1 million [12]. While this ageing raises questions about how dependency will be financed beyond 2030, the fact that France's health insurance system covers hospitalization makes it the OECD country with the lowest out-of-pocket healthcare expenses [10] is an attractive guarantee for investors. This situation applies more or less to the whole of Europe, where 10% of the population will be aged 80 or over by 2050, compared with 4% of the world's population.

Furthermore, due to the very origins of clinics and the restrictions on supply imposed by the authorizations described above, the historical structuring of the market into small, independent units has offered, and continues to offer on a European scale, the prospect of synergies for investors, guaranteeing significant growth gains. Finally, the clinic real estate market has established itself as a specific asset class that financial groups, whose business it is not, are moving away from, for developers who find in it recurring returns of between 5 and 7% that office real estate no longer offers, long-term leases and portfolio diversification[9].

Moreover, in a globalized market, the private hospital sector offers exogenous factors of attractiveness linked to the transferability of the model either to developed countries as a complement to public healthcare provision, or to emerging countries. In the case of the former, they enable us to respond to the aspirations of certain countries that are unwilling or unable to finance the development of new hospitalization capacity to meet growing demand, as in Sweden or the discussions taking place in Quebec. For the latter, the aim is to respond to population growth and, in particular, the emergence of a middle class eager for access to cutting-edge medical techniques and accommodation of the highest quality. In both cases, the potential for transferability opens up the prospect of major growth drivers and new synergies.

Final Thoughts: The Continuing Evolution of France's Private Hospitals

The dynamics of the last 30 years have led to this concentration movement, which, as in other sectors, has taken the form of leveraged buy-outs (LBOs)[13] carried out by French or foreign funds. Within these groups, intellectual medical capital and financial capital are now disjointed, calling into question the common project. While these groups, as seen above, are becoming the dominant form, alternatives coexist and play an important role in the offering of private for-profit establishments [14]. To sum up, 3 main ideotypes and one variant are emerging from this dynamic recomposition of the sector: the independent clinic, the group of clinics and its two variants, and lastly, an intermediate ideotype constituted by the cooperative group.

The long-dominant independent clinic has been supplanted by groups of clinics, of which two ideotypes can be identified:

- groups of clinics with significant physician shareholding. This ideal type is generally more tightly structured, and has a local or regional geographical reach[10].
- groups of clinics with limited or no physician shareholding. This ideal type can be found within regional groups, and is the dominant model for the sector's biggest players with international ambitions.

[9] This dynamic may, however, lead to the entry of new players in the sector, such as the AVEC group, which originally came from the real estate sector.

[10] The Vivalto Santé group, however, is a perfect example of this on a national scale.

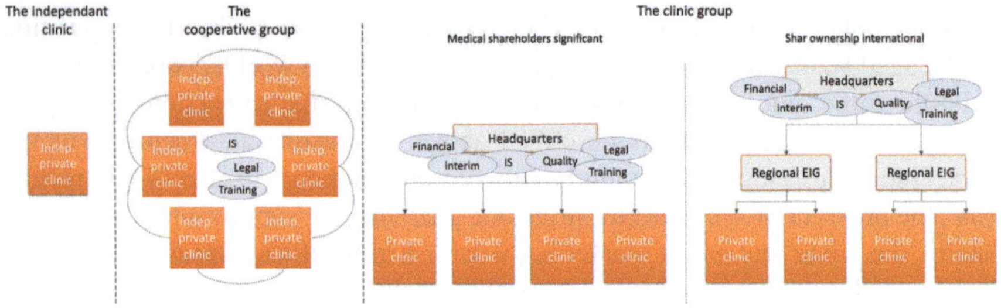

Fig. 5 The 3' ideotypes of clinics

- The cooperative group of independent clinics, an alternative ideal type, is made up of independent clinics and/or small groups of independent clinics sharing certain services in search of synergies while retaining their independence[11].

The dynamics discussed in this paper are constantly evolving, and the lines of force that led to the emergence of today's ideotypes may break down in the face of numerous present and future challenges: an aging population and the role of housing, shortages and/or quality of working life for healthcare professionals, the attractiveness of public or private not-for-profit services for patients, and so on (Fig. 5).

Finally, the holistic approach in terms of healthcare pathways, or even life paths, is attracting new players such as mutual insurance companies, banks and insurers, who have already invested heavily in the capital of the major groups. But it is also widening the field of competition, because while groups from the private clinic sector are investing in the elderly sector, or in primary care by developing health centers, for example, we are also witnessing the arrival of groups from the social or medico-social sector in the healthcare field.

References

1. Drees.: Les établissements de santé. [Healthcare Institutions]. Paris, France (2021)
2. Claveranne, J.P., Pascal, C., Piovesan, D.: Les restructurations des cliniques privées : radioscopie d'un secteur en mutation. [Restructuring of Private Clinics: X-Ray of a Sector in Transition.] Revue française des affaires sociales. Paris: La Documentation française: 55–78 (2003). https://doi.org/10.3917/rfas.033.0055
3. Faure, O.: Les cliniques privées. Deux siècles de succès. [Private Clinics. Two Centuries of success] Rennes, France: Presses universitaires de Rennes (2012)
4. Bonhomme, D., Pinaudeau, D.: Imagerie médicale: des innovations au service de l'optimisation et de l'efficience. [Medical Imaging: Innovations Serving Optimization and Efficiency] IRBM News 29. Elsevier Masson SAS: 20–25 (2008). https://doi.org/10.1016/S1959-7568(08)73445-X.
5. Schlogel, G.: Philippe Mouret: une (r)évolution par la coelio-chirurgie : le Français qui a bouleversé la pratique chirurgicale du monde entier.[Philippe Mouret: A (R)evolution Through

[11] Santé Cité brings together more than 120 MSO establishments with combined sales of over €2 billion.

Laparoscopic Surgery—The Frenchman Who Transformed Surgical Practice Worldwide] Paris, France: Sauramps medical (2017)
6. Claveranne, J.P., Pascal, C.: T2A et gestion hospitalière : la physiologie du changement. [T2A and Hospital Management: The Physiology of Change] Gestion hospitalière: 609–613 (2005)
7. Choné, P., Evain, F., Wilner, L., Yilmaz, E.: Tarification à l'activité et concurrence non tarifaire. [Activity-Based Funding and Non-Price Competition]. In: Panorama des établissements de santé, d:43–57. Paris, France: DREES (2013)
8. Cash, E., Cash, R., Dupilet, C.: La réactivité des établissements de santé aux incitations tarifaires. [The Responsiveness of Health Institutions to Pricing Incentives] 106. Etudes et Recherche. Paris (2011)
9. Moisdon, J.C., Pepin, M.: Les impacts de la T2A sur les modes d'organisation et de fonctionnement des établissements de santé. [The Impacts of Activity-Based Funding (T2A) in the Organisational and Operational Modes of Health] 97. Etudes et Recherches. Paris, France (2010)
10. Marc, C., Héam, J.C., Mikou, M., Portela, M.: Les dépenses de santé en 2019–édition 2020. [Health Expenditures in 2019–2020 Edition] Paris, France (2020)
11. Lemoyne de Forges, J.M., Apollis, B., Barlet, C., Francia, Y., Audouin, A., Seurot, L., Cristol, D., Cormier, M., Maublanc, J.V., Badin, X.: Les autorisations sanitaires—dossier. [Health Authorizations-Dossier] Revue de droit sanitaire et social mai-juin: 421–508 (2020)
12. Broussy, L.: Rapport interministériel sur l'adaptation des logements, des villes, des mobilités et des territoires à la transition démographique. [Interministerial Report on the Adaptation of Housing, Cities, Mobility, and Territories to Demographic Transition] Paris, France (2021). https://doi.org/10.1016/S0750-7658(85)80265-3.
13. Bartoli, F., Destais, N., Yeni, I., De Beauchamp, H.: Evaluation de la place et du rôle des cliniques privées dans l'offre de soins. [Evaluation of the Place and Role of Private Clinics in Healthcare Provision] Paris, France (2012)
14. Claveranne, J.P., Piovesan, D.: La clinique privée, un objet de gestion non identifié. [The Private Clinic: An Unidentified Management Object] Revue française de gestion 2003/5. Cachan: Lavoisier, pp. 143–153 (2003). https://doi.org/10.3166/rfg.146.143-153.

Replicating and Scaling a Healthcare Innovation: Theoretical and Methodological Insights

André Côté and Jean-Baptiste Gartner

Abstract Several authors note a growing gap between the development of evidence-based innovations from research projects and their implementation in day-to-day clinical and administrative practice on a large scale. One of the reasons for this is a lack of theoretical and methodological knowledge to implement the best clinical, administrative and organizational practices in other places and contexts. Scaling up requires an adaptive approach recognizing the importance of flexibility in design, appreciation of the local context, and a sensitive response to the unique needs of each environment. It requires the use of qualitative methods to examine underlying processes and mechanisms and encourages the adaptation of intervention to fit different contexts. Dissemination and scaling up of major innovations in the healthcare sector requires an approach rooted in complex systems theory which implies considering several plausible scenarios, fine-tuning innovations to local specificities, harmonizing innovation with the realities of receiving environments, and facilitating intra- and inter-organizational interactions.

Keywords Scaling up and replication · Implementation · Healthcare organization

A. Côté · J.-B. Gartner (✉)
Department of Management, Faculty of Business Administration, Laval University, Quebec City, QC, Canada
e-mail: jean-baptiste.gartner.1@ulaval.ca

Research Center for Health Services Management, Laval University, Quebec City, QC, Canada

Research Centre of the University Institute of Cardiology and Pneumology of Quebec, Quebec City, QC, Canada

VITAM, Centre for Sustainable Health Research, Laval University, Quebec City, QC, Canada

Research Center of the Hospital University of Québec, Laval University, Quebec City, QC, Canada

CISSS Chaudière-Appalaches Research Centre, Laval University, Quebec City, QC, Canada

A. Côté
e-mail: andre.cote@fsa.ulaval.ca

P. Landa et al. (eds.), *Operations Research and Artificial Intelligence in Healthcare Management*, Springer Proceedings in Mathematics & Statistics 506,
https://doi.org/10.1007/978-3-031-95659-1_19

1 Background

Several authors note a growing gap between the development of evidence-based innovations from research projects and their implementation in day-to-day clinical and administrative practice on a large scale [1–3]. In Canada, less than 40% of initiatives—stemming from pilot projects—aimed at improving health care and services are successfully replicated in another unit/department of the hospital organization. Yet, most of these innovations have a proven potential to improve the efficiency of care at the level of the healthcare system in general, and to meet the needs and expectations of patients in particular [4, 5]. These implementation difficulties are so common for service innovations that they cannot be considered a localized problem for the organizations adopting them.

One of the reasons for this is a lack of theoretical and methodological knowledge to implement the best clinical, administrative and organizational practices—resulting from pilot projects—in other places and contexts [6, 7]. "Conducting implementation research without a theoretical framework also hinders a foundational scientific goal of being able to generalize and build on findings across studies and contexts" [8]. The lack of empirical studies on replication and scaling up is also a contributing factor to this state of affairs [9]. This is why so many decision-makers and practitioners call on researchers to develop theoretical, conceptual and practical tools for scaling up innovations deemed promising in healthcare establishments [10, 11].

The purpose of this article is to shed theoretical and methodological light on the scaling up of innovation in the healthcare sector. The aim is to propose a clear and precise formulation of the concept, accompanied by a structured and contextualized approach. Finally, it aims to identify the prerequisites for scaling up an innovation within healthcare establishments. "The usefulness of all scaled-up innovations will ultimately depend on the strength of the methodology developed" [12].

2 Methods

To achieve this, we used a hybrid methodology combining both narrative review and concept analysis. Narrative reviews are used to update knowledge on a given subject, with the aim of identifying relevant publications. This type of review provides an overview of a specific topic, raising issues that are usually neglected and encouraging further research on the subject [13]. The concept analysis method aims to specify a concept and distinguish it from neighbouring concepts. It provides an operational definition of the concept under analysis, specifying its characteristics as well as its theoretical and empirical referents. The analysis consists of 8 steps as recommended by Walker and Avant in their 2011 paper [14] (Table 1).

Table 1 Presentation of the 8 steps recommended by Walker and Avant (2011), the adaptation of this method for the purposes of our study, and the themes that emerged during this study, which we will discuss in the next section

Step	Description of methodological step Walker and Avant [14]	Adapting Walker and Avant's model [14] to the realities of the study	Topics covered
1	Choosing a concept	Choosing a concept	• A real difficulty in scaling up promising innovations tested at local level • A lack of knowledge (theories and methods) for scaling up promising innovations • Few cases that could serve as examples and benchmarks The need to develop methods
2	Determine the purpose and objectives of the analysis	Determine the purpose and objectives of the analysis	Provide theoretical, conceptual and operational insight into an approach aimed at scaling up an innovation in the SSS field
3	Determining the defining characteristics	Define the concept under study	• Definition of concepts • Different types of scaling • An evidence-based approach
4	Building a model case (for example)	Identify concepts that are related, complementary, borderline or even contrary to each other	• Replication versus Scaling up • Advantages and limitations of replication
5	Constructing a limiting and opposite case		
6	Identify antecedents and consequences (i.e., outcomes)	Key concepts: Principles underlying the diffusion of an innovation	• A broad, all-encompassing definition of innovation • The preconditions (requirements) for disseminating an innovation • The prerequisites for disseminating an innovation, as well as facilitating factors • Strategic choices to be made • Actions and behaviours that reinforce success and sustainability
7	Identify all uses of the concept	Present the advantages and limitations of each of these uses	• Replication and scaling difficulties
8	Defining empirical referents	Propose theoretical and empirical referents	• Inspired by the open systems approach • Also from the logic of implementation science, just like that of learning healthcare systems, for that matter • Clear continuity/complementarity with learning healthcare systems

3 Results

For this paper, we analyzed 35 English-language scientific articles, distributed as follows: 13 literature reviews, 11 perspective papers, six case studies, three combining literature reviews and case studies, one theoretical article and one commentary. Most authors are affiliated with universities in North America and Europe (see Appendix 1 for a list of articles consulted).

3.1 Definition and Characterization of Scaling up

The World Health Organization (WHO) offers a consensus definition of scaling up, describing it as deliberate efforts to scale up the impact of successfully tested health innovations to benefit a greater number of people, and to encourage the formulation of policies and programs on a sustainable basis [15]. This definition is characterized by its all-encompassing nature, its potentially non-linear nature, its intrinsic complexity and its often-political dimension [12].

From a more concrete, application-oriented point of view, scaling up is defined as a process or method that enables an intervention that has proven its effectiveness on a small scale or under controlled conditions to be extended under real-life conditions to a larger proportion of the eligible population, while retaining its efficacy [16–18]. Innovations evaluated in the context of pilot projects must be evidence-based, or conclusively demonstrate their effectiveness, before being considered for scale-up. In addition, these innovations must represent economically viable alternatives to current practices, and be financially accessible [17, 19]. This is the definition we will use throughout this paper.

Three types of scaling have been identified in the literature: vertical, horizontal and functional. Vertical scaling is the result of political, strategic or legal imitative. It aims to institutionalize innovations through policy or legal action. Systems and structures are then adapted and resources redistributed to put in place the institutional mechanisms likely to guarantee the innovation's sustainability. Horizontal scaling (expansion) seeks to reproduce, or even expand, an innovation in similar services, sectors or organizations; the aim being to extend the innovation to new geographical areas or new target populations [20]. Functional scaling, on the other hand, aims to diversify the approach by adding new interventions to existing innovations [15]. It should be noted that the different types of scaling do not operate in isolation: spontaneous diffusion can occur in conjunction with guided scaling, and expansion is generally more effective when supported by political and institutional scaling [9, 15, 20].

3.2 Theoretical Referents

The scaling-up approach adheres to open systems theory. It is influenced by environmental factors such as gender inequalities, poverty, health system capacity and political forces [21]. The external context, including social, cultural, political and economic conditions, also plays a determining role in the success of the approach, requiring a systemic and integrated vision in planning and execution [15, 22, 23]. It is embedded in and complements the implementation sciences, seeking to systematically integrate research findings and evidence-based practices into health care and service activities. Like the implementation sciences, the scale-up approach develops strategies for adopting new health interventions in a particular setting, examining what works, for whom, and under what circumstances the innovation produces the expected results. Finally, more than implementation science, the scaling-up approach seeks to extend innovation to other contexts, enabling entire communities to benefit from the innovation [8, 23, 24]. Scaling up also aligns with the philosophy of learning health systems, contributing to the creation of more autonomous, agile and innovative health organizations. It promotes a better understanding and implementation of best practices. By developing national health learning programs, it identifies effective methods (the "what") and provides guidance on how to sustain and expand them geographically (the "how"), thus strengthening the ability to respond adaptively to health system challenges [6, 19, 25].

3.3 Replication Versus Scaling up

Some authors see "replication" and "scaling up" as similar processes [26, 27]. Others, on the other hand, see replication as an intermediate step aimed at reproducing the innovation on a small scale before going on to a global scale-up. From this point of view, replication aims to adopt and reproduce an intervention in a different environment. These interventions adjust, voluntarily or involuntarily, through contextual interactions and feedback processes, in order to reproduce the desired results in a more heterogeneous set [22, 24, 28]. Replication of a small-scale innovation under real-life conditions increases the likelihood of successful scale-up. Firstly, it provides a detailed view of the day-to-day implementation of the innovation, identifying whether and how it is applied. Secondly, it enables avoidable problems and negative side-effects to be identified and corrected before any expansion takes place. Thirdly, it provides information on what needs to be done to realize the innovation's potential, and how best to do it. In addition, it offers the opportunity to try out different delivery configurations at low cost. Finally, it acts as insurance against the risks associated with the large-scale application of an innovation that could prove ineffective or have negative repercussions, thus protecting against the waste of time and resources [22, 24]. However, replication is limited to the dissemination of an innovation without further adaptation. Consequently, it is likely to fail if the new environment differs from the initial test environment. Thus, rapid diffusion is only possible after the implementation process has been tested and adapted to the various contexts encountered in a complex scaling environment. Only when the intervention is designed to work in several contexts can it be reproduced with a minimum of further adaptation [23].

3.4 The Notion of Innovation

In the context of replication or scaling up, innovation is perceived as something new by those seeking to implement it. It encompasses not only new technologies or practices in healthcare services, but also those already in existence but unused in a specific context, making them innovations in this sense. What's more, innovation needs to be considered broadly and multifaceted, far beyond a single medical therapy, clinical practice or program component. It encompasses a range of interventions, including the processes required to build sustainable implementation capabilities. Unlike a simple, isolated solution, innovation is made up of a combination of several interdependent elements. Thus, innovation in health services is not limited to a particular technology, but also includes new delivery methods, changes in the approach to health service provision, or community-based interventions. It needs to be understood as a whole, reflecting its complexity and integration into various aspects of healthcare delivery [15, 17, 29].

3.5 Factors Facilitating the Replication and Scaling up of a Healthcare Innovation

The first, and perhaps most important, is to demonstrate the success of the innovation. Indeed, the pilot project must conclude positively with a demonstrated impact to merit the "Successfully tested" label. This implies that the interventions must be supported by locally generated evidence, confirming their efficacy and feasibility. What's more, scale-up must be aligned with the criteria of realization, relevance, and beneficial impact on the target population. However, it is crucial to recognize that not all innovations are replicable. Their potential and added value must be carefully weighed up before replicating them elsewhere. It should be noted that an innovation, even one that is effective on a small scale, may not achieve its objectives on a large scale if it is not aligned with the specific needs and expectations of the target populations. In this respect, Simmons et al. [15] propose seven criteria for determining the potential of an innovation to be scaled up, grouped under the acronym "CORRECT":

- **C**redible: Innovations must be based on solid evidence or backed by respected institutions.
- **O**bservable: Concrete results must be visible to potential users.

- **R**elevant: Innovations must solve persistent or felt problems.
- **R**elative Advantage: They must offer an advantage over existing practices.
- **E**asy to Implement: Innovations must be simple to understand and implement.
- **C**ompatible: Innovations must correspond to established values, norms and practices.
- **T**estable so that potential users can see the intervention on a small scale prior to large-scale adoption [15].

Secondly, the choice of receiving organization must be based on specific characteristics. Firstly, the members of the receiving organization must perceive a real need for the innovation, thus guaranteeing a match with the latter's objectives. In addition, the organization must have the appropriate implementation capacity, and the timing and circumstances must be right to welcome the innovation. Effective leadership and strong internal support within the receiving organization are also essential to guide and sustain the innovation. Finally, success is facilitated when the organizations disseminating the innovation and those wishing to implement it internally have similar characteristics and are physically close, thus strengthening cohesion and collaboration in implementing the innovation [15].

Successful large-scale innovation also requires substantial institutional capacity building and a guarantee of sustainability. This implies the development, establishment and maintenance of strong political support, coupled with the implementation of adequate management structures. Appropriate human and budgetary resources must be carefully allocated, and the service components essential to innovation must be put in place. Furthermore, the adoption of innovation is more likely to succeed if it coincides with a strong impetus for change and a clear fit with existing system routines. This means that the innovation must fit harmoniously into existing work and routines, and that it must enjoy broad support and limited opposition. Systematic assessment of the innovation's implications is also a crucial part of this process. All in all, these interdependent factors help to create a solid and resilient institutional ecosystem, fostering the successful implementation of programs and policies, and guaranteeing their long-term effectiveness and sustainability [26, 30].

Active stakeholder engagement is an essential component in the successful scaling of an innovation. This not only serves to ensure that needs are properly expressed and addressed, but also fosters a deeper, more nuanced understanding of the context in which the innovation is being implemented. The literature on organizational change places a strong emphasis on participatory approaches, even if, in practice, they are not always sufficiently applied. The scaling-up process, as an evolutionary process of transition, requires the deliberate involvement of the actors concerned at every phase, from conceptualization to operationalization. Influenced by their diverse beliefs, norms and affiliations, these individuals hold significant agency and can exert both predictable and unpredictable influence on the process. Their active participation thus facilitates the adoption and adaptation of the innovation, whether during the pilot phase or subsequent scaling up, contributing to a smoother and more effective integration of the innovation into the existing system [15, 31].

What's more, the successful implementation of an innovation is often linked to the existence and support of local champions. These key individuals, present at different levels of the organization or even the healthcare system, are vital, particularly during the initial phases of the innovation process. Their influence can manifest itself in several ways. Firstly, as experts in their field, they can validate the initiative, reinforcing its credibility. Secondly, their commitment denotes the importance and value of the implementation, which can stimulate acceptance within the organization. Thirdly, local champions, especially clinicians, often possess unique characteristics, such as motivation, listening skills and tenacity, qualities that can be enhanced by appropriate training. These local champions play a central role in persuading their peers, arguing that technology-supported service is effective, safe and professionally appropriate. In so doing, they act as catalysts, accelerating and facilitating the acceptance and adoption of innovation within their specific environment. Their role demonstrates the complexity and multifaceted nature of successful innovation implementation, underlining the importance of human dynamics in this process [30].

Finally, the successful adoption of an innovation will be greatly facilitated by a decentralized organizational structure. In such a framework, each department or unit can make semi-autonomous decisions, which fosters agility and adaptability. The presence of significant organizational leeway makes it possible to allocate unused resources to new projects, while supporting a culture of innovation and risk-taking where staff are encouraged and rewarded for their creative efforts. Strong leadership and good managerial relationships also nurture an environment conducive to innovation, as do opportunities for "meaning-making", where team members can collaborate to understand and interpret the meaning of an innovation [15, 22, 30].

3.6 Recommended Strategies for Scaling up

The academic literature details various strategies for scaling up a healthcare innovation, each adapted to the specific context, organizational structure and targeted objectives. The first possibility is an additive strategy, where the initial promoters plan and implement the scaling effort themselves. This approach places the entire burden of implementation on a single organization. The alternative is a multiplicative strategy, in which the initial promoters join forces with new partners to expand and promote the innovation. Here, promoters can benefit from the support and resources of the various partners, thus distributing the burden and responsibilities [6, 32]. A third choice lies in a centralized, top-down strategy, where scaling up is guided by a central authority, such as a ministry of health. While this approach can benefit from the strength of the large-scale implementation, it can also lead to rigid, uniform implementation, limiting the ability to adapt innovations to local needs. In contrast, a decentralized, bottom-up strategy can be chosen to encourage local initiative, autonomy, spontaneity, mutual learning and problem-solving. This approach allows greater flexibility and sensitivity to local realities. However, it has the disadvantage of lacking centralized reach or resources, thus limiting the ability to effect large-scale change

[15]. Each strategy has its own advantages and disadvantages and must therefore be carefully selected to align with the conditions and needs of scaling the innovation in question.

The importance of adaptability and flexibility in a scaling process is also a recurring theme in the literature. Organizations with a capacity for learning, able to adapt and think flexibly, are generally more likely to succeed than those that rigidly follow rules and emphasize standardization. This involves recognizing the need to understand and respond to the local context, using qualitative methods to explore processes and mechanisms, and tailoring intervention to best suit different contexts. Such an approach not only facilitates implementation, but also helps ensure that the innovation is genuinely beneficial and relevant to the target population. Successful intensification therefore requires a nuanced understanding of these dynamics and a willingness to adopt a balanced approach, capable of maximizing the benefits of different strategies while minimizing their drawbacks. This is a delicate challenge, requiring careful attention to detail, meticulous planning and sensitivity to the needs and constraints of each specific context [15, 31, 33].

3.7 *Actions and Behaviours that Reinforce the Potential for Success and Sustainability*

Preparing the host organization is crucial to successful scaling. Some of the challenges associated with this preparation include resistance to innovation due to previous beliefs or cultures, and competing priorities. Consensus on care objectives, alignment of practices between different services or departments, adequate dissemination of information on the aims and objectives of the innovation, and careful evaluation and adaptation at different levels of the organization can help overcome these challenges [19, 34].

In this respect, implementing an effective communication strategy is vital to promoting innovation within the receiving organization. The selection of communication methods must be adapted to the nature of the innovation and the organization's ability to assimilate the changes. Although impersonal communication strategies, such as publications and websites, are essential for dissemination, they are not sufficient on their own. Personal communication, including training programs, site visits, workshops and policy dialogues, is needed to spread innovations [35]. A mentoring and coaching program can also be key to successful scaling up. Research in the field of implementation science indicates that while training is necessary to develop skills, it is not sufficient on its own to achieve results. Training needs to be backed up by technical assistance, including coaching and problem-solving. This support not only ensures that skills are properly developed, but also that they are applied effectively and continuously, enabling the infusion of innovation on a wider scale [15, 34, 36].

In addition, meticulous planning of the time required by employees to support implementation strengthens the potential and sustainability of innovation. This includes the essential allocation of an advisory board made up of a diversity of roles and specialties to represent different perspectives and share information across the organization. This approach ensures that the different aspects of innovation are considered, and that innovation is effectively adapted and integrated into the organization, taking into account available resources and planning and execution processes. The same applies to the evaluation and monitoring process, which must be as rigorous as possible [16, 29].

Finally, the successful scaling up of a healthcare innovation requires a careful and comprehensive analysis of financial factors. This involves an accurate assessment of the costs associated with the innovation, recognition of the potential economies of scale that can be realized as the project develops, and careful planning to mobilize the necessary financial, human and material resources. In addition, it is imperative to examine the affordability of the innovation, its long-term profitability, and the feasibility of implementing it with fidelity in the existing system. These considerations ensure that the innovation can be integrated sustainably and effectively, in harmony with the constraints and opportunities of the economic and organizational context [17, 28].

3.8 Replication and Scaling Difficulties

The ability of an innovation to be replicated or scaled up is strongly influenced by its complexity. The more complex an innovation, or the context in which it is implemented, the more difficult it will be to adopt, develop and maintain successfully. This notion of complexity takes on a particular dimension when it comes to technological innovations. These can often require a significant transformation of existing clinical and organizational practices, adding further layers of difficulty and potential resistance. Thus, the diffusion and scaling up of an innovation cannot be seen as a linear mechanical process. On the contrary, they require a multi-perspective approach that considers the various aspects of the system, including operating modes, interactional dynamics and social context. When the innovation is ambitious and likely to meet resistance from the stakeholders involved, this multidimensional consideration is even more crucial to ensure successful and sustainable implementation [30, 31, 37]. In the context of innovation adoption, it is possible to identify four main types of resistance from clinicians, illustrating the complexity of implementing change in the healthcare field. The first type of resistance is linked to the introduction of a radical change in practice, such as the transfer of disease management from the professional to the patient. It may be perceived as an attack on traditional practice or professional autonomy. The second refers to the socio-material constraints arising from innovation. This may include questions about the reliability of the innovation, increased workload, or the creation of more difficult working conditions. The third type refers to clinicians' ability to exercise their professional judgment. The fourth and final type of resistance is based on the perception that innovation could reduce or limit face-to-face interactions, favouring remote communication. This can be experienced as the dehumanization of relations with patients or between professionals [30].

The literature also points to the problems most frequently encountered when scaling up an innovation. Firstly, the scheduling of activities and events for scaling may be too simplistic for the complexity of the innovation within the receiving organization. Secondly, the innovation may be insufficiently prototyped, customizable or reliable, require complex knowledge to use, or produce incomplete or inappropriate data. Thirdly, the value proposition may be imprecise in terms of quality, reliability or profitability. Fourthly, the target organizations may show little interest in the innovation, be ill prepared to receive it, or simply unable to put in place a viable strategy for its implementation. Last but not least, successful scaling requires a thorough understanding of the organizations in which the innovation is deployed. These organizations are often complex, marked by slowness, interwoven political interests, risk aversion and a propensity to seek simple solutions to complex problems [33]. In addition, they can be hampered by poorly paid staff, frequent staff changes and variable efficiency. Some administrations may wield considerable authority and operate efficiently, while others may have minimal legitimacy and be unproductive. Even within an organization, there can be significant variation, with zones of innovation coexisting with pockets of inefficiency, creating a complex and nuanced institutional landscape, where the scaling strategy needs to be carefully adapted [33, 38, 39].

4 Conclusion

Unlike a pilot project, which is often conducted in a controlled, quasi-experimental environment with the emphasis on standardization and reproducibility, scaling up requires an adaptive approach. The latter recognizes the importance of flexibility in design, appreciation of the local context, and a sensitive response to the unique needs of each environment. It requires the use of qualitative methods to examine underlying processes and mechanisms and encourages the adaptation of intervention to fit different contexts. As a result, it can be difficult to reconcile dissemination strategies that seek to reproduce a 'model' innovation in a standardized way, with the reality of heterogeneous practice settings and the unpredictability inherent in the varied contexts in which these innovations are deployed [31].

Unlike traditional 'plan-do-study-act' methodologies, which are appropriate for small-scale improvement initiatives, the dissemination and scaling up of major innovations in the healthcare sector requires an approach rooted in complex systems theory. This implies considering several plausible scenarios, fine-tuning innovations to local specificities, harmonizing innovation with the realities of receiving environments, and facilitating intra- and inter-organizational interactions. In addition, it requires encouraging collective thinking and learning, developing individual skills, promoting open-mindedness and collaboration, and constructively managing conflict. By adopting these principles, scaling up can successfully respond in a more nuanced and responsive way to the complex and evolving challenges faced by healthcare organizations [21].

References

1. Haynes, B., Haines, A.: Barriers and bridges to evidence based clinical practice. BMJ **317**(7153), 273–276 (1998). https://doi.org/10.1136/bmj.317.7153.273
2. Kristensen, N., Nymann, C., Konradsen, H.: Implementing research results in clinical practice-the experiences of healthcare professionals. BMC Health Serv. Res. **16**, 48 (2015). https://doi.org/10.1186/s12913-016-1292-y
3. Begin, M., Eggertson, L., Macdonald, N.: A country of perpetual pilot projects. CMAJ: Can. Med. Assoc. J. = J. l'Association Med.E Can **180**(12), 1185 (2009). https://doi.org/10.1503/cmaj.090808
4. Horton, T.J., Illingworth, J.H., Warburton, W.H.P.: Overcoming challenges in codifying and replicating complex health care interventions. Health Aff. (Millwood) **37**(2), 191–197 (2018). https://doi.org/10.1377/hlthaff.2017.1161
5. Dixon-Woods, M., Leslie, M., Tarrant, C., Bion, J.: Explaining matching Michigan: an ethnographic study of a patient safety program. Implement. Sci. **8**, 70 (2013). https://doi.org/10.1186/1748-5908-8-70
6. Lattof, S.R., Maliqi, B., Livesley, N., et al.: National learning systems to sustain and scale up delivery of quality healthcare: a conceptual framework. BMJ Glob. Health **7**(8), e008664 (2022). https://doi.org/10.1136/bmjgh-2022-008664
7. World Health Organization.: The network for improving quality of care for maternal, newborn and child health: evolution, implementation and progress: 2017–2020 report, Geneva (2021)
8. Kirk, M.A., Kelley, C., Yankey, N., Birken, S.A., Abadie, B., Damschroder, L.: A systematic review of the use of the consolidated framework for implementation research. Implement. Sci. **11**, 72 (2016). https://doi.org/10.1186/s13012-016-0437-z
9. Ilott, I., Gerrish, K., Pownall, S., Eltringham, S., Booth, A.: Exploring scale-up, spread, and sustainability: an instrumental case study tracing an innovation to enhance dysphagia care. Implement. Sci. **8**, 128 (2013). https://doi.org/10.1186/1748-5908-8-128
10. McEvoy, R., Ballini, L., Maltoni, S., O'Donnell, C.A., Mair, F.S., Macfarlane, A.: A qualitative systematic review of studies using the normalization process theory to research implementation processes. Implement. Sci. **9**, 2 (2014). https://doi.org/10.1186/1748-5908-9-2
11. Zamboni, K., Schellenberg, J., Hanson, C., Betran, A.P., Dumont, A.: Assessing scalability of an intervention: why, how and who? Health Policy Plan. **34**(7), 544–552 (2019). https://doi.org/10.1093/heapol/czz068
12. Ben Charif, A., Hassani, K., Wong, S.T., et al.: Assessment of scalability of evidence-based innovations in community-based primary health care: a cross-sectional study. CMAJ Open **6**(4), E520–E527 (2018). https://doi.org/10.9778/cmajo.20180143
13. Nambiema, A., Fouquet, J., Guilloteau, J., Descatha, A.: La revue systématique et autres types de revue de la littérature : qu'est-ce que c'est, quand, comment, pourquoi ? The systematic review and other types of literature reviews: what is it, when, how, why? Archives des Maladies Professionnelles et de l Environnement. **82**(5), 539–552 (2021). https://doi.org/10.1016/j.admp.2021.03.004
14. Walker, L.O., Avant, K.C.: Strategies for Theory Construction in Nursing, 5th edn. Prentice Hall, New York (2011)
15. Simmons, R., Fajans, P., Ghiron, L.: World Health Organization. Scaling up health service delivery: from pilot innovations to policies and programmes. World Health Organization, Geneva (2007)
16. Indig, D., Lee, K., Grunseit, A., Milat, A., Bauman, A.: Pathways for scaling up public health interventions. BMC Public Health **18**(1), 68 (2017). https://doi.org/10.1186/s12889-017-4572-5

17. Ben Charif, A., Zomahoun, H.T.V., Gogovor, A. et al.: Tools for assessing the scalability of innovations in health: a systematic review. Health Res. Policy Syst. **20**(1), 34 (2022). https://doi.org/10.1186/s12961-022-00830-5
18. Milat, A.J., King, L., Newson, R., et al.: Increasing the scale and adoption of population health interventions: experiences and perspectives of policy makers, practitioners, and researchers. Health Res Policy Syst. **12**, 18 (2014). https://doi.org/10.1186/1478-4505-12-18
19. Ben Charif, A., Zomahoun, H.T.V., LeBlanc, A. et al.: Effective strategies for scaling up evidence-based practices in primary care: a systematic review. Implement Sci. **12**(1), 139 (2017). https://doi.org/10.1186/s13012-017-0672-y
20. Mangham, L.J., Hanson, K.: Scaling up in international health: what are the key issues? Health Policy Plan. **25**(2), 85–96 (2010). https://doi.org/10.1093/heapol/czp066
21. McDaniel, R.R., Lanham, H.J., Anderson, R.A.: Implications of complex adaptive systems theory for the design of research on health care organizations. Health Care Manag. Rev. **34**(2), 191–199 (2009). https://doi.org/10.1097/HMR.0b013e31819c8b38
22. Damschroder, L.J., Aron, D.C., Keith, R.E., Kirsh, S.R., Alexander, J.A., Lowery, J.C.: Fostering implementation of health services research findings into practice: a consolidated framework for advancing implementation science. Implement. Sci. **4**, 50 (2009). https://doi.org/10.1186/1748-5908-4-50
23. Edwards, N., Barker, P.M.: The importance of context in implementation research. J. Acquir. Immune Defic. Syndr. **67**, S157-162 (2014). https://doi.org/10.1097/QAI.0000000000000322
24. Glasgow, R.E., Vinson, C., Chambers, D., Khoury, M.J., Kaplan, R.M., Hunter, C.: National Institutes of Health approaches to dissemination and implementation science: current and future directions. Am. J. Public Health **102**(7), 1274–1281 (2012). https://doi.org/10.2105/AJPH.2012.300755
25. Ellis, L.A., Sarkies, M., Churruca, K., et al.: The science of learning health systems: scoping review of empirical research. JMIR Med. Inform. **10**(2), e34907 (2022). https://doi.org/10.2196/34907
26. Greenhalgh, T., Robert, G., Macfarlane, F., Bate, P., Kyriakidou, O.: Diffusion of innovations in service organizations: systematic review and recommendations. Milbank Q. **82**(4), 581–629 (2004). https://doi.org/10.1111/j.0887-378X.2004.00325.x
27. Greenhalgh, T., Robert, G., Macfarlane, F., Bate, P., Kyriakidou, O., Peacock, R.: Storylines of research in diffusion of innovation: a meta-narrative approach to systematic review. Soc Sci Med **61**(2), 417–430 (2005). https://doi.org/10.1016/j.socscimed.2004.12.001
28. Barker, P.M., Reid, A., Schall, M.W.: A framework for scaling up health interventions: lessons from large-scale improvement initiatives in Africa. Implement. Sci. **11**, 12 (2016). https://doi.org/10.1186/s13012-016-0374-x
29. Milat, A.J., Newson, R., King, L., et al.: A guide to scaling up population health interventions. Public Health Res Pract. **26**(1), e2611604 (2016). https://doi.org/10.17061/phrp2611604
30. Greenhalgh, T., Wherton, J., Papoutsi, C., et al.: Beyond adoption: a new framework for theorizing and evaluating nonadoption, abandonment, and challenges to the scale-up, spread, and sustainability of health and care technologies. J. Med. Internet Res. **19**(11), e367 (2017). https://doi.org/10.2196/jmir.8775
31. Greenhalgh, T., Papoutsi, C.: Spreading and scaling up innovation and improvement. BMJ **365**, 2068 (2019). https://doi.org/10.1136/bmj.l2068
32. Bousquet, J., Farrell, J., Crooks, G., et al.: Scaling up strategies of the chronic respiratory disease programme of the European innovation partnership on active and healthy ageing. Clin Transl Allergy. **6**, 29 (2016). https://doi.org/10.1186/s13601-016-0116-9
33. Koorts, H., Rutter, H.: A systems approach to scale-up for population health improvement. Health Res Policy Syst. **19**(1), 27 (2021). https://doi.org/10.1186/s12961-021-00679-0
34. Brown-Johnson, C., Haverfield, M.C., Giannitrapani, K.F., et al.: Implementing goals-of-care conversations: lessons from high- and low-performing sites from a VA national initiative. J. Pain Symptom. Manag. **61**(2), 262–269 (2021). https://doi.org/10.1016/j.jpainsymman.2020.07.040

35. Jordon, M., Lanham, H.J., Anderson, R.A., McDaniel, R.R.: Implications of complex adaptive systems theory for interpreting research about health care organizations. J. Eval. Clin. Pract. **16**(1), 228–231 (2010). https://doi.org/10.1111/j.1365-2753.2009.01359.x
36. Braithwaite, J., Churruca, K., Long, J.C., Ellis, L.A., Herkes, J.: When complexity science meets implementation science: a theoretical and empirical analysis of systems change. BMC Med. **16**(1), 63 (2018). https://doi.org/10.1186/s12916-018-1057-z
37. Cresswell, K., Sheikh, A.: Organizational issues in the implementation and adoption of health information technology innovations: an interpretative review. Int. J. Med. Informatics **82**(5), e73-86 (2013). https://doi.org/10.1016/j.ijmedinf.2012.10.007
38. Trinkley, K.E., Ho, P.M., Glasgow, R.E., Huebschmann, A.G.: How dissemination and implementation science can contribute to the advancement of learning health systems. Acad. Med. **97**(10), 1447–1458 (2022). https://doi.org/10.1097/ACM.0000000000004801
39. Scarbrough, H., Kyratsis, Y.: From spreading to embedding innovation in health care: implications for theory and practice. Health Care Manag. Rev. **47**(3), 236–244 (2022). https://doi.org/10.1097/HMR.0000000000000323

Retention and Attraction Measures in the Quebec Health Care System During the Covid-19 Pandemic

Maude Laberge and Jasmine Sawadogo

Abstract The Covid-19 pandemic has led to many changes in the management of personnel within the Quebec health care system. Faced with the increasing burden of labor needs and the need to motivate caregivers to stay in the system, the Quebec government had to put in place various measures. Some of these measures were aimed at attracting new workers and others were aimed at retaining those already involved in the health care system. The arrival of these incentives was generally well received, but their gradual withdrawal was met with outrage by health care workers' rights groups. Our study aims to describe the measures that were introduced between March 2020 and January 2023 by the government to maintain the health care system. The study also presents the reactions that these measures generated from advocacy groups.

Keywords COVID-19 · Measures · Health system

1 Introduction

In February 2020, Quebec, Canada reported its first case of COVID-19 [1]. This date marked the beginning of a major change on many levels within the province and in the rest of the country. According to the Qubec's national institute for public health

M. Laberge (✉) · J. Sawadogo
Department of Social and Preventive Medicine, Faculty of Medicine, Université Laval, Quebec City, Canada
e-mail: maude.laberge@fmed.ulaval.ca

VITAM, Centre de recherche en santé durable – Université Laval, Laval University, Quebec City, Canada

J. Sawadogo
e-mail: laure-jasmine.swadogo.1@ulaval.ca

M. Laberge
Centre de recherche du CHU de Québec, Laval University, Quebec City, Canada

P. Landa et al. (eds.), *Operations Research and Artificial Intelligence in Healthcare Management*, Springer Proceedings in Mathematics & Statistics 506,
https://doi.org/10.1007/978-3-031-95659-1_20

(Institut national de santé publique du Québec – INSPQ), by March 2023, Quebec had more than 1,300,000 confirmed cases since the beginning of the pandemic [2]. At the same time, the province exceeded the 18,000-death mark [2].

Waves of COVID-19 patients shook the Quebec health system. Indeed, the number of hospitalizations for COVID-19 increased exponentially between March and May 2020 [2]. A de-scheduling plan for medical procedures not related to COVID-19 was implemented to face the health emergency. The context was already difficult: Quebec has one of the oldest populations in the world [3], and changes in the demographic profile of the province are generating a growing gap in which the needs of the ageing population are increasing at a faster rate than that of the capacity to deliver services.

This scarcity in resources creates pressure on healthcare providers, leading more than a quarter of those surveyed to express the desire to leave their jobs [4].

Quebec's healthcare system aims to provide accessible, quality health and social services. It is administered by local bodies such as clinics and community pharmacies, and by regional organizations such as the Integrated Centre for health and social services (Centres intégrés (universitaires) de santé et des services sociaux (CI(U)SSS)). There are 22 CISSS and CIUSSS, 4 university hospital centers, 2 university institutes and 5 health organizations serving northern or aboriginal population [5]. It is estimated that almost 7% of Quebec's working population is employed within its healthcare system. Its financing is essentially based on general taxation, which enables services to be provided free of charge in Quebec [5].

Despite these provisions promoting access to care, the healthcare system is weakened by a constant shortage of doctors, particularly in family medicine. Indeed, in 2022, Quebec had 2,8 doctors per 1,000 people, which was lower than countries like Austria (5.5), Iceland (4.5) or Italy (4.3) [6]. Health human resources (HHR) are the foundation of the system, and these include highly qualified providers with years of training, making retention key to maintain continuous services delivery. The issue of HHR retention is not limited to Quebec with other jurisdictions facing similar challenges [7]. We hypothesize that there is no one-size-fits-all solution and that the local context and the voices of interest groups (IG) may affect the choice of potential solutions.

2 Objective

The purpose of this study is to identify measures that were implemented by the Quebec government in the COVID-19 context and to document stakeholders' views and reactions.

Table 1 Websites consulted

Média		
24 heures	La Presse	Le Devoir
Le Journal de Montréal	TVA nouvelles/LCN	
Le Journal de Québec	Radio-Canada	

3 Method

We conducted a search in the grey literature to identify the measures implemented by the Quebec government during the COVID-19 pandemic. This strategy was selected because the information was expected to be mainly found on the websites of ministries, professional advocacy groups or in the main Quebec newspapers. A search of scientific databases was conducted as an exploratory strategy, but this search did not yield any usable results. We used the narrative synthesis approach [8] to transcribe the results of the research. Searches were conducted using specific key words in French, determined by consensus among the research team and based on terms frequently used in the literature to refer to government incentives. These keywords were "COVID incentives", "COVID"; "COVID guidelines"; "COVID measures", "COVID bonuses" (in French: « mesures incitatives COVID»; « COVID»; « directives COVID», « mesures COVID», « Primes COVID», respectively). Searches were restricted to the province of Quebec and the study period was from March 2020 to January 31, 2023. Finally, to exploit the grey literature more broadly, we used the keywords « mesures incitatives COVID» et « directives COVID» to perform a Google search. The media websites consulted are presented in Table 1. The institutions and interest groups (IG) identified to describe the measures are summarized in Table 2.

The documents were analyzed using an extraction grid based on the following elements:

- Name of the measure introduced
- Place of implementation
- Health professionals targeted
- Date of implementation and abolition of the measure
- Consequences of abolishing the measure

4 Results

The keyword search strategy yielded 1,703 entries of which 1,031 were from the organizations' websites and 672 were from provincial newspapers. The most comprehensive list of measures was found using Ministerial Order number 2020–035 dated May 10, 2020 [9]. Information on the purpose of the measures was mostly found on the website of the MSSS [10].

Table 2 Institutions and targeted interest groups to describe the consequences of the measures

Institutions and interest groups	Mission
Québec Ministry of Health and Social Services (MSSS)	The MSSS is the institution responsible for managing the health care system in Quebec
Centre interuniversitaire de recherche en analyse des organisations (CIRANO)	CIRANO is a multidisciplinary research center whose work aims to support the strategic decision making of decision makers, the production and transfer of scientific knowledge
Confédération des syndicats nationaux (CSN)	The CSN is a group of nearly 1600 unions, mostly in Quebec, whose goal is to ensure equity and the respect of rights in the professional sector
The Collège des Médecins	The Collège des Médecins monitors and evaluates medical practice in Quebec. Makes recommendations for the improvement of medical practice in Quebec. It may take a position, including in the media, on various health-related issues
The fédération des Médecins omnipraticiens du Québec (FMOQ)	The FMOQ looks after the professional and scientific interests of general practitioners in Quebec. It defends their professional autonomy and does everything in its power to ensure that they practice in conditions that allow them to offer their patients the optimal quality of care to which they aspire
The Fédération Interprofessionnelle de la santé du Québec (FIQ)	The FIQ is an organization dedicated to the defence of its members (nurses, nursing assistants, respiratory therapists and clinical perfusionists), but also to that of patients and the public health network
The Fédération des médecins spécialistes du Québec (FMSQ)	The mission of the FMSQ is to defend and support the medical specialists of its affiliated associations who work in the public health system, while promoting quality care and services for the Quebec population
The Ordre des infirmières et infirmiers du Québec (OIIQ)	The mission of the OIIQ is to ensure the protection of the public so that the Quebec population can benefit from safe, quality care and services provided by competent nurses with integrity
The Syndicat québécois des employées et employés de services (SQEES)	The Syndicat québécois des employées de services is a sub-branch of the Fédération des Travailleurs du Québec (FTQ) and has a majority of employees in the health and social services sector

The consequences of the measures and the positions of professional organizations were found mainly in the media. We found that measures were for the most part financial incentives (such as bonuses or salary increases) rather than professional accommodation measures. Table 3 presents the measures mentioned in the ministerial orders.

4.1 Attraction and Retention Measures

The measures were initiated in May 2020, two months after the beginning of the COVID-19 pandemic in Quebec. In our analysis, we differentiate attraction measures which were intended to encourage new or retired people to become involved in supporting the health system, and retention measures that were designed to keep employees in their jobs by encouraging them to work more and longer. These two types of measures, specifically related to the pandemic, are different from those initially in place to address the already prevalent labor shortage. Of the main eleven measures identified, seven were retention measures while four were attraction measures.

The attraction measures were mostly voluntary involvement in health support programs with good remuneration ("Je contribute" platform or a12-week intensive PSW training program specific to tasks in LTC facilities). Retention measures were usually financial compensation. Those bonuses ranged from $100 CAD to $10,000 CAD, most of which were cumulative. They applied to different healthcare providers such as nurses, health care aides, personal support workers (PSWs), and for some measures, maintenance personnel in healthcare facilities. Work during inconvenient hours such as weekends and nights was highly encouraged with incentives. In addition, additional shifts and overtime were rewarded with additional bonuses. The measures were mostly implemented in long-term care (LTC) facilities, general hospitals, and facilities or locations designated by the MSSS. Some conditions applied to be eligible to some of the bonuses such as the need to be adequately vaccinated [9].

4.2 Implementation of Measures

The announcement of the incentive measures was generally well received. These initiatives were considered relevant to motivate staff, already suffering from the heavy demands of the health system, and to enhance the value of the health professions. The former president of the Quebec Interprofessional Federation (FIQ) declared: "This is important because we need to attract people, we need to retain those who are there, and we need those who are part-time to increase their hours" [11].

On the other hand, the interest groups also pointed to the rigidity of the measures put in place and expressed the feeling that the government preferred paying the staff more rather than improving their working conditions. The FIQ considered that

Table 3 Attraction and retention measures implemented during the COVID-19 pandemic in Quebec

Summary of measures	Type of measures	Staff targeted by the measure	Start date	End date
Lump sum of $100.00 per week worked	Retention	Employees in LTC[1] centers	10-May-20	N.A
Lump sum of $200.00 for the first two consecutive weeks worked	Attraction	• Employees in LTC centers • Nurses • PSWs Health and social services workers • housekeeping attendant	10-May-20	N.A
Lump sum of $400.00 for the period of work of two weeks effectively worked consecutively and subsequent to the first 2-week period of work	Retention	• Employees in LTC centers • Nurses • PSWs • Health and social services workers • housekeeping attendant	10-May-20	N.A
Bonus of $500.00 per week to work in a socio-sanitary region more than 70 km from the provider's home when needed	Attraction	• Employees in LTC centers • Nurses • PSWs • Health and social services workers • housekeeping attendant	10-May-20	N.A
COVID-19 bonus of 8% on the hourly rate	Retention	All health care professionals	10-May-20	N.A
Additional 4% COVID-19 bonus on the hourly rate to the 8% bonus already given	Retention	All front-line health care staff	10-May-20	N.A
Implementation of a web platform ("Je contribue")[2] for people with healthcare training not currently working in the healthcare system to apply	Attraction	Nursing and cardio-respiratory staff	10-May-20	N.A

(continued)

[1] *LTC: Long term care.*
n.a: Not available.

[2] *The " je contribue " platform is a digital platform whose objective is to recruit caregivers to support the health and social services network:* https://jecontribuecovid19.gouv.qc.ca/Inscription.aspx.

Table 3 (continued)

Summary of measures	Type of measures	Staff targeted by the measure	Start date	End date
Option for employees to request payment for vacations	Retention	Nursing and cardio-respiratory staff	10-May-20	N.A
Staircase bonus of $1,000 per four-week period	Retention	Nursing and cardio-respiratory staff	10-May-20	14-May-22
Attendance bonus of $1,800 per four-week period for immunization staff working at least one day per week	Retention	Nursing and cardio-respiratory staff	10-May-20	14-May-22
12-week intensive PSWs training program	Attraction	Anyone wishing to support the health system	N.A	N.A

"The bonuses promised by the government are nothing more than sweets distributed without taking into account the fatigue of the staff, […]. It's as if fatigue could be traded for money" [12].

4.3 Withdrawal of Measures

The withdrawal of incentives has been met with difficulty. The FIQ was the IG that expressed itself the most and it perceived the government's withdrawal as a failure to address their concerns. "We had incentives with overtime paid double the hourly rate and lots of bonuses and lots of things at the financial level. Now we have none of that except overtime paid double" [13]. "The government needs to think about the effect it will have on the staff. Workers are stretched thin after two years of fighting the pandemic. We are already struggling to attract and retain staff in the system" [14].

5 Discussion and Conclusion

In many fields, the implementation of incentives is a strategy that seems to be effective in encouraging and attracting workers [15]. Prior to the COVID-19 pandemic, the Quebec government used this method to recruit nurses and PSWs as a strategy to mitigate labour shortages. In the case of the pandemic, according to the MSSS, the incentive measures allowed the Quebec health system to ensure an adequate availability of staff and the continued delivery of care and services to the population [16].

However, in the long term, incentives are costly and cannot last forever. This leads to their gradual withdrawal. Withdrawing incentives is difficult as it can lead to disruption and demotivation of staff, and to resignations because the financial compensation fails to relieve workers from the physical and mental burden [17].

Despite the difficulties associated with removing incentives, the strategy of using them has been used in many other health systems [18]. For example, in Manitoba and Ontario, risk premiums were introduced as of October 2020 to temporarily improve the wages of low-income workers in hospitals and residential care services, including long-term care homes [18].

In Australia, COVID-19 exposure bonuses were introduced for workers who had to provide their services face-to-face. These were quarterly bonuses of AUD800 for aged care facilities and AUD600 for home care for staff working more than 30 h per week [19].

In the United States, financial incentives varied by state. In Massachusetts, bonuses of between USD5 and USD10 per hour were given to individual health care workers [20]. In Arkansas, workers in facilities with at least one COVID-19 case could receive an additional USD125 to USD500 per week [21].

The introduction of incentives has been generally well received. One challenge faced by these countries is to maintain the performance of health systems and their actors while withdrawing some of the incentives that were intended to be exceptional to the pandemic situation. This analysis has documented this phenomenon in Quebec. It could be relevant to evaluate the management of this situation in other contexts to find a more appropriate strategy for governments, health care organization and insurers. Although incentives may be effective in altering behavior (in this case, retaining staff), they may not be sustainable and alternatives could be more effective in the long term. The international center on nurse migration proposed a different action plan to retain nursing staff during a pandemic. It is based on 7 actions [22]:

- commit to supporting secure staffing levels.
- commit to supporting early access to full vaccination regimens for all nurses
- conduct impact assessments on the nursing workforce
- strengthen the capacity of the national nurse training system
- improve the retention and attractiveness of nursing as a career,
- implement policies to optimize the contribution of nurses to the pandemic response
- monitor and track nursing self-sufficiency.

These elements could help other healthcare systems, such as Quebec's, to improve the retention of their healthcare staff, especially nurses.

This study, based on grey literature, provides an overview of the phenomenon of incentives during the pandemic. Future studies based on field analyses with nursing staff would enable us to reinforce and better understand our conclusions.

References

1. INSPQ.: Ligne du temps COVID-19 au Québec. [COVID-19 Timeline in Quebec] (2022). https://www.inspq.qc.ca/covid-19/donnees/ligne-du-temps
2. Données COVID-19 au Québec. [COVID-19 Data in Quebec] mars (2023). https://www.inspq.qc.ca/covid-19/donnees
3. Institut de la statistique du Québec. Le bilan démographique. [Demographic Report] (2021)
4. CIRANO.: Expérience au travail du personnel des établissements de soins de longue durée lors de la première vague de la pandémie de COVID-19 au Québec. [Work Experience of Long-Term Care Facility Staff During the First Wave of the COVID-19 Pandemic in Quebec] (2022)
5. Ministère de la Santé et des Services sociaux.: Le système de santé et de services sociaux au Québec En bref. [The Health and Social Services System in Quebec—In brief] (2017). https://publications.msss.gouv.qc.ca/msss/fichiers/2017/17-731-01WF.pdf
6. OCDE. Indicateur-Médecin. [Indicator—Doctor] (2022). https://www.oecd.org/fr/data/indicators/doctors.html
7. Ressources humaines-Mesures concernant l'attraction et la rétention des effectifs. [Human Resources—Measures Regarding the Attraction and Retention of Staff] (2022)
8. INSPQ. : Les revues narratives : fondements scientifiques pour soutenir l'établissement de repères institutionnels. [Narrative Reviews: Scientific Foundations to Support the Establishment of Institutional Benchmarks] (2021)
9. Ministère de la santé et des services sociaux . Arrêté numéro 2020–035 de la ministre de la Santé et des Services sociaux en date du 10 mai 2020. [Ministerial Order No. 2020–035 from the Minister of Health and Social Services Date May 10, 2020] (2020). chrome-extension://efaidnbmnnnibpcajpcglclefindmkaj/https://cdn-contenu.quebec.ca/cdn-contenu/adm/min/sante-services-sociaux/publications-adm/lois-reglements/AM_numero_2020-035.pdf?1589232237
10. Ministère de la santé et des services sociaux. Modifications aux mesures incitatives pour le personnel du réseau de la santé et des services sociaux et des milieux privés. [Changes to Incentive Measures for Staff in the Health and Social Services network and the Private Sector]. https://www.msss.gouv.qc.ca/ministere/salle-de-presse/communique-3476/#:~:text=Les%20mesures%20mises%20en%20place,fin%20le%2016%20avril%20prochain
11. Le journal de Montréeal. Les infirmières pourront faire jusqu'à 120 000$ par année. [Nurse Could Earn Up to $120,000 Per Year.] (2022). https://www.journaldequebec.com/2022/01/13/les-infirmieres-pourront-faire-jusqua-120-000-par-annee-1
12. "L'urgence sanitaire est utilisée de façon abusive" dénonce la FIQ. ["The Health Emergency Is Being Abused", Says the FIQ] Le Devoir (2021)
13. Le syndicat régional de la FIQ dépose ses demandes. [The Regional FIQ Union Submits Its Demand] Le journal de Québec (2022). https://www.journaldequebec.com/2022/11/07/le-syndicat-regional-de-la-fiq-depose-ses-demandes-1
14. La presse. Québec abandonnera la « prime COVID ». [Quebec Will Eliminate the "COVID Bonus"] [On line] 2022. https://www.journaldequebec.com/2022/11/07/le-syndicat-regional-de-la-fiq-depose-ses-demandes-1, 2022..
15. Gouvernement du Québec. Opération main-d'œuvre – Mesures ciblées pour certains secteurs prioritaires. [Workforce Operation—Trageted Measures for Certain Priority Sectors]. https://www.quebec.ca/gouvernement/ministere/emploi-solidarite-sociale/publications/operation-maindoeuvre
16. Main-d'œuvre en contexte de pandémie—Les mesures incitatives pour le personnel du réseau reconduites pour un minimum de quatre semaines. [Workforce During Pandemic—Incentive Measures for Network Staff Renewed for a Minimum of Four Weeks] Ministère de la santé et des services sociaux (2022)
17. Plus de 500 personnes ont quitté le réseau de la santé depuis décembre. [More than 500 Peope Have Left the Health Network Since December] Le devoir (2022)

18. Anna et al.: Risk Recognition Policies for the Long-Term Care Workforce during the First Year of the COVID-19 Pandemic: A Multi-Country Study. Cooper Reed (2022)
19. Minister Departement of health and aged care. Measures to support Senior Australians and those who care for them. https://www.health.gov.au/ministers/senator-the-hon-richard-colbeck/media/measures-to-support-senior-australians-and-those-who-care-for-them.
20. AFSCME Council 93. http://www.afscme93.org/2020/04/12/blogpost/council-93-human-services-workers-in-ma-rewarded-for-their-courage-and-dedication-during-covid-19-crisis/.
21. Empowering Arkansans. https://governor.arkansas.gov/news-media/press-releases/governor-hutchinson-announces-cms-approval-of-additional-pay-for-eligible-ltss-direct-care-workers-due-to-covid-19-emergency.
22. Conseil International des Infirmières. Pérenniser et fidéliser les effectifs en 2022 et au-delà : Les personnels infirmiers dans le monde et la pandémie de covid-19 (2022). https://www.icn.ch/sites/default/files/2023-04/Sustain%20and%20Retain%20in%202022%20and%20Beyond-%20The%20global%20nursing%20workforce%20and%20the%20COVID-19%20pandemic_FR.pdf

MIX
Papier aus verantwortungsvollen Quellen
Paper from responsible sources
FSC® C105338

If you have any concerns about our products,
you can contact us on
ProductSafety@springernature.com

In case Publisher is established outside the EU,
the EU authorized representative is:
Springer Nature Customer Service Center GmbH
Europaplatz 3, 69115 Heidelberg, Germany

Printed by Libri Plureos GmbH
in Hamburg, Germany